JUSTICE IS COMING

JUSTICE IS COMING

HOW PROGRESSIVES ARE GOING TO TAKE
OVER THE COUNTRY AND AMERICA IS
GOING TO LOVE IT

CENK UYGUR

ST. MARTIN'S PRESS
NEW YORK

First published in the United States by St. Martin's Press,
an imprint of St. Martin's Publishing Group

www.stmartins.com

The Library of Congress Cataloging-in-Publication Data is available
upon request.

ISBN 978-1-250-27279-9 (hardcover)
ISBN 978-1-250-27280-5 (ebook)

Our books may be purchased in bulk for promotional, educational,
or business use. Please contact your local bookseller or
the Macmillan Corporate and Premium Sales Department
at 1-800-221-7945, extension 5442, or by email at
MacmillanSpecialMarkets@macmillan.com.

First Edition: 2023

10 9 8 7 6 5 4 3 2 1

To my parents,
Dogan and Nukhet Uygur,
who taught me to help someone you don't know
and to fight for justice without ever saying
a word about politics.

The issue today is the same as it has been throughout all history, whether man shall be allowed to govern himself or be ruled by a small elite.

—THOMAS JEFFERSON

CONTENTS

Introduction   *1*

1. America Is Progressive   *21*

2. What Is a Progressive?   *50*

3. Why Republicans Suck   *101*

4. How We Lost Our Democracy   *141*

5. The Matrix   *195*

6. Here Comes the Revolution   *218*

7. What Happens When Progressives Win   *255*

Acknowledgments   *273*

Notes   *275*

Index   *297*

JUSTICE IS COMING

INTRODUCTION

OUR BRAINS HAVE TWO PARTS: HARDWARE AND SOFTWARE. OUR GENETICS form the hardware. For example, Albert Einstein was hardwired to be good at physics. As my high school report cards would prove, I was not hardwired in the same way. Our brains have hardware that no amount of tinkering will change.

But the rest of our brains are software: they are made up of what we are programmed to believe about ourselves and the world. Most of what we learn is benign or even positive. Your parents told you to eat with a fork and knife. So you have eaten with these utensils all your life without a second thought, because that's the coding you received at an early age. They also told you to be nice to other people—I hope! Wonderful software.

But then there is your *unconscious* software. If you watch Fox News, you're programmed to believe that immigrants are "dirty," that they create the problems in America—not the powerful people with all the money. So the guy without a dollar in his pocket who just crossed the border is the one rigging the system, not the guys at the very top? No one in their right mind could believe that. But they do! I have family members—Muslims and immigrants—who voted for Donald Trump because of the problem with Muslims and immigrants. That's some strong software. Or, more accurately, malware.

But Fox News isn't the only one doing the programming. Take health care. Single-payer, universal health care is less expensive than our private system, which deprives tens of millions of Americans of coverage. Every country with universal health care pays less per person than we do for our system. In fact, on average we pay twice as much for health care per person as other countries pay for theirs. And we get worse results! Is that what you heard about during the Democratic Party primaries in 2020? Nope. You heard the opposite. All the talk came from pundits asking Bernie Sanders one question about his health care plan: "How are you going to pay for that?"

This question is just as absurd as anything you hear on Fox News. Imagine you are about to buy an expensive car but then find one that is half the price—and a better car. You excitedly tell your friend about it and he says, "How are you going to pay for that? I think you should stick with the car that costs twice as much." You'd probably ask him to get a concussion test. But most of the country believes that our health care system is the best in the world—because the establishment media have repeated this enough that it has become part of the national software.

And yet, in Mississippi, despite the decades of our-system-is-wonderful propaganda, 62 percent of the Democratic primary voters in 2020 told pollsters that they wanted Medicare for All.[1] In *Mississippi,* a state so conservative that some Democratic candidates don't even campaign there!

Great, that means they voted for presidential candidate Bernie Sanders, who is the champion of Medicare for All, right? Nope. Because these voters were coded with another program from the mainstream media: don't elect progressives, they'll lose! So, 81 percent of Mississippi voters voted for Joe Biden, who *hates* Medicare for All.[2] These people voted against their own avowed self-interest because CNN and *The New York Times* programmed them to. That actually happened.

This book is about breaking down the myths of the right wing, the political elite in both parties, and the establishment media. It will show you how they lied to you. How they installed junk software you need to get out of your head. Myths like "The media have a liberal bias." Hilarious. I'll show you how that's not remotely true. Or how about "America is a center-right country"? Another preposterous lie that's painfully easy to debunk if you just look up the facts, as we'll see in chapter 1.

Then, why do people hold these ridiculous ideas in their heads and remain convinced of them? Because the media and politicians put the myths there and repeated them enough times that they became an operating system running in the back of your head that you aren't even aware of. In fact, big corporations, which basically own the media and both political parties, are often the ones writing the coding for these programs.

The Democrats are bought and the Republicans even more so. They don't represent us. They represent their donors. We have taxation without representation, just as we did before the American Revolution.

Here, let's take an example.

On the day I began writing this book, Utah Republican Senator Mike Lee stood up in Congress and said something stupid. That might seem unsurprising, but what he said was stupid even for him, which is saying a lot.

Lee stood on the Senate floor to comment on the Green New Deal (GND), a phrase and concept popularized by the most establishment pundit in America: *The New York Times'* Thomas L. Friedman. Later it was adopted by Justice Democrats like Alexandria Ocasio-Cortez and became controversial by definition because it was then perceived as a progressive idea. The mythmaking factory decided it would cost a couple of corporations a couple of bucks—and hence, needed to be destroyed. But at its core it's an uncontroversial position backed by 99 percent of the world's scientists and an overwhelming majority of the American people.

The GND is a plan to address the existential threat climate change poses to the world. Lee and other right-wing nutjobs act as if there is no danger and all the world's scientists are wrong. Yes, Mike Lee has it figured out better than *all* the scientists. That's likely. Back on planet Earth, temperature readings are not complicated. Anyone can read them, and they are as crystal clear as the polar caps that are melting: the average global temperature has been rising steadily for the past forty years. Not by a little, but by levels that threaten our existence on this planet. But the same Republican Party that wasn't sure whether doctors were right about vaccines during Covid-19 insists that they know better than the world's scientists.

The GND calls for public investments in things like electric cars and high-speed rail systems, the rebuilding of our crumbling infrastructure, the reduction of pollution, and the eventual elimination of greenhouse gas emissions. It pushes the country to restructure its economy toward sustainability, equality, and justice. It wouldn't just save the planet, it would create millions of jobs and potentially save the economy, too. It would help ensure a planet that is prosperous for future generations. It's win-win-win . . . *unless* you're a billionaire who profits from fossil fuels, in which case you'll probably lose some money in the short run. You'll never guess who these billionaires give campaign contributions to. One of them is—I hope you're sitting—Mike Lee! Another is Joe Manchin. Politicians of both political parties are great investments for fossil fuel executives.

Let's get some things out of the way immediately. First, there is *no* scientific debate about the reality of climate change. Human behavior is warming the planet, period. Case closed. More than 99 percent of climate scientists assert that this is our reality, and back up their assertions with factual evidence. If you think all of that is a conspiracy and that scientists from all over the world got together and decided to lie about temperature readings, you are probably deranged. You should be under compassionate professional care, not in Congress.

Second, more than 99 percent of all scientists believe in gravity—the same portion as those who acknowledge man-made climate change. If you don't believe in gravity either, I would invite you to test out your theory. Don't say I didn't warn you. The point is, if you believe corrupt politicians over scientists, we'll all be paying a pretty heavy price soon. In fact, we already are. Just ask anybody who's survived one of the mounting numbers of hurricanes, droughts, massive fires and floods, or tornadoes. It rained 60 inches in Houston during Hurricane Harvey in 2017. That's the equivalent of 780 inches of snow—65 feet of snow in one storm! It was called a thousand-year storm. Well, those record storms come almost every year now. What used to happen once a millennium now happens annually.

Third, the only reason why the existence of climate change is even publicly debated is because the fossil fuel industry bought off all of the Republican Party and much of the Democratic Party—not because the public is divided on the issue. In reality, 78 percent of Americans believe in climate change, including 64 percent of Republicans. And 65 percent believe that climate change is caused by human activity. In a functioning democracy, when two-thirds of the population agree on something, the government acts on the issue. But, alas, we don't have a functioning democracy. It got short-circuited by malware. We have climate deniers in the form of former President Donald Trump (God, it feels good to write "former"), nearly every person who appears on Fox News, Senate Minority Leader Mitch McConnell, corporate Democrats like West Virginia Senator Joe Manchin, and our old friend Mike Lee. All were bought off long ago by the fossil fuel industry.

According to an analysis by the Center for American Progress, there are 139 climate deniers in Congress. Combined, they have accepted a total of more than $61 million in direct contributions from the fossil fuel industry.[3] That's an average of $442,293 in contributions accepted by each of the 139 climate deniers. And you wonder why guys like Mike Lee stand up and parrot the talking points written by big corporations? It pays really well. Are you sure you wouldn't say it if you got paid half a million dollars? Money talks.

Does anyone in their right mind really believe that people take $442,293 and don't let it affect their decisions? Only a television pundit would believe that. And those figures are only direct contributions. Corporations spend money in other, less direct ways, too. "Fossil fuel–tied industries spent nearly $2 billion lobbying in the US from 2000 to 2016—and that was just around climate legislation," according to a report produced by the nonpartisan Public Accountability Initiative. Since 2012, those industries spent more than $333 million on federal elections alone.[4] Given the enormous cost to run election campaigns, fossil fuel industries can trust that their election contributions are greatly appreciated. A different analysis found that the average congressional opponent of the GND received *twenty-four times* more in funding from oil and gas companies than the sponsors of the GND did.[5]

How come no one on television has ever told you that? Doesn't that sound like a relevant fact when you're discussing why these politicians vote for or against something?

You know what it's called when someone gives money to a politician and asks him to vote for what they want? Corruption. That's patently obvious to all of us who live in the real world. But in the alternate reality of Washington, D.C., that's just a coincidence, and the politicians involved are all honorable people who should be revered. There is something deeply wrong with our media when they refuse to acknowledge things that are obvious to the rest of us.

Can anyone believe that fossil fuel companies spent two billion dollars to influence politicians because they care about the general welfare or like to be charitable? You are either a dullard or dishonest if you think that. Everyone can see why they spend that money—with the exception of people in the news business. Gee, I wonder if being part of multibillion-dollar corporations is affecting the news industry. It's even called an industry now. They're not in the business of making news, they're in the business of making myths. Like the myth that politicians are such honorable people that they are not affected by *billions* of dollars in political contributions.

The first bill to combat climate change was introduced in 2019 by New York Representative Alexandria Ocasio-Cortez (AOC) and Massachusetts Senator Ed Markey, both Democrats. While that bill failed to pass, elements of it were included in the Inflation Reduction Act signed into law by President Biden in August 2022. There was, and is, nothing revolutionary about the program. The term "Green New Deal" was originally used in 2007 by the predictably centrist *New York Times* columnist Thomas L. Friedman. Asked once to name his favorite columnist, Bill Clinton identified Friedman—the same Friedman who supported the Iraq War because, he said, the United States needed to send a message to the Arab world: "suck on this." There is nothing radical about the guy or his ideas, ever. By the time AOC and Markey brought it to Congress, the Green New Deal's premises hadn't changed much. Except now that legislation was possible, both Fox News and the mainstream media decided it had to be branded as radical. Fire up the mythmaking factory!

The transition from idea to passed-and-signed legislation took nearly fifteen years—in Washington, that glacial pace of change is considered normal. Think about it for a minute. A mainstream pundit proposes a solution to a public issue that literally threatens the entire planet. Then a decade goes by before anyone ever acts on it in Congress. At that point, it's branded as "radical." Its champions are called "extremists." Even in the 2020 Democratic primaries, most of the candidates said it was "not realistic." They said that based not on the substance of the GND but on the fact that they simply would not vote for it—which means the GND as originally conceived had no chance of passing Congress. The watered-down GND was shoehorned into a larger bill designed and sold as a plan to combat inflation, and only after years of negotiation with one hold-out senator—you guessed it, Joe Manchin—who nearly derailed Biden's modest ambitions to address climate change created by Manchin's political donors. There are never any political consequences for any of this negligence. The media never compare how quickly we're running out of time to save Earth with how slowly Washington is moving. The climate change band keeps playing on, paid for by the fossil fuel industry.

But back to Senator Lee. In his presentation in the most powerful deliberative body in the history of the world, how did the Honorable Senator from Utah respond to the GND—this thoughtful, moderate plan to combat the growing, life-threatening environmental crisis menacing our planet? First, he said that unlike some of his colleagues, he wasn't even worried about the effects of carbon emissions on the environment. They just aren't a problem. "I am not immediately afraid of what carbon emissions, unaddressed, might do [to] our environment, our civilization, and our planet," he explained.[6]

In other words, he began his presentation by denying the scientifically undeniable facts of climate change, a phenomenon that threatens the very planet we're on (editorial note: we do not currently have a backup planet). Apparently, it's not that big of a deal to him. Must be nice.

Then things got even worse.

Dressed in one of those bland navy suits that seem to be issued whenever individuals are elected to the Senate, Lee placed some visuals on an easel. "I rise today to consider the Green New Deal with the seriousness it deserves," he said, with his typical smug self-satisfaction. One of the images he displayed was of former President Ronald Reagan shooting a machine gun while sitting on the back of a dinosaur that was holding an American flag. "This image has as much to do with overcoming communism in the twentieth century as the Green New Deal has to do with overcoming climate change in the twenty-first," Lee said, his balding head glistening under the Senate lights.[7]

Another image he displayed was of Aquaman, the superhero, riding a giant sea horse. "Under the Green New Deal, this is probably Hawaii's best bet," he said. Why would that be? Because, Lee lied, the GND would end air travel to the island. It would do no such thing, of course, but the end of air travel was already a Fox News talking point, so Lee knew right-wing voters had already been primed to believe it. "The aspirations of the proposal have been called radical and extreme," he said. "But mostly they're ridiculous."[8]

So, Lee decided to present some environmental solutions that aren't ridiculous. Some serious, bold, well-thought-out ideas that would reverse the destruction of the planet. Plans and proposals that are anything but ridiculous or extreme. "The solution to climate change is not this unserious resolution that we're considering this week in the Senate, but the serious business of human flourishing—the solution to so many of our problems, at all times and in all places, is to fall in love, get married and have some kids," he offered. The solution to global warming could be found in "in churches, wedding chapels, and maternity wards across the country and around the world."[9]

Really. That's what he said. Without laughing. Apparently, listening to scientists isn't going to fix the problem. Having less carbon in the atmosphere is not the answer. The answer has been right in front of us the whole time: wedding chapels!

I would like to remind you that his main point was that the Green New Deal was ridiculous. Indeed. So, let's continue with his serious-minded proposal instead.

"More babies mean more forward-looking adults—the sort we need to tackle long-term, large-scale problems," he said. "American babies, in particular, are likely going to be wealthier, better educated, and more conservation-minded than children raised in still-industrializing countries."[10]

Shit, why didn't I think of that? The answer to life-threatening climate change was under our nose the whole time: more American babies!

These guys are not kidding. They are, in fact, this dumb. When the mainstream media pretend that point is not monumentally stupid, they're gaslighting you! This is not 50–50. Mike Lee is not on equal footing with 99 percent of the world's scientists. We're supposed to debate that? How do you debate a point this ridiculous? "Well, Bob, while I respect Senator Lee's proposal of throwing more American babies at the problem, hear me out on my counterpoint . . ."

Just for fun, though, let's quickly destroy the idea that American babies, in particular, are much better equipped to deal with this problem than regular old babies from Bangladesh. Americans, Congressman Lee says, are more "conservation-minded" than people from other countries. As usual for a Republican senator, that statement is not remotely true. So, let's look at the facts. A crazy idea, I know, but stick with me. The nonpartisan Center for Biological Diversity reported in 2009 that a child born in the United States would be responsible for almost seven times the carbon emissions of a child born in China. And the American-born baby would produce 168 times the impact of a baby in Bangladesh.[11] It doesn't matter how "forward-looking" Lee's imaginary American-born children would be, whatever that means. Or how wealthy—wealth usually leads to more environmental damage, given that richer people consume more resources. So does the American way of living, which is oriented around abundance, convenience, and hyperindividualism. Even among rich countries, America is especially damaging to the environment. The fact is that a young American would be responsible for 700 percent more carbon emissions than a Chinese kid—and 16,800 percent more than a Bangladeshi kid.

So, Lee's presentation wasn't just misguided. It was comically wrong. I wonder if people who agree with him on the issue aren't genuinely embarrassed. Do they think he nailed it? That he is brilliant, hilarious, and creative? If you really think American babies are the correct answer to climate change, you're so clueless that I have genuine sympathy for you, being the empathetic, progressive person that I am.

But instead of exposing these guys for the extremists they are—in other words, telling the truth about them—the media defer to them as authorities. Responding to Lee's presentation, CNN's Anderson Cooper actually said, "Both parties do this sort of thing."[12] Look, I am no fan of the Democratic Party. I don't give a damn about the parties. Who is excited by boring Democrats like Colorado Senator Michael Bennet? Nobody, literally. He ran for president and polled at 0 percent. With the polling margin of error, statistically there was a chance he was actually at –3 percent, which defies the laws of mathematics. The only people excited by him are his corporate donors. I have spent much of my life working to fundamentally change the Democratic Party as it currently exists.

But Cooper is just wrong. Both parties *don't* do this sort of thing. One party acknowledges the reality of facts like climate change—even if the corporate donors of some portion of the party encourage them to look the other way. That party introduces bold programs like the GND and has some exciting new voices like AOC, Jamaal Bowman, Ro Khanna, Cori Bush, and others on the national and state level. This party can be—must be and will be—transformed into a force for progressive politics in a way it isn't right now. But at least there's some room for hope.

The other party *doesn't believe in science.* Its members proudly declare they don't believe in facts. They even have their own "alternative facts," as former White House adviser Kellyanne Conway memorably put it. They don't believe in evidence. "Truth isn't truth," Trump attorney Rudy Giuliani declared on NBC's *Meet the Press.*[13] Let that sink in. Conservatives don't adhere to the scientific method and way of reasoning that we adopted back in the Enlightenment. Oddly, Republicans often decry the decline of Western civilization, especially as it's taught in schools. Well, if you take the scientific method out of Western civilization, almost all you have left is white noise. To be fair, that could be their intent, given that white noise might be the perfect way to describe today's Republican Party.

The problem isn't just with GOP leaders. Many of the rank and file are religious extremists. A study conducted by the Pew Research Center a few years ago found that a majority of Republican voters don't believe that humans have evolved over time.[14] That's right—most Republicans think evolution is a hoax. It's unclear if the Chinese came up with this particular hoax, or if Dr. Fauci had a hand in it.

So why did Cooper say that both parties do this? *Because he has to.* Because CNN is a business. And like all businesses, it exists to turn a profit. That's how corporate media work. CNN profits from advertising in particular. Among CNN's top-ten advertisers in 2020 were Amazon, Liberty Mutual, and TD Ameritrade brokerage. Do those sound like corporations that prioritize truth telling? Are they going to want CNN to do hard-hitting exposes on Big Tech, the insurance industry, and Wall Street? Or reporting that exposes the wrongdoings of the powerful elite in politics and boardrooms across America? Are they going to want television anchors, hosts, and correspondents to do the kind of honest journalism that might piss off some viewers—and potential customers? Of course not, they just want to move product. They want to sell to progressives *and* conservatives. Advertising executives get very touchy if you take a stand—trust me, I used to be an MSNBC host, and I've been in the room where these things are said. People have an uncanny ability to know exactly where their bread is buttered.

Drug companies are among the largest advertisers on cable news.[15] All you have to do is watch any show and count the number of drug ads. Yes, it's partly because the audience is ancient and they need help with their bladders (see, I even thought about taking this line out because some of my readers might be older and you don't want to hurt book sales—that's the influence of money!). But the issue here is that your advertisers are not going to be thrilled if you're for Medicare for All. That would drastically reduce the price of pharmaceutical drugs in this country. That might help the average American a lot, but it would certainly cut into the profits of Novartis and CNN.

Then there are the election cycles, where billions of dollars in campaign contributions go largely to . . . television advertisements! In the 2022 elections, seventeen billion dollars was spent on state and federal races.[16] And that's a midterm election, without a presidential race. Almost all of that money goes into ads running on mainstream media. If the progressive proposal to publicly finance elections had already been implemented, corporate media would not have made an extra seventeen billion dollars this election cycle—and that number goes up every cycle.

That's seventeen billion reasons to make sure right-wing mythology is not debunked and obvious corruption is never discussed on air. Mainstream media outlets don't ever talk about corruption because they are its biggest beneficiaries.

Some people say that this is a conspiracy theory. You know what's actually a conspiracy theory, pushed relentlessly by the establishment? The theory that large, multibillion-dollar media corporations are *not* interested in profit! That they exist for the public good. Some people who work in media say this with a straight face. That their organization would never be sullied by the idea of profits. I don't doubt that individual reporters have good intentions, but to say Comcast doesn't care if it makes money is beyond absurd. Before he was ousted as the head of CBS for sexual harassment, Les Moonves admitted to *The Hollywood Reporter* that his network cared more for its bottom line than for the country's well-being. "It may not be good for America, but it's damn good for CBS," he said about Donald Trump's political career in February 2016. "The money's rolling in, and this is fun. It's a terrible thing to say. But bring it on, Donald. Keep going." Yes, it is a terrible thing to say. It's fucking awful, in fact. But it's even worse to deny reality and act as if the media care about truth.

Look, these corporations are trying to reach *all* consumers, Democrats and Republicans alike. It's not going to please Republican viewers if hosts say that Republican politicians are a bunch of simpletons. That might be the truth. But they think truth isn't good for ratings. What is good for ratings is attracting the widest audience possible. And they think they best accomplish that by being inoffensive to everybody. By flattering viewers and pretending that anything is worth debating if it's said by a member of either political party. By ginning up controversy about things— like the reality of climate change or whether Barack Obama was born in America—where no controversy over the facts actually exists. In 2017, then–CNN president Jeff Zucker actually told a reporter, "The idea that politics is sport is undeniable, and we understood that and approached it that way."[17] In sports, of course, you need more than one legitimate competitor to have drama. The teams need to be evenly matched. Even better if you can add conflict and drama between personalities. And so, CNN had to create legitimacy, conflict, and drama when none existed, truth be damned. Just as long as everyone keeps watching. Post-Zucker, the new regime at CNN says it wants more "fair and balanced" reporting and a less politicized tenor to its programming. Yet almost no progressives have been invited on air. Strange, I thought they wanted to be more balanced. No, they just mean they're going to become even more in favor of corporate interests. Calling news with a corporate bias "objective" was the best trick the media ever played. Corruption is the goose that lays the golden egg for the media as well as politicians. You know who doesn't want to rock the boat? The guy who owns it. For media corporations that thrive under this current system, it's their boat and they don't want anyone rocking it. Expecting media executives to disrupt the conservative status quo is a fool's errand. To them, America is a center-right country, and that's that. They are deeply sensitive about offending advertisers and conservatives.

And do you know what it's called when you prioritize political sensitivity over facts? Political correctness. The reason the mainstream media aren't honest about the root of the problem, namely the Republican politicians and voters, is because they are worried about ratings and advertisers. They don't want to offend a big chunk of the country and lose viewers, readers, and ad dollars. So they cover up the ugly face of the Republican Party. Though they whine about it incessantly, ironically, it's conservatives who are the biggest beneficiaries of political correctness.

Now, you might be wondering why CNN didn't mind telling the truth about Donald Trump. He's a Republican. They normally bend over backward for Republicans. For example, during the 2016 primaries, everyone on TV was in love with Marco Rubio. He is the prototypical establishment politician: completely synthetic and utterly controlled by corporate donors. So, of course, he was the darling of mainstream media. They were almost trying to collectively will him into winning the 2016 primaries. Ross Douthat of *The New York Times* wrote back then, "The entire commentariat is going to feel a little silly when Marco Rubio wins every Republican primary."[18] Oops.

The press used to love Lindsey Graham when he was helping John McCain start the Iraq War. Speaking of which, John McCain was in favor of every disastrous war we ever started and every monstrous tax cut for the rich that redistributed the wealth to the top. But to this day, everyone on cable news, including almost every host on MSNBC, is absolutely smitten with the man. They wouldn't be honest about him if their lives depended on it. If you're in mainstream media, you're aghast now—how could anyone take McCain's name in vain? Well, did he or did he not advocate for every horrible war? That's the definition of a warmonger. And every one of those was a colossal error. Yet the media loved McCain back then and they still love his memory today.

But Trump was different.

In the beginning it was all good theater, as Moonves explained. Then, when things got serious, when he won, all of a sudden, CNN wasn't neutral anymore. Now, mind you, I never thought they should be neutral! I'm glad they finally gathered up the courage to tell people what kind of a monster and liar he is. But I think they should count the lies of every politician, not just Trump's. The reason they broke their coveted vow of neutrality is because Trump started threatening the status quo. And that is an even bigger imperative for corporate interests: We must protect the system that brought us to the top! Nothing should fundamentally change!

Why do you think Joe Biden promised that to donors? The status quo is the one thing the donor class—in other words, the ruling class—wants to protect the most. When Trump started bothering the establishment, instead of this being an amusing and profitable sideshow, it unleashed the corporate media.

Of course, there are no secret memos written inside news headquarters to attack Trump. As I'll explain later, it's the invisible hand of the market. Everyone's interests are aligned with money, so everyone leans to the green. When the system is threatened, the incentives and disincentives built into the system kick in. It's almost like your antibodies attacking a virus. It happens naturally because of the way the system is set up.

That's why, eventually, CNN anchors could tell you that Trump was a ridiculous liar, but they still wouldn't say it about Mike Lee. In this case, Senator Lee was just as ridiculous as Trump, if not more so, but Anderson Cooper couldn't bring himself to say it. Instead he gave half the blame for that insane speech to the Democrats! Neutrality, right or wrong!

Yes, but we've mainly been talking about television. They're less serious people. How about the esteemed print journalists working at institutions that pride themselves on their sober analysis of the news? Take *The New York Times,* the self-proclaimed "paper of record." Its job, like the job of every other news outlet, is to report the truth without fear or favor. Right?

Wrong. Instead, the *Times'* editors believe it's their job to make the paper popular. "A paper whose journalism appeals to only half the country has a dangerously severed public mission," said Liz Spayd a few years back, when she was the newspaper's public editor, sort of an ombudswoman position. After the high-minded stuff about public mission, Spayd explained the paper's real motivation: "A news organization trying to survive off revenue from readers shouldn't erase American conservatives from its list of prospects."[19] That might work if American conservatives were reasonable and open to facts. But that approach fails with today's right wing. And it grants these same conservatives—who, again, don't acknowledge climate change, vaccines, or the Americanness of Obama or Kamala Harris—a veto on accuracy and truth. That neutral mentality means you'll turn your media outlet into a dish detergent that's harmless enough for everyone to buy. There's just one problem: the media's job is not to be an attractive brand but to tell the truth. They're supposed to deliver facts, not tell readers and audiences what they want to hear.

What people like Liz Spayd fail to realize—or don't want to admit—is that conservatives won't be content until every media outlet just reprints Republican National Committee press releases. Conservatives don't want fair, accurate, hard-hitting reporting that is skeptical and subjects Republicans to scrutiny. They want someone who will tell them that injecting disinfectant into your body might cure Covid, Tom Hanks might eat babies, and climate change is a fantasy dreamed up by the Chinese. That Black people have all the power in this country while white people can't catch a break. That two gay people getting married will destroy our culture by giving everyone equal rights. The media shouldn't surrender to these demands. Imagine that an unnamed senior administration official says two plus two equals six and a mathematician says it's four. The job of *The New York Times* is not to call it five to try to make everybody happy. Facts are stubborn things, as John Adams said.

This isn't a new problem. In his 1996 book, *Breaking the News*, *The Atlantic*'s correspondent James Fallows pointed out that the media fetishize "balance" above all other values, including accuracy—because it makes people in media feel they are being objective. In reality, the objective answer to combating climate change is not the midpoint between reducing carbon in the air and American babies. Neutrality is by definition not objective. It's an arbitrary midpoint between two political positions. The purpose of being neutral is to achieve political correctness rather than factual correctness. This is inarguable. Yet no one in media acknowledges it.

By the way, what if both sides are wrong? Then neutrality is the midpoint between two wrong points. This is obviously ridiculous. Yet it is universally accepted as the gold standard of journalism in the mainstream press.

Conservatives understand this phenomenon, and so they have whined about liberal bias since the civil rights movement. "If people are complaining from all sides, the editors reason, it must mean that they've got the balance just about right," wrote Fallows, speaking about newspapers and magazines that prioritize balance at the expense of accuracy.[20]

Twenty-seven years after he made that observation, the same problem still plagues us. The mainstream media are obsessed with "balance" and impartiality. Instead, they should prioritize actual correctness. If someone says it's raining and someone else says it isn't, the job of the media isn't to report that people disagree about the weather: its job is to stick its collective head out the window and see if there is any goddamned rain.

Imagine if this same neutrality standard were used by sports reporters. "The Yankees and Red Sox played earlier today. The Yankees say they won, and the Red Sox say they won. I guess we'll never know." Report the damn facts, not what the two sides want you to report.

Instead, what happens is that GOPers like Mike Lee are invited onto the influential Sunday news shows and treated like reasonable people. Not just reasonable but smart, thoughtful, well-intentioned leaders who have important, well-considered information to share. The media insist on presenting "both sides" to every issue, even when that issue is whether water is wet. "I think if we show we take conservatives seriously and we take ideas seriously . . . we get a lot more moderates paying attention to what The New York Times has to say," said a former top Times editorial page editor, James Bennet.[21] The party that went along with a "fake elector" scheme to try to overturn a democratically held election isn't filled to the brim with serious ideas. If they have one, great! You don't have to—and you shouldn't—dismiss their ideas out of hand. But you don't have to pretend that half of their positions are reasonable to fill your neutrality quota. Bennet talked about moderates as if they exist within the GOP. There are no longer any moderates among Republicans—all the moderates have already become Democrats and taken over that party.

Think I'm being unfair to the GOP? Well, no other major political party in the Western world doubts the science of climate change or argues against universal health care—American conservatives are unique in this regard. In fact, today's Republican Party is unique in most of its extreme ideas and personalities. "Conservative America has become an outlier in the Western world because of its growing radicalization over the past three decades," writes McGill University professor Mugambi Jouet in his book *Exceptional America*.[22] He didn't make that claim out of thin air. A German nonprofit organization called the Manifest Project compared the policy platforms of more than one thousand political parties on five continents since 1945. "According to its 2016 manifesto, the Republican Party lies far from the Conservative Party in Britain and the Christian Democratic Union in Germany—mainstream right-leaning parties—and is closer to far-right parties like Alternative for Germany," the *Times* wrote, summarizing the project's findings. "The difference is that in Europe, far-right populist parties are often an alternative to the mainstream. In the United States, the Republican Party *is* the mainstream."[23] And that study was released in 2016; Republicans now are even further radicalized.

What's amazing is that Republicans no longer hide their corruption and extremism. Instead, they boast about it. House Republican Chris Collins from New York said this about Trump's tax 2017 giveaway to the ultra-wealthy: "My donors are basically saying, 'Get it done or don't ever call me again.'"[24] He actually said that. Out loud. In public. That he was working exclusively for his donors. And he wasn't the only one who said the quiet part out loud. Senator Lindsey Graham (R-S.C.) told reporters that failing to pass the bill would drain his coffers. "The financial contributions will stop," he said.[25] How is that for clear? A sitting United States senator said he wants to pass a bill that reduces taxes on the rich because otherwise his financial contributions from those same people will stop. That's pretty much quid pro quo. Steven Law is the head of the Senate Leadership Fund, a super PAC affiliated with then–Senate Majority Leader Mitch McConnell (R-Ky.), and he was equally clear: "[Donors] would be mortified if we didn't live up to what we've committed to on tax reform."[26] The donors would be mortified if they didn't get what they paid for! How is this not bribery?

Trump took every bad instinct that the Republican Party had and amplified it. Corruption was put on steroids as he funneled political money into his properties and demanded foreign leaders give him personal favors in exchange for changing American foreign policy. And he took racist dog whistles the GOP was using and turned them into human whistles that we could all hear. From the 1960s until the Trump era, conservative leaders couched their language in code words. Lee Atwater, a top Republican campaign operative during the 1980s, explained how the game went:

> You start out in 1954 by saying, "N—r, n—r, n—r." By 1968 you can't say "n—r"—that hurts you, backfires. So you say stuff like, uh, forced busing, states' rights, and all that stuff, and you're getting so abstract. Now, you're talking about cutting taxes, and all these things you're talking about are totally economic things and a byproduct of them is, blacks get hurt worse than whites. . . . "We want to cut this" is much more abstract than even the busing thing, uh, and a hell of a lot more abstract than "N—r, n—r."[27]

For decades, GOPers lived by this strategy. Richard Nixon talked about preserving "law and order," which told voters that he would clamp down on crime—and civil rights protests. Ronald Reagan talked about "states' rights" in 1980 in Mississippi, near where three civil rights workers were murdered in 1964. In 2008, John McCain said that Barack Obama would turn the IRS into a "welfare agency." All of these statements were racist—and all were deniable in that intent. That was the deal between Republicans and the media—the politicians said racist things without mentioning color, and the media told everyone they were crazy for hearing racist things as racist. Trump ripped up this contract (just as he ripped up actual contracts with small-business owners when he didn't want to pay them, and presidential documents that were supposed to go to the National Archives, and who knows what else).

What people forget is that Trump was, for a time, popular with Black people and Latinos. *The Apprentice* featured people of color as smart, ambitious, aspiring businessmen and -women—beyond the stereotypes that have historically dominated their portrayals in American film and television. In the show's fourth season, the overall winner who became "The Apprentice" was an African American Rhodes Scholar. Trump was more popular with minorities than white viewers because he seemed to ignore the color of contestants in favor of their abilities. Of course, this was the work of the NBC producers who actually put the show together, but it played well for Trump.

If he'd wanted, Trump could have run for president as a forward-thinking Republican who appealed uniquely to people of color. But Trump knew that wasn't what conservatives really wanted. They didn't want someone reaching out to Black people, immigrants, and Muslims. They wanted someone who would insult people of color. They didn't want small government, faithfulness to the Constitution, or anything else that the media and right-wing intellectuals had sworn for generations that they cared about. They wanted racism, cruelty, and authoritarianism. That's who they were, and Trump knew it.

I sometimes think about that famous quote everyone puts on their Instagram feed, by the late poet Maya Angelou: "When someone shows you who they are, believe them the first time." The Republican Party shows us every day what it is. I'm talking about all of them: the leaders, the activists, the pundits, the voters. It is a party built on corruption that attacks anything and anybody that brings you facts—college professors, the media, scientists, experts in a variety of fields, and now even doctors. In other words, any neutral or objective authority that brings you facts, data, or information. You know who is opposed to facts? Someone trying to lie to you.

But look, as a political candidate and then president, Trump got good ratings. Oh, not *approval* ratings—he's been the most hated presidential nominee and president in modern American politics. No, he got good television ratings. The press never tired of Trump's act, and the truth is that most Americans didn't, either. Trump is entertaining. He is ridiculous. He is outrageous. The thing is, the news media shouldn't be infatuated with entertainment and entertainers. It shouldn't be about ratings and viewers and clicks and web traffic and listeners. But it is. And Trump knows it.

Throughout his political career, Trump kept upping the ante—saying more and more batshit-crazy stuff and getting correspondingly more and more media coverage for it. It was an addiction for news executives, and they are still hooked. Trump got about *five billion dollars* in free media coverage during the 2016 election.[28]

But as you'll see here, the Republican Party had already gone down a dark path by the time Trump arrived on the scene. It had laid the foundation for the extreme direction he would take. And the media had covered it up all along. It wasn't just because they were intimidated by Republicans. It's also because the mainstream media in America are part of the corporate machinery that has taken over the country. Republicans are the party of Big Business. The media had a vested interest in their winning. The more the GOP won, the more tax cuts and deregulation media companies received. The GOP was good for business.

In fact, there are two different story lines here. One is conservatives versus progressives. As you'll see throughout the book, that's a relatively easy competition for progressives to win. Most of the country agrees with us on nearly every policy issue, the younger generations are overwhelmingly progressive, and progressive ideals are woven into the fabric of American society. America is indisputably progressive.

The harder battle to win is the one against the establishment. This is outsiders versus insiders. The rebel alliance versus the corporate machines. As you'll see here, we live under corporate rule, but we don't know it. The media serve as the Matrix that plugs us into a completely skewed version of reality. They are the great protectors of the status quo. Populists have to unplug our fellow citizens from that machine and fight back against the establishment.

These fights will not be easy, but the good news is that our victory is inevitable. Progressives always win at the end. That is the story of human history. Change is the only constant. So, change is coming—and bringing justice with it.

1

AMERICA IS PROGRESSIVE

IT'S THE CORRUPTION, STUPID

HERE'S A QUESTION YOU'RE LIKELY TO HAVE: IF PROGRESSIVE POLICIES ARE so popular, why don't they get passed into law? Why isn't America run by bleeding-heart liberals who have enacted a social safety net to make the country look something like Sweden or Denmark? Good question!

Here's a good answer. During Bill Clinton's successful 1992 presidential run, his fast-talking strategist James Carville famously put up a poster in their campaign headquarters. The slogan on the poster said, "It's the economy, stupid." It was meant to concentrate the team's focus on the top issue. The economy was all that mattered if they wanted to win the election. Anything that deviated from that issue was a useless distraction at best and a costly diversion at worst.

Well, if you want to understand how American politics works now and for the past four decades, you need a sign in every office that says, "It's the corruption, stupid." Progressives aren't out of power because they lack good ideas; they're out of power because of the insane amount of money corporations are allowed to pour into our elections to buy off politicians. Because Republicans use tactics like gerrymandering and voter suppression to rig elections. Because conservatives know that their ideas are unpopular with Americans—as we'll see, they've always known this—so they devise and utilize tactics that deliberately thwart the majority.

That's why Donald Trump said in the lead-up to the 2020 election, "They had things—levels of voting that, if you ever agreed to it, you'd never have a Republican elected in this country again."[1] He was referring to Democratic proposals to allow for more vote-by-mail, same-day registration, and early voting in response to the coronavirus epidemic. As usual, he said the quiet part out loud. Republicans have been trying to block people from voting since the 1960s. They know something you don't—if everyone voted, "you'd never have a Republican elected in this country again."

But Trump's not the only one. His frank admission about Republicans needing to suppress votes became contagious. South Carolina Senator Lindsey Graham said after the 2020 election, "If we don't do something about voting by mail, we are going to lose the ability to elect a Republican in this country."[2] You know what the other name for "voting by mail" is? Voting.

Trump and his entire family voted by mail. And, weirdly, bragged about it. But they don't want most Americans to do it because they know that Republicans are deeply unpopular. More so than even the Democrats know it. In fact, they've known it for a long time.

Paul Weyrich, who was arguably the most influential conservative of his time (or any time) and who started the Heritage Foundation, the Moral Majority, and the American Legislative Exchange Council (ALEC), said in 1980, "I don't want everybody to vote. . . . As a matter of fact, our leverage in the elections quite candidly goes up as the voting populace goes down."[3] Why would all these powerful conservatives want as little voting as possible if they actually thought this was a center-right country? Because they know much better than anybody else how progressive this country is.

The fact is that progressive ideas to this day are amazingly, wonderfully popular. Every time Americans show that with their votes or by taking to the streets in huge numbers—think of the Women's March or the more than twenty-five hundred Black Lives Matter protests in May and June 2020—the media act surprised that so many people out there are not happy with the status quo. They shouldn't be surprised. Neither should politicians. But the media are clueless, and most of our politicians are so corrupt they couldn't care less about what the American people want.

Let's start with a simple example. Progressives want a universal background check on guns. Sometimes you'll read in print publications and hear on cable television news shows that gun control is unpopular in this country. "People mistakenly believe that most Americans support gun control efforts," *U.S. News & World Report* told us in 2016. "They don't."[4] Now, do you want to know how many people support universal background checks? Polls show that anywhere between 88 and 97 percent of Americans are in favor of them![5] That's virtually the entire country, including Republicans, conservatives, rural Americans, Evangelical Christians, and all other demographics who are supposed to be infatuated with guns. In 2008, even then–presidential candidate Barack Obama famously referred to some of them as "clinging" to their guns. Well, most Americans don't cling too tightly, if you look at the numbers—at least when it comes to background checks. Even 83 percent of gun owners and 72 percent of NRA members want background checks on sales of all firearms.[6] Want to know why? Because almost no one wants criminals buying guns . . . except gun manufacturers.

You might say: Well, if virtually the entire country agrees with implementing background checks, can that really be considered a progressive proposal? Fine: Would you call it a conservative one? Of course not. Every Republican politician is against it. And they say that their voters don't want background checks. That's just not true. Are conservatives opposed to some forms of gun control? Yes, of course. But are they opposed to universal background checks specifically? No, not even close. Only the executives at the NRA hate them. But opposing background checks is now the official conservative position because of . . . corruption. It's that simple. It's because of money. Lots and lots of it.

It doesn't matter how corrupt some Republican politicians are—background checks were passed into law anyway, right? I mean, do we really have a democracy if our Congress can't pass something 97 percent of voters want? As you might have guessed by now, universal background checks have not passed. As of May 2023, even after the mass shootings in Sandy Hook, in Las Vegas, in Parkland, in Buffalo, in Uvalde, and in many other schools, places of worship, and communities, the Senate has failed to pass background check legislation. America has the most gun-friendly laws on the planet. We don't even change them after our kids beg us to because they've seen their classmates murdered right in front of their eyes. Not even then. Our system is fundamentally broken. The voters are deeply progressive, but our legislators are right-wing zealots because elections are decided by donors far more than they are by voters.

Let's get something straight: there *is* a silent majority out there. But it's not the silent majority that Richard Nixon spoke about in 1969, when he reached out to people he thought privately supported him in his campaign to continue the Vietnam War and make war on the hippies. No, today America has a silent majority of progressives.

I can just hear members of the traditional press reading this and flipping out. "Come on, how can you say the country is not conservative? That's outrageous." Yes, compared to some Northern European countries, we could stand to be a little more liberal. But compared to the rest of the world, we are one of the bastions of liberalism. In fact, the United States has almost always led the world in being progressive. Our citizens are far more progressive than our government, especially these days. But even our government, as flawed as it has been, has at times taken some of the most progressive actions the world has ever seen. We developed the New Deal, which at the time was a model for a strong social safety net; created the United Nations; rebuilt Europe through the Marshall Plan; pushed for human rights throughout the world; established the idea of freedom of speech and of the press; and the list goes on and on. We are a progressive country and we should be proud of it.

Look, Americans are just not fundamentally conservative. We believe that when there is a disaster like Hurricane Katrina or Covid-19, people should help one another, and that it's the government's job to be there for its citizens when they are in need. We believe it is the government's job to regulate the markets (which simply means to establish some fair rules everyone plays by) so that the free markets are not left unfettered. We believe that aggressive wars in foreign lands turn out to be bad ideas, as does alienating our closest and longest-standing allies. We don't like torture. We believe in a strong minimum wage. We don't like cops beating on people, let alone killing them. We believe that women have the right to choose whether or not to give birth, regardless of what the Supreme Court or Republican politicians believe. And we fundamentally believe in a social safety net, as established in programs like Social Security and Medicare. Hell, even Obamacare is popular, and it's substantially worse than health care in any other wealthy country.

Since the national press has been brainwashed by conservatives for several decades now, perhaps wittingly, and the center-right myth is all they've ever told you, it might take some convincing for you to adjust to this. So let's look at the facts.

GREEN NEW DEAL

When the Green New Deal was first unveiled, it was incredibly and immediately popular. More than 80 percent of registered voters supported it, according to a poll conducted by the Yale Program on Climate Communication and the George Mason University Center for Climate Change Communication. Among Democrats, of course, support for robust action against climate change is nearly universal. More than 90 percent of them are on board with the GND. But there is bipartisan love for the planet. Most Republicans supported the GND—64 percent. Before the propaganda attacks by the media started, nearly two-thirds of Republicans supported the Green New Deal! As a headline in *The Hill* put it, summarizing the study, "Majorities of Both Parties Support Green New Deal."[7]

Hold on. Isn't the country insanely polarized? Aren't we more divided than we've ever been? Well, yes and no. Yes, we seem to deeply dislike and misunderstand each other. Most people have picked a team, and it's very hard to move their loyalties from that team. But when you look at the individual issues, all of a sudden the polarization disappears! When it comes to the GND—and much else, as we'll see—this famous polarization just doesn't exist in reality. It's a great mythical creature, like the Loch Ness Monster, the Abominable Snowman, or the reasonable, moderate Republican senator.

That Yale/George Mason polling on the GND wasn't an outlier. "More than 80% of Americans support almost all of the key ideas in Alexandria Ocasio-Cortez's Green New Deal," reported *Business Insider,* which did its own polling.[8] "People Actually Like the Green New Deal" was the title of an op-ed column in *The New York Times* written by Sean McElwee, cofounder of Data for Progress, a nonpartisan think tank that conducted polls on the GND.[9] Voters had more than a passing interest in legislation targeting climate change, too. Battling climate change was the top issue for Democratic voters, a CNN poll found in 2019.[10] It was a higher priority for them than even health care or gun control.

And among young people, the numbers are also great. Millennials who supported the Green New Deal outnumbered millennials who didn't by a nearly 30-point margin, one poll found.[11] In March 2019, American students were among the 1.6 million young people in thirty cities worldwide to protest for more action on climate change.[12] In September 2019, young people again marched in the streets—organizers said there were 250,000 marchers in New York City alone. They chanted in unison: "We vote next!"[13] Indeed, they did. Voter turnout among eighteen- to twenty-nine-year-olds increased by 11 percent in 2020 and made the critical difference in the 2020 election.[14] The additional young voters in the swing states single-handedly won the election for Joe Biden. And they're just getting started.

Establishment types were amazed that the GND polled so well. Wasn't it a crazy plan introduced by that Communist bartender, AOC? Actually, Republicans know that young people are concerned about climate change—and they're worried, because even young conservatives care about the fate of the planet, and that won't sit well with the GOP's donors. According to *The New York Times*, "a new Harvard University survey of voters under the age of 30 found that 73% of respondents disapproved of Mr. Trump's approach to climate change (about the same proportion as those who object to his handling of race relations). Half the respondents identified as Republican or independent."[15] The piece quoted a former Republican National Committee staffer as saying, "We're definitely sending a message to younger voters that we don't care about things that are very important to them. This spells certain doom in the long term if there isn't a plan to admit reality and have legislative prescriptions for it." Frank Luntz, the influential GOP pollster, was reported to be circulating a memo to congressional Republicans saying that climate change was a "G.O.P. vulnerability and a G.O.P. opportunity" because, he said, "Americans believe climate change is real, and that number goes up every single month."

That's why Republicans were nervous about Lee's spectacle that we discussed in the introduction. "Mockery doesn't get anybody anywhere," Representative Brian Fitzpatrick (R-Pa.) told *Politico* after Lee made an idiot out of himself, the entire party, and the conservative movement. "We should be offering solutions," he continued.[16] But of course, that's the one thing they can't do. Republicans won't be offering solutions, because they are puppets whose strings are pulled by their donors. Just about the only constituency in America that dislikes the Green New Deal is the fossil fuel companies. "Corporate America Is Terrified of the Green New Deal," as a headline in *The New Republic* put it.[17] As usual, corporations are pretty much alone in that.

I know what you're thinking—yes, the Green New Deal was popular when it was first introduced, but after the media, Republicans, and even most Democrats savaged it, it must be terribly unpopular by now. Nope. To Joe Biden's credit, he took almost all of what was proposed in the GND and put it into his initial climate plan, before he had to water it down in order to appease fossil-fuel-backed senators—this was one of the biggest successes of the Unity Task Force that was set up after the Democratic primaries. He even kept the ambitious two-trillion-dollar price tag for the program. It wasn't perfect, but progressives were pretty thrilled at how close it was to their original proposal. So, how did that climate plan poll right before the election? Sixty-six percent of Americans wanted it![18] Get used to seeing that two-thirds number. Even with all the propaganda in the world aimed against them, two-thirds of Americans are consistently progressive.

So did the GND pass? Of course not. The remnants of our climate change proposals were sprinkled into the Inflation Reduction Act of 2022, but they were accompanied by provisions that allowed the fossil fuel industry to cause even more harm to the planet. If the GND is so popular, why was it gutted by Republicans and even some Democrats? Because Corporate America runs the GOP completely—every single Republican senator voted against the climate change proposals. But that's not enough in a deadlocked Senate, so they needed some corrupt Democrats to help—and those are very easy to find in Washington. Just pay a politician enough money and they'll kill any legislation you want. In this case, it was Senator Manchin who rode to the rescue for corporate donors. But was there really a quid pro quo? You hear on cable news that these politicians are very honorable people, right? Have you ever seen a television anchor ask a politician if his vote was based on the money he took from donors? Of course not. That would question their integrity!

Well, I'm sure you're going to be shocked to find out that two of the top-five career donors to Joe Manchin are energy companies. *The New York Times* reported that energy companies increased their bribes (they call them "campaign contributions" out of politeness to politicians) to the greasy Senator Manchin while the dealmaking was taking place: "Natural gas pipeline companies have dramatically increased their contributions to Mr. Manchin, from just $20,000 in 2020 to more than $331,000 so far this election cycle, according to campaign finance disclosures filed with the Federal Election Commission and tallied by the Center for Responsive Politics."[19]

Gee, I wonder why he voted against popular proposals. He was literally paid to. And it's not like they were subtle about it. Here is CNBC's description: "Sen. Joe Manchin's reelection campaign raised nearly $300,000 from corporate political action committees and executives days after the conservative Democrat said he would oppose President Joe Biden's $1.75 trillion social and climate spending package, according to a CNBC analysis of Federal Election Commission filings."

Days after! Brazen. But if you think that's bad, look at how obvious Republican donor Ken Langone was: "Thank God for Joe Manchin. I'm going to have one of the biggest fundraisers I've ever had for him. He's special. He's precious."[20]

Precious!

Did the media then shred Manchin for this over-the-top corruption? Nope. They rewarded him with an endless torrent of stories where he was called "moderate." Sounds so reasonable! To be fair, the moderate position in Washington is corruption.

It's important to note that this is not an issue we largely lost on because of a vote by an unexpectedly corrupt Democrat at the end. No, none of the powerful people in either party were ever really in favor of the GND. This handwriting has been on the wall the entire time. So-called "centrists" have always been horrified by the GND. Howard Schultz, the Starbucks CEO, who flirted with a presidential run because he was positive the interests of the rich were not being fully represented, declared that "the Green New Deal is fantasy."[21] Billionaire former NYC Mayor Michael Bloomberg said the GND was "pie in the sky" and "never going to pass" Congress.[22]

Isn't it funny that corrupt politicians will say that deeply popular proposals will never pass Congress because of other corrupt politicians? And they'll say it with a straight face as a real reason why we shouldn't do reform. Yes, they might be really popular with the people—but what do you think this is, a democracy? They never say the proposals are unpopular, they just say they will never pass Congress.

Then maybe we shouldn't change the proposals—we should change Congress.

But am I being fair? At least Democratic leaders were always in favor of fighting climate change, right? Well, here is what Democratic House

Speaker Nancy Pelosi said about the Green New Deal when asked by a reporter in 2019: "The green dream, or whatever they call it, nobody knows what it is, but they're for it, right?" She said, "It will be one of several or maybe many suggestions that we receive." She was never in favor of it. This was always theater. Pelosi also neglected to mention that she and "her top four lieutenants collectively took over $790,000 from oil, gas and electric utility interests during the past two years," which the industry journal *E&E News* reported, citing data from the Center for Responsive Politics. Pelosi also forgot to mention that her husband, Paul Pelosi, owns stock in Clean Energy Fuels Corp., which sells natural gas infrastructure and fuels—and had a partnership interest in Odyssey Investment Partners LLC, a venture capital firm that's invested in Cross Country Pipeline Supply Co. Inc., an oil and gas business. *E&E News* found those ties, too.[23]

It's the corruption, stupid.

And corruption dictates how the political process works in the United States. Here's the pattern: A majority of Americans support something major that's very progressive, like the Green New Deal. They see what's happening in their lives and their country and understand that these progressive policies can make things better. Big money and the establishment rightly see that as a threat to them. So they team up to fight anything that might upset the status quo. Politicians, funded by these forces and most of the time emerging from the same background, do their bidding. Then the media call the corrupt politicians who killed the popular proposal "moderates" to clean up their reputations. They pretend the least reasonable people in Washington are the most reasonable. You can call this reputation laundering. Corporate and right-wing media alike declare that it was great for America that the proposal Americans desperately wanted was killed. Voters get angry and confused but don't know where to turn. End scene.

The policies that are proposed and implemented by Congress, the White House, and the various agencies of the federal government are much more right wing than the American people would like to see. And the reason for that is the same reason that our political system is in shambles: money in politics. It's the corruption, stupid.

Let me show you, through the numbers, that the country is progressive not only on the environment but on nearly all the issues.

FACTS ARE STUBBORN THINGS

Do you know how many Americans believe we should raise taxes on the rich? That number can't be high, right? If we're a right-wing country, we definitely wouldn't raise taxes. Correct answer: 76 percent.[24] Three-quarters of the country wants to raise taxes on the rich. Yet the Trump administration did the exact opposite. It passed a two-trillion-dollar tax cut for corporations and the rich. Trump's tax law reduced the individual tax rate of the top earners—which was already the lowest of any country in the developed world—from 39.6 percent to 37 percent. That might not sound like much, but we're talking about billionaires and multimillionaires here. When you have a billion dollars, 2.6 percent is twenty-six million dollars. The corporate tax rate was cut even more, from 35 percent to 21 percent. With these and a few other goodies for his friends built in, Trump's law reduced revenue—which the government needs to function—by $1.9 trillion. You hear Republicans say all the time that they care about deficit reduction, and their claims are further echoed by the media, which relentlessly repeat this claim. This $2 trillion hole in the budget obviously added enormous amounts to America's debt.

Did the media scream in unison, as they always do when it's a policy that helps you, "How are you going to pay for that?!" Nope. Did they call out the Republicans for being liars and hypocrites who never cared about the deficit? Nope. Did they make it sound like a radical proposal that was opposed by three-quarters of the country? Nope.

Someone's going to have pay down this giant tax cut one day. And I promise you, it won't be the people who got the tax breaks. It'll be the 76 percent of Americans who wanted the exact opposite policy! Remember, they wanted tax *increases* on the rich, not tax *cuts*. And Washington, as usual, gave them what the rich and powerful wanted instead.

Wait, we're not done with the rich yet. Eighty-two percent of Americans think wealthy people have too much power and influence in Washington. Eighty-two percent![25] How about Big Business? We're told every day in the press that Americans want business-friendly politicians because they want jobs. That turns out to be more mythology. Eighty-four percent of Americans think large businesses have too much power. Republican politicians hate the idea of trying to regulate businesses at all, let alone regulate the amount of power they have. Too bad for them that more than eight out of ten Americans disagree.

Seventy-six percent of Americans want to *increase* Social Security benefits, even if it means increasing taxes paid by wealthier Americans.[26] Social Security is progressive, preserving it from Republican cuts is progressive, increasing benefits to this entitlement program is progressive, and raising taxes on the rich to pay for it is definitely progressive. What does that make 76 percent of the country then?

Maybe you're saying, "Well, older Republican voters also like Social Security." That's true. That's why even they are more progressive than they realize. No one would argue that a giant government-run program that provides public money for your retirement is a conservative idea. Conservatives fought against it when it was proposed. Conservatives have been trying to cut it ever since. They just can't, because even their own voters love Social Security. You know why? Because, on that count, even conservative Republicans are actually left wing. They just don't know it. In fact, 73 percent of Republican voters also said we should raise taxes on the rich to pay for more Social Security benefits!

Do you know what percentage of eligible voters want a federal jobs guarantee? Hold on: The government is going to guarantee you a job? In this supposedly center-right country? The number has to be low, right? Wrong. It's 64 percent.[27] If we were really a center-right country, that number would top out at 25 percent, max. I bet if you asked television pundits, they'd guess around 10 percent. Can anyone make the argument the country isn't left wing when a nearly two-thirds of Americans want the federal government to *guarantee* jobs?

Right now, we are one of the few countries in the world that doesn't mandate that employers provide time off to families when they have a new baby. That's not because Americans don't want paid family leave. Eighty-four percent of voters want a national paid family and medical leave law.[28] Including 74 percent of Republicans! And yet almost all Republican politicians are against it. Why are Republicans opposed to nearly three-quarters of their own voters? It's the corruption, stupid.

In a real democracy, you would never have that kind of enormous gap between public opinion and public policy. But unfortunately, the mainstream media aids and abets this phenomenon by constantly telling everyone we're a right-wing country when the exact opposite is true.

Okay, but those are all economic issues. The country is at least socially conservative, right? Actually, 71 percent of Americans think same-sex marriage should be legally valid.[29] I'm pretty sure seven out of ten people is a majority. And again, we've won over the Republican voters here, too: 55 percent of them also want to recognize same-sex marriages.[30] Republican politicians have now proposed hundreds of anti-LGBTQ+ laws at the state level over the last five years, but their voters are getting more progressive on this issue. Even though a majority of their own voters now want same-sex marriage to be legal, in 2022 Republican representatives voted against the Respect for Marriage Act by a margin of 169 to 39 anyway.[31] Fifty-five percent of their voters wanted it, but 81 percent of their politicians voted against it. Welcome to America. This is what passes for democracy now.

What's undeniable though is that on social issues, we have seemingly unstoppable momentum with the voters. That's why Fox News is screaming every night that conservatives are losing the culture wars. Even the recent reactionary right-wing proposals and comments about racial and gender issues are, in a sense, the desperate overreaction of a side that is losing the country.

Speaking of progressive Republican voters, 84 percent of them want to legalize marijuana![32] Overall, 88 percent of Americans are in favor of legalizing marijuana for recreational or medicinal purposes. When you take out the people who think pot should be for only medicinal purposes and leave the people who want it just to get high—that's still 59 percent of the country! Anyone want to say legalizing weed is a conservative position? Nixon started the War on Drugs. Reagan industrialized it. And the Republican Party has been demagoguing on this issue for my whole life. Yet, 84 percent of their own voters disagree with them on this policy, too. On how many issues can the country be overwhelmingly progressive before you start to think maybe—just maybe—America is in fact center-left?

Fine, fine, but how about the issues where we are most divided: race and immigration? Now, this is going to not only show a split country but one where conservatives finally have an edge, right? Maybe even a decisive one, since Trump and the Republicans got into power by bashing immigrants and people of different races and religions. Let's take a look.

How many Americans think cops treat Black people and other minorities differently than whites? The beloved cops. The protectors of the realm and all things conservative. Sixty-seven percent.[33] That includes 63 percent of white Americans who say police are less fair to Blacks. Two-thirds of the country basically admits our cops are racist! Jesus Christ, where is this center-right country I keep hearing about? And those numbers were compiled before Americans saw with their own eyes the gruesome deaths of Tyre Nichols and George Floyd at the hands of the police.

Sixty-eight percent of Americans think the country's openness to people around the world is "essential to who we are as a nation."[34] There's that two-thirds number again. Only 29 percent agree with the conservative position that "if America is too open to people from all over the world, we risk losing our identity as a nation." I think everyone in that 29 percent watches Tucker Carlson. But instead of being the silent majority, they are the loudmouth minority.

Sixty-two percent of Americans say immigrants strengthen our country "because of their hard work and talents."[35] Only 28 percent of Americans think immigrants are a burden "because they take our jobs, housing and healthcare." When asked whether immigration is "a good thing" or "a bad thing," 70 percent of Americans said immigration was positive for America and only 24 percent said it was bad for the country.[36] It's funny that only a quarter of the country is conservative on an issue where virtually all the media declare the country to be center-right. This must be what Kellyanne Conway meant by the term "alternative facts."

Yes, but if you asked them about a specific policy regarding immigrants, would the numbers be different? How about the most critical one—should *illegal* immigrants be allowed to stay in America and become U.S. citizens? There's no way that's a majority, right? A stunning 83 percent of Americans say they should be allowed to have U.S. citizenship as long as they meet some basic requirements.[37] Was that at all clear to any of you from media coverage of this issue?

How about Medicare for All? Every corporate Democrat and every television pundit agrees that you can't be in favor of this policy if you want to win elections. Really? One of the first polls ever done on Medicare for All registered it at 70 percent popularity![38] Even a majority of Republicans said they wanted it—52 percent. Medicare for All doesn't seem unpopular; it seems to be the opposite. Television pundits gorging on ad money from health insurance and drug companies made up a half-lie that Americans would lose our private insurance if we went with this new system. What they didn't tell you is that you would get better insurance! That's a pretty important fact to leave out.

To be sure about that fact, I spoke to Senator Michael Bennet (D-Colo.), whom we discussed earlier. Bennet is a strident opponent of Medicare for All. He's the type of guy who, instead of saying "Hello" when you meet him, greets you with a warning that you'll lose private health insurance if we switch to Medicare for All. I asked him if, under Medicare for All, an American would have no health insurance at all. He said, "No, you would have the Cadillac Plan." Wait, what? I asked him again, and he repeated that health care coverage under Medicare for All would be "awesome" and the "Cadillac Plan." I turned to Dave Weigel, then at *The Washington Post*, who was standing next to me in the media scrum, and asked if there was something wrong with my hearing. No, he confirmed that one of the biggest opponents of the progressive proposal actually thought it would be "awesome."

After the second Democratic presidential debate in 2019, I caught up with the good senator in the spin room again. I repeated our earlier conversation and asked him if cost was the issue behind his opposition to Medicare for All—since there must be some explanation for why he's opposed to the policy. He said that yes, there was: it costs too much. I asked him to acknowledge that at least we would have better coverage. That's when he yelled at me (yes, Michael Bennet can raise his voice, but only at journalists, apparently) and stormed off. Facts are inconvenient for people who mindlessly repeat myths and who are usually buffered by a friendly press that has the same agenda as they do. You rarely, if ever, hear pundits admit that Medicare for All would replace private health insurance with something better, not worse. Instead, they yap endlessly about how it would take away your private insurance, thereby heavily implying that you would lose your health care. How many times do news anchors have to mislead you before you start to think maybe they're not in the news business?

After the beating Medicare for All took by the leaders of both political parties in the 2020 election (both Trump and Biden were adamantly against it) and all of the negative coverage it received on-air, in 2020 it still polled at 69 percent. No matter how much everyone in power pretended it was too far left, seven out of ten Americans still said they wanted government-run health insurance.[39] Yes, but that's all theoretical. If we applied that giant government program in real life, people would hate it! Right?

Wait a minute, we have a form of Medicare for All right now. You know what it's called? Medicare. That's been around for decades for people over sixty-five. Since America is supposed to be a center-right country, people will obviously hate that enormous government program. Especially after all these years of that instrument of socialism being forced upon the good, conservative people of America. You see where this is going, because at this point you're beginning to realize how progressive this country actually is. Seventy-seven percent of Americans said Medicare was a "very important government program."[40] Every poll of Medicare finds it to be enormously popular. In fact, 85 percent of Americans think it should be a *high priority* for the federal government to *expand* Medicare to include at-home health care.[41] And 84 percent say Medicare should be *expanded* to include dental, vision, and hearing. That includes 79 percent of Republicans.[42] Apparently, America loves socialism!

But really, we kind of do. And why have you never heard a cable news anchor tell you that the two most popular programs in the country are the handiwork of big government? In fact, it's giant government. Social Security and Medicare are colossal government programs—and the American people love them! That's an actual, verifiable fact. Isn't it super weird that you never heard it framed that way by anyone on television in your entire life?

It's as if everyone on TV is serving the interests of giant multibillion-dollar corporations because they work for giant multibillion-dollar corporations. More on this later, because it's the most underreported story in America. But why wouldn't media report about their own corruption? Oh!

Finally, we get to the mack daddy of all divisive issues: abortion! This is the one that is finally going to shut me up and show that the country is center-right, yes? Come on, this must be the one issue conservatives win in the polling, right? America has the most restrictive laws on reproductive rights of any country in the developed world, and we're more restrictive on the issue than many countries in the developing world, too. And it just got intensely more restrictive after the Supreme Court decision to overturn *Roe v. Wade*. Plus, this is the cause that right-wingers care most about, so they must have convinced their fellow Americans with their passion. Besides which, they don't need to convince anybody, because this is a right-wing country! Love it or leave it!

Actually, 71 percent of Americans opposed overturning *Roe v. Wade*.

Even 50 percent of Republicans agreed. Again, those numbers were compiled before the Supreme Court decision. After the decision, the right wing was jubilant—they were finally ascendant! A poll done several months after the decision showed that only 29 percent of the country supported it. Wait, where is that mythical center-right country we've all heard so much about? And there's that 29 percent number again. Almost all the polls show that conservative positions come in anywhere between 26 and 29 percent (look above).[43] They're just a loud minority who are used to getting their way.

In fact, after the decision, conservatives in Kansas rushed to make abortion illegal. And they had the perfect circumstance. There were heated Republican primaries drawing a lot of GOP voters to the polls but almost no competitive Democratic primaries in that cycle in Kansas. There were as many Republicans voting that day as Democrats and independents combined. And it's Kansas! The epicenter of the center-right! They lost 59–41. In what was a shocking result to the media, the people of Kansas did exactly what the polling indicates. They voted overwhelmingly progressive. Not only Democrats and independents, but tons of Republican voters switched over and voted to protect reproductive choice. It won by 165,000 votes! And the only reason you were surprised when you saw it was because the media have lied to you for your whole life. This is not remotely a center-right country. It's progressive, everywhere!

"Everywhere" sounds like an exaggeration, right? For example, there's no way voters are going to vote for abortion rights in Kentucky or Montana! Wrong again, mainstream media. Ballot initiatives trying to take away abortion rights in both of those states failed in 2022. The right wing has lost so badly on abortion that Republican legislators in Ohio panicked that the voters were going to take away their restrictive abortion ban and proposed legislation that would move the threshold for winning a ballot initiative to 60 percent.[44] If you're the majority, why would you worry about the other side getting well over 50 percent of the vote? They tried to limit democracy in Ohio because even Republican politicians know their policy positions are deeply unpopular.

After all this, you have to ask yourself, where the hell is the center-right? If seven out of ten Americans want abortion to be legal—and if conservatives win on no other big issue—what sane analyst could call this country conservative?

But if you're not convinced already, I've got one last doozy for you. What percentage of Americans think corporations simply make "too much profit"?

What business is it of ours how much profit corporations make? Why do you want the government to interfere with that? I don't think I even agree with that. What does "too much profit" even mean? If Americans were to agree to this, we would be challenging the very core of capitalism. If the Republicans and the media were right, this question would be roundly rejected by the American people. Even the most stubborn pundit would have to agree.

Well, it turns out that the percentage of people who agree is not two-thirds! It's just 59 percent.[45] Seriously, wow! Nearly six out of ten Americans say companies just make too much damn money. I could give you dozens more examples, but my case is closed for now. If you still don't understand that America is a progressive country, you are assiduously ignoring the facts and no amount of information will help you.

PAID FAMILY LEAVE

Let's take one more look at an individual issue, to give you a sense of how deeply our politicians are disconnected from the voters. Paid family leave is uncontroversial everywhere else in the world. Literally every country in the developed world has it. Except one. Us. In fact, almost *every* country in the world has it, including the majority of low- and middle-income countries.

That seems strange, doesn't it? What sets us apart? Is it that we're the best country in the world and we've figured out you don't need a single day off after delivering a baby? Are we superhuman? Do we think it's somehow more moral or decent to send women back into coal mines or assembly lines the day after they give birth? Does it toughen them up? Or is it possible that we're the country where corporate rule is most dominant and that those corporations have paid off our politicians (and media) to be brutal to us and make it seem normal? Let's find out.

If disdain for time off after birth is somehow in our moral fiber, we would see that paid family leave is very unpopular in the country. Certainly, if we're a right-wing country, we wouldn't want it! Welfare state!

Are you trying to soften up these mothers? Maybe the American people are shouting in unison, "We don't need no stinkin' time off after delivering a stinkin' baby. We're America tough! And we're number one!"

As you might have guessed, only a cable news anchor could possibly think something so absurd. In 2017, there was a poll that showed that 82 percent of Americans wanted paid family leave.[46] But to be fair, that was before it was proposed in President Biden's signature program, Build Back Better. That piece of legislation was eviscerated. Even when the remnants of it were passed in the Inflation Reduction Act, paid family leave was not included. Not popular enough! So, if you polled that same issue in 2022, the number of Americans who are in favor of it is probably way down, right? They didn't even include it in the least controversial parts of the bill.

Good news, Navigator did conduct a poll on it in 2022, after this proposal was roundly defeated in Washington. So, we know exactly what Americans actually think of this issue now. Paid family leave came in just as popular as before! It turns out that 80 percent of Americans love the idea! In fact, only 12 percent were opposed.[47] The poll I cited in an earlier section has it at 84 percent approval. Another YouGov poll has paid maternity leave at 82 percent approval.[48] There is no dispute: every poll, before and after the national conversation about the issue, has the same numbers—Americans absolutely love the idea of paid family leave. So obviously the politicians reconsidered and legislation was passed right after all those polls came out, right? Of course not. I know, this is becoming a bit of a sick joke. Our politicians just won't do anything we want. It's so frustrating that you almost have to laugh at how absurd it is.

There is almost no chance that the American government would do something the American people want (this is a literal statement, according to studies, as you'll see later in the book). In every poll, Americans tell you that they are overwhelmingly progressive, and then the media tell you the opposite. "Don't believe your lying eyes, you're center-right!"

Wait, we're not done with the Navigator poll yet. It turns out 70 percent of Republicans want paid family leave! Since paid family leave was part of the original Build Back Better bill, everyone in Congress had a chance to vote on it. You want to guess how many Republican senators voted for paid family leave? Yep, zero. Remember, 70 percent of their own voters want it. But alas, none of their politicians do.

By law, in Britain, mothers get thirty-nine weeks of paid family leave after birth. Not thirty-nine days, thirty-nine weeks! In Sweden, they get sixty-four weeks off. Fathers can even take off thirty-four weeks in Sweden. In Japan, mothers and fathers can get fifty-two weeks off. Mothers in America get *zero* days off. The idea of a father taking time off for parental leave is considered a joke in America. Which father in their right mind would care about their babies, amirite?

If you're thinking, "Wait a minute, I got paid family leave when I had my baby," congrats, that means you're likely an executive. Only 15 percent of the American workforce gets paid family leave provided by their companies, and those are almost all white-collar jobs, most in management. It's not provided by the government, as it is in other civilized countries, it's provided at the mercy of employers. And usually, those employers provide it because they want to be competitive with other companies in getting the most highly coveted executives. But it's back to the mines for the rest of you.

Well, maybe we're just poorer than we realized. Maybe Sweden and Japan have it so much better than us because they have so much more money. Nope. The United States has one of the highest GDPs per capita in the world, significantly higher than Sweden, Japan, or almost any other nation that has paid family leave. In fact, our GDP per capita is about three times the size of Estonia's. How many weeks off do women get in Estonia? Eighty-two! In America, we claim we can't afford one day off for mothers who just delivered. Meanwhile, Estonia can afford it—easily. The reality is that we're the one country that is by far the most vicious to our workers, even when we can afford to do better.

Remember, it's not in our culture. We don't want this kind of brutal capitalism. We're progressive on this issue, as we are on almost every issue. On this policy, even a huge majority of Republican voters are progressive. We were very clear—four-fifths of us want paid family leave. But we have no chance of getting it. Because our Congress is owned by corporate donors. And they're not interested in your well-being, they're interested in your productivity. You're a widget to them, and the politicians stand with them to get you back in line if you dare complain. If you think that's too harsh, let me ask you a simple question. If 80 percent of people want a policy and their so-called representatives refuse to give it to them, do you really live in a democracy?

And if no one in the press thinks there is something deeply wrong with this, do you really have a free press? Or do you have one that's owned and not at all free to tell the truth?

Corporate interests own both our politicians and our media; all we're left with is the illusion of freedom.

THE TELLING TALE OF OBAMACARE

Time after time, voters say they want something progressive and politicians give them something conservative—because their donors demand it. "Corporate managers are whores," a right-wing congressman in the 1970s admitted. "They don't care who's in office, what party or what they stand for. They're just out to buy you."[49]

You see this process play out over and over. Let's look at an in-depth example that's sure to come up again—health care. In 2008, Barack Obama ran his presidential campaign in a way that highlighted his health care plan. It called for guaranteeing eligibility for health insurance for all Americans. It was announced that the plan would cut nearly in half the number of people without health insurance, from thirty-four million to eighteen million. Obama's plan was repeated loud and clear to voters—it wasn't a secret.

Obama's plan was more conservative—meaning that it relied on more private health care providers and covered a smaller portion of the population—than any health care system that exists in any other industrialized country, from Japan to Canada. That's because the plan drew heavily from the health care program that was passed in Massachusetts by Governor Mitt Romney. Yes, that Mitt Romney, the guy so enthralled by right-wing ideas that he once infamously promised to double the number of people in the prison at Guantánamo Bay and wanted to make conditions so bad for undocumented immigrants that they'd "self-deport." He might seem moderate by comparison to Trump these days, but Romney was doing hateful talking points before Trump even thought about politics. Romneycare was, in turn, inspired by a plan created by the Heritage Foundation, an ultraconservative think tank. So what Obama was proposing was originally a Republican plan.

Notice that the 2012 presidential campaign was between Mitt Romney, who was in favor of Romneycare, and Barack Obama, who was in favor of Obamacare, which was originally Romneycare. There was a lot of sound and fury, but they were essentially arguing for the same plan. Do you remember anyone in the mainstream media telling you that? Isn't it weird that they didn't? The illusion of choice, indeed.

Of course, the fact that Obamacare was originally a Republican plan didn't stop Obama's campaign opponent in 2008, John McCain, and other Republicans from branding the plan as a Commie nightmare. McCain called it "big government at its best."[50] He also said, "I want to make sure that we're not handing the health care system over to the federal government, which is basically what would ultimately happen with Senator Obama's health care plan. I want the families to make the decisions between themselves and their doctors, not the federal government."[51]

By the way, Obamacare has been the law of the land for over a decade now. Did the government get between you and your doctor? Was the health care system handed over to the federal government? Do you now have to go to the DMV to see your doctor? No, none of those things happened. When is America going to get tired of Republicans constantly lying to them?

At least the 2008 presidential election offered voters a clear choice on health care. McCain's plan was to cut Medicare and Medicaid to offer tax credits to Americans to buy health insurance. That plan wouldn't dent the uninsured rate and would tax workers—instead of employers—if they got their health insurance through work. It was a draconian plan to roll back even the shitty health care system that Americans had at that time. The only beneficiaries? The insurance companies, of course!

Presented with this stark choice, Americans overwhelmingly voted for Obama. Not only that, but they gave Democrats a majority in the Senate and the House. Exit polls showed that one in three voters said they were worried about being able to afford health care—and those voters went for Obama over McCain by two to one.

As Barack Obama was about to be elected with what appeared to be a mandate, *National Journal,* an influential D.C. magazine, asked if it was "the end of the Reagan era." *The Wall Street Journal* warned that this could be "a change we haven't seen since 1965 or 1933 . . . a liberal supermajority." Sam Tanenhaus, a moderate journalist at *The New York Times,* declared in a cover story for *The New Republic* that "conservatism is dead."[52] Everyone seemed to agree that Obama's victory clearly illustrated that Americans had turned in a liberal direction and were supportive of the new president's program for reform.

As promised, once in office, Obama and the Democrats introduced the Affordable Care Act, nicknamed "Obamacare." It was the private-public plan that Obama had campaigned on. In a normal, functioning democracy, it would have sailed through the legislature and become law swiftly, in whole, as it was designed. Oh, sure, maybe a few tweaks to the bill here or there, but the public should get what they clearly wanted. Right?

Spoiler alert: that didn't happen. What did happen is that the lobbyists and corporations went to work. They saw a positive development about to happen to millions of Americans and were determined to wound it, if not stop it. They descended on Washington in record numbers, like a pack of lice determined to destroy a healthy head of hair. "About 1,750 businesses and organizations spent at least $1.2 billion in 2009 on lobbying teams to work on the health care overhaul and other issues," NPR reported.[53] That's "billion" with a *b*. In one year, in one place. Those dollars went to companies like Patton Boggs LLP, Alston & Bird LLP, Holland & Knight LLP, and the Podesta Group, Inc.—names that don't mean anything outside Washington but are household names inside the Beltway. The money spent to kill Obamacare was, to that point, a record amount.

That wasn't all. Members of Obama's administration met behind closed doors with representatives from the prescription drug industry. The drug reps promised they wouldn't oppose Obama's legislation, and Obama's team promised to push a bill that didn't take a big cut from Big Pharma, despite all that the president had said publicly. Veteran health care journalist Jonathan Cohn summarized the demands the drug industry made: "It strongly opposed letting the federal government negotiate directly with drug companies over price, the way governments in other countries do; it didn't want to give the government rebates on drugs it purchased for Medicare recipients; and it didn't want to let Americans buy cheaper drugs overseas."[54]

The industry got its way on all of this. The legislation was stripped of these provisions, which would have made health care more affordable for tens of millions of Americans and saved the federal government untold amounts of money. In return, the White House got buy-in from one of the most important special interest groups in Washington. If Big Pharma had opposed Obamacare, it could have killed the bill. Illinois Senator Dick Durbin once admitted about Congress that "banks . . . frankly own the place."[55] Well, it's not only banks. Big Pharma also owns a big chunk.

Still, even some in Congress were outraged at the behind-closed-doors agreement, which epitomized everything Obama had said on the campaign trail about the evils of Washington. "We have all been focused on the debate in Congress, but perhaps the deal has already been cut," Representative Raúl Grijalva, cochairman of the Congressional Progressive

Caucus, told reporters when he found out about the Obama team's deal.[56] Indeed, it had. Former Labor Secretary Robert Reich called it "extortion." One official in the know told *The New Republic,* "No matter how much high-handed talk there is [in Congress] of reining in Pharma, in the end, they always get their way."[57]

The Chair of the Senate Finance Committee was then a guy from Montana named Max Baucus. "Lobbying disclosure filings for the first quarter of 2009 reveal that five of Baucus' former staffers currently work for a total of twenty-seven different organizations that are either in the health care or insurance sector or have a noted interest in the outcome," the nonpartisan Sunlight Foundation found. Over his career to that date, Baucus had received $2,797,381 from the health sector and $1,170,313 from the insurance sector.[58] This was the main guy writing the bill. The reform bill.

Does anyone think that the health care and insurance industries gave the guy writing the bill about health care insurance $3.9 million because they care about the general welfare? If you do, you're a schmuck. And probably work in mainstream news. You wonder why progressive policies don't pass in a country that is clearly center-left? Even a guy like Obama, who was supposed to be the savior of the Democratic Party—and a Marxist, if you believed Fox News—cut a dirty deal with Big Pharma because . . . frankly, they own the place. And the top Democratic senator who wrote the bill practically worked for the health care industry. He took millions from them, and almost all of his ex-staffers literally worked for them.

It's the corruption, stupid.

A right-wing congressman in the late seventies explained how it worked: "The irony here is that although the public perceives us as carrying business's water, much of big business is really supporting our enemy. Many of these groups are more about buying access to incumbents than to any philosophical principles."[59] So, it turns out Donald Trump isn't the only one who says the quiet part out loud. This conservative politician was accurately pointing out that Big Business doesn't just buy Republicans, they buy everyone in D.C.!

People in Washington know that money dictates their behavior, but nobody is supposed to say it. The media told you Obama was a saint, and he might be a good man in his personal life, but money ruled everything in the Obama era, just as it did during Republican administrations. The system is built on corporate money. No amount of pleasantness is going to fix that. And to be honest, Obama didn't even really try to fix it. He just played within the same corrupt rules that he found when he got there. He was a relatively efficient bureaucrat, but real change was nowhere to be found.

Progressives fought valiantly for one more provision in Obamacare: the public option. It was a no-brainer. It just provided government-run health insurance as an option. No one had to buy it. You would only use it if it was cheaper and better than your current health insurance. It was killed by Joe Lieberman in the Senate. A Republican? Nope. A Democrat, who was Barack Obama's mentor while he was in the Senate.

The health care bill was eventually watered down until it barely looked like what Obama had promised on the campaign trail. It was a photocopy of a photocopy of a photocopy that bore only a slight resemblance to the real thing. Still, it was a lot better than nothing. It expanded coverage and promised to lower the number of uninsured people, which it eventually did. That's why Republicans said the law was like "Armageddon" that would "ruin the country" (then–House Minority Leader John Boehner); would "destroy the country" because America would have to "dramatically cut the military because we can't pay for it" (former Pennsylvania Senator Rick Santorum); and promised to be "the end of America as you know it" (Fox News clown/host Glenn Beck). Representative Paul Broun of Georgia said that if Obamacare passed, "a lot of people are going to die." My personal favorite is Texas Representative Louie Gohmert predicting that one in five American women would die as a result of Obama's law. Twenty percent! That would be a genocide. In effect, he thought Obamacare would kill thirty-three million women in America! And we're supposed to take Republicans seriously. These guys actually said these things. Seriously. Look them up.[60]

Fun side note: Louie Gohmert also said Obama was helping to "jump-start a new Ottoman Empire."[61] Do you remember when the Turks took over America? Because if I missed it, I'm going to be really pissed. This was my one chance!

Yet the media say the points Republicans make are as valid as Democrats', and that we should all call it 50–50. Does that mean we're 50 percent of the way toward the Ottoman Empire? Have 16.5 million women died because they got more health care?

But despite all the Republicans' best, amply funded efforts to deny Americans health care, the Affordable Care Act was passed into law. Once it was enacted, of course, none of the insane predications came to pass. The law caused the uninsured rate to plummet to 12.6 percent in 2016—still far too high, but about half of what it had been before the ACA. And those enormous costs that conservatives said would fall on Americans? The nonpartisan Congressional Budget Office found that the ACA *reduced* the budget deficit by $143 billion between 2010 and 2019 by doing things like encouraging Americans to use preventive care instead of waiting to go to the emergency room. There were no deaths related to Obamacare, let alone deaths in the numbers promised by conservatives. Somehow, America avoided losing one-fifth of its women, even though it increased affordable health care coverage for millions.

Republicans, of course, didn't care about any of this. They never cared about the deficit, they never cared about rising health care costs, and they certainly never cared about helping Americans get health insurance. Anyone who believed otherwise got suckered. Not one conservative pundit or politician who had been proven deeply wrong apologized or even mentioned how wrong they'd been. And the media never held them to account. In fact, Rick Santorum afterward got a job as a senior analyst on CNN.

Republican politicians were high on their own supply. They believed that the American public despised Obamacare as much as they did. They thought most people really hated health care organized by the government because it somehow violated their "freedoms." Once Trump became president and Republicans controlled both houses of Congress, they moved to repeal Obamacare, as they'd always promised.

Of course, the media and skittish Democrats declared that Trump's election meant that Obamacare was dead. "Obamacare As We Know It May Be Done For," a CNBC reporter determined.[62] *Reason* magazine, a libertarian publication, concluded that the "Affordable Care Act's Unpopularity Helped Trump Win 2016 Election."[63] A Harvard University professor who worked in the Senate to help pass Obamacare told *Vox*, "They have [dealt] a death blow to the Obamacare health coverage expansion."[64] *The Fiscal Times* wrote that "the Failure of Obamacare Helped Turn the 2016 Election."[65] Even a supporter of the ACA, the labor historian Nelson Lichtenstein, wrote that "it seems likely that after seven years of intransigent hostility to Obamacare, Republicans can maintain the discipline and momentum necessary to deregulate the insurance industry, curtail Medicaid expansion, and slash subsidies to those of modest income buying policies on the state insurance exchanges." He added, "Whether all this will amount to a rapid collapse of the ACA, especially the exchanges, or a more protracted devolution and defunding remains the only question."[66]

The Trump administration, of course, was packed with former lobbyists for the health care industry. Eric Hargan, the deputy secretary of Health and Human Services, represented the health insurance company UnitedHealthcare at the law firm he worked at prior to joining HHS. So did Paula Stannard, the senior counselor to HHS Secretary Thomas Price. HHS Chief of Staff Lance Leggitt had forty health care industry clients in his previous work. These are just a few of the many ways in which Trump's government was stuffed with corruption.

Republican donors wanted action from their employees, the politicians. "Get Obamacare repealed and replaced, get tax reform passed," a major Texan donor named Doug Deason told the GOP. Deason refused to hold a fundraiser for Republicans until he got what he wanted. "I said, 'No I'm not going to because we're closing the checkbook until you get some things done.'" If that sounds more to you like a parent withholding allowance from an entitled teenager to punish bad behavior, you're on the right track. Deason told them, according to the Associated Press, "You control the Senate. You control the House. You have the presidency. There's no reason you can't get this done. Get it done and we'll open it back up." A different lobbyist, an operative for the Koch family, said, "If they don't make good on these promises . . . there are going to be consequences, and quite frankly there should be."[67] There are going to be consequences. This guy was talking like he's Tony Soprano and Republicans in Washington are his crew members. Which, in a way, they are. And like Tony's crew following orders, they aren't much concerned with how many innocent people they hurt.

If that sounds like corruption, it's because it is. Openly talking about how you will or won't pay off politicians can only be done in a system so decayed that members of the donor class believe there are no consequences for publicly talking about how they buy our government. A lobbyist openly threatening politicians brings no consequences to either party. It's just understood that, well, this is how politics works in Washington. And we're told that if we don't think that's right, we're just naïve.

Republican politicians did as they were told and moved to repeal. Good mafiosos don't ignore orders from their bosses. They introduced bills to strip millions of Americans of their health care. But then something happened that nobody expected—nobody except those who understand that Americans are actually progressive. In February 2017, supporters of Obamacare turned up at town halls held by Republicans in Congress. And it turned out that there were a lot of supporters. And they were pissed off that their health care was going to be taken away so that some lobbyists could cash an even bigger paycheck.

In deep Republican territory—Utah, Tennessee, Iowa, Kansas, Kentucky—they came in large numbers. Thousands. They yelled at their representatives and screamed at them, "Do your job!" Here's what a thirty-two-year-old in Antioch, Tennessee, told Representative Diane Black: "I have to have coverage to make sure I don't die. There are people now who have cancer that have that coverage, that have to have that coverage to make sure they don't die. And you want to take away this coverage—and have nothing to replace it with! How can I trust you to do anything that's in our interest at all?"[68]

It was a damn good question. And it was one that Republicans had no answer for, one that they hadn't even prepared for. Some of them apparently had never considered that Americans might enjoy having health care. Being forced to actually confront the views of their constituents was frightening to them. So frightening that GOP lawmakers began avoiding their town halls. In some cases, they stopped holding them altogether, citing "security concerns." Our old friend Louie Gohmert said that "groups from the more violent strains of the leftist ideology . . . are preying on public town halls to wreak havoc and threaten public safety."[69] The politicians opted instead for town halls over the phone or on Facebook Live. That way they could control who attended or who spoke. You wouldn't want to actually give voice to your voters in a democracy, would you?

Displaying his usual perceptiveness, then–White House Press Secretary Sean Spicer said, "There is a bit of professional protester, manufactured base in there. . . . It is a loud, small group of people, disrupting something in many cases for media attention."[70] That was the standard GOP talking point—that these were crowds funded by wealthy Democrats. After all, funding protesters to shout down politicians is something Republicans would do. It's something they did do. Years earlier, when Obamacare was being passed, conservative activists poured hundreds of thousands of dollars into local efforts to prevent Democrats from passing health care reform. Remember the Tea Party? Supposedly the party of reform and revival of the American revolutionary spirit? Well, wealthy right-wingers like the Koch brothers were spiking the tea by pouring money into the movement, but making it look like a grassroots uprising. And the media bought it, of course.

But 2017 wasn't 2009. And taking away people's health care makes them a lot angrier than trying to expand health care coverage, a phenomenon psychologists call "loss aversion." These new protests were genuinely organic and spontaneous. And even Republicans knew it. "Protesters at GOP town halls won't accomplish much by adopting a hard line and shouting for reform," a columnist at *U.S. News and World Report* had lectured Americans.[71] She was wrong. Enough Republicans caved and voted against repealing the ACA.

One more fun fact: the decisive vote to keep Obamacare was cast by . . . John McCain, the man who had run an entire presidential campaign against it.

It turned out that Americans liked Obamacare. At least more than we liked not having it. Americans liked government making our lives better and healthier. We liked controlling health care spending and insuring more people. We liked having fewer Americans die when they couldn't pay their bills. We liked . . . progressive policies.

While some Republicans were genuinely surprised that Americans liked better health care coverage (it's funny every time), others always knew that if Obamacare passed, people would like it so much that they could never get rid of it. You know why? Because even Republicans know how progressive Americans are. And how well our policies work. They've been trying to get rid of Social Security and Medicare for decades and have never even come close. They know if you let Americans have access to progressive policies, we'll never go back! And it's not just America that loves progressive health care policies; no country that has implemented universal health care has ever switched back to privately run health insurance. It'd be political suicide for conservatives in those countries to even suggest it. People love progressive policies everywhere.

Nevertheless, the media were shocked at this development. They couldn't believe that Americans might be on board with a landmark progressive law, so much so that it couldn't be repealed even with solid Republican majorities in both houses of Congress. This problem is widespread within the Washington bubble. Inside the Washington bubble, the Republicans are always right, the Democrats are always out of touch with the average man. Republicans represent "real Americans," while Democrats represent elitists. Every issue is framed from the conservative perspective, and progressives are continually portrayed as some fringe group outside of the "mainstream of America." There is a reason for this talking point that America is center-right—it is a way for the Republicans to control the agenda even though they have been voted out of power. It is a warning to Democrats from the D.C. establishment—you'd better not actually be progressives and work on behalf of people outside the nation's capital.

Of course, it would help if people knew what being a progressive actually means.

2

WHAT IS A PROGRESSIVE?

UNFORTUNATELY, THE WORD "PROGRESSIVE" HAS BEEN USED IN AMERICAN politics as an empty vessel. People put whatever meaning they want into it. Corporate Democrats almost all claim to be progressives when running in primaries. Almost all of the twenty-seven Democrats running for president in 2020 called themselves progressive at one point, even though some of them were miles away from being so. The mainstream media loved to parrot this because it covered up the important differences between actual progressives and corporate politicians who are completely opposed to our policies.

By the way, you too would cover up the differences between policies if you were sure the other side's policies are definitely more popular. In the primaries, I wanted everyone to know that Joe Biden proposed to cut Social Security several times and Bernie Sanders did the opposite. The corporate media didn't want you to know that, so they never covered the fact that Biden had offered up Social Security cuts half a dozen times throughout his career. Would they have shown the same courtesy to Donald Trump? Or Bernie Sanders? You know that they likely would have eviscerated those politicians if they had ever talked about cutting the most beloved program in America.

Of course, at the same time, the media want to scare you by saying Bernie Sanders is a "socialist." But certainly no one would dispute that he is a progressive. So, which one is it? We got the sense that Biden was progressive enough on the policies people loved but was "moderate" whenever that appeared to be an electoral advantage. Bernie was a progressive along with everyone else, but a socialist anytime that appeared to be an electoral disadvantage. I don't mind the candidates playing these games—they're politicians. I get it. But the media shouldn't help them obfuscate their positions.

The reality is that "socialist" and "progressive" are not the same thing.

And, as usual, the Republicans are even worse when it comes to this issue. They define a progressive as anyone who would scare the bejesus out of you. According to them, a progressive is someone who wants to maniacally control your life, tell you that you can't eat hamburgers, and make sure you live under the jackbooted tyranny of government! They're unintentionally hilarious. If we had a functioning media, every time someone said this in public they would be roundly mocked as a clownish blowhard, not treated as if they were making a legitimate political point.

But even if you asked progressives what their defining principles are, I'm not sure most of our voters, or legislators, could name them. They know some of the policies that now define the movement, like Medicare for All and the Green New Deal. But those are policy proposals, not what it means to be a progressive.

That's what I'm going to boldly attempt to do here. I believe these three principles lie at the core of progressive thought: Expansion of the circle of liberty. Equality of opportunity. And justice for all.

I know what you're thinking: "You can't do that. You just took the most basic American principles and appropriated them for the progressive movement." First of all, yes, I can. Second, Republicans absurdly lay claim to words like "freedom"—and they don't even mean it. Third—and most important—it's absolutely true, as you'll see here.

If you say that's not fair because it sounds like progressives are more American than anyone else, that's true, we are. That's why you should be a progressive (and some of you probably are and don't even know it). We actually believe in the principles that formed this country. America hasn't always lived up to those principles, but progressives are the ones who steer the American ship back on course. We are the conscience of this country.

EXPANSION OF THE CIRCLE OF LIBERTY

Let's start with expanding the circle of liberty. Well, doesn't everyone believe in that? No, not at all. Historically, conservatives have fought to make sure Black people don't have the same rights as white people. They also fought to make sure women didn't have the same rights as men. And gay people didn't have the same rights as straight people. Those are indisputable facts. You can say, "Yes, well, that's true, but conservatives don't believe that anymore." Really?

First of all, they elected Donald Trump, and an overwhelming majority of Republicans supported him to the bitter end, including the 93 percent of Republicans who voted for him in the 2020 election. The anticipated break from Trump's hateful rhetoric by the so-called moderate Republicans never came. Because there are no moderate Republicans. It's a mainstream media myth. The average Republican voter is just as hateful as Trump. That's why the party picked him in the first place!

Trump is constantly attacking all the groups I mentioned. His administration argued in court that people in the LGBTQ+ community should not be protected under Title VII—that would mean they could be discriminated against in employment. So they literally would *not* have the same rights as straight people! Think about that—Trump went to court and spent taxpayer money in a desperate fight to make sure gay Americans could not have the same rights as straight Americans. Republicans hate the idea of equality. It is an inarguable fact that they fought it tooth and nail. And this was not in the 1860s or 1960s, this was in 2020.

Then there are the attempts to ban transgender people from bathrooms . . . and high school sports teams . . . and the military. Transgender Americans who say they love this country so much they're willing to die for it have been rejected as defective by Trump and the Republicans. The GOP literally says they should not have the same rights as all other Americans in this regard. How can you be clearer than that? Republicans are not for expanding liberty to those Americans, they're not for equality of opportunity for those Americans, and they're not for justice for those Americans. They are indisputably the party of hate and inequality.

If you're reading this and think, "Well, transgender people shouldn't have the same rights as me, either. They're weird and different"—thank you for proving my point. You prefer discrimination over equality. You just don't believe in America as much as we do.

Republicans have proposed nearly 670 bills across the country trying to codify discrimination against LGBTQ+ individuals in just the last four years.[1] That includes 238 bills proposed in the first three months of 2022 alone! Well, maybe they just represent the feelings of real Americans. Nope, a poll conducted in 2021 showed 71 percent of Americans think gay marriage should be legal.[2] And a whopping 83 percent think LGBTQ+ Americans should be protected from discrimination at the workplace, in housing, and in public accommodations.[3] But the Party of Hate doesn't care what most Americans think. They're trying to appeal to the most vicious end of their base. So, Florida Governor Ron DeSantis not only proposed a law banning the mere mention of gay people in schools in his state, he got it passed. Saying Republicans are in favor of gay Americans having equal rights is just flat out lying on behalf of Republicans.

Then there is the "total and complete shutdown of Muslims" entering the country. What part of any of this sounds like conservatives want everyone to be treated equally? If your answer is "Yes, but Muslims are dangerous and should be treated differently"—thank you for proving my point again! You don't believe in equality for all. Just own it.

Progressives, on the other hand, have fought for equal rights for all minorities, including women and LGBTQ+ Americans, throughout history. I know that the media want you to think progressives are weak and feckless by nature. To be fair, that does accurately describe Democratic leaders, who are all hopelessly "centrist." How do you fight for your side from the center? But the opposite is true for actual progressives. We have won every single one of those fights for liberty and equality. We are the ones perfecting the union.

Conservatives scream that everything should always stay the same, including hateful parts of our heritage, like statues of Confederate generals and, yes, discrimination. If it's old, conservatives love it. And there is nothing older than discrimination.

To be honest, humanity has been fighting off the "others" since the first day we formed tribes. All other tribes were the enemy, and that got woven into the culture. And the rest of history has been a battle between progressives trying to expand the circle of people we consider part of our tribe and conservatives fighting that idea tooth and nail. They scream into the void—keep the tribe small.

An interesting question was asked in a Cato Institute Survey in 2021— do you view yourself more as a global citizen than a citizen of the United States? Fifty-eight percent of "very liberal" respondents said they viewed

themselves as global citizens, and 75 percent of "very conservative" respondents said they do *not* view themselves as global citizens.[4] There you
have it—larger view of the tribe for progressives and smaller view of the
tribe for conservatives.

In 1981, Princeton philosopher Peter Singer wrote a book called *The
Expanding Circle*. The book argued for a system of ethics that begins
with caring for oneself, and then expands—first to one's family, then to
one's community, country, civilization, and, eventually, all of humanity. It's a circle of empathy, and the job of human beings is to expand
that circle to include all of us. Not just ourselves, or our family, or even
our community, important as those are. We should care about all living
creatures, because they exist. Singer uses the metaphor of an escalator:
selfishness at the bottom, extreme altruism at the top.

But that's not how conservatives see it. They might change Singer's
analogy from an escalator to a step ladder. They want to keep their
ladders of empathy short and their circles of compassion tight. But it's
not like they don't have empathy for anyone else. To be fair to conservatives, they are not all sociopaths like Donald Trump. They love
and fight for the people they consider to be in their tribe—people in
their family, religion, community, church, and, often, race. But when
it comes to the "others," that's where they get tribal. They think we're
soft and naïve. "The others will hurt us, we must keep the circle small
so we can protect our own!" On the other hand, progressives think
all humans are created equal. I wonder which of those principles got
written into our founding documents? Oh, right, the progressive part.
That's part of why I say progressives are more American.

FOUNDING FATHERS

This is another part where brainwashed conservatives will say that it's
outrageous to think our founding fathers were progressives. First, they
started a literal revolution against an established system. It doesn't get
any more progressive than that. Second, they demanded equality instead
of setting up a new kingdom where they would be royalty. They gave
up their own power to give rights to others. That's at the heart of being
progressive. They completely overturned an existing societal structure,
threw the culture, norms, traditions, and heritage of that system in the

garbage, and lit it on fire. Conservatives of the time hated the founding fathers! They were radicals!

But if you still don't think they were liberals, you can look at their direct quotes.

> All too will bear in mind this sacred principle, that though the will of the majority is in all cases to prevail, that will to be rightful must be reasonable; that the minority possess their equal rights, which equal law must protect, and to violate would be oppression.
>
> —Thomas Jefferson

> As mankind becomes more liberal, they will be more able to allow that those who conduct themselves as worthy members of the community are equally entitled to the protection of civil government. I hope ever to see America among the foremost nations in examples of justice and liberality.
>
> —George Washington

If George Washington saying that he hopes America becomes the foremost liberal nation on earth doesn't convince you, how about this doozy:

> We hold these truths to be self-evident; that all men are created equal; that they are endowed by their creator with certain unalienable rights; that among these are life, liberty, and the pursuit of happiness.
>
> —Thomas Jefferson, Declaration of Independence

Is there any validity to the revisionist history that the founders were conservative, that they wanted to keep the current system and traditions in place? That's absurd on its face. No one who likes the current system leads a revolution against it. So the next time you hear a Republican call a progressive a radical, understand that should be a badge of honor. The people who founded this country were undeniably radical. Thank God!

In the end, did the founders do a perfect job of creating true equality for all? Of course not. The hypocrisy of slavery and so many other atrocities of the time speak for themselves. Calling African Americans three-fifths of people and designating them as property is not exactly how you establish equality for all (understatement of the year!). Critiques of the founders are legitimate and justified. But they did start us down a road of equality and wrote that principle down as the cornerstone of our country. It's hard to uproot cornerstones.

Was establishing equality their ultimate goal? There might be some dispute about this (from people on the left, actually), but I think based on what they wrote and what they did, it sure looks like that was their intention. And they knew they were falling short, so they asked the country to continue to become more liberal. Then they made sure you could amend the Constitution so that you could continue to "form a more perfect union." There are no conservatives who go around imploring people to change the way things are done!

JESUS!

You know who else was a radical who wanted to completely upend the traditions and mores of his times? Jesus Christ! If a present-day progressive went to Wall Street and attacked the bankers the way Jesus did the money changers when he threw them out of the temple, they'd be arrested, ostracized, and called a . . . radical. Occupy Wall Street had nothing on Jesus of Nazareth.

Jesus said it wasn't going to be just rich men who got all the glory, it was going to be the majority of people—the poor! That's how you expand the circle of liberty. The conservatives of the time not only fought him, they killed him! It wasn't the Jews or the Romans who killed Jesus, it was conservatives. Not all of the Jewish population agreed, and not all of the Romans agreed, but the conservatives wanted that heretic eliminated. He was transgressing on their heritage and traditions!

Jesus wanted to throw out the established system and bring equality to the masses. He took care of the poor, the needy, the homeless, the prostitutes, and the sick. Fox News would have shredded him for being a do-gooder liberal. They would have said he didn't believe in family values for consorting with prostitutes (but Donald Trump having several porn star mistresses, on the other hand, is rock and roll!). They would have said he was a radical liberal who didn't understand supply-side economics. They would have lectured Jesus about how great it is to give all the money to the rich because it will eventually trickle down to the poor.

Jesus, on the other hand, said, "I tell you the truth, it is hard for a rich man to enter the kingdom of heaven. Again I tell you, it is easier for a camel to go through the eye of a needle than for a rich man to enter the kingdom of God."

That would not have played well with Sean Hannity. Imagine what Hannity would say about a modern-day Democrat who said that we should take all the money from the rich and give it to the poor. Fox News and the Republican Party would have tarred and feathered Jesus. Or maybe crucified him.

Isn't it amazing that when modern-day charlatans who call themselves prosperity preachers say the exact opposite of Jesus Christ, they are celebrated by the Republican Party? They say that God wants you to be rich. I'm not sure Jesus got that memo. And, of course, God wants you to vote for the party that gives tax cuts, and every other break, to the richest among you. They say this with a straight face as if they're on Jesus' side.

Here's what Jesus actually said: "If you want to be perfect, go, sell your possessions and give to the poor, and you will have treasure in heaven. Then come, follow me."

Is there any chance that they wouldn't have called him a Communist at the Republican National Convention? Even AOC doesn't tell you to sell all your possessions and give everything to the poor. Jesus would have made Karl Marx blush.

Modern-day Republicans would call that redistribution of wealth and class warfare. Jesus might have answered, "You're damned right it is!"

I'll never be half the progressive Jesus was. I don't think you should immediately give away everything you own to the poor. I don't spend my days washing the feet of the homeless or prostitutes. He wasn't just a better man than us, he was a better progressive, too.

The idea that conservatives are on Jesus' side is hilarious and ridiculous. Do they believe in turning the other cheek? Do they believe in taking in immigrants, as Jesus did? Do they believe in redistributing wealth? They don't believe any of these things. They are the world's worst Christians. To add insult to injury, they even worship a golden calf. The statue of the Charging Bull on Wall Street is their new idol.

Expanding liberty is what brings together everything that progressives fight for. Universal health care, LGBTQ+ rights, criminal justice reform, higher taxes on the wealthy, foreign policy that prioritizes human rights, student debt relief, free college, reproductive freedom, affordable childcare, racial justice—what unites all of it is a desire to give everybody a chance to live the American dream. It's that simple. We want everyone in this country to have a shot at life, liberty, and the pursuit of happiness. Not just some, or a few. Not just white people, or Christians, or men, or heterosexuals. Everyone. All Americans deserve opportunity, because they are Americans.

EQUALITY OF OPPORTUNITY

The second tenet of progressivism is closely intertwined with the other two tenets. We want equality of opportunity for everyone. Not equality of results! The more opportunities people have, the better results we'll have for everyone. Through that opportunity we'll have expanded liberty for more Americans. It's also a matter of justice that everyone gets a shot at the American dream, not just the elites.

Right now, that dream is accessible only to some—and that's not how America is supposed to work. According to the best estimates, the top 0.1 percent control 20 percent of the country's wealth.[5] Notably, that's the highest share since 1929, the year the stock market crashed and the Great Depression began. Radical inequality is ultimately unsustainable and leads to massive upheaval, such as depressions and worse.

Right now, the top 1 percent have 39 percent of all the wealth, whereas the bottom 90 percent of Americans (that's nearly all of us!) have just 26 percent of the country's wealth. That means the top 1 percent has one and half times the amount of wealth that *three hundred million* people have. The bottom half of Americans combined actually have a negative net worth, since they owe so much money to others (mostly huge corporations like banks, credit card companies, and payday lenders, which charge people ridiculous levels of interest).

But it gets worse. In 2017, the American billionaires on the Forbes 400 list had as much money as 64 percent of the country combined.[6] That number is likely much higher now. Just a few hundred people have more money than over two hundred million Americans!

And inequality keeps getting worse. In 1980, the top 0.1 percent had 7 percent of the country's wealth; now it's at 20 percent. That's more money than the bottom 85 percent.[7] The tiny sliver of the rich has more wealth than an overwhelming majority of the country. Notice the money keeps getting redistributed to the top, not the bottom. This is what actual class warfare looks like. The top 0.1 percent have tripled their wealth since 1980, while the rest of us have stagnated. That wasn't an accident. The campaign contributions of the very wealthy led to lower taxes and other legal advantages for them that robbed everyone else of equality of opportunity.

But the problem isn't just the results, it's where those results came from. Where did they originate? They came from a system that constantly rewards the already wealthy and powerful. For example, more than one-third (36 percent) of Harvard's class of 2022 are legacy students—relatives of people who went to Harvard.[8] A mediocre person whose daddy went to Harvard has a far, far better chance of getting into that school than an A-plus student whose parents are mechanics or teachers. And it's hardly just Harvard. Across the top thirty schools in the country, one study found that children of alumni "had a 45 percent greater chance of admission" than other applicants.[9]

The right wing is constantly complaining about affirmative action. That's a tiny issue compared to the giant "legacy" exception to the so-called meritocracy at the top schools. At this point, I don't love affirmative action because it stigmatizes the success of minorities so much that it's become potentially counterproductive (though it was desperately needed in the beginning). But if you're in favor of ending affirmative action but not legacy admissions, you're an obvious hypocrite. Saying disadvantaged minorities shouldn't get a leg up but the wealthiest people in the country should is absurd. And ridiculously un-American.

By the way, legacy admissions aren't the only way rich people get their kids into top schools. Jared Kushner's dad didn't go to Harvard, and Jared wasn't a very good student, so obviously there was no way he could get in. Except, in an amazing coincidence, Charles Kushner donated $2.5 million to Harvard and his son got in just a little while later.[10] And conservatives say the system isn't fair because too many poor minorities are let in!

The disparity that starts at birth often continues throughout your life, unfortunately. The best numbers suggest that there are 336,160 people in America who live on two dollars a day or less.[11] And, crucially, that number doesn't include people who are homeless. Homeless people can't be reached for research. The Department of Housing and Urban Development estimates that more than 580,000 people sleep without shelter every night.[12] Their fathers are definitely not buying them spots at Harvard.

THE MYTH OF MERITOCRACY

In America, one of the most powerful myths is the myth of meritocracy. It's essential to the idea of the American dream. But it is also essential to maintaining income inequality. First, let me add an important caveat here: I love the idea of a meritocracy. I want to wish it into existence. I also like that it is an essential part of the American idea—because then maybe we can make it real.

I understand that many of these American myths are basically marketing campaigns meant to lull people into a false sense of complacency and equivalency. But the upside of them is that they are woven into our culture. That gives us a chance of bringing them to life, if we can just show people how to do it right.

I also understand that moving up the income ladder through merit is not impossible. In fact, no one understands that better than my family—because we actually did it. That was largely due to my father's heroic work but also due to how much more progressive Turkey was than America (no, you didn't read that wrong; I will explain later). But just because my father did it (largely in a different country) doesn't mean everyone can or that it's easy. Back when I was a Republican, I remember having a debate with my cohost on *The Young Turks* at the time, Ben Mankiewicz, about how my dad lived the American dream, so I knew for sure it was possible. He said, "Did you ever consider that your dad might be exceptional? That it's not fair to ask everyone to be able to do the Herculean task he did?" No, I had not considered that. But it was an excellent point. Obviously, the better way to go is to make the dream possible for more people, not to make it a nearly impossible obstacle course.

Now let me tell you why the myth of meritocracy is dangerous, even if it has upsides and in rare cases might be achievable. The myth holds that you achieve success purely through merit. Well, by definition, that means that everyone who has achieved success deserved it! And anyone who didn't also deserved their fate.

What does that do? That validates the current income inequality not as some sort of injustice that has to be fixed but as the exact opposite—the definition of justice. Those folks got to the top by working hard and achieving success. If you complain about that, you're the one being unfair. What do you want—to achieve success without merit?

The reality is that many of the people at the top did not achieve success through merit. Some achieved it through simple inheritance. For example, about 30 percent of the Forbes 400 inherited more than fifty million dollars. I'd have a lot of merit, too, if Papa left me fifty million bucks. Over 20 percent of the Forbes 400 inherited all the wealth they needed to make the list.[13] In other words, they literally did nothing to earn all their money. Nothing. A significant percentage of the wealthy "earned" their fortune through the hard work of their parents' dying.

Then Republicans turn around and say if you work at Burger King you should pay the highest possible taxes in your income bracket (also true if you're a dentist or an accountant), but we should eliminate the estate tax so that Paris Hilton doesn't have to pay *any* taxes on the money Grandpapa left her! Why? Because your hard work to become an accountant, and earn what you do, doesn't have much merit because you're not spectacularly wealthy. But her wealth proves she has all the merit in the world. Now can you begin to see what a load of crap this is?

Having worked at a couple of large corporations, I also know that executives who rise to the top don't necessarily get there through hard work or amazing accomplishments. Usually the skill set that helps them the most is how good they are at internal office politics. Is that the great meritocracy we're constantly bragging about? "Well, Bob earned it by kissing the right amount of ass and blaming others for his mistakes at work, so obviously he deserves all the wealth that he is getting at the top of that corporate ladder." Really?

To be fair, there are plenty of great executives and entrepreneurs—and even people who do wonderful things with the money they have inherited. But the idea that wealth equals merit is utter nonsense.

So, when progressives look to change the system so that more people have access to the opportunity that can lead them to similar accomplishments, conservatives cry, "Class warfare!" No, class warfare is when the rich set up an unfair system that doesn't allow anyone else to cross the bridge they did to get there. It's class warfare when they take away educational opportunities for your kids and when they steal the American dream from underneath you. It's not class warfare when we ask to set up a fair system that allows all of us to have a shot at success, too.

But the idea that America already has a meritocracy allows the wealthy to flip the truth on its head and say that people who are asking to set up a more equitable system are the ones who are being unfair and trying to take what others made. They say it's sour grapes. Because they "earned it" and you didn't—and you just want to take it from them. How do we know that? Because everyone gets what they have through merit! If you don't already have money, you must have merited nothing! And if they already have money, they must have merited it—and now you're the bum trying to take something you didn't earn.

The myth of meritocracy is required in order to dress up the injustice of income inequality with the appearance of justice—so that people think that everyone gets exactly what they deserve.

Since it's not pretty to say that ordinary people shouldn't have the same opportunities as the wealthy, conservatives have to pretend that progressives want absolute equality of outcomes. According to the conservative pundit Victor Davis Hanson, progressives desire "government-mandated equality of result rather than that of opportunity" and believe that "egalitarianism should encompass nearly all facets of life."[14] What the hell is he talking about? I've led a progressive news show for two decades and talked to the leaders of almost every progressive group in the country, and I've *never* heard any progressive say something like that.

I've never heard a progressive say, "Boy, I'd love to control everyone's life. Then we can take their stuff and give it out equally to everyone, even if they didn't earn it." These are paranoid delusions. And it's sickening that media in America have treated them as if they are legitimate political points.

Progressives just do not believe in what Hanson calls "radical egalitarianism or a society of absolute equals."[15] Only in conservative fantasies do we call for everyone to wear identical uniforms, eat together each morning, and work in the fields all day. Actually, that sounds like what corporations make their workers do. Progressives don't believe any of that. In fact, in our ideal world, everyone would have enough opportunity to pursue whatever is their individual dream. And conservatives would leave us alone.

But these are the fairy tales conservatives tell themselves to avoid confronting our simple request to live up to our country's founding ideals. If you're trying to do awful things like deprive people of health care or keep entire communities locked in poverty, it's far easier if you convince yourself and your allies that your opponents are descendants of Chairman Mao and that you earned everything through a perfect meritocracy.

I saw this great video online about a race.[16] Everyone started at the same point and they had to run a hundred yards, and whoever got there first got a hundred dollars. Meritocracy! Except before the race started, they asked people who had access to a private school to take two steps forward. Then whoever didn't have to help their parents with the bills took another two steps forward. And this went on and on until some folks were near the finish line and some were still all the way back at the starting point. Then they started the race!

I'm not sure I've seen a better analogy for how American society is currently constructed. And you'd have to be nuts to think that's a meritocracy. This is a powerful way of presenting how some of us have such an enormous leg up before the race even starts. As the video explains, the people in the back are allowed to race, and some of them will catch up to others, but the race is fundamentally unfair. Someone near the finish line won, of course, because it was just too easy for them. But in our society, that person turns around and tells everyone else they earned it and that the rest of us didn't merit winning. It's one thing to have a huge advantage; it's another to not recognize it and yell at the rest of us that we didn't deserve any success.

But it just doesn't sell as many burgers and jeans to say America is fundamentally unfair. Again, I want to emphasize I don't want it to be like that. I want to believe in America. I love the idea of a meritocracy, and I want to work toward getting there. We're never going to get it perfect, and people will always start in different places in the race, but we can make it better, much better. The best way to fix the myth of meritocracy is to fix the system, so we can be the country that we say we are. Let's live up to our marketing!

BLACK-AND-WHITE ISSUE

So how can we create an actual meritocracy?

Education is an enormous part of the answer, and so is access to decent and universal health care. But let's start with the bare minimum—fair treatment by the government.

Progressives believe that the amount of wealth your family possesses shouldn't affect how you're treated by state institutions: the courts, police, immigration authorities, elected officials, or government agencies. In 2015, a judge famously handed a six-month jail sentence and three years of probation to Brock Turner, a Stanford University student who'd been convicted of three felony counts of sexual assault (he raped a woman behind a dumpster), because "a prison sentence would have a severe impact on him" and he had suffered bad press.[17] In asking for a lenient sentence, the student's parole officer lamented that the rapist had lost his swimming scholarship. There was a Black guy in Louisiana serving a life sentence for stealing hedge clippers in 1997.[18] I don't think anyone was concerned about his swimming scholarship.

Ethan Couch killed four people while driving drunk in Texas, but he didn't have to serve a day in prison because his attorney argued he had "affluenza"—a condition that makes rich people not realize the consequences of their actions because they have gotten away with everything their whole lives. This defense worked! Because in America, everyone knows that rich people can get away with anything.

Does this sound like a meritocracy to you? Meanwhile Black men are being choked to death over loose cigarettes and twenty-dollar bills that look a little fishy. You want to create equality of opportunity? Have the justice system treat everyone equally. Right now, in America, that seems unimaginable. From the progressive perspective, that is the bare, bare minimum.

Do you have any idea how elated minorities, the poor, and even the middle class would be if our justice system just held the rich accountable, the same as anyone else? What does it say about the current sorry state of our country that almost no one reading this believes that's remotely possible? If you're one of the few who think it is possible or easy, then you are very likely rich and have no idea how good you have it.

Now imagine if our justice system didn't lock up (let alone kill in the streets) thousands of Black men every year for minor offenses, like drug possession. Imagine the lives they could lead, the families that could be saved, the money that could go back into the economy. If you're one of those ancient conservatives who still thinks people should be locked away for "doing drugs" (sounds so scary!), then understand that you would have locked up most of our modern-day presidents. Politicians like Bill Clinton, George Bush, and Barack Obama blithely admitted to doing drugs, but they had no repercussions at all because they were among the elite. There was no way Obama was going to get locked up for smoking marijuana at Columbia, nor was Bush getting locked up for all the things he did at Yale. The poor get life sentences, the rich get a big laugh about their wild days in college.

Right now, we have 2.2 million people in prison. That's a stunning 500 percent increase since 1980.[19] There are over 1.5 million people incarcerated, on probation, or on parole for drug crimes.[20] Some drug crimes can be very serious, but arresting people for possession of marijuana is completely nonsensical. And, as we showed you in chapter 1, the American people don't want to do that! But someone is arrested for simply possessing drugs every twenty-five seconds in America anyway. The prison industrial complex is doing great! Can't say the same for the rest of us. You don't have much liberty or opportunity if you're in prison. All this carnage is over the equivalent of having a Coors Light.

Crime is real. Serious criminals must do serious time. Protecting victims is also an issue of justice. You also don't have any opportunity if someone kills you. We have to do right by everybody. Justice isn't just for some; we need justice for all. The injustice happens when rich and privileged folks get away with the most serious crimes, while minorities and the poor have their freedom taken away for trivial offenses.

Now let's talk about race. White Americans and Black Americans smoke pot at nearly the same rate. Do you want to guess who gets locked up more? If you guessed white people do, you're either disingenuous or shockingly unaware of the facts. Most people know that white people are going to get arrested at a lower rate in this country for almost any crime. But do you know *how much more often* Black folks were locked up for the same crime? They were arrested at 3.7 times the rate of white people.[21] Same crime, same amount, and Blacks arrested at a massively higher rate. Why? Because cops target minorities! They don't go trolling Dartmouth's campus to lock up the children of the wealthy and powerful. Cops heavily patrol areas that are African American and target that community as a matter of course because that's what they're taught to do. Minorities and the poor have no power, so they're easy targets for the police.

Would Bill Clinton have become president if he had served five years in San Quentin for drug possession (a crime he has admitted to)? Of course not. Every time we send the police to target, harass, beat, and arrest Black men for drug possession in this country, we rob them of opportunity for the rest of their lives.

Imagine what you would have been able to accomplish—or not

accomplish—if police were constantly checking for what you were doing wrong. My guess is not very much. I got in a lot of fights when I was younger, and I did other dumb things that could have landed me in jail. My guess is most of you did, too. But you didn't have cops parked up your ass 24/7 if you aren't Black or poor. How many times could they have robbed you of all your future opportunity for any of your transgressions?

I was interviewing Chuey Martinez, a popular radio and TV host out of Los Angeles, and he told me that when he was a kid, he used to have his report card at all times in his backpack. Why? Because the cops would pull over poor Latino kids two or three times a week in his neighborhood, and he would show his report card to them to prove that he wasn't a criminal—as they had assumed. That's one of the saddest things I've ever heard. Imagine living through that when you were a kid. If you didn't prove yourself innocent at every turn, they would take away all your future opportunity.

When I was interviewing Wendy Osefo, who is both a professor at Johns Hopkins and one of the cast members of *The Real Housewives of Potomac,* she told me a similar story. In instances where she's taken relatives to the emergency room, she's often had to tell all the doctors and nurses how educated her family members are, because she's worried they will think her relative's life might not be worth saving if the staff thinks they are a Black "thug." This is an instinctual reaction to living a lifetime's worth of white indifference to your life. That's why the movement is called Black Lives Matter: because for minorities in this country, unless they can clearly prove they aren't bad people, they are treated as if their lives don't matter.

Now, if you didn't grow up a minority in this country, you likely never experienced that. You probably also never saw anyone experience that. That's what is called white privilege. It's an unfortunate term because it makes it sound like a poor white kid from Nebraska is rolling up in a limo and asking his buddies for Grey Poupon. But it just means that you have the privilege of not being constantly treated as guilty—and you didn't even know it. Because that shouldn't be a privilege. Everyone should have equality of opportunity.

Does the progressive position here sound like "radical egalitarianism," or are we just asking for basic, minimum-level justice? If you think common decency for everybody is too much to ask for, you might be a conservative.

But the Socialists . . .

Yes, but we hear all the time that Democrats are socialists. Whether it's Bernie, who calls himself a democratic socialist, or Joe Biden and Barack Obama, who want nothing to do with that title, they're all labeled socialist and worse by Fox News and every Republican in every race. Donald Trump even called Kamala Harris a "Communist" right before the 2020 election. Desperate times call for desperate measures.

So what is the big difference between socialism and the government we have today? What fresh hell do we have planned for you guys once us "socialists" take over?

The real answer is that there is almost no difference between European-style socialism and what we have now in America. The two biggest differences by far are universal health care and some sort of paid family leave. Wow! Sounds like we're going to round people up and . . . give them health care! And maybe even let them take care of their newborn babies in peace. Heaven forbid! We wouldn't want that kind of Marxism around these parts.

The reality is that all these labels are silly. Almost every government on earth has a mixed economy. Some portions of the economy are run by private interests and some portions are run by the government. Before you spit out your tobacco chew and say, "Not around here, they don't," let me ask you a question. Who runs the military? I'll let you take a minute with that one.

Oh, right, the government does. The government also runs the police, the fire department, the post office, and about a thousand other things. By the way, it wasn't always so. In this country we used to have privatized fire departments. I know what the free-market purists are thinking—yes! If you didn't pay for private insurance, your house should burn down! And if your family is inside, we'll throw bootstraps at them. Personal responsibility!

Well, like I said, we tried that before. And here's what happened. Once one house didn't have insurance and their house burned down, so did everyone else's in the neighborhood. It turns out fires are hard to contain. That's why fire departments have to be public and cover everybody. If we don't stick together, we all burn together. In other words, *fucking socialists*! Amirite?!

Now, if you grant me that privatized fire departments are a particularly bad idea, I don't think you'll disagree much if we apply the same idea to the police or the military. Letting someone get murdered—or raped—because they didn't have private police insurance might be the only idea worse than letting the neighborhood burn down because you wanted to show Bob he should have paid more for his fire insurance.

But then wait a minute, what if your neighbor doesn't have a fire or an intruder to contend with, but has the coronavirus? Do you think it's a good idea to not treat him because he didn't have enough money for insurance? Well, in the middle of the pandemic, we decided that was a terrible idea. But there are thousands of other infectious diseases—do you think it's a good idea for us not to treat the guy standing next to you who has Ebola because he couldn't afford the deductible?

It's not just infectious diseases, though. Yes, it's true, your kid's cancer won't spread to me. But I'm not enough of a monster to let her die because you didn't have enough money for the premiums. Yes, you can go to the hospital if your daughter breaks her arm—it'll bankrupt you and you'll probably lose your house, but they will treat her. But if she has cancer, they won't! Or at least not right until she's about to die, then you can take her to the emergency room.

I had a friend who found out all of a sudden that he had stage-four colon cancer. Luckily, he had insurance (look at the Russian roulette we're playing—"is my friend going to die?" is the question that goes through everyone's head as we hold our breath and ask if he has insurance). So he's fine, right? You likely have private insurance, so you know that's not the whole answer. Health care providers are going to try to deny you lifesaving procedures so they can make more money. And in his case, the specialist who could operate on him was in Denver instead of Kansas, so he was out of network! This is the absolutely insane system we live under, that we are brutalized by.

By the way, his wife switched jobs and the new insurance did cover the doctor in Denver, so if you were wondering if our privatized insurance system murdered my friend, luckily, in this case, it didn't.

Back to your neighbor's daughter—if she has cancer, you can't take her to the emergency room. If your neighbor is poor enough, they can get Medicaid. But God help them if they're middle class. That's the scenario under which we literally let her die. Jesus Christ, what kind of sick society are we running?

Of course, public health insurance is just as necessary to saving our lives as public fire insurance and public police departments. To think otherwise is just counterfactual. The only reason why we accept it now (although, as every poll shows, the actual American people want to change it—it's just that our corrupt politicians won't let us) is that we have been spoon-fed endless propaganda (mainly by the mainstream media) that it is acceptable and humane to let your neighbor die if they can't afford the right kind of health insurance. Well, it isn't. It's barbaric.

How Are You Going to Pay for That?!

Then, of course, the media—and the corporate Democrats and Republicans—will jump in with, "Yes, but how are you going to pay for that?!" In order to understand how disingenuous this question is, you have to know one simple fact—every other developed nation on earth has universal health care, and it costs, on average, half of what our system costs! The media has lied to you so often, you're almost not going to be able to believe that. So google it. Seriously, look it up. You're going to be amazed that *every other developed nation on earth guarantees health care to all its citizen*s. And pays *half* of what we do!

But honestly, what's more amazing is that the media keeps asking how we're going to pay for something that costs half of what the current system costs. "Oh, you're paying a hundred dollars a month for your car insurance. And now you want to pay fifty dollars?! How are you going to pay for that?" they ask with a goddamn straight face. I don't know, how about I pay for it with the fifty bucks I was already paying and keep the other fifty bucks? It would appear that would solve the problem. Call me a genius!

They say, "Well, that's not fair. The American system is already so bloated that we couldn't possibly save half of the money like other countries do. In fact, a study paid for by the massively right-wing Koch brothers showed we would only save two trillion dollars a year by switching to Medicare for All."[22] Oh, I didn't know your case was that compelling. So we get everyone as much health care as they want—and we *only* save two *trillion* dollars? Remember, the original question was "How are you going to pay for that?"

And the media wonder how they lost all credibility with the American people.

Okay, fine, that talking point didn't work. So, let's try another one. Wait, why is the media in the business of trying one talking point after another against a certain policy proposal? I thought they claimed to be neutral. Did they seem neutral to you in the 2020 race? I literally can't remember one cable news anchor saying one positive thing about Medicare for All.

No, wait. Could the billions of dollars that mainstream media outlets get from drug company and insurance company commercials have something to do with it? Well, that sounds conspiratorial—as if multibillion-dollar corporations care about profits or something. Swear to God, they say this with a straight face. I had a reporter ask me once if I was saying there was a conspiracy by these corporations to make a profit. Not exactly what I would call a conspiracy.

Did you know videos about pharmaceutical companies get demonetized on some social media platforms? The ostensible reason is that you don't want to run a drug company ad before a video that bashes drug companies. Look, at least there is some logic behind that. But what does that do? It lays the media incentives bare (at least it's more honest), and it clearly disincentivizes anyone from making videos telling you how the drug companies have bought off your government. There's no money in that. Literally.

Back to their talking points. "But isn't that a takeover of the whole medical system? I don't want the government picking my doctor for me!" I love this one because it packs so many lies into one small argument.

First, think about it: Doesn't your insurance company pick your doctor now? A lot of us can't go outside of network for a doctor. Isn't that limiting what doctors we can see? If the government did that, the right wing (and corporate media) would be up in arms. "Don't get between me and my doctor . . . unless you're an insurance company!" Huh?

Second, under Medicare for All, no one can limit what doctor you see. You have unlimited health care coverage. I know it seems too good to be true. Google it—every other developed nation has it. They're scandalized that we're so barbaric we let our own citizens die if some insurance company isn't making enough money off them.

Remember my friend who couldn't get a specialist to save his life when he had stage-four cancer because the doctor was in Denver and not Kansas? Sounds like they got in between him and his doctor. And they did it to make a buck off denying him coverage. Do you even know what the business model of health insurance companies is?

They make money by taking more from your deductibles, premiums, etc., than they pay out in health care expenses. That's basic business. Your revenues have to be higher than your costs. But in this case, *their* costs are the health care that saves *your* life. Well, they want to minimize those costs. So, one way to do that is to deny you health care as much as possible.

The top health insurance CEO made $36.5 million in 2019. None of the top seven CEOs in the industry made less than $15 million. That money could have gone to your health care, but instead it went into their pockets. And that's just the CEOs. Do you know how much profit the health insurance industry made in 2020? It was $31 *billion*.[23] All of that could have been saved, but instead it went to *middlemen* who provide no benefit at all. Now are you beginning to see why our system costs twice what others do?

Third, Medicare for All is only for health *insurance*. It doesn't socialize any of the rest of the health care system. The hospitals, doctors, and other health care providers are still all in private hands. The UK has a system that nationalizes all of health care. But that's not what we're fighting for! We're just talking about health insurance, like fire insurance or car insurance. If you made car insurance public, that wouldn't mean Uncle Sam is making your car.

Did you get that sense from the media coverage? If you're a progressive who follows the news religiously, you almost certainly knew this. But I guarantee you a lot of people reading this right now are thinking, "Yeah, why didn't they tell me it was just the insurance? And why the hell were they talking about a government takeover of my doctor if it's just my insurance?" Let alone the lie about not being able to see any doctor you want.

Fourth, let's note the irony of conservatives complaining about the government getting between you and your doctor when their signature issue is abortion, where they want the government . . . to get between you and your doctor.

"But wait, Cenk, what does all this health insurance talk have to do with equality of opportunity?" Well, you don't have any opportunity if you're dead. And you also don't have much opportunity if you're spending all your disposable income on just staying alive or if you're stuck at a terrible job because you're scared to death of losing your insurance.

I'm not being glib. Really, it's wonderful to get an education and to be safe from crime and all the other things that give you a fair shot at success. But you can't do any of that if you're sick or dead. The wealthy have unlimited access to health care, so they not only have better health, they also have better opportunities in life that good health opens up.

If you can't afford your insulin shot, you're not busy trying to figure out which corporation you're going to take over next, you're busy trying to figure out how to survive. And some of you won't make it. Hard to live the American dream if you're already dead.

Again, this is not hyperbole. Forty-five thousand people die each year in this country because they don't have health insurance.[24] In all other developed nations, that number is zero! Forty-five thousand people is a stadium full of people. That's how many people die *every year* because they didn't pay the ransom to a private insurance company. The health insurance industry is like the villain Bane in the Batman series. He says, I'll kill a stadium full of people unless you pay me my profits! Then he kills them anyway!

Our system allows the health insurance companies to get all the profits *and* shoot the hostages.

JUSTICE FOR ALL

How could "justice for all" be part of the progressive agenda? "That's in the Pledge of Allegiance, so it applies to all Americans." Does it? "Conservatives love the idea of justice, too." Do they?

On social justice, conservatives have fought against equal rights for all Americans for as long as this country has existed. Progressives pushed for equality and justice—conservatives pushed back. In the civil rights era, when progressives were campaigning and protesting for equal rights, why did they have to protest if there was no one on the other side? Oh, right, there were a lot of people on the other side. In fact, the civil rights groups were massive underdogs and had been losing for a hundred years straight. So who were the people on the other side? Were they liberals? Of course not. They were people fighting against change—conservatives!

So, are conservatives in favor of justice for all? No, not at all. They've fought tooth and nail for injustice for centuries. This is a historical fact. When you think of nearly any injustice in this country where people were denied the right to vote or to enjoy their basic human freedoms or to even be in the same room as other human beings, it was conservatives who fought with all their might for injustice rather than justice. Fact.

Now, does that mean that conservatives are always wrong on every issue? No. Admit that you thought I was going to say yes. In a rational society, conservatives and progressives balance each other out. Is every change a good change? No, not necessarily. Change to give people more rights is almost always a good thing, but change in regulations isn't always a net positive, for example. It's possible that progressives would go too far and overreach on an issue and then it would be helpful for conservatives to reel them back in. It hasn't happened, at the national level, in this country for the last forty years, but it's definitely theoretically possible.

California might have just provided a recent example. Democrats have a supermajority in California. And generally speaking, it's pretty heavenly out here. Of course, there are still many societal issues that we have to deal with in California that afflict the whole country. But in total, it's a great place to live, and we're an enormously wealthy state. If what California has is socialism, then there should be a gold rush toward socialism. There's a reason why California keeps growing exponentially.

If you call California socialist and it's the richest state in the nation, aren't you accidentally doing an ad for socialism? Apparently, socialism is an amazing economic model that leads to tremendous wealth. Thanks for letting everyone know!

But does this mean the state always gets it right? Of course not. Recently it passed AB5, which forces companies who use gig workers to turn them into full-time employees after certain thresholds are passed. This was supposed to protect workers, but for some, it wound up limiting their opportunities. For example, it stated that freelance writers can only write thirty-five articles for a website before they have to be hired as full-time employees. This was to protect those writers and get them benefits, vacations, and health care. But even though it was done with good intent, it didn't work. Companies imposed strict rules on anyone they were going to hire full time, and they cut off everyone else. A lot of gig economy workers, like rideshare drivers, hated it because it took away their freedom to drive anywhere, anytime they wanted. Some gig economy workers were cut off entirely from their steady source of income. Since there were fewer writers and drivers, prices skyrocketed. And consumers hated that.

The road to hell is *not* paved with good intentions, it's usually paved with very bad intentions. But sometimes good intentions take a wrong turn. That's where conservatives can be helpful in achieving balance.

How much should we all pay in taxes? Well, that's a perpetual balancing act between liberals and conservatives. So, conservatives, don't feel too bad, you can have a role, too! Am I not merciful?

But on the issue of social justice, there is not as much nuance. Basically, a fair summary is that conservatives suck. And everyone knows it. They still brag about it to this day. Their latest target is transgender people and how apparently they need to be stopped from using the wrong bathroom or competing on the wrong high school and college sports teams. Is this a real issue, let alone an emergency in America? Come on. No one thinks that. So, why are we talking about it? Because it's considered a "wedge issue." What is that? That's something conservatives use to drive a wedge between us and then take advantage of the fear and loathing of "the others" that they have created.

Every reporter knows what a wedge issue is. But none of them tell you that it's used almost exclusively by conservatives and it's a way of dressing up bigotry.

So, I ask you, defender of conservatives, is the right wing in favor of letting transgender people use the bathroom of their choice (freedom) just like anyone else (justice)? The answer is a resounding no! That's what I thought. Still fighting against equal rights and justice for all. It's a new target but still the same hateful ideas and the same cheerleading for injustice.

How about economic justice? Do tax cuts for the rich sound like economic justice? Do subsidies for the biggest oil companies, banks, and multinational corporations sound like economic justice? To be fair, pork barrel politics and corrupt crony capitalism are more of a Republican thing than a conservative thing. Am I not merciful?

But as explained above, progressives fight for equality of opportunity, which leads to economic justice. Whereas estate tax cuts lead to the children of billionaires becoming even bigger billionaires and greatly exacerbate economic inequality.

Republicans are even against raising the federal minimum wage. They often say there should be no minimum wage. If we raise the minimum wage to fifteen dollars an hour, it will raise the wages of over thirty-three million Americans by over ninety-two billion dollars. These are all hard-working Americans. You don't get minimum wage unless you're working!

This law wouldn't get any of these folks to parity with the wealthy, but it would lessen the impact of economic inequality. In fact, it would lessen it by ninety-two billion dollars.

The current federal minimum wage is $7.25. You know how much income that is for a full year's worth of work? $15,080, if you don't take a single day off. And Republicans say that's too much! The progressive proposal would only get you to $31,200 a year. That's still barely making it. But does it bring you more economic justice than what you currently have? Of course. It's empirical.

Now, let me give you a sense of how devastating the economic injustice in America has been—and how much money it has cost you personally.

First, the good news. For thirty years, from the late 1940s to the late 1970s, we had economic justice in this country! So, it is, in fact, possible. As the World Economic Forum explains, "Between 1948–1979, the percent growth in productivity and wages were relatively similar, with an increase of 108 percent and 93 percent, respectively." That means as you worked harder, your wages went up. That's exactly how it's supposed to be. That's what justice looks like. And we had it here in the United States for a long time. But then something changed drastically. In chapter 4, I'm going to explain what that change was—the beginning of corporate rule. And I'm going to show you exactly how and why that change happened. For now, let me show you the horrible injustice that change caused. The World Economic Forum explains what happened next in America: "The growth from 1979–2018, however, has been drastically different. While net productivity has continued to increase by an expected 70 percent, hourly compensation in the country is less than a fifth of that at just 12 percent."[25] That means you were just as productive and worked just as hard, but you didn't get the rewards of that labor. While your productivity continued to soar, they stopped increasing your wages to match it.

To show you what that looks like, see the graph on page 76.

The Economic Policy Institute calculated that if your wages had kept up with your productivity in that same time period, the median hourly wage, adjusted for inflation, in 2017 would have been $33.10.[26] Remember, this is not minimum wage—this is the median wage for all American workers. Instead, the median hourly wage in America in 2017 was $23.15. That looks like a big difference—about ten bucks an hour, for every hour worked, for the average American worker.

The gap between productivity and a typical worker's compensation has increased dramatically since 1979

Productivity growth and hourly compensation growth, 1948–2021

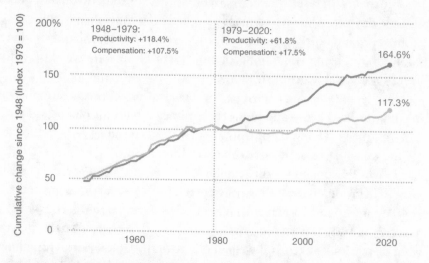

1948–1979:
Productivity: +118.4%
Compensation: +107.5%

1979–2020:
Productivity: +61.8%
Compensation: +17.5%

164.6%

117.3%

Notes: Data are for compensation (wages and benefits) of production/nonsupervisory workers in the private sector and net productivity of the total economy. "Net productivity" is the growth of output of goods and services less depreciation per hour worked.

Source: EPI analysis of unpublished Total Economy Productivity data from Bureau of Labor Statistics (BLS) Labor Productivity and Costs program, wage data from the BLS Current Employment Statistics, BLS Employment Cost Trends, BLS Consumer Price Index, and Bureau of Economic Analysis National Income and Product Accounts.

Economic Policy Institute

So, what does that come out to per year? According to an *In These Times* calculation, that meant the average worker in the U.S. lost $17,385 that year because their wages hadn't kept up with productivity.[27]

Holy shit! They've been taking about $17,000 a year out of your pocket for all that time! Imagine how much more you could afford, and how much better your life would have been, if you had that money. That's what economic injustice looks like.

How much did American workers lose in 2017 alone because the wealth was redistributed to the top? According to those same calculations, $1.78 trillion. The people at the top of the economic ladder have been taking trillions of dollars out of our pockets every year, as the corporate media covered their tracks. Both mainstream and right-wing media—the two arms of corporate media—distract us with culture wars while they execute this robbery, year after year.

Where did all that extra money that should have gone to you go instead? Corporate profits, of course (see graph on pages 78–79).

This is class warfare done in the dark of night. But when we ask to go back to a place we used to have—an America where everyone was treated fairly—they say *we* are waging class warfare. How dare we not accept our position—beneath them? "Now run along, everybody, and make sure you fight each other instead of us." Yes, as you see in this book, a lot of our fights are progressives versus conservatives. But this one, the granddaddy of them all, is more corporate elites versus the rest of us. The establishment versus the populists.

Again, in chapter 4 I will lay out exactly how this happened and who did this to you. But for now, suffice it to say that, unfortunately, conservatives fought for this system to remain exactly as it has been for the last four decades (largely because of how right-wing media and politicians lied to them), and progressives have been fighting desperately to get you back to economic justice.

Okay, it turns out that conservatives are generally against social and economic justice, but what about criminal justice? "Conservatives love law and order." Do they?

They like law and order when cops are breaking up Black Lives Matter protests. But did they like law and order when Donald Trump broke countless laws while in office and after he left office? Nope, hated it! When the FBI raided Mar-a-Lago to retrieve classified documents Trump had stolen, they wanted to defund the FBI. "How dare they try to enforce the law?!" said the people who pretended to be in favor of the rule of law.

And if conservatives liked law and order on January 6, 2021, they sure had a funny way of showing it. They claim they love law enforcement. Once you Taser someone and drag them half-conscious down a flight of stairs, I don't think you get to say you love them anymore.

How about when Black Americans ask for reform in the justice system? Who is on the other side? For example, earlier in this book I showed you the disparity in marijuana arrests. White and Black people smoke it at the same rate, and Black people get arrested at 370 percent the rate of white folks. There is obviously no reason in the world to think that's fair.

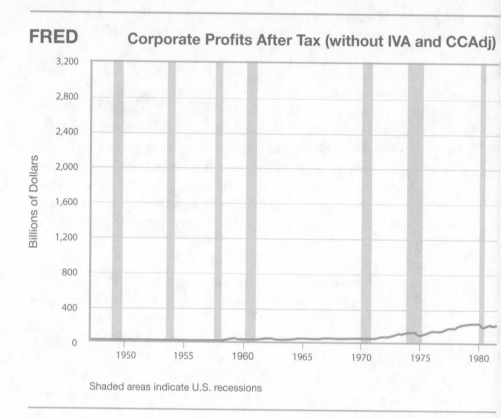

FRED   **Corporate Profits After Tax (without IVA and CCAdj)**

Shaded areas indicate U.S. recessions

If you think that's just, you might be a racist. But guess what? That's the current state of law enforcement! As a society, by not changing it, we are collectively saying we do think that's fair. That's not something from two hundred years ago. That's not something that everyone naturally agrees to change. As things stand now, conservatives are fighting to keep the current system—with that unbelievable injustice—intact!

If you're a conservative protesting that my facts are unfair to you, then I propose that you join us in fixing that horrible injustice. And you'll find out when you call your local Republican representative that they are on the other side of the issue and have no intention of changing any of those numbers.

So when we say progressives are for justice for all, it's literal. And yes, we do have a much better stake to that claim. If you say that makes us more American, I agree.

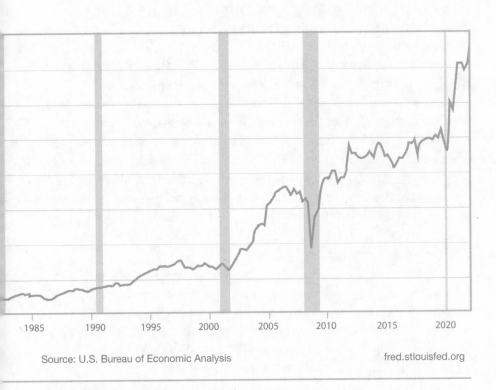

1985   1990   1995   2000   2005   2010   2015   2020

Source: U.S. Bureau of Economic Analysis   fred.stlouisfed.org

FREE COLLEGE

Large concentrations of wealth among a small portion of the population—our current state of affairs—inevitably lead to extreme unfairness in everyday life. So extreme that it makes a mockery of freedom. Liberty is useless if individuals are not free to access the fruits of liberty. This is not a new idea. Sometimes right-wingers like to pretend that there was a reasonable Democratic Party and an American left that they once liked and that these were moderate, patriotic, and capitalist—but somewhere along the line, progressives abandoned their noble tradition and embraced radicalism. Maybe it was Jimmy Carter who lured Democrats away from their love of America and its traditions of free enterprise. Maybe it was Bill Clinton. Maybe it was Obama. Maybe it was all three.

But the truth is that my explanations for the values underlying

progressivism are not new at all. Bernie Sanders and Elizabeth Warren haven't invented anything. Here's what FDR said in 1936: "Liberty
requires opportunity to make a living—a living decent according to the
standard of the time, a living which gives man not only enough to live by,
but something to live for."[28] Roosevelt said this in his speech accepting the
Democratic Party nomination for president for the second time.

He continued: "For too many of us the political equality we once had
won was meaningless in the face of economic inequality. A small group
had concentrated into their own hands an almost complete control over
other people's property, other people's money, other people's labor—other
people's lives. For too many of us life was no longer free; liberty no longer real; men could no longer follow the pursuit of happiness."[29] Liberty
was no longer real—FDR knew that the ultimate impact of extreme inequality was to crush the American dream. That economic fairness was
a prerequisite to freedom.

That's why, in 1941, he said that "freedom from want" was one of the
fundamental freedoms of human existence, alongside freedom of speech,
freedom of worship, and freedom from fear. He defined freedom from
want as "economic understandings which will secure to every nation a
healthy peacetime life for its inhabitants."[30] Establishing those economic
understandings is what lies behind the progressive vision. Fighting for
economic opportunity is not a new or radical idea. Democrats have believed in it for decades, and it has always been intensely popular with the
American people. It wasn't an accident FDR won four terms in office.

There are simple steps Americans can take to make this country a place
where everyone has a shot at making it. Take college education. It's been
called "the great equalizer" because it has the effect of "dramatically reducing the correlation between parents' income and the adult incomes of
their children," as the ultra-establishment Brookings Institution put it.[31]
Going to college is a way to seriously dent American inequality. Good news,
right? Wrong. In practice, college has been labeled "the great stratifier"—
because a kid is far, far likelier to attend and graduate college if his or her
family has money. If everyone could attend college for free, then it could
close the equality gap, but the current system makes that gap wider!

And if a student in college does come from a low-income background,
he or she is likely to be saddled with huge debts for decades. So higher education in this country actually furthers wealth disparities, making life
even more unfair for the lower and middle classes.

That's why progressives push for things like free college. Because it gives people a fighting chance at a decent life! It's that simple. Average student debt is now thirty thousand dollars per student, triple what it was in the 1990s.[32] These loans prevent graduates from buying houses and cars, moving jobs, starting businesses and families, saving or investing—and prevent many people from going to college or graduating in the first place. Bloviating on Fox News in June 2019, the pundit and minor *Ferris Bueller's Day Off* star Ben Stein sputtered that a plan for free college was "fantasy thinking, child's play . . . highly irresponsible . . . a wild attack on the whole idea of responsibility."[33] Stein explained that if he were a parent (he apparently forgot he actually is one), he would teach his children about personal responsibility. He neglected to mention that all the Nordic countries—Denmark, Sweden, Norway, Finland, and Iceland—provide higher education free of charge to their citizens. They seem like perfectly responsible, upstanding folks. He also failed to mention that Amazon didn't pay a cent in taxes for the more than $11.2 billion revenue it generated in 2018.[34] Hey, what happened to personal responsibility?

The issue of free college is also personal for me. My dad, Dogan Uygur, was a dirt-poor farmer in southeastern Turkey. In the 1960s, Turkey provided free college for anyone who could score in the top tier of national standardized tests. My dad worked incredibly hard to get into college, while still working on the farm. He lived the American dream, but in Turkey. Later he got his graduate degree in mechanical engineering in the States and could afford the small amount that cost by selling pots and pans in Hoboken. Imagine paying for college tuition that way these days. Now, not only is college not free, it's extremely expensive for most. But my dad wouldn't have had even that opportunity in graduate school here if college in Turkey weren't free. Are conservatives and cable news anchors really going to tell us that Turkey could afford to do that in the sixties but the mighty United States of America, the richest nation on earth, can't afford to do it now?

My dad went on to set up his own business and create hundreds of jobs in Turkey and America. Then I set up my own business, with his help, and I've hired hundreds of people here in the United States for my media company, TYT (*The Young Turks* was the name of both our flagship show and our company for years, but now the company is known as TYT—you can find out more about the network at tyt.com). Collectively, my dad and I have created countless jobs. Investing in bright young students isn't just the morally right thing to do, it's also the smart thing to do for the economy.

My dad and our entire family got to live this wonderful dream because he was able to go to college for free (you can read my dad's amazing life story in his book *The Original Young Turk*).[35] If it weren't for that opportunity, right now I'd still be a farmer in a small town near the Syrian border. Now can you see why I'm a progressive? In a sense, progressive policies saved my life.

I already got my shot at living the dream. For God's sake, let's give that same fair chance to all our kids.

How to Create Income Inequality

The rich use their money not just to buy better health care, education, and housing—they use it to buy the government. About 85 percent of Americans don't give any money to politicians, political candidates, or political parties, according to the Pew Research Center. And of those 15 percent, most donate less than $100. And almost all donate less than $250.[36] Well, who the hell is donating the money then? Politicians are getting it from somewhere. A record $5.2 billion was pumped into the 2018 midterm elections.[37] More than $1.1 billion went into super PACs alone (thanks, *Citizens United*). And that record was quickly crushed in the next midterms, in 2022, where $17 billion was spent.[38] So where did all the cash come from?

Well, from the billionaires, of course. In 2018, most super PAC money—nearly 80 percent—came from donors giving more than $500,000.[39] Anyone who can afford to funnel half a million dollars into a super PAC is someone a politician wants to know. "Donors get their phone calls answered, is one way of thinking about it," according to Ian Vandewalker, a senior counsel at the Brennan Center for Justice. "We like to think of our democracy as being one person, one vote—the majority rules. But just being rich and being able to write million-dollar checks gets you influence over elected officials that's far greater than the average person."[40]

Americans know their government is rigged. The public is well aware that big money has captured government. What they don't know is the precise ways it's been captured, or the effects of this capture. They don't see the details of how the wealthy use their money to rewrite the rules of policy. They just know it happens.

Let's dive into policy for a second. A person who makes twenty thousand dollars a year is twenty *times* likelier to be audited than a person making four hundred thousand dollars, the investigative news website *ProPublica* found.[41] Why? Because Republicans targeted the IRS with budget cuts—the agency's budget was slashed by almost three billion dollars since 2010[42] (the recently passed Inflation Reduction Act will increase the IRS's budget by eight billion dollars a year over ten years, with the specific intention of improving enforcement against wealthy tax evaders—it received exactly zero Republican votes in the Senate[43]). Before the new law passed, the IRS had fewer employees than it did in 1953, when Eisenhower was president. These cutbacks did what Republicans wanted—the agency's auditing of the ultrawealthy plummeted. But the GOP insisted that the IRS maintain its scrutiny of anyone who claims the Earned Income Tax Credit (EITC)—and whose average annual income is less than twenty thousand dollars. When Democratic Senator Ron Wyden from Oregon asked the IRS why it was concentrating on poor people, the agency responded that doing so was "the most efficient use of available IRS examination resources." Auditing low-income people is mostly done by mail and with low-level staff. Auditing the rich, on the other hand, takes much longer, with higher-level staff required. And "the rate of attrition is significantly higher among these more experienced examiners" because of cutbacks, the IRS said. "Congress must fund and the IRS must hire and train appropriate numbers of [auditors] to have appropriately balanced coverage across all income levels," the agency continued.[44] It's exactly the opposite of what the GOP's funders want—that's why they instructed all Republicans to vote against supplying the IRS with more auditors, every time.

What's amazing is that, by definition, anyone receiving the EITC is working—these aren't even people who have disabilities preventing them from working, a class of people the GOP despises. These are the working poor, people who receive such low wages for their work that they live in poverty. Conservatives want them scrutinized for every penny. They say it's about cracking down on "tax cheats" and "welfare queens."

But the bitter irony is that nobody cheats on their taxes the way the rich do. A comprehensive analysis in the *National Tax Journal* found that the ratio of people lying about their income "generally increases with income," peaking among taxpayers with incomes between half a million and one million dollars.[45] "The top 0.1 % have become expert in shifting and relabeling their income in response to tax incentives," Bloomberg News determined. "When it comes to paying taxes, the rich are different."[46] Remember when Trump was exposed by *The New York Times* for not paying any taxes? He had been publicly accused of this many times (correctly so, as the *NYT* story showed). "That makes me smart," he said, when asked about it during a debate with Hillary Clinton. His comment was controversial, but it shouldn't have been—he was just being honest about what a man thinks when he comes from a background of inherited wealth that was itself amassed through tax cheating, as the *Times* reported.[47] Trump's notorious remark was indicative of how the rich think—only suckers pay their fair share.

Since it's estimated that 70 percent of the underreporting comes from the top 1 percent of earners, auditing the rich winds up bringing in a lot more money than it costs. The Treasury Department estimates that for every dollar the government spends on the IRS, it gets back six dollars through enforcement and three times more on indirect revenue, including the deterrence those audits have on people who were thinking of cheating on their taxes. So, every dollar you cut from the IRS costs the country twenty-four dollars.[48] Who the hell would do that? Why would you make such an obviously terrible accounting choice? Well, it depends on your goal, doesn't it? If your goal is to be fair to everyone or to raise more money for the government so that we won't have such huge deficits, then cutting the IRS budget would be penny wise and pound foolish. But if your goal is to protect the rich, then congrats, you did it again!

The Congressional Budget Office is more conservative than the Treasury Department and estimates that if we put $20 billion extra into IRS enforcement over a decade, we would get $61 billion in return.[49] If we put in an extra $40 billion in resources, we'd gain $103 billion. That's not complicated math. If I told you that if you give me $40, I'll give you $103, first of all, you wouldn't believe me because that deal is way too good. But if you did believe me, how often would you make that deal? Correct answer: very often! But for so long our government did the opposite. IRS revenue agents had been cut by one-third over the last ten years. The result—audit rates for people earning more than $1 million fell by 81 percent! Mission accomplished.

But the more tax cheats flourished, the more politicians got campaign contributions and the more the rest of us were screwed. And what did Republican minority leader Kevin McCarthy promise to do as his first order of business if the GOP won the House in 2022? "We're going to repeal 87,000 IRS agents."[50] Remember, under the Inflation Reduction Act, these agents were specifically aimed at auditing only people who made over $400,000. McCarthy added, "Our job is to work for you—not go after you." He didn't explain that he didn't mean you, the American voter. He meant his job is to work for his donors, not go after them. This is exactly what you would do if you wanted to protect those wealthy donors. So they got what they paid for.

This double standard in auditing—scrutiny for the poor, lax oversight for the wealthy—didn't happen by accident. It's not just the natural way of the universe, as conservatives like to claim about inequality. This happened because Republicans did the donors' bidding and used the government to let rich people have an easier time cheating on their taxes. It was an active decision to rig the system in favor of the rich.

To be fair to the Democrats, they did pass the Inflation Reduction Act, which has the provision to audit the rich. It might be rare, but you do have to give Democrats credit for actually doing the right thing in this case and proving there are still some differences between the parties, even on economic issues.

Overall, the ways in which the deck is stacked against working people are countless. They exist across every policy area, not just taxation: health care, defense, the environment, minimum wage standards, labor rights, voting rights, all of it.

And unstacking that deck—creating a game where all people have a fair shot at winning—is what motivates progressives. That's what it's all about—a fair chance for all of us.

THE 47 PERCENT

Conservatives have concocted bizarre explanations for why progressives believe what we believe. According to *Newsweek* contributing editor Peter Roff, it's all about politicians buying votes. "They're out to win votes by promising stuff to key voter blocks that would be free to them," he wrote.[51] This explanation fails to acknowledge that if the Democrats are out to buy votes, they're doing a pretty bad job of it; they lost to Donald Trump in 2016, the greatest act of political incompetence in this nation's history. Then they almost lost to him again in 2020, *after* he suggested we inject bleach into our bodies to cure Covid-19. Republicans continue to either have a majority in one of the houses of Congress or enough members to block all progress, despite almost every conceivable advantage for the Democrats. The GOP controls fifty-seven out of the ninety-nine state legislative chambers and has twenty-six governors to the Democrats' twenty-four. In the Obama years, the Republicans picked up a thousand seats nationwide in state and federal races. If Democrats are trying to win elections by "buying" votes, they might want a refund.

And this charge of buying votes comes from the party that promises donors . . . tax cuts! That's the granddaddy of vote-buying schemes. Except in that case, they buy the support of the donors—and the millions the donors give to Republican politicians buy the rest of the election.

Roff's analysis is a convenient way to avoid reckoning with the popularity of social programs. Most Americans like taxing the wealthy, because they know that the wealthy rig the game. Members of the media are constantly surprised by the popularity of progressive positions, because they prefer the status quo—after all, it's good for them! It's how they got to where they are. They're trying to protect their status. The word "status" is even in the phrase "status quo." If you already have status, you love the status quo.

In March 2019, CNBC's senior economics reporter Steve Leisman wrote, "From government-mandated paid maternity leave to tuition-free college, the CNBC All-America Economic Survey reveals a *surprising* American appetite for some very progressive policies" (italics mine). Surprising to whom? To out-of-touch media elites, I guess. He continued, "On some of the issues, the survey even found majority Republican support." Well, yeah, so does every other poll—pundits like him just have their heads lodged too deeply in the sand (or elsewhere) to know that.

Leisman even quoted a Democratic pollster who was shocked by the findings: "'I feel these types of proposals will be more closely debated and perhaps more closely supported within the public than maybe we would have anticipated,' said Jay Campbell, a partner at Hart Research Associates. Campbell said he was not expecting the widespread support for tuition-free college and Medicare for All. 'The fact that so many independents do come down in support of these two policies was surprising to me,' he said."[52] That's the political establishment—persistently befuddled that progressivism is popular, no matter how many times they find out.

Sometimes conservative politicians will be honest and say they know the public is progressive. During the 2012 election campaign, a tape of Republican presidential nominee Mitt Romney speaking at a fundraiser was leaked. Romney said what he really felt: "There are 47 percent of the people who will vote for the president [meaning Obama] no matter what. There are 47 percent who are with him, who are dependent upon government, who believe that they are victims, who believe the government has a responsibility to care for them, who believe that they are entitled to health care, to food, to housing, to you-name-it. That that's an entitlement. And the government should give it to them. And they will vote for this president no matter what." He ended by saying, "I'll never convince them they should take personal responsibility and care for their lives."[53]

Sometimes Romney's speech is remembered as a "gaffe" because it did in fact hurt his campaign. But it was a gaffe only in the journalist Michael Kinsley's definition: when a politician accidentally tells the truth. Romney was just being honest. Like most conservatives, he thinks half the population are leeches who want to sit around on their couches while the other half works hard and forks over their huge tax payments to them.

Another example was when Romney gave a speech at Ohio's Otterbein University and advised the students to just start their own businesses. Right, good point. They were wondering where they were going to place their capital and were thrilled to hear of the right investment vehicle. Oh, right, they have no money because they're millennials and are not loaded like the Romney family. But Romney's assumption was that they would either start their own businesses because they are driven or wouldn't because they're part of the 47 percent who are lazy. No, you schmuck, they don't have any money.

Then Romney made it worse. He gave an example of a buddy of his who started his business with a small loan of twenty thousand dollars. Now, if you're trying to start a business that one day will grow into a large enterprise, he's right, that's not a lot of money. But if you're talking to a bunch of students who are worried to death that they are not going to get that starting assistant marketing rep job and instead are going to have to work one more summer at Burger King, telling them to get a small loan of twenty thousand dollars to start a competitor to Burger King is not useful advice.

But as we would find out later, Romney was an amateur when it came to not being able to relate to the common man. Donald Trump came along and made a mockery of trying to understand the average man, as he has made a mockery of everything he has touched.

Trump told the story of how he was a self-made man because his dad gave him a "very small" loan of one million dollars (in 1975!). It's not clear if he put up his pinkie to his mouth à la Dr. Evil when he said "one . . . million . . . dollars." Who the hell thinks that's a small loan?

Donald Trump, the world's most ironic populist.

Of course, that story isn't true, either. Trump's dad, in reality, gave him $413 million! He bungled most of that away as he was playing a successful businessman on TV. He filed for six bankruptcies, several of which his dad bailed him out of. Mr. Self-Made Man had to go crying home to Daddy on many occasions to get more money, a lot more money.

In one case, his dad had to send his lawyer to buy three million dollars' worth of chips at one of Donnie's casinos and walk out the door, so it looked like his poor, bungling, incompetent son had made an extra three million dollars. Not exactly the kind of advice you can give at a graduation speech.

Texas Governor Ann Richards had a great line about George W. Bush's unearned confidence: "He was born on third base and thought he hit a triple." Since Trump is significantly less intelligent than even Bush, Richards's saying might be adopted to "Trump was born on third base and thought he kicked a field goal."

But the most salient point is that neither Romney nor Trump can see past their enormous privilege to realize that's not how the other half—or 47 percent—live.

And while they pretend now that Romney's comments were awful, conservatives defended him at the time because, after all, he had only said what they all really thought. Radio host Rush Limbaugh said, "This could be the opportunity for Romney, and for that campaign, to finally take the gloves off and take the fear off and just start explaining conservatism, start explaining liberty to people and what it means. And explain that they don't need to be in that 47 percent. There's no reason for them, for everybody, to essentially have given up on their future in this country. There's no reason for it."[54] CNN pundit Erick Erickson said, "The Romney campaign should double down on what he said. They should own it. The trouble for the left and media (but I repeat myself) is that most Americans agree with Mitt Romney."[55] They didn't agree with Romney, of course. He lost by 3.5 million votes. Trump also lost the popular vote, twice—by 3 million and 7 million. But, of course, he won the presidency once anyway and almost won it a second time because of our insane Electoral College system. This system is rigged in a hundred ways to help the rich, even when their ideas are enormously unpopular and their candidates get fewer votes.

MAKERS VERSUS TAKERS

Right-wingers believe progressives are progressives because we hate working for a living. Progressive ideas are popular because they're about giving freebies to lazy people, and most people are lazy, they think. As then–conservative avatar Paul Ryan said in 2010, "We're going to a majority of takers versus makers in America and that will be tough to come back from that." That wasn't a one-off statement of Ryan's. In 2011, he said, "Before too long, we could become a society where the net majority of Americans are takers, not makers."[56] In the view of the Republican Party's most celebrated budget thinker in a generation, most Americans have no interest in contributing productively to society—they are just bums.

Conservatives see Black people as particularly lazy. Think that's an exaggeration? Soon after the election, Romney explained to donors why he lost. "The Obama campaign was following the old playbook of giving a lot of stuff to groups that they hoped they could get to vote for them and be motivated to go out to the polls, specifically the African American community, the Hispanic community, and young people," he said. "In each case they were very generous in what they gave to those groups."[57]

So white people—who took the bodies, the work, and often the lives of Blacks in this country as they enslaved them, so they wouldn't have to do their own work—are the makers? And Blacks are the takers? Whites stole the labor of Blacks to *make* this country and then accuse them of being takers! This is what professional-level gaslighting looks like.

Hell, Romney made even more racist slanders than that during the campaign. In July 2012, he delivered a speech to the National Association for the Advancement of Colored People (NAACP). Now, African Americans have voted overwhelmingly for Democrats in presidential elections since FDR and were overwhelmingly supportive of Obama. If Romney wanted to persuade them to vote GOP, he had an uphill climb. But that wasn't the purpose of the visit—he was there so he could later boast to conservatives that he was willing to tell off lazy Black people to their faces. "The unemployment rate, the duration of unemployment, average income, median family wealth are all worse in the black community," Romney told the NAACP, as if the organization wasn't dedicated to rectifying exactly those problems.[58] He railed against government programs, implying that Black people's supposed dependency on them keeps the community down. He rightly received boos and a harsh NAACP statement after he left. And then the next day, he bragged to a group of donors that he'd given Black people some harsh truths. "I hope people understand this, your friends who like Obamacare, you remind them of this, if they want more stuff from government tell them to go vote for the other guy—more free stuff," he said. "But don't forget nothing is really free. It has to [be] paid for by people in the private sector creating goods and services."[59] In the conservative mind, that's what Black people, liberals, and Democrats want—free stuff that other people produce.

Of course, that viewpoint ignores the many advantages that Americans like Romney have enjoyed to make them rich—including taking the wealth produced by Black people for, oh, four hundred years. It assumes a fair and level playing field that has never existed. Do you think Donald Trump Jr. would be wealthy without his father putting him on the payroll? Please. The guy can barely dress himself. Trump himself received over four hundred million dollars (in today's dollars) from his father through tax dodges, *The New York Times* found. "Trump participated in dubious tax schemes during the 1990s, including instances of outright fraud, that greatly increased the fortune he received from his parents," the newspaper reported.[60] Trump and his siblings set up shell companies to hide millions of dollars in gifts from their parents. He helped his dad take illegal tax deductions worth millions. He undervalued their real estate holdings by hundreds of millions. As a result of all this, they ripped off the government for hundreds of millions of dollars in uncollected taxes. But we're the takers?

The progressives-are-lazy thesis also fails to account for the existence of wealthy progressives, from FDR to Hollywood types who post cringeworthy videos of themselves singing badly to John Lennon's "Imagine." Conservatives have nicknamed them limousine liberals, latte liberals, and, in England, champagne socialists. These people are progressive, conservatives say, because they can afford to hypocritically lecture about poverty and exploitation while living in luxury. According to *American Greatness,* a pro-Trump journal, "Today's elite limousine liberals are above all products of the modern university and its corresponding corporate culture. The money makes them 'limousine,' but the university education makes them liberal. . . . The well-to-do neighborhoods of educated elites increasingly mirror the identity politics ethic of the university, where students learn the correct way of thinking on sexual inequality, gay marriage, transgender rights, and the gamut of diversity issues. They can enjoy their wealth without guilt precisely because their hearts are in the right place."[61] Except that, by definition, wealthy progressives are voting to reduce the amount of wealth they have through higher taxes. If they vote for progressive candidates and take other progressive actions, they are putting their money at risk—precisely the opposite of hypocrisy. Progressives cannot win in the right-wing imagination: if they're low income, they're progressive because they are lazy and want the government to take care of them instead of working. If they are rich, they're just guilt-ridden elites who are hypocrites if they don't give away all their money. The right-wing talking points demean us either way. And the mainstream media have validated those points by treating them as legitimate all these years.

The right wing constantly comes up with framing language that sticks in the popular imagination and is then reinforced by the media. Everyone who follows politics has heard of limousine liberals. For far too many people, that is the image of a wealthy progressive. This is part of why I can't stand the current leaders of the Democratic Party. They never fight back. They never fought back against that framing, and they never, ever do their own framing of Republicans.

Look at how easy it is. Next time someone in media accuses anyone of being a limousine liberal, the Democrat on the air should say, "You mean that someone who is wealthy and helps others is a limousine liberal? Well, what do you want them to do—not help anybody? Do you want them to be greedy, like the Republicans? Would that make it better? If you were a halfway decent person, you'd be praising them for using their money for good!"

You could also counterattack by calling anyone on the right who is rich but greedy a Rolls-Royce Republican. The kind of person who wouldn't even pass the Grey Poupon from one limo to another (apparently, I loved that old commercial). For decades now Democrats *could* have been saying Rolls-Royce Republicans are the worst kind of people, who made their wealth by crossing a bridge of opportunity and then burning that bridge down after they crossed it. This also has the advantage of being true.

It's not that wealthier Americans are more likely to be liberal, it's that highly educated people are now voting in much greater numbers for Democrats. This might have something to do with the Republican Party's assault on science and truth. A lot of middle-class and even wealthy folks came out in force for George Floyd, the first time that white people have turned out to join African Americans in civil rights protests at this scale in the history of this country. In fact, inequality is so out of control that a small group of wealthy people formed an organization called "Patriotic Millionaires" that calls for higher taxes on the ultrarich. It has more than two hundred members in thirty-four states, according to *The New Yorker*.[62] They lobby Congress, write op-eds and open letters, speak to the media, and meet with politicians. They pushed Obama to let George W. Bush's tax cuts expire, and the group's founder speaks in blunt terms about the human costs of plutocracy, saying about other multimillionaires and billionaires, "You want people to suffer and die earlier, because your greed is more important to you than another human being." This straight talk is no less true because it comes from the mouth of a class traitor, to use a term leveled at FDR.

Conservatives discourage wealthy people from being progressives because they want all wealthy people to look out exclusively for themselves (more on this in the next chapter). And they want the rich to pour some of their money into government structures that help other rich people get even richer. Nobody with a pulse doubts that we have government of the rich, by the rich, and for the rich. What's interesting is that Trump even admits it. "I love all people, rich or poor, but in those particular positions, I just don't want a poor person," he said about his cabinet.[63] He actually said that out loud. More than once—on a different occasion, he said, "I want people that made a fortune because now they're negotiating with you. It's not different than a great baseball player or a great golfer."[64] And he got what he wanted—he organized the richest cabinet in history.[65] And of course, instead of looking out for you, they enacted policies like tax cuts and regulatory rollbacks that made themselves even richer. What was that about wanting free money from the government?

CORPORATISM

The irony of all this is that progressives aren't antibusiness at all—we're more probusiness than conservatives are. What! Doesn't every news actor on cable tell us that Republicans are the party of business? Of fiscal responsibility and limited government?

Well, maybe they do. But they're lying or wrong or both. Republicans and centrist Democrats aren't probusiness. They're corporatists. When I heard the word "corporatist" many years ago, I laughed. I thought, "What a funny, made-up, liberal word." I call myself a capitalist, and "corporatist" seemed vaguely antibusiness, so I was put off by it.

Well, as it turns out, it's a great word. It perfectly describes a great majority of our politicians and the infrastructure set up to support the major corporations in the country. It is not just inaccurate to call these people and these corporations capitalists; it is, in fact, the exact opposite of what they are.

Capitalists believe in choice, free markets, and competition. Corporatists believe in the opposite. They don't want any competition at all. They want to eliminate the competition using their power, their entrenched position, and, usually, the politicians they've purchased. They want to capture the system and use it only for their benefit.

Truthfully, I don't blame them. They're trying to make a buck. And it's a hell of a lot easier making money when you don't have competition or truly free markets or consumer choice. All these corporations would absolutely love it if they were the only choice a consumer had.

Blaming corporations for this is a little silly. It's like blaming a man for breathing or a scorpion for stinging. That's what they do. In fact, they are legally bound to make their best effort at not just beating the competition but eliminating it. Lack of competition leads to making more money (presumably for their shareholders, though realistically it winds up being more for their executives these days). And that's exactly what's happened. In the past twenty years, 75 percent of industries have become more concentrated—with fewer companies hogging more of the market share.[66] The number of public companies in the U.S. has declined from nearly 7,000 in 1995 to just 3,530 in 2020.[67] That's a major reason why the profits of those large companies that do survive have skyrocketed—after-tax profits as a percentage of GDP was 11.24 percent in 2022,[68] up from 4.8 percent in 1980.[69] It makes sense—less competition means more money for the big corporations.

But as the ancient proverb goes, "Don't hate the player, hate the game." We have to understand how this system works and then account for the abuses that are likely to arise from it. I don't hate the scorpion for stinging, but I also wouldn't put a bunch of them in my house. And I wouldn't take kindly to someone else putting them there, either.

The sensible approach would be to recognize the problem and figure out a way to avoid or minimize it. Money always finds a way in, but we can at least be cognizant of the issue and try to combat it. We must do this as citizens who care about our democracy, but we must also do it as capitalists.

I believe in the capitalist system. I think it makes sense, and it is attuned to human nature. People do not work to the best of their ability and take only as much as they need. Usually, they work as little as humanly possible and take as much as they can. Unfortunately, that's natural. Capitalism helps to funnel these relatively normal impulses in a positive, maybe even productive manner.

But in order to have capitalism we must have choice. If consumers do not have different companies to choose from, if the markets aren't truly free and there is no real competition, then you kill capitalism. Corporations are a natural by-product of capitalism, but as soon as they are born, they want to destroy their parents. Corporations are the Oedipus of the capitalist system. They want to screw their mom, capitalism. And kill their dad, democracy. And money in politics is the weapon they have chosen to kill our democracy (more on that in chapter 4).

In order for capitalism to work, corporations must not be allowed to succeed. When I was growing up as a young Republican dork, I was told that "regulation" was a bad word. Sensible people were for less government regulation. Socialists were for more government regulation because they liked big government controlling the markets and your life. Most of all, they loved red tape that inhibited business.

To this day, I still shudder when I hear the word "regulation." It sounds so nasty and socialist. That's the power of brainwashing. Here's the only problem: it turns out we—as humans and corporations—totally and completely need regulation. Without government regulation, the excesses of the market go unchecked and create financial meltdowns. We have been trained, or programmed, to believe that government is a bad thing and the less you have of it, the better. Until your house is burning down, then, all of a sudden, government help—in the form of the fire department—seems like a pretty good idea.

The reason we have government is because it serves roles that we need in society: police, fire department, public education, common defense, and financial regulation of the markets. If you don't have a check on insider trading, the rich get richer and the average guy gets screwed. But so does capitalism. If there are no rules and no referees, then the cheaters will run amok until they build monopolies and end free markets. Even Adam Smith warned about this. The great irony is that regulations are not meant to hurt capitalism, they're meant to protect it. It turns out regulations are not the enemy of capitalism, but its defender.

You know another word for regulations? Laws. Everyone knows that if you take away law enforcement, you get more crime. We don't want cops who enforce nonsense laws or enforce them in a way that's fundamentally unfair, but we still need cops. The citizens have to be protected. That's just as true in the economic world. You don't want regulators who enforce nonsense regulations or enforce them in a way that is fundamentally unfair, but you still need regulators. The citizens have to be protected.

Regulators are the cops of the business community. And their job is to make sure guys in fancy suits aren't robbing us either.

So, we need cops, not just on Main Street, but on Wall Street, too. In fact, that's probably where we need them the most. And not just at the Securities and Exchange Commission. We need more regulatory agencies that watch over the financial industry to protect the interests of all of us. Right now, the industry is out of control. We can't wait for another meltdown like the 2008 financial crisis to hit us before we make changes.

Of course, the right answer is balance. Too much government regulation does slow down business and can inhibit growth. Too little regulation means there is no one to watch over the excessive risks that corporations take for short-term profit, leading to economic collapses. Every progressive since William Jennings Bryan has been calling for a "mixed economy," with government and business working on behalf of the public instead of only business.

Balance is what progressives call for. There are no Communists—who actually do want to eradicate private enterprise—who call themselves just progressives, or vice versa. Because the two things are very different, despite what Republicans tell you. Bernie always makes sure to emphasize that he's a democratic socialist for just that reason—to show that he understands that socialism can't and doesn't work without democracy. It's Bernie's opponents who ignore the crucial democratic component of his philosophy—Bernie never does.

When Senator Sanders, Elizabeth Warren, or anyone else calls for breaking up the banks that ruined our economy or giant companies that have monopolized markets, it's not just to protect the average American, it's also to protect small *businesses*. "In rural America, we are seeing giant agribusiness conglomerates extract as much wealth out of small communities as they possibly can while family farmers are going bankrupt and in many ways are being treated like modern-day indentured servants," Sanders said in May 2019.[70] That's not an attack on the farming industry, that's a warning that we have to improve it so that it can also serve family farmers. Conservatives and the media have never understood this—it is progressives whose ideas will preserve capitalism, if it's done right. Capitalism without rules is just theft, like a rigged casino. After the stock market crashed in 1929, the hypercapitalist President Herbert Hoover said, "The only trouble with capitalism is capitalists; they're too damn greedy." Progressives know better—people will be as greedy as you let them be. The only way capitalism can be saved is by reforming it. The trouble with capitalism is unchecked capitalism, which immediately turns into corporatism.

DEMOCRATIC SOCIALISM

Right after the 2020 elections, conservative Democrats like Abigail Spanberger came out and blamed progressives for their near defeat. First of all, I thought conservatives believed in personal responsibility. I'm pretty sure it was her responsibility to win her own race, not AOC's. Second, she said Republicans called her a socialist because of progressive members of her caucus. Has she been around the last forty years? They call every Democrat a socialist in every election, no matter what. They called Obama a Marxist. That's hilarious—and had nothing to do with AOC (who was student at the time) or progressives.

But most important, what in the world does Spanberger mean by "socialism"? She was joined by Conor Lamb and Jim Clyburn immediately thereafter in piling on against the so-called socialists in the party. Of course, every anchor on cable news then joyously joined in the chorus, almost singing now, "It was the socialists!"

You want to hear something funny? No one ever defined what they meant by socialist. No anchor ever asked anyone what it meant. In all my life, I have never once seen anyone on TV actually ask this very simple question, "Hey, we're constantly calling people socialists, what does that mean?"

I guarantee you if you ask any Republican, establishment Democrat, or cable news pundit to define it, not one could. They couldn't even come close. But to be fair, it's not an easy thing to define because it means so many different things to different people. What we do know for sure is that Bernie Sanders calls himself a democratic socialist. That's a start, because we can look at his policy proposals for guidance.

As we discussed before, in reality, almost every country has a mixed economy. Some things, like the fire department, the military, and Social Security, are public, and other parts of the economy, like the burger business and the jeans industry, are private. Almost everyone on the planet agrees that this is how government should run. The private sphere does what it does better than the government would—do you really want a government burger? The government is better suited to run the fire department. As we discussed earlier, I'm pretty sure you wouldn't want your neighbor's house to burn down because he missed his monthly fire insurance payment (on the other hand, I don't know your neighbor).

So, what *extra* policies is Bernie Sanders pushing for in his dangerous democratic socialism? Yes, he wants higher taxes on the wealthiest Americans and Big Business. As we discussed in chapter 1, so do a great majority of Americans. But that doesn't really affect whether any part of the economy is private or public. So let's focus on those parts of his proposals.

Most famously, he is for Medicare for All. That's universal health care. That's the system that every other developed country in the world uses. And again, it's also what a huge majority of Americans want. It is not making the entire health industry public, it is only making health *insurance* public, which it already is for all Americans over sixty-five. Wow, sounds really scary! What if we all had health insurance?! Argh. No wonder all the cable anchors are so worried.

He also wants to make college education free. Ahhhh! You mean like the GI Bill that gave millions of Americans a free education and built the strongest middle class the world has ever seen? Wow, that too sounds dangerous. The professors are liberal enough without having them work for the government. Wait a minute. Don't the ones at great state colleges like the University of Texas, University of Michigan, Rutgers University, University of California at Berkeley, University of North Carolina at Chapel Hill, and many more all work for the government already? Ahhhh!

When did Bernie say he was turning all universities into public ones? Oh, right: never. He's not going to force Harvard or Stanford to go public. They can keep their forty-billion-dollar and twenty-seven-billion-dollar endowment funds, respectively. They can keep mainly admitting privileged students whose parents went there before. All he's saying is that the government should pay for your tuition if you go to a *public* university. You can't be serious, that can't be it, you're thinking. But it really is. Those schools are already public, and instead of the government charging students tuition, it wouldn't. Wow.

But wait a minute! How are you going to pay for that?! That must cost a fortune. Nope. Just seventy-five billion dollars a year. If that sounds like a lot of money, it isn't for the U.S. government. That's just 5 percent of what we spent on the Iraq War. We could have given every kid who wanted a college education a chance to get it free and still had 95 percent left over if we hadn't needlessly invaded Iraq. Can you imagine? Are you sure this democratic socialism is as scary as everyone says it is?

Well, let's go to the final program that would be added by the government. Brace for impact. Paid family leave! Ahhhh! It doesn't even turn anything public. It's just a government subsidy, like the ones oil companies and farms get. Ahhhh! But instead of the money going to oil executives, it goes to pay for your wages for a short while when you have a baby. Ahhhh!

Chris Matthews suggested that if Bernie Sanders won, you might get taken out to Central Park and shot.[71] Instead, you might be taken out to the park and given health care and childcare. That doesn't sound quite as scary.

DEMOCRATIC CAPITALISM

I use a different name instead of democratic socialism. I call my proposal for a mixed economy "democratic capitalism." Okay, so what's that?

Almost the same thing. Remember, almost all developed countries, except us, have the same mix of public and private as Bernie suggests (and as I suggest here). By the way, quick note, none of those countries have fallen into the ocean. They are all fine. People are having delicious strudels in those countries as we speak. All the ridiculous, preposterous Republican campfire stories are obvious lies. Norway and Taiwan did not burst into flames as soon as they made contact with socialism. What I'm calling democratic capitalism is nearly the same thing, because almost all developed governments on earth have similar systems.

So why did I bother giving it a different name? Let me explain.

First of all, "democratic capitalism" sounds better. Not to the younger generation, but for older Americans it gives them peace of mind. You explain it by saying it's capitalism checked by democracy. Oh, my God, it's as comfortable as an old blanket on your favorite couch on a fall afternoon. Who isn't going to love that?

And when you explain all the policies, you know what it sounds like? Democratic capitalism. Private industry hires you, but the government makes corporations treat you like a human being. A private company pays your salary, but the government makes it guarantee a little time off when you have a baby. Capitalism checked by democracy. I rest my case.

At the end of the day, it doesn't matter much if someone calls herself a socialist or a capitalist if their positions on critical issues are progressive. Framing is important for winning elections. But when someone is in office, the only thing we all care about is the policies.

But there is one more reason I call it democratic capitalism. I don't actually believe in socialism, or more accurately, what socialism is confused for—communism. I believe in private industry. I believe money is a strong incentive for people. Competition is not always the right motivator, but in business it usually is. Communist nations have produced exactly zero thriving industries so far, at least while they were still Communist (the Chinese economy, for example, is *nowhere* near communism now). Countries we call socialist, on the other hand, support perfectly good markets. For example, Ikea and Volvo come from a socialist country called Sweden. But those markets are composed of . . . private industry checked by the government.

I also believe people should be allowed to own private property. You know what percentage of Americans agree with me? Approximately 110 percent. So I don't really want to head anywhere near the direction of banning private property, and neither do most progressives. More young people are actually sympathetic to communism these days (which is a bit shocking to us middle-aged Americans), but overall their numbers are still minuscule. And they don't call themselves progressives or socialists. You know what they call themselves? Communists.

I want to head in the direction of checking capitalism with democracy. Companies look out for themselves, and the government looks out for us. You know why? Because it's your government! That's how it's supposed to work in a democracy—where you elect people to represent you in your government. And they represent you by making sure different things don't hurt you or screw you over, the way big businesses do! The public sector, on your behalf, serves as a check on the excesses of private industry. Doesn't that sound just right?

See, I told you, you're a progressive!

3

WHY REPUBLICANS SUCK

REPUBLICANS WEREN'T ALWAYS THE PARTY OF HATE. IN THE BEGINNING, THEY were the good guys. They were, in fact, the progressives. You know who really, really expanded the circle of liberty? Abraham Lincoln. But when present-day Republicans call themselves the Party of Lincoln, that's unintentionally funny.

Now, here's what no one else in the media dares to say but is obviously true. When someone tells you that Republicans are the Party of Lincoln, they are either completely ignorant of all politics or lying to you on purpose. But our media never has the courage to call out Republicans for all their obvious tricks and lies.

So, if Lincoln was in fact a Republican, how can it be a "lie" to say they are the Party of Lincoln? Because the parties switched positions—massively and unmistakably—especially on the issue of race. Everyone who follows politics even minimally knows that. There is a clear reason they switched and a defining moment when it happened.

THE SOUTHERN STRATEGY

The parties switched places on race when Lyndon Johnson bullied, cajoled, and convinced his party, which was filled with Dixiecrats (racists in the South who hated that the Republican Party freed the slaves), to vote for the Civil Rights Act and the Voting Rights Act. This infuriated racist voters in the South. So, when Johnson declined to run for president in 1968, Richard Nixon and his allies came up with a strategy that was explicitly racist, meant to pick up those votes for the Republican Party, so that they could win that election and others to follow on national, state, and local levels.

It's called the Southern Strategy. Everyone in politics knows it. Everyone knows the entire point of the strategy was and is racism. Everyone is aware that it was a political calculation. But finish the thought—what was the calculation? Nixon and his team concluded that the Republican Party would pick up more votes and have a better chance of winning the Electoral College if it became clearly the more racist party. The Southern Strategy was the original identity politics.

You could tell from his White House tapes how racist Nixon was personally—but this wasn't about that. This was just strategy. An active decision that Republicans could win the South if they attacked the Civil Rights Act and the civil rights movement. If the GOP became the Party of Hate instead of the Party of Lincoln, it would get more votes and be able to hold on to power more effectively.

I've never seen anyone in politics dispute that. In fact, two former heads of the RNC, Ken Mehlman and Michael Steele, have both acknowledged the racism implicit in the Southern Strategy and apologized for it.[1] But during the Trump years, the GOP went back to that same well—and it turns out, it still wasn't dry. Republicans didn't appeal to the South by endlessly talking about how much they liked peach cobbler. They did it by opposing every reform meant to end discrimination. Literally everyone in media knows this. Yet the media never share with their readers or viewers that the Republican Party made an *active* decision to become racist! It wasn't even that the tide of history took them there, it was that the awful people running the Republican Party decided racism was a better political strategy. And they have stayed on that course ever since.

Unfortunately, they were right. This strategy was depressingly effective for a very long time. Part of the reason it worked so well was that there was no backlash against or opprobrium for the party that chose to be racist. The media would refer to the Southern Strategy but never finish the thought—hey, America, the Republican Party is the racist party! Oh, God, we wouldn't want to offend the racists. Republican voters have been trained to believe in lies, such as that the Southern Strategy is about Southern culture. They never clarify which part of the culture they're referring to, outside of the racism—is it the grits that got them all those votes? In a sense, Republicans have been believing ridiculous conspiracy theories, such as that the Civil War wasn't about slavery, for decades now. For a party that delusional, was it that surprising that Donald Trump could get them to believe complete absurdities?

That's what the press and Democrats never understood about the appeal of Donald Trump to Republican voters—they didn't mind the lies, they wanted to be lied to! They wanted to be told they were still special, that their race made them better than others, and that they deserved to have power forever just because of who they are. They needed that sense of unearned entitlement. And if you're looking for someone to tell you lies, who better than the biggest liar in the country? Trump will tell you any lie you need to hear to get what he wants out of the deal. His ability to lie at that scale was not the bug, it was the feature.

But this agreed-upon national fiction wasn't just for Trump or Republicans. In order for the advertisers and the media companies to be happy and profitable, they too had to make an active decision—they had to ignore the racist elephant in the room. They didn't want to offend their viewers, many of whom wanted to be against civil rights but not be called racists. I was a Republican growing up. I had to find out on my own that Republicans were racists. The media lied to me—very actively—by omitting this very relevant fact. If, when my family came to this country, someone had explained to us what the Republican Party did and what its strategy was, we would have never joined it. But the press was too cowardly and greedy to tell the clear, unvarnished truth.

Because the press never reported on the obvious lies of the Republican Party, we wound up voting for people who based most of their ideology and political strategy on being racists, oftentimes against people like me and my family.

Unsurprisingly, Black folks in this country eventually got the memo about the Republican Party. They didn't need the media to tell them anything, because those racist policies affected their daily lives. It was largely white folks who never got the memo. Some would have been discomforted or made angry. Some, however, would have welcomed the information, but since it never touched their lives and the press covered it up, they never knew they were voting for racists their whole lives.

So, you shouldn't give up on all Republicans. All of them have also been lied to, as I was. Believe it or not, many have no idea what their party stands for. For example, if the entire media were ever honest about the

Republican Party's true intentions—to get people to vote for tax cuts for the rich—they'd immediately lose half their voters. In the old days, mainstream media would debate whether giving all the money to the rich was a good idea, with serious discussions of supply-side economics and the Laffer Curve (most appropriately titled curve ever—the idea that you give all the breaks to the rich because a tiny amount will trickle down to the rest of us is laughable). Think about that—for decades, the most predominant economic idea in politics was to help the average American by . . . giving everything to the rich! That's an idea you're supposed to debate? But the mainstream media didn't want to offend the powerful by pointing out that this was an obvious sham, so they earnestly debated it for decades. That gave the idea enough legitimacy to provide cover for endless tax cuts that led to trillions in wealth redistribution to the top. This is what passes for journalism in America. And now the right-wing media have become the greatest defenders of the rich by creating every cultural distraction you can think of to make sure Republican voters don't realize the robbery that's happening in the background. While Tucker Carlson was having you debate the gender of Mr. Potato Head, the GOP robbed the national treasury of another two trillion dollars, in the form of the Trump tax cuts. And again, half the Republican voters never even noticed.

The truest thing Hillary Clinton ever said was her famous line on the "deplorables":

> You know, to just be grossly generalistic, you could put half of Trump's supporters into what I call the basket of deplorables. Right? The racist, sexist, homophobic, xenophobic, Islamophobic—you name it. And unfortunately there are people like that. And he has lifted them up. . . . But that other basket of people who are people who feel that government has let them down, nobody cares about them, nobody worries about what happens to their lives and their futures, and they are just desperate for change. It doesn't really even matter where it comes from. They don't buy everything he says, but he seems to hold out some hope that their lives will be different.[2]

The media often report on the first part of that statement, but ignore the second half. As you can see here, I pull no punches on Republicans. I'm happy to take them on and fight them just as viciously as they fight us. But half of them are redeemable, if we could ever get them to listen to something outside of right-wing or mainstream media. If progressives could get past that wall of propaganda, we could show half the Republican Party that they actually agree with us on economic issues.

Today, things have changed at least a little bit, because progressive voices are stronger and louder. We're not letting the press bully us into silence. In the past, the mainstream media would call you a radical and say you were on the fringes if you openly talked about how racist America was. A lot of people in the press will still be scandalized by this as we speak. They'll think it's outrageous to say the modern Republican Party's defining characteristic is racism. They would never say that! Even though they all know what the Southern Strategy is. At this point, protecting the feelings of Republicans is built into their DNA. But with progressives fighting back and the demographic shift in this country, we're going to find out soon if the clock is finally going to run out on the Southern Strategy. It looked for a while as though the clock had already struck midnight, but Trump reset the clock in a completely unexpected way. He didn't just bring racism back, he made it popular again.

Now, are all present-day Republicans racists? No, as I just told you, many of them have no idea what's going on. And there are other factors that could affect your decision to be a Republican. For example, you could be greedy. One of the few demographic categories Trump won in 2020 was people making over one hundred thousand dollars. This is surprising, because he got clobbered among well-educated voters, who tend to be wealthier. But one force was strong enough to compel even educated people to vote for the obvious con man—greed. Remember, the point of the Republican Party for at least the last century has been to get rich people everything they wanted.

Now, you might be thinking, "Wait a minute, didn't you just tell me that the point of the Republican Party was to be racist?" No, that's their strategy for getting more votes, but that's not their objective. Racism is the tool; greed is the goal.

The Republican Party's slogan should be: come for the racism, stay for the tax cuts.

The whole point of getting more votes is so they can pass more bills to help rich people! How do I know? Because that's almost the only thing they ever do.

Reagan passed huge tax cuts that funneled trillions to the wealthy. To give you a sense of how large the Reagan tax cuts were, the Trump tax

cuts gave away $1.9 trillion and were the size of 0.9 percent of our gross
domestic product (GDP). Reagan's 1981 tax cut alone was the size of 2.89
percent of our GDP—almost three times the size of the Trump tax cuts![3]
Then he did another round of tax cuts in 1986 that reduced the top rate
from 70 percent when he came into office all the way down to 28 percent
when he left. Not to be outdone, George W. Bush passed $5.6 trillion in tax
cuts, the lion's share going to the wealthy, as usual.[4] That was the amount
the Bush tax cuts cost just between 2001 and 2018—and the costs keep
mounting as we speak (to be fair, Barack Obama made those tax cuts far
more expensive by rendering them permanent—and that deal was negotiated for him by his Vice President, Joe Biden). Then Trump passed another
$2 trillion in tax cuts for the wealthy. You see a pattern? Well, if you don't,
you have problems with your vision, and probably live in Washington.

Here's one more for you, the exception that proves the rule. George
H. W. Bush said, "Read my lips! No new taxes!" But since the deficit was
in horrible shape and it was clearly the patriotic thing to do to rescue the
country, he was forced to raise taxes. Republicans hated him for it! They
immediately abandoned him, and he lost the next election. They rejected
him because he forgot the whole point of the party. As Trump would put
it, patriotism is for suckers and losers. The GOP donors and power bro-
kers screamed in unison—give us the goddamn money! And chased him
out of town.

If you're a right-winger, there might be other reasons you like the Republican Party, but even you know the party is for the rich. In fact, it's a
minor miracle that a party that for over a century has been serving only
a tiny percentage of the country has been so successful in a democracy.
It's as if a party set up to serve Asian Americans exclusively kept winning a majority in most elections. That makes no sense. Except Asian
Americans are 5 percent of the country; the super-rich are just 1 percent.

So how do they do it? Well, they've got to trick you into voting for
them. We already discussed one way to do that—racism. And think about
how perfect that is. If you're poor, you might already have class resentment, so they just have to misdirect it a little. This is the oldest trick in
the book. Don't look up, look down. Then you sprinkle in envy, the most
toxic of human emotions, and provide the answer—it's "the others" who
are causing all your problems. You're better than them! Well, how do
you keep them down to make sure you stay better than them? Racism!
Perfect. That way, even if some minorities are more successful than you,

you rest easy with the comforting thought that they can *never* be better than you by definition because of their race.

LeBron James had the N-word spray-painted on his twenty-million-dollar mansion in Los Angeles. Someone wanted to teach him a lesson—no matter how much fame, success, or money you have, I still get to feel better by putting you "in your place." Remember the controversy during Obama's first term about Harvard professor Henry Louis Gates Jr.? Cops harassed him on his own porch and arrested him for disorderly conduct for breaking into his own house! Gates was a public figure, well known in Boston, and one of the most respected professors in the country. They put him in his place! In his recent book, President Obama explained that when he made a mild defense of Gates, it cost him more white voters than anything else he had ever done.

There's a reason why Republicans keep going back to the well on racial resentment. It works. In the Gates incident, only 29 percent of white respondents thought the arresting officer had acted "stupidly." But a stunning 58 percent of white respondents thought it was Professor Gates who had acted "stupidly."[5] Obama's approval ratings declined precipitously because he thought it was wrong to arrest the Black professor for entering his own house.

But race and greed are not the only things in the toxic Republican stew. Perhaps their largest weapon is . . . religion. It doesn't matter what else we do or how we rob you blind, because we're the Party of God. By the way, Hezbollah is also the Party of God—that's what "Hezbollah" means in Arabic. They're the folks who bombed our marines in Lebanon in 1983, for God, of course, among hundreds of other bombings. Whenever God talks to anybody, he apparently only tells them to bomb things. George W. Bush once told the French president that he wanted to bomb Iraq because he was concerned about "Gog and Magog at work" there, according to his interpretation of the Bible. To be fair, God also seems to be asking people to cut taxes for the rich on a pretty regular basis.

I thought Jesus said to turn the other cheek, not to bomb other people or invade their countries. And if you actually read the Bible or chapter 2 of this book, you would know that Jesus wanted the rich to give away all their money. All of it. To the poor. No mention of cutting the capital gains tax in the New Testament. I double-checked.

Since the teachings of Jesus Christ are diametrically opposed to right-wing ideology but the GOP needs to use religion to trick people into voting for it, what do the Republicans need? A magic elixir that can solve all their problems. And they found it in—abortion.

THE BIGGEST LIE OF ALL

There are two critical facts you have to know about the abortion issue. One is that the people who run the Republican Party have never actually cared about abortion. It was a callous strategy to use religious people as fodder for their political ambitions. The idea was to get people angry about one particular moral issue—but never fix it—and keep dangling that carrot over their heads so that they keep voting for your interests. Otherwise, there aren't enough rich people to win elections!

This phenomenon is why Republican politicians panicked a little bit when *Roe* was overturned in 2022. There goes their carrot! When asked if the GOP would call for a national ban on abortion, now that it could, Senate Minority Leader Mitch McConnell said, "Most of the members of my conference prefer that this be dealt with at the state level."[6] All of a sudden, McConnell is shy and reserved? He never hesitates when there's a war to start or tax cuts to be passed, but when they finally have the one policy they pretend to care about the most at their fingertips, he doesn't want to act on the national level. These guys are so obvious.

Republicans were afraid of losing their foot soldiers. They need an army to win elections. An unthinking army that would take their word on faith alone. Aha! Who forms their worldview based on faith alone? Religious folks. Target acquired.

When *Roe* was first decided, evangelical Christian leaders didn't even object. It took them five years before Paul Weyrich figured out the Republicans could use that issue to get religious voters to vote unquestioningly for any damn thing GOP leaders wanted.[7] Before they realized they could use it for electoral advantage, evangelical leaders and the Republican Party didn't even have a position on abortion! For five long years. In 1978, Weyrich ran an experiment for the Republican National Committee to use abortion as an election issue. It worked! And they won four local elections for Republican candidates in Iowa, New Hampshire, and Minnesota. That's when they realized they should pretend to care about the issue.

If you think about it, abortion was the original QAnon-like conspiracy. These days QAnon says that you have to vote against Democrats because they are child molesters! Now, as absurd as that sounds to any rational person, followers believe it with all their hearts. They actually believe that children are in mortal danger and they have to protect them!

What would you do if you truly believed that? Pause to think about it. If I thought children were actually being molested and then murdered, there isn't anything I wouldn't do to stop it. Now you know why QAnon adherents are radicalized. What would be too radical to do to save children from molestation and murder?

If you think, "Yes, well, that might be a small sliver of the Republican Party, but not a big enough contingent to be politically relevant," you are disastrously wrong.

As of 2022, 25 percent of the Republican Party believes that "the government, media and financial worlds in the US are controlled by a group of Satan-worshipping pedophiles who run a global child sex-trafficking operation."[8] I know it's unbelievable, but it's true! Overall, 16 percent of all Americans believe this insane theory—that's over fifty million people! But it gets worse. An even bigger number—28 percent of Republicans—say that there is a "storm" coming that is going to wipe away the elites and restore the "rightful leaders."[9] That sounds scary. Who are the rightful leaders? And who designated them that? And what do they mean by a storm that wipes people away? Well, don't worry, they get more specific. The same 28 percent of Republicans say that "because things have gotten so far off track, true American patriots may have to resort to violence in order to save our country."

You didn't read that wrong, and it is an exact quote. These are the questions that were asked verbatim in a Public Religion Research Institute and the Interfaith Youth Core poll done in May 2021. Yes, nearly three in ten Republican voters think it might be time to "resort to violence" because they are worried that the Democrats are Satan-worshipping pedophiles.

But wait, it gets worse. It always does. Another 55 percent of Republican voters weren't sure! To be fair, they "mostly disagreed" with the statements—but they didn't completely disagree. Which part was the accurate part? I'm afraid to ask. The pedophile ring, the Satan worshipping, or the harvesting of children's blood? Oh, yeah, they also believe that. There is a QAnon conspiracy that the elites harvest the adrenaline that is present in the blood of frightened children. To be specific, they believe a video exists of Hillary Clinton and her top aide wearing the mask of a dead child's face as they drink the child's harvested blood.

What would you do if you thought the other side was molesting children and then drinking their blood? Well, you might be confused, because it'd be the first time you'd ever heard of such a thing, so it would be hard to have a rational reaction. But seriously, what wouldn't you do if you thought some people were doing child sacrifices? What wouldn't you do to save those children?

This is a trick as old as time. It is called blood libel, and it has been used to drum up anti-Semitism for thousands of years. People who wanted to attack Jews would convince the faithful that Jewish people were kidnapping Christian children and drinking their blood.

The minute people believe that, they are hooked forever. Those people are weaponized as the most hard-core political participants. Who cares about trade policy or infrastructure bills if the other side is kidnapping and raping children? Now do you see how powerful this is?

That's also exactly what Republican Party leaders did with abortion! They convinced religious voters to be Republicans because Democrats were . . . murdering children. Republican voters have been letting the rich rob them for decades because they thought they were saving innocent children from being murdered. That's exactly what "pro-life" advocates believe. Why did you think they were so angry and radical? It's the same exact idea as QAnon—what wouldn't you do to save babies from certain death?

But in the case of abortion, it wasn't a bunch of lunatics online that dreamed this up. It was guys in suits. And they did it so they could rob you more effectively.

Wait a minute, isn't there at least truth to the Bible being against abortion? I hope you're sitting. No, there is no truth to it! It's made up. The Bible is actually pro-abortion!

I know this is a tough pill to swallow. This is where I almost lose you—"Come on, Cenk, you challenged a lot of our orthodoxies and you had some interesting facts to back you up, but not this one! This is one of the bedrocks of American politics. Are you saying the entire country got it wrong? And all the religious leaders as well?" Yes, that is what I'm saying, and I'm about to prove it.

Let's go to the Bible and find out who is right. Actually, let me do a magic trick. Let me insert a passage in the Bible that will prove me right. It'll be a passage where God clearly calls for an abortion and *a priest* performs it. Well, there's no way in the world that's in the Bible, so this will have to be the best magic trick you've ever seen.

I'll call it Numbers 5:11–31.

11 Then the LORD said to Moses, 12 "Speak to the Israelites and say to them: 'If a man's wife goes astray and is unfaithful to him 13 so that another man has sexual relations with her, and this is hidden from her husband and her impurity is undetected (since there is no witness against her and she has not been caught in the act), 14 and if feelings of jealousy come over her husband and he suspects his wife and she is impure—or if he is jealous and suspects her even though she is not impure—15 then he is to take his wife to the priest. He must also take an offering of a tenth of an ephah of barley flour on her behalf. He must not pour olive oil on it or put incense on it, because it is a grain offering for jealousy, a reminder-offering to draw attention to wrongdoing.

16 "'The priest shall bring her and have her stand before the LORD. 17 Then he shall take some holy water in a clay jar and put some dust from the tabernacle floor into the water. 18 After the priest has had the woman stand before the LORD, he shall loosen her hair and place in her hands the reminder-offering, the grain offering for jealousy, while he himself holds the bitter water that brings a curse. 19 Then the priest shall put the woman under oath and say to her, "If no other man has had sexual relations with you and you have not gone astray and become impure while married to your husband, may this bitter water that brings a curse not harm you. 20 But if you have gone astray while married to your husband and you have made yourself impure by having sexual relations with a man other than your husband"—21 here the priest is to put the woman under this curse—"may the LORD cause you to become a curse among your people when he makes your womb miscarry and your abdomen swell. 22 May this water that brings a curse enter your body so that your abdomen swells or your womb miscarries."

"'Then the woman is to say, "Amen. So be it."

23 "'The priest is to write these curses on a scroll and then wash them off into the bitter water. 24 He shall make the woman drink the bitter water that brings a curse, and this water that brings a curse and causes

bitter suffering will enter her. 25 The priest is to take from her hands the grain offering for jealousy, wave it before the LORD and bring it to the altar. 26 The priest is then to take a handful of the grain offering as a memorial offering and burn it on the altar; after that, he is to have the woman drink the water. 27 If she has made herself impure and been unfaithful to her husband, this will be the result: When she is made to drink the water that brings a curse and causes bitter suffering, it will enter her, her abdomen will swell and her womb will miscarry, and she will become a curse. 28 If, however, the woman has not made herself impure, but is clean, she will be cleared of guilt and will be able to have children.

29 "'This, then, is the law of jealousy when a woman goes astray and makes herself impure while married to her husband, 30 or when feelings of jealousy come over a man because he suspects his wife. The priest is to have her stand before the LORD and is to apply this entire law to her. 31 The husband will be innocent of any wrongdoing, but the woman will bear the consequences of her sin.'"

Wait a minute! Holy cow, is that really in the Bible? Well, go to a Bible near you. Any Bible. Open it up go to Numbers 5:11–31. You see, I'm a magician! I put it in there. How did I do that? There's no way that was in there the whole time and no one told you about it, right? Well, as you might have guessed by now, this trick was very easy because it's not a trick. They lied to you the whole time!

The passage very clearly says that the priest will give you a potion to cause a miscarriage—that is, induce an abortion! It's not a natural miscarriage. They induce it with what passed for medication then. And it is done for a purpose. It is meant to evacuate the fetus if it does not belong to the husband. That is verifiable, 100 percent abortion—as featured in the Bible!

This is God's commandment, and the person who carries out the abortion is—a priest!

Now, did any religious leader in your lifetime read you this passage? Hm, I wonder why they didn't. Did anyone on television ever tell you this amazing fact? This fact that would alter all of American politics if the whole country knew it? Nope, they never said a word, either. Now are you beginning to see that people in power might have had a vested interest in deceiving you?

Now, those people will scramble and say, well, the Catholic Church cites another passage (Psalms 139:13) that says, "You knit me in my mother's womb." That says nothing about abortion! God also knit the fetus I mentioned above in her mother's womb and then aborted it as soon as He thought the husband got cuckolded! Hmm, why are they contorting passages that don't talk about abortion and ignoring the very clear passage that authorizes—and even *encourages*—abortion? It's almost like they have an agenda.

Well, if you wanted to pass trillions of dollars in tax cuts, would you tell people that the rich should get even more money at their expense, or would you tell them the lives of little babies are depending on it?

Same old tricks, same old party. Now do you see why I get furious with the media? Okay, the Republican Party leaders have a vested interest in this lie. I understand perfectly why they cooked it up. I understand logically how it helps them for people to fervently believe this lie. But why did the media—which assert that they are truth tellers and objective—hide this most crucial fact from you? Because as I explained earlier, if you're a multibillion-dollar corporation, you have no interest in being the liberal media. You have interest in protecting the status quo, the current power structure, and helping the Republicans deregulate your industry, lower your taxes, and assist you in swallowing up your competition.

But would a multibillion-dollar corporation really act based on a profit motive? Isn't it funny that they got you to believe that they wouldn't?

CROOKS

But we haven't reached the worst part yet. Wait, how could anything be worse than a deeply racist party or maniacal liars who trick people of faith to rob them of their money and votes? It's why they do it and who they serve.

Republican politicians are masterful at a psychological phenomenon called projection. Whatever they are doing behind the scenes, they project it onto their opponents. Normally, this part of human psychology is subconscious. With Republicans, it is not. It's done on purpose, for a very good reason. If you attack first with what is actually your number-one problem, when the other side counterattacks it'll look defensive, and they'll look guilty. So that's why Republicans are always saying that

Democrats are controlled behind the scenes by secret donors like George Soros. Because that's exactly who they're controlled by—secret donors behind the scenes.

Now, the GOP probably didn't expect to get this lucky—the craven Democratic leadership never even bothered to counterattack. So, if you ask most Americans which party is more elitist, Democrats would probably lose that fight. And to be fair to the American people, the Democrats *are* elitists and are controlled by donors. But to be fair to the truth, the Republicans are even worse!

George Soros has nothing on the Koch brothers, the late Sheldon Adelson, or the Mercer family. These guys give way, way more to Republicans than Soros does to Democrats. I would definitely take all their money out of politics, including Soros'! Otherwise we don't have a democracy, we have an auction. But if anyone tells you how bad Soros is, ask them if they want to end private financing of our elections to stop that awful problem. If they're an average Republican voter, they'll agree. But if they're a Republican politician, they'll never agree in a thousand years. They love the system that brought you George Soros. They wouldn't change it if their (political) lives depended on it—because they do. They'd never win another election if we ended private financing of elections. The whole party is built on corruption.

Which brings us to a fun and important question: Who are worse, Republican voters or Republican politicians?

Republican Voters versus Republican Politicians

In the Republican Party, there are two different sets of people—the voters and the politicians. As you might have discovered, I'm not within a thousand miles of politically correct, so I don't mind telling you that they're both awful. But they're awful for different reasons.

What do the voters want? That's really easy, because they just told you with their votes. In the 2016 presidential primaries, they had seventeen different Republicans to choose from. They could have picked the pure conservative firebrand (Ted Cruz) or the most efficient conservative bureaucrat (John Kasich); they could have voted for the patrician (Jeb Bush) or the young, dynamic conservative (Marco Rubio), etc. No, they decided to vote for the ugliest, loudest, most bigoted son of a bitch they could find.

Trump's hateful rhetoric, like his lies, wasn't the bug for Republican voters, it was the feature. When he went after "The Squad," the four young progressive women in Congress (AOC, Ilhan Omar, Ayanna Pressley, and Rashida Tlaib—all Justice Democrats) and said they should go back to their countries, he *gained* five points among Republican voters. Trump consistently maintains the support of 90 percent of Republicans. He got 93 percent of their vote in 2020! Voters have had plenty of opportunity to see what a lying, vain, xenophobic scam artist he is. Since the media were in love with Republican voters—with their incessant refrain that this is a "center-right country"—they thought that those wonderful, decent voters who represent "real" Americans would reject Trump in 2020. But they didn't. They loved him! They were here for it. In fact, now many of them won't listen to anyone but Trump.

Remember, Trump is a lifelong con artist. If GOP voters had wanted a kind and gentle Republican, that's what he would have pretended to be. He became more and more vicious in his racism and cruelty because he sensed that's what his base wanted—and he was right. So it's not that Republicans are now more hateful because of Trump. In a sense, Trump is more hateful because of Republican voters. Like a good performer, he's giving the crowd what they want!

In fact, Sam Nunberg, one of his closest advisers, explained how Trump used him to figure out what conservative voters most desired. Nunberg explained:

> I listened to thousands of hours of talk radio, and he was getting reports from me. . . . When I started putting him on conservative talk radio in 2013, Mark Levin's show and guys like that, they kept asking him about immigration. . . . That was our focus group. . . . Every time Trump tweeted against amnesty in 2013, 2014, he would get hundreds and hundreds of retweets.[10]

This is what digital media professionals would call A/B testing. You try A and see if it works, and if doesn't you move on to B and test that. Well, Trump tested bigotry and it tested through the roof. Nunberg told reporter Joshua Green that "it was intuitive by him to use immigration as a new wedge issue."[11] Remember that a "wedge issue" is something used by politicians to divide us based on identity politics. So Trump tested his racism methodically and chose the more hateful approach because it was getting a better response from Republican voters.

This is who conservatives are, and this is what they believe. Their actions and their votes, not the words of their pundits, reveal what conservatives actually want. If you stroll through bookstores in D.C., you can find a whole shelf of tomes with titles like *The Conservative Sensibility* and *Conservatism: An Invitation to the Great Tradition*. The ideas in them bear only a passing resemblance to what conservatives actually do in practice. Sometimes right-wing intellectuals and upper-level party flunkies like to imagine that they're part of some highbrow, sober, bow-tied tradition that dates back to Edmund Burke. That's hilarious. The guy they just voted for said we should inject disinfectant into our bodies to cure Covid. He thought it might have been a good idea to nuke a hurricane. He thought passing a dementia test meant that he was a "very stable genius." Highbrow, intellectual conservatism? Come on, that's hysterical, there's no such thing among Republican voters.

Remember all those television segments where the pundits would tell you that the Republican voters wanted policies like free trade and deregulation of the banking industry? They were just making that up out of whole cloth. There was never any poll that showed that. If you told an average Republican voter that he was in favor of free trade, first, he would ask you what that is, because, in reality, he has no idea. Does he really know that means outsourcing his own job? And then once you explained to him what free trade actually means, he would tell you he hates it. And lo and behold, Trump came out *against* free trade—and Republican voters loved him for it! The corporate media were lying to you the whole time. They were just telling you what they wanted and pretending that Republican voters wanted it.

Now after all this, you might be surprised that I think Republican politicians are even worse than their voters! Why? Because at least what's described here is the real, unvarnished opinions of the voters. In a democracy in a giant, diverse country, you're not going to have an electorate of angels. You have to debate, cajole, convince, and defeat the other side. I think there are good guys and bad guys, but at least they're all real. And that's how democracy works. We have to work with the electorate we have, not the one we wish we had.

And at least Republican voters have progressive economic instincts, even if they don't know it. They also distrust the establishment and are rooting for the average American worker, in their own way. I can work with that. I'll fight their demons and look for their better angels. If you look super hard, you might even find them.

That's not the case for elected Republican officials. At the national level, they have absolutely no redeeming qualities.

Unfortunately, Republican politicians don't even believe in democracy. That was true even before they tried to literally end democracy in 2020. They are craven, callous followers of the donor class. They're glorified water boys for the rich who will do anything they are ordered to do, no matter how corrupt and harmful to the country and the world.

A first-of-its-kind study published in March 2019 by Harvard Law School used Federal Election Commission records to compile a database of all the political contributions made by over thirty-five hundred CEOs of S&P 1500 companies from 2000 to 2017. The study found that Republicans received twice as many contributions from CEOs as Democrats did. More than 90 percent of CEOs of energy companies donated heavily to Republicans—gee, I wonder why Republicans deny climate change?[12]

So what do Republican politicians believe in? Protecting privilege. That's it. That's what modern conservatism is about. According to the political theorist Corey Robin in his book *The Reactionary Mind*, that's what conservatism has always been about, since Burke's days. Keeping the lower orders in check so that their social betters can continue ruling and amassing privileges. "That is what conservatism is: a meditation on—and theoretical rendition of—the felt experience of having power, seeing it threatened, and trying to win it back," writes Robin. "Historically, the conservative has favored liberty for the higher orders and constraint for the lower orders."[13] This explains why the Republican Party promotes itself as devoted to small government, even as it pushes policies that are about massive government intrusion in people's lives: mass incarceration, the state taking control of women's bodies when they're pregnant, state-mandated discrimination against members of the LGBTQ+ community, and a gluttonous military that gorges on endless wars. None of that is anywhere near small government. They want big government for you, but small government for themselves. To the rest of us, that might look hypocritical, but it doesn't to them. They want power, period. So, using the government to restrain "the others" and then having the government back off when it comes to them is consistent—they want the power, either way. They couldn't care less about the conservative movement's intellectual foundations. There are no ideological conservative principles other than those in the imagination of a handful of Republican "intellectuals" in D.C. It's a Frankenstein party stitched together from the resentful, the willfully uninformed, and the greedy.

In the end, I'll take the Republican voters over their politicians because at least they're honest. They hit you from the front and don't hide their intentions. Plus, they also hate corruption. As awful as the right wing can be, they're still leagues above the people claiming to represent them but secretly working for the elites.

CENTER-RIGHT MYTH

So why don't Democrats fight back more aggressively against the GOP if I'm right about how radical the GOP is? Because they have also bought into the mythology that we're a center-right country. It's maddening because it leads to unilateral surrender on what is actually winning ground for us.

There's a ton of research showing that politicians and the mainstream media consistently overstate the conservatism of the American electorate. In 2018, three political scientists from Columbia University and the University of California at Santa Barbara, Alexander Hertel-Fernandez, Matto Mildenberger, and Leah C. Stokes, asked the most senior staff members in Congress to judge what the public in their district or state believed when it came to five hot-button issues: repealing Obamacare, raising the minimum wage, requiring background checks on gun sales, regulating carbon dioxide, and investing three hundred billion dollars in infrastructure projects. The academics then compared the responses with large public opinion surveys to determine what the public actually wanted. The senior staffers are the ones who write the bills, prepare hearings, and organize the schedules of their bosses—that is, they are the people who actually do the work in Congress. If anyone in the country is attuned to public opinion, it should be these folks.

That wasn't the case. It wasn't even close. "Across the board, we found that congressional aides are wildly inaccurate in their perceptions of their constituents' opinions and preferences," the political scientists determined. On all five issues they were asked about, the senior staff members in Congress believed that their voters were far, far more conservative than they actually were. For instance, 92 percent of the staffers underestimated public support in their state or district for background checks for gun purchases. Every single Republican—100 percent—believed that voters would be more likely to oppose these commonsense gun-control measures.[14] Maybe that shouldn't be a surprise—Republicans long ago sold their souls to the NRA. They had to buy into the idea that people don't want any gun control so they could sleep at night.

But 85 percent of Democratic aides also underestimated how much their voters wanted background checks.[15] Remember that the next time your crazy, Fox News–watching uncle tells you how congressional Democrats are far-left zealots. It turns out even these allegedly antifa-loving Democrats are way more conservative in their assumptions than the *average* voter!

Think about how amazing that is. The average American voter thinks that Republicans are wrong on almost every issue—but the Democrats disagree! They think Republicans are more popular than they are. Wow! Now can you begin to see why progressives might have a huge advantage on the issues and lose elections anyway? The most incompetent, self-defeating people in the country have been put in charge of the Democratic Party. Of course you'll lose if you think you're going to lose before the game even starts.

The same trio of researchers then looked at why Washington aides were so far off when it came to guessing public opinion. The first reason they came up with was the staffers' own (right-wing-leaning) beliefs. "Aides usually assumed that the public agreed with their own policy views," the academics wrote in the *Times*, summarizing their research.[16] Since people working in Congress have relatively conservative beliefs, staffers assumed that voters back home do, too. Nope.

The other reason why staff members overestimated public conservatism was "interest groups." "Aides who reported meeting with groups representing big business—like the United States Chamber of Commerce or the American Petroleum Institute—were more likely to get their constituents' opinions wrong compared with staffers who reported meeting with mass membership groups that represented ordinary Americans, like the Sierra Club or labor unions," the political scientists determined.[17] And who do you think aides meet more with—representatives from Big Business or from environmental groups? The Chamber of Commerce or the

Sierra Club? Here's a hint: it's the one with a gazillion dollars to spend bankrolling politicians, not the group trying to save the caribou.

Yes, they actually convince themselves that the American Petroleum Institute really knows what the American people want. And has the best interests of American citizens in mind. No one can be that stupid. And it turns out, they're not. They're basically being paid to have that position.

It wasn't just meetings that fueled the problem. "The same pattern holds for campaign contributions: The more that offices get support from fossil fuel companies over environmental groups, the more they underestimate state- or district-level support for climate action." As we showed you earlier, Congress members get a lot of financial support from fossil fuel companies—and, lo and behold, they're convinced everyone loves dirty energy! Conducting good polling actually costs money and takes time. "Since most congressional offices cannot regularly field public opinion surveys of their constituents," the political scientists explained, "staff members depend heavily on meetings and relationships with interest groups to piece together a picture of what their constituents want. And if offices hear from only deep-pocketed interest groups, they are likely to miss out on the opinions of ordinary Americans."[18] That's *exactly* what's happening.

This research built on other studies that reached similar conclusions—except that earlier research had shown that political elites *everywhere* in the country thought their voters were more right wing than was true. In other words, this is a problem that exists far beyond Washington. In a study published in 2018 in the *American Political Science Review,* two political scientists at Northwestern University and Stanford University, David E. Broockman and Christopher Skovron, surveyed 1,858 state legislative politicians. They looked at both incumbents and candidates—those in power and people running for office. And then they compared the results to data on public opinion from the Cooperative Congressional Election Study.

What do you think they found? The state politicians "believed that support for conservative positions on these issues in their constituencies was much higher than it actually was. These misperceptions are large, pervasive, and robust."[19] Of course! Large, pervasive, robust—those three words succinctly describe the levels of wrongness of policymakers around the country. Again, Democrats were part of the problem; they, too, believed that their voters were more right wing than was actually the case. Their mental software was also rewritten to believe the myth that we are a right-wing country. "Democrats and Republicans both overestimate their constituents' conservatism on every single issue, with the one exception that Democrats very slightly underestimate support for the conservative birth control religious exemptions policy," the authors of the study found.

Here's another reason why Washington thinks the country is center-right: conservatives are much more likely to contact their legislators than progressives are. "In the 2012 American National Election Studies (ANES), Republicans were 28% more likely to say they had contacted their representatives than Democrats, and in the 2008 CCES Republicans were 39% more likely to have said they contacted their representatives than Democrats," according to the article in the *APSR*. Republicans don't just contact Republican politicians more than Democratic voters do—they contact *Democratic* politicians more, too. So, *all* officeholders hear from conservatives more often. This is why it mattered when ordinary people showed up to yell at Republicans trying to take away their health care in 2017, and when people took to the streets in the wake of George Floyd's murder in the summer of 2020—politicians just aren't used to hearing from people holding progressive opinions. If you're ever wondering whether your efforts contacting Congress members actually make a difference, remember this.

Of course, the other—and much larger—reason for politicians' conservative bias is that they are constantly hearing from industry lobbyists and wealthy donors. They live inside a conservative bubble where right-wing business interests are always right and ever present. And, oh, yeah, *the corruption.* Whether or not politicians and their staffers already believe this mythology that the country is right wing, it also doesn't hurt that their pockets are stuffed with legalized bribes from corporations and the wealthy.

So that's the national and state levels. What about local? "All politics is local," Tip O'Neill famously said. That's not really true anymore because of television and the internet, but every book in politics is obliged to use that line at some point. Nonetheless, let's look at the local level, because that's also important. That's where almost everyone gets their political start.

Well, the same two academics who published that study in the *APSR* did some different research at the local level, surveying county leaders of both parties. "We find that both Democratic and Republican party leaders perceive public opinion in their counties as more conservative than it really is (compared to data from large public opinion surveys), a disconnect that may help explain Republicans' greater enthusiasm for extremely conservative candidates and Democrats' (relative) restraint when it comes to more extremely liberal candidates," they wrote.[20] They found that Republican county leaders believed that candidates far to the right of the median voter would do much better than a centrist in an election—which explains how you get so many far-right nutjobs running for office. But whether it's national, state, or county level, both Republican and Democratic officials always agree the Republicans must be right. The only people who don't agree are everyday Americans.

Why is Washington more right wing than the rest of the nation? Well, because that's where power and the establishment reside, of course. Power is by nature conservative—it wants to protect its privileged position. That's not nefarious, it's natural. It's inevitable, actually.

This is not a new phenomenon. Frederick Douglass explained in 1857, "Power concedes nothing without a demand. It never did and it never will." Are most powerful people going to agitate for change? Of course not. That's so obvious that someone in media must have told you about that already, right?

So why do members of the press—who hilariously pretend they are truth tellers—hide the fact that Washington is by its nature conservative? Because they're also super powerful and don't want to change a thing. Why would you want a new system if you're already on top in the old system?

Of course the media are going to say that the country doesn't agree with progressives—that might lead to change that costs them their current position. Some cable news anchors make up to forty million dollars a year. They're not going to undermine a system that gives them all that. Expecting them to do anything but fight against change is just naïve.

There's one more, rarely discussed reason why Washington is so conservative. In 2018, a political scientist at Southern Methodist University named Ryan Murphy estimated the levels of sociopathy in each of the forty-eight contiguous states, along with the District of Columbia. He did that by taking state-level data on personality traits and comparing them with indicators for sociopathology—the markers of sociopaths, such as boldness, meanness, and "disinhibitedness" (think of the obnoxious guy dancing to "Cotton Eye Joe" on a bar table at two in the morning with a beer in each hand, or a guy who keeps telling people he is a "very stable genius"). What he found shouldn't shock anyone paying attention to the news. "The District of Columbia is measured to be far more psychopathic than any individual state in the country," Murphy wrote in a working paper. "I had previously written on politicians and psychopathy, but I had no expectation D.C. would stand out as much as it does," he told a reporter.[21] Yes, Trump might be a special case of sociopathy—according to *The Atlantic,* he told his Chief of Staff, General John Kelly, as the general was standing over the grave of his son who had died in battle, "I don't get it. What's in it for them?" You'd have to be pretty disinhibited to say something like that. Trump also said fallen soldiers were "suckers" and "losers."[22] But Trump is not alone. It turns out D.C. is full of these egomaniacs with no empathy for others. "Psychopaths have an awfully grandiose way of thinking about themselves, and D.C. has numerous means of seeking and attaining power," Murphy told the reporter.[23]

It's clear that Washington looks after its own and favors policies that hurt other people. And because the movers and shakers in D.C. are conservative in their orientation, they assume the rest of the country is also that way. In Trump's parlance, they view anyone who *isn't* selfish as a sucker or a loser. Democrats have bought into this system and abandoned any progressive positions they might once have supported because they're chasing a ghost—a center-right country that doesn't exist.

But before the greedy, the bigoted, and the psychopaths took over, the Republican Party wasn't always nuts. Of course, there was Lincoln, when it was a completely different party. But you don't have to go back that far. In his farewell address, President Dwight Eisenhower, who governed from 1953 to 1961, famously warned us of what he called "the military-industrial complex." Presidential farewell addresses sound themes that departing leaders find crucial. Eisenhower could have spoken about anything. The Cold War was at its height. The civil rights movement had commenced in 1955. Ike always fretted about fiscal conservatism, so he could have talked about that. Instead, he chose to speak about big corporations dominating the government. He said, "In the councils of government, we must guard against the acquisition of unwarranted influence, whether sought or unsought," by that dangerous union of defense corporations and the armed forces. If Eisenhower said that now, the media would say he's weak on national security and hates the troops. But he was a Republican, back when there were Republicans like him, moderates who valued the safety net, our international allies, and, well, sanity. It was hardly just Ike—Richard Nixon established the Environmental Protection Agency and the Occupational Safety and Health Administration. Ronald Reagan, the avatar of conservatism, had positions that were so far left he wouldn't have won in a Democratic primary because of his "radical left" policies—he sold arms to Iranian terrorists, negotiated with the Evil Empire known as the Soviet Union, pulled marines out of Lebanon after Hezbollah killed nearly three hundred of them, and *gave amnesty to undocumented immigrants!*

This is not to say Nixon and Reagan were progressives. They definitely were not. Remember, Nixon started the avowedly racist Southern Strategy. But consider how far right Washington has moved without anyone noting it. As the country became more and more progressive, the elites got more and more conservative.

The whole center of political gravity has shifted to the right—including Democrats. The progressive tilt of the Democratic Party dates to the late nineteenth century. The Democrat William Jennings Bryan ran for president the first time in 1896. "Despite his loss that year, and in two subsequent races, his party embraced the pro-regulation, antimonopoly, pro-union stand of this eloquent politician called 'the Great Commoner,'" writes Michael Kazin, his best biographer.[24] With the New Deal and an unprecedented four presidential victories, Franklin Roosevelt entrenched progressive ideas as central to the Democratic Party, and indeed the country, until the 1970s.

Starting in the seventies, however, the Democrats moved slowly away from the commitment to progressive goals that had turned them into the party with unshakable majorities in Congress. We'll see why in chapter 4, but for now it's enough to say that segments of the business community never warmed to the New Deal, and starting in the 1970s they consciously steered America in a more corporate-friendly direction. They succeeded, and by the end of Jimmy Carter's administration (1977–1981), many Democrats, including Carter, were more conservative than Republicans had been just a few years earlier. By the time corporate donations ran through the veins of most Democrats, we had lost the whole party.

Barack Obama and Joe Biden bragged about deporting more undocumented immigrants than anyone else (until the 2020 primaries, when that became a political liability for Biden), and Obama would not have dared to propose the same exact amnesty that Reagan did for undocumented immigrants. He would have been labeled a radical and would have had no chance of winning the Democratic primary in 2008. If you can't see the massive movement of the political spectrum to the right in D.C., you're trying really hard not to see it.

The press has been normalizing the radicalization of the Republican Party for decades now. They hid the Southern Strategy, fawned after fake Republican politicians, and never told anyone that Washington had become way more right wing than the rest of the country. Instead, they pretended that America was center-right and had signed up for all those Republican policies, like . . . cutting taxes on corporations and deregulating industries. I'm sure the fact that every major media organization lobbied for those exact policies was a wild coincidence.

MAKE YOUR CASE!

Now you are beginning to see why Republicans still win so many elections despite having very unpopular ideas. They have almost the entire power infrastructure helping them, from campaign contributions to corporate media. But we haven't gotten to the most important factor yet: the unilateral surrender of their opponents, the feckless Democrats.

In a Jonah Ryan–inspired ad for an Indiana Senate race, former Democratic Senator Joe Donnelly is carrying an ax, splitting wood in a lumberjack shirt, proudly declaring, "I split with my own party to support funding for Trump's border wall!"[25] Get it, he's splitting wood and splitting with his party. Yeah, no one else liked it, either. The fake Republican he was trying to be in that ad lost to the actual Republican in the race.

Donnelly went on, "The liberal left wants to chop defense spending. No way!"[26] I'm not kidding, this was in a Democrat's ad. No, you're not the crazy one. Telling people your side sucks and the leader of the other party is awesome is not in fact good political strategy. But people in Washington very earnestly believe that it is. They're mad right now reading this, muttering to themselves, "This is juvenile analysis. You have to go right wing in Indiana to win. Everyone knows that." Yes, everyone in Washington actually believes telling the voters how correct the other party is on all the issues is good politics—Joe Donnelly's and every other conservative Democrat's losses notwithstanding. It apparently never occurred to them that if you tell voters how great Republicans are, they might believe you and vote for them!

Wait, I'm not done. Donnelly went on to say—in that same thirty-second ad—that he "voted to extend the Bush tax cuts."[27] He also gave Ronald Reagan a handie, but he didn't mention that in the ad. But would you be really surprised at this point if he had? I've never seen this good an ad for your political opponent. "Remember everybody, the other party and the other guy are awesome, but could you please vote for the inferior version anyway?" This passes for sage political strategy in Democratic circles. Unsurprisingly, Donnelly, despite all his advantages as an incumbent, lost to his Republican counterpart by six points. The voters did exactly what he told them to do—vote for the Republican.

My publishers, in order to avoid liability, are going to want me to tell you that Joe Donnelly did not in fact give Ronald Reagan a hand job. Sorry, Joe. Better luck next time.

Mark Pryor, on the other hand, was a conservative Democratic senator so dominant that he ran unopposed in 2008. It's hard to remember now, but Arkansas, home of Bill Clinton, was a Democratic state for a long time. By the time Pryor was running for reelection in 2014, the political tide had shifted in Arkansas as the Southern Strategy had fully run its course. Now, the former titan was concerned about the race. So he ran an ad where he was literally cradling the Bible. He was trying to outflank the Republicans on the right! He was more devout than they were; he would rule by the Bible even more than they would. He said in the ad, "I'm not ashamed to say that I believe in God, and I believe in His word. The Bible teaches us no one has all the answers. Only God does. And neither political party is always right."[28] In other words, I'm really defensive about being a Democrat. You should start looking into the other guy, because I just told you that he might be just as right as I am. They're literally paying for ads that are making them less likely to win. And congrats to Mark Pryor, it worked! It did make him less likely to win. In fact, he lost by seventeen points! This is embarrassing.

Good news. Claire McCaskill, another conservative Democratic senator, was running in Missouri in 2018, and she had a winning issue! Increasing the minimum wage was very popular in the state, and as luck would have it, it was on the ballot. And this time the polls were right, it passed easily, 62–38. That's a twenty-four-point landslide. So McCaskill cruised to victory, right? Nope. She never campaigned on the minimum wage issue. That was a Democratic position and, in her mind, by definition, a losing issue. Oops. She lost by six. That's a thirty-point difference in performance between the Democratic issue and the Democratic candidate. That's the perfect picture of a party in the midst of a needless surrender. If Democrats had any idea how popular their own positions are, they might not pretend to be Republicans.

If this looks like the pathetic strategy of a defeated, impotent party, that's because it is. There was no four-dimensional chess, as Washington media claim Democratic leaders play; there was just nothing but losses as far as the eye can see. In the Obama era, when they had a popular president and an advantage on every issue, they lost . . . a thousand seats nationwide![29] The Democrats lost a stunning 816 state legislative seats in less than a decade. Is that even possible? They lost 13 governorships, 12 seats in the Senate, and 64 seats in the House. They bled out the party at a time when they should have been ascendant. They ran away from their own winning issues and were led by their inept and corrupt consultants like lambs to the slaughter. All across the country, they told everyone the Republicans were right—and people believed them.

Imagine if you went into a car dealer and the salesman told you, "Look, I've split with my own dealership." You'd instantly wonder what was wrong with the cars. Why did he have to do that? And why is he telling me to watch out for his own place of work? He split with them! Jesus, he's got an ax. Then the salesman leans in and says, "You know the dealership across the street? I paid for one of their cars!" Remember, Donnelly literally said he had voted to pay for Trump's border wall. Is there any chance you'd buy a car from that salesman?

The salesman continues, now creepily, "My dealership wants to take the doors and seat belts off the cars! These cars are dangerous. But don't worry, like I said, I bought a car from the other guys." Actual ad: "The liberal left wants to chop defense spending. No way!" He is implying his own side is literally dangerous!

As you're trying to awkwardly backpedal out of there before you find out if the ax is a prop or not, he screams, "Then I bought another car from them!!" Actual ad: "I voted to extend the Bush tax cuts." If you're new to American politics and totally confused at this point, yes, Bush is also from the other party.

Does a single person reading this think Donnelly had any chance of winning with that insane strategy? But remember, in Washington's Alice in Wonderland world, this is considered not just good but indisputably correct strategy. "Only radical leftists wouldn't agree to run ads saying how great their opponents are," they say, as if they don't live in an alternate reality.

In 2020, instead of a Blue Wave down ballot, there wound up being a Red Undercurrent. Biden won, but Democrats lost seats in the House and did far worse than expected in the Senate. A lot of good candidates were also washed out in that undercurrent. Kara Eastman had almost beat Don Bacon the last time around for a seat in Congress and, despite running a strong campaign, lost by four points in 2020. She is a strong progressive running a race in the middle of Nebraska. This is where the mainstream media jumps in and says, "Aha, progressive candidates did poorly." That is lying by omission. That leaves out the critical part—conservative Democrats lost by far more! Max Rose is a conservative Democrat in New York. He was often on national TV to yell at his own party and tell people how right Republicans were. His voters believed him. He lost by six points.

Did you ever hear anyone on cable news talking about how conservative Democrats throughout the country got eviscerated? Nope. What you heard instead was how AOC might have cost the Democrats the election. What? Every progressive incumbent who was for Medicare for All won their race, including in several swing districts. They ran strong and beat the undercurrent. Establishment Democrats ran to the right and got annihilated.

In the 2022 midterms, Democrats were thrilled with how well they did—and they lost the House! There is perpetually a low bar for Democratic leaders in D.C. Yes, they were supposed to lose by a lot more (congrats?), but they did lose. Without the House, they can't get anything passed. And notice who did well and who didn't in that election. John Fetterman ran as a strong, populist progressive. He crushed Dr. Oz, even after he had a stroke! Let's be honest, he could barely speak at their debate—and he still picked up a Republican seat. Remember Max Rose, the conservative Democrat from New York, who keeps bragging about how right wing he is? How did he do in 2022, when he ran again? He lost by twenty-four points.

You have heard me tell you in this chapter how awful the Republican Party is. But if that's true, why do Americans keep voting for Republicans? Now you know—they have more money to buy more ads, the media implicitly and explicitly help them with their framing, and even their own opponents surrender to them without a fight. Imagine if the voters actually knew who the Republicans were; if they just read what's in this book, the Republicans would probably never win another election in this country.

So the next logical question is "Why don't their opponents tell people? Isn't that kind of their job? To oppose these folks?" No, that's not how they view it. Politicians get their power from their ability to raise the most amount of money. That's because 95 percent of the time, whoever raises more money wins. They logically conclude that money is the key to success. From there on out, all they do is serve money.

When Democratic donors push toward a more tolerant society, that's great. But when they also tell Democrats to lower their taxes and reduce regulation, that's not so great. Will Democrats be corrupted by money and serve the donor class as well? Of course! They're people. And on top of that, they're a particular type of people called politicians. So, what does this produce? A system where both Republican and Democratic donors are telling the politicians to look out for the interests of the wealthy. And you're never going to guess how this movie ends . . . politicians on both sides agree to enormous tax breaks for the wealthy over and over again. Shocker!

If Democrats try to fight Republicans on economic issues, their donors get very upset. Raising the minimum wage cuts into their profits; raising the tax rate on carried interest cuts into their profits. So there won't be any of that. Democrats are not allowed to attack their opponents on the single most important topic—their economic interests.

Can you begin to see why Democrats have been surrendering for all these decades? They were told to stand down.

If a Democratic politician talks in favor of Big Business—or "understands" the business "community"—they will get a ton of cash. Anyone who wants to regulate the business community gets no cash. Gee, I wonder how corporate Democrats gained control of the party.

If you were building a devious machine to create the illusion of a battle while you snuck the loot out the back door, what two sides would you pick? You would pick a very strong side that constantly makes unreasonable demands. And then you would build a whiny, huffing and puffing, weak party that constantly finds a way to lose in humiliating fashion to the stronger party. It makes a good show of there being conflict and rights being fought for. It also puts the stronger party in a position to get their maximum demands as the other side mumbles, "There was nothing we could do."

Then build a press that is the organ grinder's monkey that parrots for them, "There was nothing they could do." And so it was decreed! You would hear it on all the TV sets and in all the columns written by old savvy journalists. "There was nothing they could do," the message would echo. Until the people started to believe that the weaker party really does fight for them, even though it never wins. The party members sometimes win for themselves and get a lot of power and status, but they never win on issues that affect you. But you would believe to the end of time that . . . there was nothing they could do.

That's how that devious system would be set up. And obviously, that's our current system.

I swear to God, I can hear now the establishment Democrat crowd mumbling as they read this, "That is not a very sophisticated analysis, there really was nothing they could do." Sophisticated, indeed.

Neutralizing the Democratic Party as the controlled opposition was the smartest thing the ruling class ever did. It was a stroke of genius. It's one thing to pick a side. It's another to pick both. If you build a system on money, cash will be king. Any wise king would create a pretend opposition to placate the masses, to give a good show of fighting for them.

This chapter is about how much Republicans suck. So why am I telling you about how much Democrats suck? Because that explains the mystery of how the backward party that serves the interests of the rich wound up winning so many elections. The game is rigged, and you'll never guess by whom: the people who paid for the game. Say it with me. Of course!

Only a rube would try to rig an election by putzing around with the ballots. No, you rig it way before the election even starts. You pay the contestants on both sides and get the exact result you want no matter who wins. Now, that's a sophisticated robbery!

In this case, playing the role of the Harlem Globetrotters are the Republicans, and in the role of the Washington Generals are the Democrats. One side is paid to win, and the other side is paid to lose. And it's a fun show for everybody. But the guys with all the money are the ones who paid both teams. They chose the Republicans to be the Harlem Globetrotters in this story, so they are.

WHY WAS DONALD TRUMP SO POPULAR?

First, let's get it straight—he wasn't. Trump was never popular with the whole country. In fact, to be fair to America, the majority of us disliked him all the way through. Trump never crossed 50 percent in popularity in the country. In Gallup polling, he didn't cross that mark once![30] Never, at any point, did the majority of this country say we wanted Trump to be our leader (unfortunately, in our "democracy," the Electoral College is more important than majority rule). At several points, he fell into the 60 percent unfavorable range! And often with over 40 percent saying their opinion was strongly unfavorable. That means six out of ten Americans didn't like him and four out of ten hated him.

Remember, Trump lost the popular vote in both elections. He lost the 2016 election by three million votes. Yes, he won the Electoral College, and that's what counts in America, but it doesn't erase the fact that fewer people voted for him. Using that as evidence that he's popular is like saying, "Yes, three million fewer people voted for him, but he won a game of badminton!" Congrats! But that misses the point of this conversation.

By the way, on Election Day in 2016 his popularity was only 36 percent![31] He was deeply unpopular on his best day. Literally. His disapproval numbers on Election Day 2016 reached 61 percent. That's stunning. It's also a terrible indictment of our system for electing a president. Six out of ten Americans clearly didn't want Trump, and he won anyway. Of course, he also had the great fortune of going up against someone who was almost as unpopular as him. Trump was the least popular candidate on Election Day in American history, then Barry Goldwater, and then Hillary Clinton. Two out of the top-three least popular candidates in history ran against each other in 2016. But think about that: he lost by three million votes not to someone who was very popular, but to someone who was very unpopular.

Then, in 2020, he got clowned by seven million votes. Then cried and cried for months about voter fraud that didn't exist. Then lost five dozen court cases. And never once presented any evidence that there was fraud that could have overturned this election. Facts are optional for him; they shouldn't be for us. It is indisputable that he is deeply disliked in the country, even for a politician.

The idea that Trump was broadly popular was a mirage. It was never true, or even close to true, even on his very best day. On the other hand, Republican voters loved him! That part is true. He is their daddy. They looked up to him with complete reverence. Trump could do no wrong. It's almost as if he could shoot someone on Fifth Avenue and get away with it.

Even after five years of Trump's hellish behavior and even after seven hundred thousand deaths from Covid, they still loved him! In the end, 93 percent of Republicans voted for Trump in 2020. All the Lincoln Project ads didn't work. All the former Republicans yelling at him on TV didn't work. He said the noise from wind causes cancer—and they still loved him. Nothing was too absurd. No lie was too big. No horribly offensive comment was too problematic. They fell in love with Trump, and nothing could break up their romance.

In fact, even after the rioting at the Capitol on January 6, an overwhelming majority of Republicans said that it wasn't Trump's fault. Two different polls had 69 percent of Republicans saying Trump had little or no responsibility for the riot. In a Yahoo! News/YouGov poll in August 2021, only 9 percent of Republicans said Trump was responsible for the attack.[32] Well, if it wasn't Trump, who the fuck was it? Did Walter Mondale get them to attack the Capitol? Was it Chuck Grassley or Bob Dole? No, they rioted because Trump told them that the election was stolen from him, not from Nancy Pelosi. It's absolutely absurd to debate who inspired the riot on January 6.

But don't worry, Republicans did eventually find out who the real culprit was. Fifty-two percent of Republican voters thought Joe Biden was responsible for the riot![33] He apparently wanted a riot to overturn his own election! I know it seems impossible to believe, but a *majority* of Republicans actually believed this. An entire political party had lost its mind.

In other words, they were madly in love with Trump and he could do no wrong. A violent attack on our democracy was a small price to pay for fealty to their beloved.

During the break-in at the Capitol, the crowd chanted, "Hang Mike Pence." They had brought zip ties and nooses. Journalists reported repeatedly hearing plans to murder the Vice President throughout the day. That was Trump's *own* Vice President! A PBS/Marist poll showed that only 15 percent of Republicans thought Trump should be removed from office after that. Eighty-three percent thought it was no big deal, he should remain in office.[34] The things that we do when we're in love.

So, finally, the big question—why?

They love him because they are him. Everything is identity politics. Trump is the prototypical privileged white male with a right-wing perspective. He has lived off unearned privileges and the labor of others. He feels entitled to everything and doesn't care what "the others" think. He is angry and frustrated, just like they are. Trump followers have a unique blend of an unbridled entitlement complex with a heavy dose of toxic victimhood. Is there a better representative of that than Donald J. Trump? The racists and bigots among Republican voters especially loved Trump. Racists have fragile egos. That's why they need to believe they are superior to others—because deep down inside they know for sure that they are not. Racism is their insecurity talking. They bully others but get super touchy if anyone criticizes them. Man, how could they not pick Trump? He is their mirror image. I don't know if he lucked into it or if he is just the best con man in American history, but he gave that particular crowd exactly what they wanted—someone just like them who finally comes out on top!

They weren't voting for him; they were voting for themselves.

Plus, he fights for them! That is so critical. Important note before we move on: he doesn't actually fight for them. That's a joke. He thinks they're suckers and losers to be taken advantage of, like any fool who would trust him. He has always said it is smart business to take advantage of investors who trust him—and stiff them. That's exactly how he feels about his own voters, too. Trump, in reality, fights only for himself, and by extension his wealthy benefactors. But he has the *appearance* of fighting for his voters. And they really, really believe that he does. And they love it!

He told the establishment and the elites to fuck off. A lot of people have been waiting for that moment their whole lives. And I'm not sure I blame them on that count.

Populism works, even if it's fake. Right-wing voters in this country, like everyone else, have had their wages reduced, their jobs shipped out, their dignity stripped; they've been left to survive on crumbs. But unlike everyone else, they believe they're entitled to the best jobs, so they're extra pissed. And unlike everyone else, they are not used to injustice. So they think they are being uniquely victimized.

This provides an opening for a con man like Trump to swoop in and say, "Now, let me tell you who did this to you!" Boy, does he have their attention at that point. Now think about what his answer is going to be to that crowd. What would you do if you were a con man? You would give the crowd what they want, so they love you and trust you.

So, what do right-wingers in this country want? They want to blame "the others"! That is what they have been conditioned to believe. Circle the wagons; everyone on the outside is a mortal threat. When someone comes along and says "the others" caused all your pain, the crowd goes nuts. And a cult begins.

What is the right wing's favorite pastime? "Owning the libs." What is that? Blaming "the others" for all your problems and incessantly attacking them. And for a party and a candidate that wanted to divide and conquer, that was the perfect vehicle to get right-wing votes and get everyone to fight each other. The ideal distraction while they snuck the money out the back. Like a two-trillion-dollar tax cut for the rich.

Who did Trump target first? Latinos crossing the border who are here to . . . take your job! They are a threat to you. Your self-respect at work was not stripped away from you by the multinational corporation that employs you, it was taken by the guy who looks different from you and just crossed the border illegally to steal your job! There's no way that's not going to work. It was catnip for conservatives.

Then you turn to Muslims. Ahhhh!!!! They're coming for your lives, and one man has enough courage to stop it all until we figure out what the hell is going on!

He doesn't just think like them, he talks like them. They don't know what the hell is going on, either. They're so confused that they think the guy who just crossed the border without a dollar in his pocket is the one with all the power. They passed a law in Oklahoma banning sharia law, as if the caliphate were knocking on Tulsa's door. I don't know that anything has ever described the conservative voter in America better than "let's stop everything until we figure out what the hell is going on."

I got news for you: they're not going to figure it out. That's part of why they are always opposed to change.

Now, the same message wouldn't work as well with left-wing voters. Why? Because even though they face the same frustrations, they have not been culturally trained to believe that it is the fault of people beneath them in the social hierarchy. That line of thought makes no sense to them. If you told them instead that it was the giant corporations that are squeezing the life out of them, they would believe that much more readily.

Quick side note: Who do you think is more likely to be right? The one who thinks the brown man without any money is the one pulling all the strings or the one who thinks it might be the multibillion-dollar corporations that have all the power? At the end of the day, facts are facts. And I'm given to understand that facts don't care about your feelings. One side is definitely more correct than the other. Billions of dollars are stronger than no dollars. You'd have to be a lunatic, or a Republican, to argue otherwise.

In fact, even though the right-wingers love the anti-others talk, they still know in their gut that the real answer is that power resides with money. Hating immigrants is good sport and satiates them for a while, but they know that there are some among the elites who are working against them. The problem is that Republican politicians know their own donors are the richest executives in the country. So they need to distract people with a scapegoat within the elites. Who do you think they're going to pick for that role? Unfortunately, the people who are always picked for that role in history. So behind the scenes and in coded language, the right wing is sending out the message that the real problem is . . . the Jews.

The massive well of anti-Semitism in this country is like a lake of oil waiting to explode under us. That is why the number-one boogeyman in right-wing circles is . . . George Soros. If it weren't him, I guarantee you it would be someone else Jewish. When right-wingers talk of the "global elites," it's almost always code for the Jews. Now, in the real world, there are elites. But they're Christian, Muslim, Jewish, Buddhist, you name it. Just look at the executives of any private equity company and you'll see the elites are very diverse. But that doesn't make for a good story line for the right-wing mind. Screaming "it's the Jews" is a perfect fit.

You couldn't scream that in public in 2016. It was still a bridge too far, but they were warming up to it as more and more Republicans came out of the hate closet. I've been saying on air for years now that they were soon going to drop the coded language and get as brazen with anti-Semitism as they did with racism under Trump. Unfortunately, Kanye West proved me right with his talk of "death con 3 on Jewish people." And other ghouls and goblins followed quickly thereafter.

But back in 2016, saying it out loud would have caused Republicans a lot of trouble. Remember, Trump's largest donor was Sheldon Adelson, who was Jewish. The right-wing crowd really believed that someone was pulling the strings behind the scenes (we even interviewed a Trump fan with an enormous tattoo on his back of George Soros pulling the strings as a puppeteer, another old-school anti-Semitic trope), but the Trump guys couldn't say that when they were on Team Adelson. They had to find just the right code words to strike the balance. To wink and nod at their audience while still having plausible deniability.

That's why every speech and every other ad that Trump ran in 2016 talked about . . . the global elites. Now, you can say, "Hey, he has a daughter who converted to Judaism. His son-in-law and former chief adviser is Jewish. He has a lot of close Jewish friends." First, there is no one close to Trump. He is so self-absorbed, the idea that he would care about hurting the feelings of one of his so-called friends or family members is hilarious. Second, he doesn't have to believe it! He just has to say it. Remember, he's a con man. The whole point is that he's giving the crowd what they want—someone to blame for their problems, someone to hate.

In fact, this talking point was the result of Trump doing more A/B testing in front of his crowds. If you notice, he constantly contradicts himself. I think he's doing it unconsciously, but it winds up accomplishing the goal, especially if you're a con man with no principles. So Trump will test out two different messages—even in the same speech. And then he'll go with whichever got the most applause. And the "global elites" killed it for him!

Walter Masterson is a comedian who does interviews with MAGA and QAnon followers—while dressed up like them, so they think he's on their side. He told me in a recent interview that when he turns off the camera, they invariably say the real problem is the Jews. For conspiracy-minded people who have no idea what the hell is going on and hate people who are not like them, who did you think they were going to blame? Masterson says that no matter where the conversations start, if you go down the rabbit hole deep enough, it always ends with blaming the Jews.

Remember QAnon's claim that the elites are drinking the blood of children. That's blood libel that's been used against Jewish people forever. It's the same exact idea with the word "elites" replacing the word "Jews." The code is not that subtle.

I interviewed David Duke in 2015 on *The Young Turks*. He was so excited about Trump, and I wanted to see what was underlying the extremist fervor for this one candidate. I thought Duke would rant against Latinos, since immigration was the hottest issue on the campaign trail. I thought he'd go after familiar targets like African Americans, Muslims, and gay Americans. Nope. The only thing he wanted to talk about was . . . the Jews. No matter what I said, he would say the Jews are responsible for it. The stock market reacts to what are called leading economic indicators. David Duke is a leading hate indicator. It starts at the extremes and works its way toward the mainstream. These are scary times.

Again, does Trump hate the Jews? I have no idea. I know he believes ridiculously anti-Semitic tropes. He told a gathering of Jewish Republicans, "No one likes to negotiate more than this room." Jesus. He's so old-school bigoted, he doesn't even know he's bigoted. But that's not the important part. The important part is that he is giving the right-wing crowd what they want! They wanted to blame "the others" and "the Jews." And Trump thought, I'll be your huckleberry. Ask and ye shall receive.

He is their id and their champion. Why wouldn't they love him? Again, they picked him out of seventeen candidates in 2016. It's not like they didn't have plenty of other choices. Everyone in media projects their own views onto Republican voters. So they kept saying that it was basically an accident of fortune. The cable news pundits kept talking about if Rubio had dropped out earlier or Jeb had run a "better" campaign, the result would have been different. No, it wouldn't have. The only way they could have run a "better" campaign is if they were more racist and bigoted. That's not an exaggeration. You saw it with your own eyes. Trump was clearly the most hateful of the candidates. It wasn't even close, and neither was the election. He won the nomination hands down. And they've loved him ever since.

Coup-Coup for Cocoa Puffs

On the show, I will sometimes say that people, often right-wing people, are cuckoo for Cocoa Puffs. Like the old ad that we loved growing up (unless you're young, in which case, trust me, we all loved it). It just means someone is crazy. Well, as I was writing this book about how Republicans and their voters are cuckoo for Cocoa Puffs, something interrupted my work—the Republicans going coup-coup for Cocoa Puffs. As we know, when Trump lost, he would not admit defeat. He wanted to hold on to power even if that meant ending democracy. A lot of people were surprised, but as you saw in this chapter, they shouldn't have been. This was not an aberration. This was the natural course for the Republican Party.

This is a party that made an active decision to be racist to try to get racists' votes. I hate to break it to you, but the driving ideology of racism is not equality or justice. It's the opposite. They don't want justice for everyone. And certainly not equality. So a party built on racism would of course favor tyranny over democracy. It was built on raw power and assertions of innate supremacy over others. What part of that sounds like a democracy?

As I was writing about how Republicans hated democracy, they tried to burn ours down.

On January 6, 2021, some of the rioters even brought Confederate flags. Bringing nooses and Confederate flags is not subtle. It's a nod to where their heart still lies—in the old South, where white right-wingers were firmly in charge. The Republican Party has kept that flame alive for decades now. How did it do that? By using . . . the Southern Strategy. I saw this comment online after the January 6 riots: "After 159 years, they finally did it! They stormed our Capitol."

Republicans built a party to appeal to entitled racists who never liked democracy or equality in the first place and then feigned surprise when those exact people showed up. The people who stormed the Capitol on January 6 felt entitled to be in power. As a minority in America, I have never felt that kind of entitlement. I can't fathom thinking that I was owed power, even if my side didn't win. That's such a foreign concept to me. But in the right-wing mind, they can't imagine us in *their* House. So they came to take it back.

In a sense, this was the day they'd been hoping for their whole lives. They couldn't wait for someone like Trump to give the order to march. Trump promised: "Will be wild!" He threw a party for them! This is why they're so loyal to him and never question what he says. He's giving them exactly what they have always dreamed about. He gave them permission to take back power with force, like the good old days. Remember, 52 percent of Republican voters blamed the riots on . . . Joe Biden. That's what a majority of the Republican Party is—cuckoo for Cocoa Puffs. What level of lunacy do you need to think Biden caused those riots—against himself? Well, that's exactly the level of lunacy the *majority* of Republican voters are at now.

But they're not just crazy. They are deeply un-American. They think they should be in charge no matter what, no matter who wins, no matter how democracy works, no matter the Constitution, no matter the very idea of America. They never believed in it! It was always an inconvenient relationship they felt forced into. They have been trying to break up this marriage for 250 years, because we have irreconcilable differences. They don't like the idea of democracy, and that's what we built the whole country on.

Remember, the Confederate flag was the emblem of the people who declared war on America. That's quite literal. So, if you see a right-winger waving that flag, he is waving the flag of traitors who hated America. The Confederacy killed 120 times more Americans than Al Qaeda did on 9/11.

I remember an old line Joe Scarborough used against Muslim radicals once (absurdly, in his case), "They hate us because they hate us." It's the "us" in that sentence that's the problem. Republicans don't think *they* are *us*, so they hate us because they hate *us*.

To them, there is no hypocrisy in claiming that they are for America while hating the idea of equality. Because they meant democracy for them, not for us. They never viewed us as part of them. So it's not hypocritical to them. They never thought we were their equals, who deserved the same rights as them. *They have never thought that!* In their worldview, they are supposed to be above us. To us, that's logically inconsistent with the idea of America; to them, that is America. And always has been.

So, after Biden won the election, when they realized that they were no longer going to get their way, what did they resort to? What they always resort to—violence. Who do you think did slavery? Who do you think did the whippings and the beatings and the lynchings? Who do you think started the Civil War? And did it to be able to keep the privilege of controlling other people's lives with violence? Who do you think did the cross burnings? Who threw Emmett Till's body into a river with barbed wire around his neck? The people who did that kind of violence, over and over, were conservatives. Almost every time. They attacked the rest of us—Native Americans, Blacks, Latinos, Asians, Muslims, Jews, women—repeatedly for their own gain. And they always won. Can you not see why they felt entitled? Can you not see why they felt enraged?

They used to run this house with a heavy hand, and now they had to listen to the rest of us. Oh, they hate it. It bothers them to their core. To them, the good old days were when they could end all that with a whip or a noose. And guess what they brought to the Capitol? A noose.

They had always believed in violence. They worshipped at the altar of guns well before the riots and the militia terror attacks began. The Second Amendment was meant to protect state militias. In the South, the state militias had a different name—slave patrols. Why do you think they're so obsessed with the Second Amendment? It's cultural, a symbol of their beloved oppression of others.

Not every proponent of the Second Amendment believes this, of course. And not every Republican thinks this way, as I've now explained several times, but a lot of them do. And that's why they showed up with bells on when Trump told them to march on the Capitol.

Trump cooked up a batch of toxic Kool-Aid, made of violence glorification, unearned entitlement, and fear and loathing of the others. On January 6, 2021, thousands of conservatives assembled, with great excitement, to drink that Kool-Aid. But none of that could have worked if the Republican Party had not already laid the foundation for exactly this type of party for decades.

4

HOW WE LOST
OUR DEMOCRACY

[We must] crush in its birth the aristocracy of our monied corporations, which dare already to challenge our government to a trial of strength and bid defiance to the laws of our country.

—*Thomas Jefferson*

THE RISE OF THE MACHINES

WHEN AMERICA WAS FOUNDED, THERE WERE ALMOST NO CORPORATIONS. THEY existed in the British Empire, and it was partly those corporations that led our founding fathers to revolt against the empire in the first place. It was the British East India Company's tea that the American patriots threw into Boston Harbor. The revolution was against that company almost as much as it was against the crown. So, when the United States was first formed, the founders had to decide whether they were going to allow corporations at all. Most of the founders despised them because they saw them as accumulated power unaccountable to the people.

As you can see from Jefferson's quote above, they viewed corporations as challengers to democracy. They understood that if left unchecked, corporations would naturally look to seize power. And they did. That is, in fact, exactly how we lost our democracy and the machines took over. This is the story of how corporate power gradually captured our government and now runs this country.

At first, state governments started allowing cities, schools, and some charitable organizations to be incorporated. This seemed innocent enough, and there was some logic to it. Then, in the 1790s, they finally allowed business interests to form corporations. But the states were very careful. Every charter had to be granted by the government. You could not start a corporation without getting the permission of the people's representatives. Sounds a little like democratic capitalism. And there was an expectation that those businesses had to serve the community, otherwise the democratically elected officials would not allow incorporation.

James Madison said in 1827, "Incorporated companies with proper limitations and guards may, in particular cases, be useful; but they are at best a necessary evil only."[1]

So how in the world did these corporations, which were despised by the founders of this country and were so carefully guarded against, wind up taking over the whole government?

The short answer is, through the courts. No elected body ever gave them the powers that they now possess. In the old days, if executives at companies wanted to influence a politician, they had to bribe them. And risk going to jail. A lot of them did anyway, but the problem was kept under control for a long time. But then corporations found a way to take over the Supreme Court and rewrite (or reinterpret) the laws so that they could control the government, rather than vice versa.

Jefferson and Madison were right, and so were Andrew Jackson and Teddy Roosevelt. If you allowed capital to accumulate in concentrated masses, its possessors would have overwhelming power. They would then logically use that power to take over the government so that they could direct the public's resources toward themselves. And, of course, use the government to crush their competitors. This is what we now call crony capitalism or corporatism.

You've seen me take apart conservatives in this book. So you know when I compliment them, it is not to find a false balance. I have no inclination to do them any favors. But, as it turns out, they are right about a couple of things. First of all, activist judges absolutely ruined this country. The part they might not know is that it was Republicans who came up with the idea of activist judges. In fact, it was specifically a lawyer for the Chamber of Commerce who came up with the idea of inserting "activist" judges into the Supreme Court so that corporations could take over the government. His name was Lewis Powell. In a minute, you'll see the devastation he wrought.

Conservatives are also right to warn about accumulated power. They just missed the right target. They think big government is the source of

power. And in the old days it used to be. But now the roles have been reversed. Now all the power is in the hands of Big Business, which uses the
elected officials as its minions to do anything it wants. If you are concerned
about concentrated power, your top concern should be how corporations
took over our government—and now have all the money *and* the power.

So, when the left wing or the right wing is fighting against "the establishment," whether they know it or not, they are fighting against Big
Business and its political servants. Once the Supreme Court allowed corporate interests to spend unlimited money on politics, companies did the
most logical thing in the world—they bought the government.

Some liberals and Democrats will be deeply offended reading this
part of the book. I think they'll be even more offended than conservatives. Because I'm about to criticize some of their beloved politicians, who
they have been taught by mainstream media are demigods and the purest
people on earth. There's nothing that will offend a mainstream Democrat more than criticizing Barack Obama or Nancy Pelosi. Well, buckle
up and brace for impact.

But before we get to Obama, Bush, Biden, and all the corporate-
controlled politicians of today, we have to go back and see what went
wrong. How did we go from a country that was so wary of corporations
that each one had to ask permission from the people to exist to a place
where it feels sometimes like people need permission from corporations
to exist? In other words, how did the machines take over?

That's what a corporation is, really—a machine. Despite what the United
States Supreme Court might say, corporations are not, in fact, people. They
are not endowed by their creator with inalienable rights. We are their cre-
ators. They are legal fictions. That means they are created by the law for
a specific purpose. In other words, they are machines built with a specific
objective.

The main reason why entities had to be incorporated in the first place
was so that they could act as one organization instead of a loose collection of people. They needed limited liability. If you were going to open a
school, and every person working at that school was going to be held in-
dividually responsible by the law for anything that went wrong, it created
significant problems for working together. So Madison was right, we did
need to set up some structure that resembled a corporation to limit liability, so that these organizations could function as one unit and effectively
exist. But he was also right that it was at best a "necessary evil" and one

you had to be very careful with! Well, we weren't. And those machines rose up and took over.

THE FIRST HORSEMEN OF OUR APOCALYPSE

There are four seminal cases in Supreme Court history that ruined our democracy. They were all crooked decisions, meant to help facilitate a corporate takeover of our entire government. If you think that statement sounds hyperbolic, you are wrong. It is literal, and you are about to see the evidence for it.

First, in 1886, the executives of the Southern Railroad Company decided that there was a better use for the Fourteenth Amendment than giving rights to freed slaves. They thought it was better used to give corporations rights—in fact, the same rights as human beings. At the time, that was thought to be preposterous. So the Supreme Court ruled against them in the landmark case *Santa Clara County v. Southern Pacific Railroad*. But if you're a legal scholar right now, you're thinking, "Wait a minute, that's the case where the Supreme Court did the exact opposite. It gave corporations personhood." Well, not exactly.

The justices of the court clearly said that they would not rule on the idea of corporate personhood. They decided the case on different grounds. One of the justices, Stephen J. Field, was very mad about that because he was working with corporations. In fact, he was friends with the owner of that particular railroad company and would leak internal court deliberations to its lawyers. In other words, he was a crook. When his colleagues on the court wouldn't let corporations have these new outrageous "rights," he wrote a furious dissent. But then something strange happened.

Back then the court reporter would write a quick summary of the case. This would be done well after the case was decided and had no force of law. It was just an attempt at a legal summary by a clerk. But at the time, the clerk position was held by J. C. Bancroft Davis, who until recently had been the head of the Newburgh and New York Railway company. The Supreme Court clerk who had run a railroad company was responsible for summarizing a case about railroads. Now, how is that for a hell of a coincidence? But wait, it gets way worse.

Davis wrote in the summary that the court had ruled that "corporations are persons within . . . the Fourteenth Amendment." Wait, no, they didn't! They explicitly did not write that, and Field's angry dissent proves it beyond a shadow of a doubt.

Well, innocent mistakes happen, and sometimes not so innocent ones. But what difference does it make, since it has no force of law? It's literally a clerical error. Well, here is the genius of the crooks. Several years later, Justice Field quotes the incorrect summary in a different case as precedent. And then it becomes one! Voilà, watch as democracy magically disappears in front of your very eyes.

Field wrote that corporations had personhood; "It was so held in *Santa Clara County v. Southern Pacific Railroad*." He knew that was an outright lie. He had written the dissent! Well, did it work?

Precedent is when a court makes a definitive decision in a case and future courts rely on it as the law of the land going forward. When Field lied about the precedent but no one corrected him, it became Supreme Court precedent through the latter decision. From then on, courts started quoting Field's statement as if it referred to something real. Then, through the magic of precedent, it became real.

Stephen J. Field was the first activist justice. He would not be the last.

This was the beginning of the corporate takeover of our country, but the next step didn't come for a long time. In fact, in the late nineteenth and early twentieth centuries, we entered the Progressive Era. This was when we built the greatest middle class the world has ever seen and passed the most popular laws in American history. We actually had a functioning democracy! Until 1978, when the corporate machines figured out how to stop us.

WHEN PROGRESSIVES WERE LIONS

Progressives dominated in Washington and around the country for decades! From 1931 to 1994, Democrats controlled the House for all but four years, in the early 1950s. Teddy Roosevelt, Woodrow Wilson, and FDR were maybe the three most progressive presidents the country has ever seen, and they all governed within a thirty-eight-year span. In the 1912 federal election, all four of the major candidates were progressives! "Above all, there was the question of how to curb the excesses of big business, symbolized by the great trusts, which had accompanied the rise of industrial capitalism," one historian wrote about that year's campaigns.[2]

FDR won four—yes, four—presidential elections. And more than any
president before or since, he embraced the label and spirit of what it means
to be a progressive. His first campaign came during the Great Depression, still the most devastating economic collapse in American history.
In May 1932, Roosevelt made a speech that many historians consider to
be the best statement of the philosophy behind the package of reforms
that he called the New Deal. "Do what we may have to do to inject life
into our ailing economic order, we cannot make it endure for long unless
we can bring about a wiser, more equitable distribution of the national
income," he said. "The country demands bold, persistent experimenta-
tion. It is common sense to take a method and try it: If it fails, admit it
frankly and try another. But above all, try something."[3] That's a pretty
good explanation of the progressive creed. We are willing to boldly try
change. We are willing to do and try almost anything—beyond violat-
ing anyone's basic human rights—to achieve freedom and justice for all
Americans. And we won't stop until we get there.

In addition to evangelizing on behalf of liberalism, Roosevelt had another notable quality: he was politically aggressive. He didn't shy from
a fight. The stakes were the future of America, and they were high. He
acted like it. In 1936, right before his second election, he spoke about
the twelve years of Republican rule that preceded his 1932 victory: "We
know now that Government by organized money is just as dangerous as
Government by organized mob." Here's what he said next:

> Never before in all our history have these forces been so united against
> one candidate as they stand today. They are unanimous in their hate for
> me—and I welcome their hatred. I should like to have it said of my first
> Administration that in it the forces of selfishness and of lust for power
> met their match. I should like to have it said of my second Administra-
> tion that in it these forces met their master.[4]

Can you even imagine any present-day Democratic president—let alone
kumbaya types like Bill Clinton, Barack Obama, or Joe Biden—delivering
such a passionate defense of political combat? Welcoming the hatred of
his opponents? Mastering his political adversaries? A Democrat? We must
be talking about a different party. Joe Biden would rather make out with
a Republican than fight one. Imagine him saying he welcomes the hatred
of Republicans. Never! It's the exact opposite of who he is.

Even in his speech in Philadelphia in 2022 where he took on "MAGA Republicans," he went out of his way to say that MAGA was not the "majority of Republicans." That's empirically untrue. They're 93 percent of Republicans. As usual, the leader of the Democrats wanted to help Republicans look more reasonable. He continued, "I know because I've been able to work with these mainstream Republicans."[5] Joe Biden is forever bragging about how much he likes to work with the GOP. He is of today's era of Democrats, whose raison d'être is to agree to whatever the Republicans want. But in an earlier era, back when Democrats won endless elections and actually passed laws, they loved fighting Republicans!

Democrats today quote FDR, but they definitely don't mention the quotes cited here. They're more likely to tell you how much they respect the Republican Party than to say the GOP represents "the forces of selfishness and of lust for power." After Joe Biden won the 2020 election, both he and Nancy Pelosi gave speeches hoping for a *stronger* Republican Party! We are told that if you are not very polite to Republicans, you will lose elections. Really? Because FDR won four of them and he welcomed their hatred.

In fact, pundits predicted a close election in 1936. But three days after Roosevelt said these words, he won the highest share of both the popular and electoral vote in the history of the two-party system. With 60 percent of the vote, it's still the biggest electoral victory in the country's past. More than seventy-five years later, even Republicans don't think they can eliminate Social Security, insurance for banks, or other essential government programs. "In the United States at this time liberalism is not only the dominant but even the sole intellectual tradition. For it is the plain fact that nowadays there are no conservative or reactionary ideas in general," the critic Lionel Trilling wrote in 1950.[6]

At different times in this book, you're going to think I'm exaggerating because people in politics can't be this obtuse and wrong, could they? And those poor reporters I keep beating up on, they must know some history, right? They're going to know that Democrats won a lot more elections and dominated Washington when they were far more combative, right?

Nope. I was involved in a situation that proves almost perfectly how clueless mainstream media are and how they have no sense of history whatsoever. Part of the reason the Democratic Party is in disrepair (having nearly lost to a buffoonish clown twice) is because its representatives listen to mainstream reporters telling them—do not fight back!

Do they really say that? Well, when I ran for Congress in 2020, I had a great meeting with the *Los Angeles Times* editorial board. That was important to me because Democratic voters these days give tremendous weight to what "legitimate" and "established" mainstream media publications say. Many Democratic voters in California check who the *L.A. Times* endorsed before they vote. So I was thrilled to have a great exchange of ideas with the journalists on its board. I was sure my opponents did not have anywhere near the command of the policies that I did. They usually talked about anodyne nonsense like how they supported the local fire department and really liked veterans. Wow, how bold! You left out puppies and kittens. Yes, we all support those things, but what do you think of actual legislation we might vote on at the federal level? In my debates and exchanges with the other candidates, they avoided policy discussions as if they were an awkward ex-boyfriend trying to connect with you on Facebook.

So, was the editorial board impressed by my grasp of policy? It seems that they were! Did they largely agree with me on the solutions? It seems that they did! So, did they endorse me? Of course not. Why? Because I would fight Republicans too much! That has got to be hyperbole, right? Well, read it for yourself:

> But while we agree with [Uygur] about the corrupting influence of money in politics and some other subjects, we find his pugnacious style off-putting and not conducive to a more civil Congress.[7]

I do declare! The club would have its feathers quite ruffled if someone were actually "pugnacious" to Republicans, i.e., the opposing party. You know, the one that's destroying the country? Yes, at the time Donald Trump was president, but they thought *I* was too uncivil. Did it ever occur to them that you might want to fight back against bullies like that? Nope. At a time when Republicans were ripping the Democrats apart—including with insane conspiracy theories about how they were all child molesters—here were the mainstream media imploring Democrats to not fight back. They prefer civility!

I guess if you're comfortable—and don't want to change anything—you'd also prefer civility. In fact, you'd prefer slumber. Mainstream media are now almost all billion-dollar companies. They've created a culture that seeps into good people trying to do the right thing. And that culture is one that cherishes the status quo and views any change agents as radical interlopers. The sirens sound, the civility police emerge, and any progressive *fighting* for change is labeled illegitimate and not to be trusted. Everyone, hurry back to sleep.

This has come at great cost to the Democratic Party. But it has also come at great cost to the truth. FDR was quite uncivil. He welcomed hatred! He beat the Nazis. He was a combative antifascist, quite literally, as he took us to war against fascists. You know what's a shorter term for an antifascist like FDR? Antifa. That's what "antifa" stands for, it's short for "antifascist." He tore apart the greedy bankers. In the 1960s, when fighting to pass landmark civil rights legislation, LBJ would chew you up and spit you out. He'd lean on you so hard, you wished you'd never gotten into politics. Democrats kicked ass for their voters. Recasting them as Mister Rogers is an affront to truth itself. It's so obviously wrong that it's stunning that so-called reporters can't see it.

If you wanted to see a model for success in the Democratic Party, would you look at pushovers like Mike Dukakis, John Kerry, Harry Reid, and Chuck Schumer, or would you look to fighting heroes like FDR and LBJ? The answer is obvious, unless you're a reporter. They say that Democrats should be soft like their losing candidates, and not fight like the winners did. Civility above all!

If your objective is Democratic victories, civility is the last thing you want. But if your objective is protecting the status quo, where corporations rule everything and control all our politicians, then civility is perfect.

During the Progressive Era, Democrats were so strong that even Republicans believed that liberalism was a permanently leading feature of the American political landscape. In 1954, Dwight Eisenhower, a moderate Republican, wrote to his brother: "Should any political party attempt to abolish social security, unemployment insurance and eliminate labor laws and farm programs, you would not hear of that party again in our political history. There is a tiny splinter group, of course, that believes that you can do these things. Among them are . . . a few Texas oil millionaires, and an occasional politician or businessman from other areas. Their number is negligible and they are stupid."[8] They are still stupid, but their numbers are larger now. Partly because of how gracious and civil we have been to them.

Progressive policies seemed poised to rule eternally. The presidential campaign of 1964 provided perhaps the starkest, most direct contrast between liberalism and conservatism. Lyndon Johnson campaigned on using government to eliminate poverty, work on behalf of the oppressed, and help the elderly lead decent lives. Republican challenger Barry Goldwater was a committed conservative—a rare genuine believer in small government. "Extremism in defense of liberty is no vice," he famously declared at the GOP convention. Voters disagreed—LBJ won in a landslide.

Noam Chomsky has called Richard Nixon "the last liberal president" because even he was forced to accommodate himself to the realities of progressive power and sign legislation establishing the Environmental Protection Agency, wage and price controls, expanded welfare, and increased Social Security, Medicare, and Medicaid benefits. Nixon, of course, being a stalwart conservative, would have loved to do away with social programs, not expand them. But progressives so dominated politics that he felt he had no choice but to bend a knee to them.

Beginning in the 1970s, however, things began changing. Progressives began losing power. Conservatives resurrected themselves from near oblivion. Along with the presidential victories of Reagan, Bush, and Trump, GOP revolutionary Newt Gingrich brought Republicans to power in the House in 1994, and they controlled it until 2006, as well as from 2010 to 2018. And they won it back again in 2022. The story with the Senate is much the same, except the bloodletting began earlier, when Republicans gained power in 1981, on Reagan's coattails. But again, this GOP dominance is new. "The last half of the 20th century saw significant Democratic control at the state legislative level as well as Congress, right up until the '94 revolution," *The Atlantic* reported.[9]

Now, it's not as though all those Democrats in Congress and state legislatures were perfect progressives at the time, but the progressive culture dominated so much that there was a time when even some Republicans were progressives. One prominent example was Mitt Romney's father, Michigan Governor George Romney. But progressives gradually disappeared from political power in the United States. They completely vanished from the Republican Party and eventually lost power even within the Democratic Party. America became governed almost entirely by conservatives, so-called moderates, and neoliberals.

And so, inevitably, politicians began separating themselves from progressive policies and even the term itself. Eventually being identified as a liberal was considered so electorally toxic that when George H. W. Bush branded Michael Dukakis as one, it was a slur. Democrats began defining themselves as "New Democrats" to show they weren't like those other Democrats, who supported things like expanding freedom and equality for all voters. From Barack Obama to Joe Biden, from Nancy Pelosi to the Clintons, establishment Democrats ran away from progressive policies like their lives depended on it. That's because of what happened next—and how it made it seem like their political lives did depend on betraying progressive values.

HOW WE LOST THE DEMOCRATS

Here's the question the media won't ask: What changed? Did Americans collectively decide they hated things like affordable health care coverage and clean air? Did they fall in love with tax cuts for billionaires and unlimited corporate spending in elections? Of course not. So what in the world happened to cause this sea change in America?

The answer to this question came to me from Ralph Nader. Remember him? You might know him as the guy Democrats despised for running as the Green Party presidential nominee in 2000 and costing Al Gore the election. I've even had him on our show and gotten into an epic shouting match over that. Or you might remember him being a constant thorn in the side of the Democratic establishment for the last twenty years.

But there was a time when Nader was such a giant in politics that he used to boss the establishment around. He bullied Republicans into compliance on a regular basis. That can sound impossible to anyone born in the 1980s or later, but it's true. He was an unknown Connecticut lawyer before publishing a book in 1965 on auto safety. *Unsafe at Any Speed* was one of the most impactful books of the twentieth century. It showed how the auto industry was deliberately resisting measures that would save millions of lives because they wanted their cars to crash—that led to people buying more cars and car parts, after all. The book inspired congressional hearings that led to the National Highway Traffic and Motor Vehicle Safety Act. His successful public campaigns for seat belts and driving only when sober collectively saved tens of millions of lives over decades! The guy was a legend—and was treated as such back then.

Nader then issued a report on the Federal Trade Commission, a government agency so beholden to corporate interests that it was bad even by Washington standards. That led President Nixon, who was nothing if not attuned to public opinion, to fire the FTC director and replace him with someone who actually did his job and immediately took on big companies.

Nixon also signed legislation creating the Environmental Protection Agency and the Occupational Safety and Health Administration, and strengthened other legislation to counter corporate power. Not all this action was due to Nader, but a lot of it was!

As Rick Perlstein observes in his book *Reaganland*, Merriam-Webster's dictionary added the word "consumerism" to its third edition in 1971. Nader was on the cover of *Esquire* magazine. George McGovern considered tapping him to be his vice presidential candidate. More laws favoring consumers were passed under President Gerald Ford, Nixon's successor. Nader was among the most beloved people in the United States. Five days before Carter's inauguration, he hosted *Saturday Night Live*. Now he'd have trouble getting invited to one of the show's after-parties.

I've hosted Ralph Nader on *The Young Turks* several times, but ironically, it was at a fundraiser for a progressive cause in L.A. that I found out the secret to his rise and fall. I asked him in a more personal setting how we'd gone from a world where he was among the most powerful people in America, where even Richard Nixon was afraid to oppose progressive legislation inspired by him, to one where he is now considered a pariah and a radical. It didn't just happen in his lifetime, it happened to *him* in his lifetime. His answer at the time seemed strange. He just said, "It was Tony Coelho."

You're probably asking yourself the same question now that I was asking myself back then: Who the hell is Tony Coelho?

Coelho is one of those people whose name is not well known but who is in fact deeply consequential to our lives. As a member of Congress from California, Coelho in 1980 was named chairman of the Democratic Congressional Campaign Committee (DCCC), which raises money for the party so they can win more seats in the House. He convinced the Democratic leadership that the party needed to take money from business groups. "That's where we ran into a brick wall and never recovered," Nader told me. It turns out corporate cash was unsafe at any speed.

Honestly, when I heard this, I was skeptical. The explanation sounded simplistic, but it was intriguing. How could one relatively obscure man have changed politics so much? As I did research, I was staggered to find out how right Nader was. Nader didn't change between 1965 and today. The Democrats changed. And that empowered Republicans to take over.

So let's return to Nader's heyday, when the movement he helped lead was so powerful that, for a time, it managed to go toe-to-toe with corporate power—and win. "We don't have a business community," Perlstein quotes an executive as saying in the mid-1970s. "Just a fragmented bunch of self-interested people."[10]

What they needed to do was unite in their collective self-interest. One person unhappy about Nader's mini-revolution was a guy named Lewis Powell, a geeky business-friendly lawyer who represented clients in big tobacco and served on Philip Morris's board of directors. He thought Nader's consumerism was leading America toward socialism (of course). In 1971, he wrote a memo that changed America.

It turns out, Powell led to Coelho, who led to Democratic ruin. So, what was in that goddamn memo?

THE MEMO THAT CHANGED THE WORLD

Lewis Powell wrote his confidential memo at the request of his friend and neighbor, the education director of the U.S. Chamber of Commerce. He called it "Attack on American Free Enterprise System." As its title indicates, the memo argued that liberals, leftists, and the media were intent on destroying American freedom. "The single most effective antagonist of American business is Ralph Nader, who—thanks largely to the media—has become a legend in his own time and an idol of millions of Americans," Powell wrote. "Business, including the boards of directors and the top executives of corporations great and small and business organizations at all levels, often have responded—if at all—by appeasement, ineptitude and ignoring the problem."[11] Back then corporations were the serial bunglers instead of the Democrats. It was a fantastical time indeed.

To even the playing field, Powell recommended that business groups and leaders pool their resources and coordinate to fight back against socialism. "Strength lies in organization, in careful long-range planning and implementation, in consistency of action over an indefinite period of years, in the scale of financing available only through joint effort, and in the political power available only through united action and national organizations," he wrote.[12]

It's difficult to overstate how effective Powell's memo was. Big Business's assault on our government and economic fairness starts here. The memo should have been called "Attack on the American Worker." Writes journalist Jane Mayer: "It was Powell's memo that electrified the Right, prompting a new breed of wealthy ultraconservatives to weaponize their philanthropic giving in order to fight a multifront war of influence of American political thought."[13] She calls the memo "a virtual anti–*Communist Manifesto* for right-wingers."[14] Instead of inspiring European workers and intellectuals, however, Powell's memo galvanized the corporate machines.

Powell was in some ways a community organizer, it's just that his community was that of multinational corporations. He knew that if they spent their considerable resources on accruing "political power," it would be fairly simple to take over America. Unfortunately, he was right.

The entire corporate lobbying complex and think tank apparatus that dominates the conservative world dates back to Powell's memo. He explained how its members could give their pursuit of profit the appearance of a scholarly endeavor to inject their positions into the political ecosystem.

> The first essential is to establish the staffs of eminent scholars, writers and speakers, who will do the thinking, the analysis, the writing and the speaking. It will also be essential to have staff personnel who are thoroughly familiar with the media, and how most effectively to communicate with the public.[15]

This led to "think tanks" providing scholarly explanations of why corporations should get everything they wanted from the government. Funny that in all that "thinking," not one of their "scholars" ever concluded that maybe corporations shouldn't have all the power.

These are the guys who have been doing "the thinking, the analysis, the writing and the speaking" in Washington for the last fifty years. And yet all the media take them seriously and quote their work as if it's legitimate, educational, and unbiased. There is literally a memo—perhaps the most famous memo in political history—that tells you that they are going to trick you with their fake, bought scholars. Yet everyone in media still used them as sources for decades—and still do. Is there a single journalist in the country? Have any of them heard of this memo that explains how they're all going to be co-opted as useful idiots?

The think tanks this memo led to not only provided "ideas" for the Reagan, Bush, and Trump administrations and conservative media like Fox News but also a steady stream of personnel who had already proven their loyalty to their corporate masters.

The Heritage Foundation opened its well-funded doors in 1973. The

Chamber of Commerce's membership doubled between 1974 and 1980, and its budget tripled. The membership of the National Federation of Independent Business doubled between 1970 and 1979.[16] The American Enterprise Institute's budget was less than one million dollars in 1970; by 1980, it was $9.7 million.[17]

By the way, that quote about planting the people "who will do the thinking" was from a section of the memo called "What Can Be Done About the Public?" Indeed, what should Big Business do about the meddlesome public and their damned democracy? Well, they decided to buy the government "of the people, by the people, and for the people" and turn it into a government "of the corporations, by the corporations, and for the corporations." And if the public had to be duped along the way, then that literally was the cost of doing business.

In fact, Powell explained, "The type of program described above (which includes a broadly based combination of education and political action), if undertaken long term and adequately staffed, would require far more generous financial support from American corporations than the Chamber has ever received in the past."[18] Well, they got that generous support, and Powell proved prescient. It was relatively easy to buy politicians and trick half the country into voting for them on a regular basis. And it turned out to produce a great return on investment.

Speaking of duping people, Powell went on to say that corporate interests should sneak speakers on to college campuses and demand equal time and the right to speak. These are the same exact talking points that people like Charlie Kirk and Ben Shapiro still use decades later. Powell wrote, "The Chamber should insist upon equal time on the college speaking circuit. . . . The two essential ingredients are (i) to have attractive, articulate and well-informed speakers; and (ii) to exert whatever degree of pressure—publicly and privately—may be necessary to assure opportunities to speak."[19] In other words, hit them with a healthy dose of corporate propaganda, and if they refuse, scream from the rooftops about cancel culture.

Here's another oldie but goodie that Powell created: "The threat to the enterprise system is not merely a matter of economics. It also is a threat to individual freedom."[20] How many times have you heard conservative ideas—i.e., corporate propaganda—framed as advocating for "freedom"? That was Powell, too. He planted that thought in millions of people's heads fifty years ago. And backed by enough corporate money,

it worked! Now unlimited corporate power equals freedom! Propaganda
is a hell of a drug.

You have to remember that this memo was written in 1971, when
progressives were in charge. Corporations believed they were the downtrodden. I know that sounds impossible to believe today, but listen to
what Powell wrote about how badly corporations were getting their asses
handed to them back then:

> Yet, as every business executive knows, few elements of American society
> today have as little influence in government as the American business-
> man, the corporation, or even the millions of corporate stockholders. If
> one doubts this, let him undertake the role of "lobbyist" for the business
> point of view before Congressional Committees. The same situation ob-
> tains in the legislative halls of most states and major cities. One does not
> exaggerate to say that, in terms of political influence with respect to the
> course of legislation and government action, the American business ex-
> ecutive is truly the "forgotten man."
>
> Current examples of the impotency of business, and of the near-
> contempt with which businessmen's views are held, are the stampedes
> by politicians to support almost any legislation related to "consumer-
> ism" or to the "environment."
>
> Politicians reflect what they believe to be majority views of their con-
> stituents. It is thus evident that most politicians are making the judgment
> that the public has little sympathy for the businessman or his viewpoint.[21]

Doesn't that sound amazing? Look, I'm also a businessman. I run TYT,
a midsize business that employs about a hundred people. So I don't want
businesses or all company owners to be treated unfairly. But right now,
corporate lobbyists have such an unbreakable stranglehold on our government that the "impotency of business" interests in Washington sounds
fantastic. The idea that politicians would represent the "majority view
of their constituents" and have "little sympathy for the businessman or
his viewpoint" sounds like a dream that couldn't possibly come true in
today's America.

Don't ever let anyone tell you that progressives or Democrats are weak
by nature. No, we used to own our opponents. They feared us. They were
so sad at how much power we had and how little they had—until Powell
convinced Big Business to use its money to crush us and kill off our de-

mocracy. Now we live under the rule of the machines and can't believe we ever had representatives who fought for us. The media have lulled us into thinking that that time never even existed, that it was all a dream. But it wasn't, it was real.

You just read how corporate interests used to be scared to death of us. Understand that when people tell you that you can't ever have any power, it's a trick. It's a lie told to make you complacent. There was, in fact, a time in America when you actually ran this country!

Who did Powell want to target first with what he called "A More Aggressive Attitude"?

There should be no hesitation to attack the Naders, the Marcuses and others who openly seek destruction of the system. There should not be the slightest hesitation to press vigorously in all political arenas for support of the enterprise system. Nor should there be reluctance to penalize politically those who oppose it.[22]

Well, how would you reward or penalize your political opponents? With money spent on political ads, of course. And hence, the modern era of money in politics was born.

Powell explained that this is what corporations do already—convince or trick people into buying their products through ads. He said, "If American business devoted only 10% of its total annual advertising budget to this overall purpose, it would be a statesman-like expenditure."[23] It turns out they didn't need 10 percent of their ad budget; politicians could be bought for much cheaper than that.

Between 2010 and 2015, the top two hundred most politically active companies spent a stunning $5.8 billion influencing politicians. That's a lot of money to invest in a product—in this case, our government. So how did they do? Did they get a good return on investment? The government in that same period gave those same corporations $4.4 *trillion* in government support! That's nearly a 100,000 percent rate of return on their investment. Holy cow, Powell nailed it. Best investment ever. Buy the U.S. government and have them do your dirty work for you.

Now wait until you see Powell's role in the execution of this plan. It's going to blow your mind.

If we're being honest, Lewis Powell was a genius. He correctly assessed the situation, came up with an effective battle plan, and routed

the competition. His victory was merciless. And what was his crowning
achievement that made all of this possible? The courts! Remember, he
was a lawyer. So he suggested to the Chamber of Commerce that it was
most important to influence the judicial system.

> American business and the enterprise system have been affected as much
> by the courts as by the executive and legislative branches of government.
> Under our constitutional system, especially with an activist-minded Su-
> preme Court, the judiciary may be the most important instrument for
> social, economic and political change.[24]

You ready for this? Two months after he wrote this memo, Richard
Nixon put him on the Supreme Court! Not someone like him or someone
who had similar ideas; no, he put Lewis Powell himself on the Supreme
Court. This is what I call Nixon's Revenge. Nixon was getting so thoroughly beaten by Ralph Nader, of all people, that he was passing some
of the most progressive legislation we've had in this country—again, it
was Nixon who formed the EPA and OSHA! But, unfortunately, Nixon
got the last laugh by putting the architect of the corporate takeover of
our government on the Supreme Court.

In essence, Lewis Powell said to the Chamber of Commerce: Why don't
we take over the Supreme Court? Nixon said: Good idea, why don't you
do it! So he put Powell in a position to execute his own plan. And wait
until you see what Powell decided on the court! Unfortunately, Nixon
and Powell were right; it made all the difference.

How Hope Was Lost

Remember that Powell wrote his famous memo in response to huge progressive victories in Washington. In 1971, we were still kicking ass and
passing terrific laws. That year was crucial in another way: Congress introduced the Federal Election Campaign Act (FECA). It was among the
most sweeping campaign finance laws in American history. FECA man-
dated increased disclosure requirements for politicians, political action
committees, parties, and candidates in federal elections. "By giving the
American public full access to the facts of political financing, this legislation will guard against campaign abuses and will work to build pub-

lic confidence in the integrity of the electoral process," Nixon said as he signed it.[25]

After Watergate revealed the extent of financial criminality in the political system—it turns out Nixon wasn't quite as horrified by campaign abuses as he'd claimed, since he was one of the people doing it in the first place—Congress enhanced the law in 1974, establishing government subsidies for presidential primary campaigns. This had been a desire of every progressive president since Teddy Roosevelt. The amended bill also restricted individual spending on campaigns, parties, and PACs. The climate in 1974 was so strong against corruption that Republican President Gerald Ford didn't dare not sign the bill.

Reactionaries didn't take that lying down, of course. Literally the day after the amendments went into effect, New York Senator James Buckley, a member of the Conservative Party, joined with others in filing a lawsuit. They argued that the campaign finance laws violated inalienable rights, including to freedom of expression and due process. Republicans understood their only pathway back into power was to ride the coattails of corporate money and power. They needed that cash to convince people to vote against their interests. Without it, they were getting killed in the fact-based world.

In 1976, the Supreme Court agreed with them and began the destruction of our democracy. In the case *Buckley v. Valeo*, the court took an ax to the laws, which were designed specifically to thwart the corruption that comes from private financing of elections. Congress had concluded that if private interests financed elections, politicians would work for private interests, and not the public interest. Congress has never been more correct. The Supreme Court, on the other hand, said that the state's interest in preventing corruption was not as important as the interests of individuals to be able to express their opinions through money, lots of money.

"The Act's expenditure ceilings impose direct and substantial restraints on the quantity of political speech," the court ruled.[26] It struck down limits on candidates' election spending. It changed the ways in which Congress appointed the commissioners of the Federal Election Commission. It weakened the spending disclosure and reporting rules. And most consequentially, the decision destroyed all restrictions on spending by outside groups. So, decades before *Citizens United,* this is how the floodgates of money were opened.

Buckley v. Valeo "set the structure of modern campaign finance law," according to Demos, a liberal think tank. "The ruling eliminated many of the strongest protections against wealthy individuals and institutions translating economic might into political power, and has helped sustain a vicious cycle of political, economic, and racial inequality that endures today."[27]

The decision is considered a landmark because it established a new precedent that any future legislation would have to overcome. Ellen Weintraub, chair of the Federal Election Commission, said, "From where I sit, American politics took a very wrong turn in 1976, when the Supreme Court ruled in *Buckley v. Valeo* that spending limits of any sort were unconstitutional." She continued: "The idea of reversing *Citizens United* has captured some of the public's imagination but flipping *Citizens United* achieves little as long as the *Buckley* decision stands."[28]

Buckley v. Valeo, the most important Supreme Court decision you've never heard of, was supported in its entirety by only three of the eight justices (Justice Stevens had just arrived on the court and recused himself). One of them was, of course, Lewis Powell. Without changing the laws or amending the Constitution, Nixon and Powell used the court to change the Constitution through interpretation—and they gave the wealthy virtually unlimited power to legally bribe politicians.

Powell had told the Chamber of Commerce that business interests could use an "activist-minded Supreme Court" as the "most important instrument" in acquiring power.[29] He was right. This was an end run around democracy. Pack the courts with activist judges in favor of the wealthy, and they'll change the laws with just a couple of people on the bench.

They created a right to spend *unlimited money* in politics. That's what "activist-minded" judges do. They don't write the law; they change the law to whatever they want. In this case, they changed it to allow for unlimited bribery.

Justice Byron White, in his dissent, warned that unlimited political spending would be "a mortal danger against which effective preventive and curative steps must be taken."[30] No such steps were taken. Instead, we continued to go backward. And the "mortal danger" to our democracy grew.

So the *Buckley* decision became the second horseman of our democracy's apocalypse. *Southern Pacific Railroad* had brought the corporate machines alive by declaring them people, i.e., living entities with the rights of natural-born people. *Buckley* allowed them to arm themselves by using unlimited cash in politics.

The new corporate court was not done yet. In 1978, the Supreme Court ruled on a case called *First National Bank of Boston v. Bellotti*. The bank joined with other huge corporations in arguing that they should be allowed to spend funds on advertising to influence the outcome of referendums. Blocking corporations from spending money on politics seems sensible, right? Otherwise, companies, with their enormous resources, can just flood the world with political propaganda. They can overwhelm everyone else with the amount of money they have. Do you think a politician is going to listen to you or the guy with all the money? With corporate money they could buy enough ads to trick thousands, or even millions, of people. So why would they care about just one voter? A politician would be crazy to try to get voters one by one when they could get them by the thousands with ads paid for by corporate interests.

In a 5–4 decision, the justices decided that corporations had the same rights to free speech as human beings! "The inherent worth of the speech in terms of its capacity for informing the public does not depend upon the identity of its source, whether corporation, association, union, or individual," the majority wrote.[31] The court said that intangible entities such as corporations had the same rights as people, including freedom of speech.

Remember, corporations are legal fictions. They are entities created by law to serve a specific purpose. They're not actually real. They don't have flesh and bones. They're not alive. They can't die. They have no human rights because they're not actually human. They don't have natural rights because they don't exist in nature. They are, in essence, machines we created. They are not "endowed by their Creator with certain unalienable Rights" because we are their Creator!

Not anymore. Not in America. According to the corporate-captured court, they are the equivalent of humans. They have First Amendment rights to speech. Money is speech. Unlimited money is even more speech. So they have the unalienable right to shower our politicians with as much money as they want, or just enough to buy their votes. Guess who cast the deciding vote? Yep, Lewis Powell. Guess who wrote the majority opinion that allowed for unlimited corruption? Lewis Powell.

Bellotti became the third horseman of our apocalypse. It connected the generic rights of corporations as people started in *Southern Pacific Railroad* to the specific right of spending money in politics created in *Buckley* to the concept of freedom of speech (the most American of rights!). These corporate machines could now spend unlimited money in "speaking" to politicians and "speaking" to the public in the form of political ads. The consequences of this decision were that Big Business could spend directly on elections. Corporations didn't just have generic speech rights; they could spend money on defeating specific ballot initiatives, and eventually specific campaigns and candidates. That allowed them to buy politicians one by one. "You can do what we tell you and we'll spend millions to make sure you get elected, or you can defy us and we'll spend millions to make sure you lose." If that sounds like the kind of deal a mob boss would give someone, you're starting to understand what happened to our representatives in government. They were made an offer they couldn't refuse.

Now there were almost no brakes left in the car. This allowed corporations to buy our government wholesale and declare that they had done it in the name of "freedom." Just as Lewis Powell taught them to.

The *Bellotti* decision was part of a case that involved ballot initiatives, but the constitutional rights that were created were so broad that subsequent decisions extended the application to nearly every corner of politics. The decision paved the way for later courts to gut any law that curbed the tremendous power of Big Money to dominate the political system. Republicans rejoiced! They loved their activist judges. Now they could finally compete! It didn't matter if the American people didn't agree with them, they could just lie to them in the ads and get them to vote against their own interests. If they could get them to buy expensive watches or bags they didn't need, getting them to vote for the wrong guy would be a piece of cake! "The Court's decision also laid important groundwork for later gains in free speech rights, most famously *Citizens United*," according to the Institute for Free Speech, a corporate-funded D.C. think tank.[32] Indeed. The groundwork for the complete corporate takeover of our government had been set. From then on, it was a long slide into oblivion. By the time *Citizens United* came around, the horse had long been dead. But the court shot the dead horse anyway. That decision shredded the carcass of our representative government with a Gatling gun, but our democracy had already perished in 1978.

Since then, we have seen the rise of the machines. Corporations went from the downtrodden underdogs that Lewis Powell described in 1971 to the behemoth that has swallowed our government whole. Different machines give to different politicians for their specific interests. Drug companies give to politicians who sit on health committees. Real estate interests give money to state governments that pass zoning laws. Banks give money to people who sit on the financial committees, and every other committee, just to be safe. After all, they're banks—they have nearly unlimited money. This is all out in the open. It's so brazen, but no one is minding the store. Almost all the politicians take corporate money, and hence, obviously, serve corporate interests. The only people who haven't figured this out yet are our media. Oh, right, our corporate media. I suppose they would have a vested interest in not figuring it out. As Upton Sinclair famously said, "It is difficult to get a man to understand something, when his salary depends on his not understanding it."

Remember the charts I showed you in chapter 2, where wages stopped growing along with productivity? Remember what year they started to diverge? It was 1979, the year after the 1978 *Bellotti* decision. Before that decision, your wages grew along with your productivity. After *Buckley* and *Bellotti* went into effect, productivity kept growing, but wages came to a screeching halt. Now, do you remember where all the money went instead? Corporate profits.

Mo' Money, Mo' Problems

By the time we got to 2022, corporate lobbyists so thoroughly controlled Washington that politicians openly talked about how congressional seats and chairmanships were up for sale. Mo Brooks, a very conservative congressman from Alabama, during a campaign event laid out exactly how this system of bribery works.

> I'm sure that you are very much concerned about why our Congress is so unresponsive to the regular needs of American citizens, why some of these policies that come out are so bizarre, so unfair, so skewered against regular Jane and Joe Citizen. The reason is simple. Special interest groups run Washington, and I don't mean that metaphorically, I mean, literally. Now, here is how it happens. In the House of Representatives—I use that as an example because that's where I work—if you want to be chairman of a major committee, you have to purchase it. And the purchase price for a major committee, say like Ways and Means, minimum bid is a million dollars. I'm talking literally here. I'm not talking metaphorically.[33]

He just said it. This is like a description of a crime scene in one of those *CSI* shows on television. He is explaining in public how bribery works in the U.S. Congress. He's also telling you that the average person has no voice at all in Congress. The special interests have won completely. Remember how Lewis Powell had lamented, "Politicians reflect what they believe to be majority views of their constituents"? Well, mission accomplished. They don't anymore. Powell's plan worked, better than he could have imagined.

But wait, it gets worse. In this era of unlimited corruption, it always gets worse. Here is more from Mo Brooks:

> So where does a congressman come up with a million dollars to be chairman of one of these [powerful] committees? You can't get it from Joe and Jane Citizen because Joe and Jane Citizen back home, they're not going to be contributing that kind of money. They don't have it . . . And so you have to get it from the special interest groups. And with the special interest groups, there is a quid pro quo. If you don't do what they tell you to do, they won't give you the money that finances your chairmanship.

Isn't that amazing? That speech was recorded by independent journalist Lauren Windsor for her program *The Undercurrent*. But if it's that brazen, how come you never heard of this admission by Congressman Brooks? And you never heard that politicians have to purchase their committee assignments and do as they are told by corporate interests? Well, Representative Brooks explains that, too:

> Now, the national media knows about this. Both political parties do it. So neither party rises to the occasion and makes this a major public policy issue that would increase exposure about what's getting done. But if you want to know why our government is not properly facing the challenges that are in front of the United States of America, that more than anything else is the reason.

Mo Brooks gave this speech well after I started writing this book. He laid out my case perfectly for me. It was a stunning admission. And he explained that the national media knew it. So I hosted Lauren Windsor on *TYT* to ask her how much pickup this explosive report had received in the national media. She said that it had received absolutely none. She said reporters and editors told her that "everyone already knows this." So she googled it. There wasn't a single national media story written about how you buy committee chairmanships and how you then have to do as you're told by the corporate interests that have purchased your fealty. Not one.

Everyone in power knows that there is a quid pro quo system of bribery in place and that the American people have no say in their own government—but none of them ever tell you. To be fair, if you were being bribed, would you tell anyone? And if you were a giant corporation that was the largest recipient of all that money—in the form of billions spent on political ads in the mainstream media—would you tell anyone? It's also difficult to get a man to say something, if his salary depends on him not saying it.

MORTAL DANGER

Back in the 1970s, as our democracy was being dismantled by the courts, there was one person on the Supreme Court who consistently understood what was happening and kept warning the court and the country to turn around: Justice Byron White. His judicial philosophy was to decide the case based on the facts in front of him. He had warned about the "mortal danger" of money in politics in *Buckley*. In *Bellotti* he was the first to warn about the corporate machines. He understood they were legal fictions, but if you allowed these entities, which had enormous resources, to spend those resources on politics, they would do what was obvious—buy the government. He wrote in his dissent, "The State need not permit its own creation to consume it."[34] But no one listened.

By the time we get to the infamous *Citizens United* decision in 2010, the system had already been completely taken over by corporate cash. What *Citizens United* did was take the faucet of money coming in from companies and attach it to a fire hose. That decision said that corporations could spend unlimited money to directly advocate for or against the election of specific candidates. This was the progeny of *Bellotti*, which initially said that corporations could spend money on ballot initiatives. *Citizens United* said they could spend unlimited money through independent expenditures. This is the current legalized bribery regime we have in place. The fourth horseman had arrived, and the political apocalypse ensued.

Our government was consumed by corporations, exactly as White predicted.

Now, what do you think is going to happen if an issue could cost billions of dollars for a corporation and it needs to influence the politicians who are voting on the issue? Every clear-headed, noncorrupt person knows the corporation is going to do the logical thing—it's going to spend as much money as necessary to buy every politician voting on that issue. If the tax cut or the subsidy is worth billions of dollars, spending one hundred million dollars buying every senator is chump change. You'd be nuts not to bribe the politicians. It's now legal, and your profits depend on it.

Did you know the U.S. government cannot negotiate the price of drugs it buys for government programs like Medicare? I don't even know what that means, it's so ridiculous. So, drug companies can charge whatever they want, and the government has to pay it. Even though the government is their customer, it has no say over what it must pay. This is unheard of in actual capitalism. Adam Smith would look like the man in the iconic painting *The Scream,* by Edvard Munch, if he saw this monstrosity. Why is this absurdity allowed? Because the drug companies own the government. We're the only country in the world that does this with drug prices because we're the only country that has legalized bribery.

The drug companies have also long fought for other enormous financial interests in front of Congress. Take OxyContin. The company that sold OxyContin knew that it was so addictive it would sell like hotcakes. And it did. And hundreds of thousands of people died. OxyContin is an opioid. It's called an opioid because its base is . . . opium. A government website describes it this way:

Opioids are a class of drugs that include the illegal drug heroin, synthetic opioids such as fentanyl, and pain relievers available legally by prescription, such as oxycodone (OxyContin®), hydrocodone (Vicodin®), codeine, morphine, and many others.[35]

The government knew it's the same thing as heroin but still let them sell the stuff! It was only when private citizens and states began suing the company that the federal government got involved. Bottom line, the drug companies are the politicians' bosses. And their supplier, if you will. We became addicted to opioids because the politicians became addicted to campaign cash. When we legalized bribery, it was only a matter of time before every other vice was legalized. A drug as addictive as heroin became legal and was sold by guys in suits. Brazen criminality was disguised as a legitimate business interest. Remember what Justice White called money in politics? A "mortal" danger. He turned out to be more right than anyone could have realized. Through products like OxyContin, the corruption was literally killing us.

The drug companies also needed their patents extended, to squeeze more money from those who needed their drugs and so that they could maintain high prices without competition. They also needed to kill single-payer health care, i.e., Medicare for All. They have billions, perhaps trillions, of dollars on the line when Congress votes on all these issues. So, unsurprisingly, they are the number-one industry that contributes to politicians, even more than the banks and oil companies.

At one of his talks, I heard the legendary journalist Bill Moyers tell the story of what the game of baseball would look like if it were like our government. Before the batter steps up to the plate, he hands the umpire ten thousand dollars. Would anyone trust that umpire to call balls and strikes fairly? Maybe he's a great guy and he wouldn't be affected by it, but I wouldn't count on it. And it certainly looks bad. Everyone would instantly lose faith in the game if that were allowed. Every batter would pay the umpire. Even if the first umpire's judgment wasn't affected, the next one's would be. We all know this. Well, I should be more accurate: everyone except the people covering politics in the national media knows this. The very people who are supposed to be telling you what's going on in politics are the ones who can't figure out the most basic thing about politics. It's almost as if the billions that drug companies and all other corporations spend on advertising in modern media might affect their judgment as well. That's why it takes an old-school journalist like Moyers to tell you the obvious truth.

But even Moyers's example undersells it. In American politics, before the politicians vote, they're not handed ten thousand dollars, they're handed millions. Casino magnate Sheldon Adelson once spent over a hundred million dollars in one election. Then he did it again. And again. Why? Because he got a great return on investment!

You could accuse Adelson of many things, but you'd have to admit he was a savvy businessman. He was unlikely to spend all that money without expecting anything in return. In fact, he was expecting many, many things in return. Let's see if he got them.

THE ADELSON PRIMARY

In the 2016 election, before any Republican voters got to weigh in through actual voting, there was a far more important contest. Almost all the Republican candidates went down to Vegas to kiss the . . . ring of Sheldon Adelson. They knew how much he had spent in the last presidential election—$155 million! Adelson had given $98 million in publicly traceable money and, according to reporting from *The Huffington Post*, another $57 million or so in dark money.[36] He had given $20 million just to Newt Gingrich's PAC (and he didn't even win the primary!). And another $30 million to Mitt Romney's PAC. GOP candidates in 2016 weren't going to miss out on these juicy, legendary bribes. So they all had to interview with the man who was actually going to select the president. It was so brazen, even the press finally noticed and called it "The Adelson Primary."

The owner of the Las Vegas Sands Corporation was going to pick the president. Do you think his interests in maintaining his casinos' profits might weigh into his decision? Did you know that even though it has "Las Vegas" in the name, Adelson's corporation made most of its money in China, where it dominated the very lucrative gambling center of Macau? So the profits of a company mainly operating out of China were going to determine who might be the next U.S. president. Yeah, this makes sense. To no one, except politicians.

Wanna guess who won the Adelson Primary? Yep. Donald J. Trump.

Later, Trump would break the irony record by running his campaign on the anticorruption slogan "Drain the Swamp." To be fair to Trump, he did at least drain the desert of all the bribes you could imagine. Adelson would go on to put $25 million into Donald Trump's campaign in 2016 and another $75 million in 2020.[37] Adelson wound up giving $242 million to Trump and the Republican Party since the rise of Trump. Brazen, open bribery. And Trump ran on draining the swamp!

With one month left to go in the 2020 election, Sheldon Adelson accounted for 90 percent of the money that went to Trump's super PAC Preserve America. Now, do you think Trump was going to be principled and ignore hundreds of millions of dollars in bribes? Or do you think he did exactly as he was told to keep the bribes coming? Well, let's find out.

Speaking of bribery, Adelson was accused of bribing foreign officials in order to get approvals for his casinos overseas.[38] The irony is that it is illegal in the U.S. to bribe *foreign* officials, but it is not illegal to bribe U.S. officials in the form of campaign contributions. So Adelson paid Trump to make the case go away. And lo and behold, four months into Donald Trump's presidency, Adelson paid a paltry $9 million fine, and the case was put to bed. To give you a sense of scale, the "consultants" Adelson had paid off in China took $62 million in bribes, in flagrant violation of the Foreign Corrupt Services Act. If Adelson paid $62 million in bribes, how much do you think he made from those deals? The correct answer is a hell of a lot more! Compared to the profits that could have easily stretched into the hundreds of millions of dollars, if not billions, that $9 million fine is a joke. It's a rounding error. Yes, but this was deeply illegal—and in the civil settlement, Adelson's lawyers admitted he did it! So did Adelson go to jail for bribery? I'll give you a moment to catch your breath from laughing your ass off. Of course he didn't go to jail for bribery—because he had bribed the people making that decision!

If you had done it, would you have gone to jail? Of course you would. But that's because you haven't spent millions buying off American politicians.

Then Adelson had a long laundry list of demands for Trump. Did Trump address those as well? Everyone reading this knows the answer already. Again, to be fair to Trump, are you sure you would have been able to resist hundreds of millions of dollars? Even if Trump played it strictly within the rules (good one!) and actually spent the money on his campaign, he could—and he did—funnel millions into his own properties under the guise of using them for his campaign offices and campaign events. That was a way of skimming off the top of those campaign contributions, so the money not only helped him accrue power but also went into his personal bank account. And that was the relatively legal part.

What else did Adelson get in return? Well, he wanted to crush the unions in his casinos. He was worth thirty-five billion dollars when he passed away in 2021, but he thought the janitors and cocktail waitresses in his casinos made too much money. This was a direct way he could make his money back from the investments in the seedy politicians he greased—use the government to block anything that would raise the wages of his employees, especially unions. Check. No problem. Unions got nothing passed while Trump was president. Adelson saved millions!

Adelson also wanted to wipe out the main competition for his casinos. So he wanted to ban internet gambling. Now, I love this part. He said he was "morally opposed" to online gambling. Let's get this right. Gambling inside his casinos is perfectly moral but gambling on someone else's website is deeply immoral. That's some quality trolling.

I think old Sheldon was having fun with this. He probably realized that the American media were never going to call this what it obviously was—corruption—so he was messing with them. He went on to say that online gambling was "a train wreck, it's a toxicity, it's a cancer waiting to happen."[39] When you lose all your money to him, it's apparently far less toxic.

When asked why he was so animated about this particular issue, he said, "I can afford to be honest and moral without taking money into consideration, and that's what I'm doing." There's some chance the phrase "laugh out loud" (lol) was coined at that moment.

Then he was on a roll. "I am in favor of [gambling] as a form of entertainment, but I am not in favor of it exploiting the world's most vulnerable people."[40] At the Las Vegas Sands Corporation, they were deeply concerned about the most vulnerable people. They didn't want them exploited anywhere else but within the morally safe confines of their casinos. He added, presumably while laughing uncontrollably, "I know I am a Republican, and I am not supposed to be socially sensitive, but I am very socially sensitive."[41]

And lo and behold, in late 2018, the Justice Department issued a memo declaring that online gambling would be illegal. According to *The Intercept,* "The new memo insisted that most forms of online gambling are in fact illegal under the Wire Act."[42] Of course it did.

Ironically, Adelson wasn't taking any chances. Online gambling could have single-handedly ruined his brick-and-mortar casinos. It could have cost him billions. So now you can begin to see why all the money he invested in politicians was a savvy move.

Sheldon wasn't done by a long shot. He also wanted the U.S. embassy in Israel moved from Tel Aviv to Jerusalem. Yep, that was him. Trump probably threw that in, *if he acted now,* like an extra Ginsu knife. But Adelson had showered him with so much money that Trump couldn't stop kissing his ass. After he nearly set off a war in the Middle East for him, he capped it off by awarding Adelson's wife, Miriam, the Presidential Medal of Freedom. I'm not kidding. That's our highest civilian honor. He threw it in like a tchotchke. A parting gift after the deal is done. Does anyone in their right mind really believe that the wife of the largest political donor in America happened to coincidentally deserve that Presidential Medal of Freedom? They're making a mockery of our country.

But wait . . . there's more. Trump, of course, passed a giant $1.9 trillion tax cut. Want to guess who benefited from that tax cut? Yep, Sheldon Adelson—and the Las Vegas Sands Corporation. It's impossible to determine how much Adelson saved personally out of his vast fortune because of all the different tax cuts. He likely benefited from cuts to personal income taxes, pass-through income taxes, the alternative minimum tax, and, of course, the estate tax (just in the nick of time). But those were all peanuts compared to the two main events.

Trump lowered the foreign-earnings tax. You could repatriate overseas profits at a rate of 15.5 percent for cash and 8 percent for reinvested earnings. That means you could pay only 8 percent instead of the 35 percent normal corporate tax rate. Guess where the Las Vegas Sands Corporation had made most of its profits? Overseas! The corporation got to bring back an enormous amount of profit with almost no taxation. That saved the company billions! Now you can begin to see why investing a couple of hundred million dollars in crooked politicians was the easiest gamble of Adelson's life. Corrupt politicians in America are a sure bet!

Finally, the cherry on top (or maybe three, like in a slot machine) was the giant corporate tax cut. Rates were lowered from 35 percent to 21 percent. Now, everyone got paid on this one. Yes, the Las Vegas Sands Corporation will likely save billions in the long run from this tax cut. But it's not alone. The corporate machines collectively save *trillions* of dollars from this tax cut. No wonder the machines took over the government. They could—and they did—turn it into their private casino, where they always win and we always lose.

Sheldon Adelson's casino company might be a spectacular example of American political corruption. But it is definitely not the exception, it is the rule. Everyone does it. There are awful conspiracy theories that George Soros is the puppet master behind all our politicians because of how much he has given the Democrats. That particular theory has anti-Semitic undertones (and overtones). But rational people know that this isn't about any race, religion, or ethnicity. The Mercers did it. And so did the Koch brothers. And the Wilks brothers. And it goes on and on. They're all from different backgrounds, and they all have different corporate interests (the Wilks brothers want more fracking; Koch Industries sells products ranging from toilet paper to oil). It's a fucking auction. And the only color anyone cares about is green. You can call it the Green Old Deal.

But the entities that stood to gain the most from this corrupt system aren't even people. They're corporations. They're machines. We programmed them to maximize profit. Then Lewis Powell taught them how to buy the government. Now they are buying our government to maximize profit. What else would they do?

In fact, if a corporate executive doesn't legally bribe American politicians to get tax cuts and deregulation and any other fantastical thing his corporation wants, then that executive would have to be fired. He or she has a fiduciary responsibility to maximize profits. It's not optional. There is no morality clause. Shut the fuck up and maximize profits. Otherwise, we'll get someone else to drive the machine. And the machine makes more money if the government is on its side. It can use the bribes to zap its competitors, protect its monopolies, deregulate its energy grids, authorize more fracking, prevent the negotiation of drug prices, and, of course, lower all their taxes. The machine needs it. It must get it. And it has. It doesn't really matter who the driver is, let alone what race or religion the driver is, it just matters that the machine is fed. This is our current system. Now do you see why we need a revolution?

We Want the Money, Lebowski!

In the classic Coen brothers movie *The Big Lebowski,* the fumbling villains keep telling the protagonist, Jeffrey "The Dude" Lebowski, that they "want the money" no matter what happens. Even when it is discovered that they no longer have their hostage, they declare in their vaguely German accents, "We still want ze money, Lebowski!"

Unfortunately, this became the story of not just the Republican Party but the Democratic Party as well. No matter what happened in elections—whether taking corporate money was good long-term strategy or not—the politicians still wanted the money, Lebowski! They forgot it was supposed to be a tool for winning elections. Instead, they became singularly focused on it.

To be fair, until recently they were right. In the 2004 election cycle, the candidate with more money won their House election 97.54 percent of the time.[43] Can you see now why politicians are obsessed with money? If you could outraise your opponent, you had over a 97 percent chance of winning! That's a lock. By the way, this number didn't depend on whether you were a Democrat or Republican, liberal or conservative. No ideological position mattered. No legislative achievement mattered. The candidate's virtue didn't matter. These were all peripheral. At most they all added up to 3 percent. The rest was all money. If you had it, you won. If you didn't, you looked for a new line of work. Corruption was complete.

So, are things much better now? What percentage of House candidates do you think won in 2016 when they had more money? It was 95.41 percent. Shit, that didn't get much better. This is where the money obsession comes from. In *Trainspotting,* Ewan McGregor's character explains why he and his friends do heroin: "What they forget is the pleasure of it. Otherwise we wouldn't do it. After all, we're not fucking stupid . . . take the best orgasm you've ever had, multiply it by a thousand, and you're still nowhere near it."[44] That's how politicians think about cash. They're not fucking stupid, it just works so well. Take your best-performing policy plank and multiply it by a thousand and you're still nowhere near the power of money in politics.

After the Justice Democrats formed and scored some stunning upsets, like a little-known bartender in Queens knocking off the fourth-most-powerful Democrat in the House, we started evening the odds a little bit, and by the time we got to 2020, the House candidates with more money were winning *only* 87.71 percent of the time.

But does this all have an effect on policy? This is where we go to a Princeton study that will crush your soul until you read the end of this book and find out how to fight back. A study conducted by Princeton Professor Martin Gilens and Northwestern Professor Benjamin I. Page in 2014 reached this conclusion:

> Multivariate analysis indicates that economic elites and organized groups representing business interests have substantial independent impacts on U.S. government policy, while average citizens and mass-based interest groups have little or no independent influence.[45]

You want to know what that means? It means the corporate machines and the elites have won. They have a "substantial impact" on what legislation actually passes. We, regular citizens, have "little or no independent influence." That means we don't matter at all. This is in a so-called democracy. The overwhelming majority of voters have *no influence* on policy.

So if you ever felt like politics is bullshit and your voice doesn't matter, this is why. Your gut instinct was, unfortunately, right. Legendary comedian George Carlin had it figured out better than anyone else when he said:

> The real owners are the big wealthy business interests that control things and make all the important decisions. . . . They own all the important land. They own and control the corporations. They've long since bought and paid for the Senate, the Congress, the statehouses, the city halls. They've got the judges in their back pockets. And they own all the big media companies, so that they control just about all of the news and information you hear. They've got you by the balls. They spend billions of dollars every year lobbying—lobbying to get what they want. Well, we know what they want: They want more for themselves and less for everybody else.[46]

The Princeton-Northwestern study confirms this. They looked at 1,779 survey questions on policy issues from 1981 to 2002. That's a very large sample size and a very long period of time. So the conclusions they reached are far more likely to be right. The results were not an anomaly. This is actually what happens in our government.

And remember, *Citizens United* was in 2010. As I told you earlier, our democracy was lost long before that. The years these professors studied ended in 2002, and the results were already crystal clear. Corruption had completely taken over the body politic.

They explain:

> When a majority of citizens disagrees with economic elites and/or with organized interests, they generally lose. Moreover, because of the strong status quo bias built into the U.S. political system, even when fairly large majorities of Americans favor policy change, they generally do not get it.[47]

That's amazing. If the great majority of Americans want something and the elites don't, the elites win almost every single time! In fact, statistically, whether the masses really wanted something or really didn't want it didn't matter at all! It didn't move the needle. Statistically irrelevant. Does this look like a democracy to you? Our democracy is statistically irrelevant.

How about the economic elites and organized business interests? How did they do? "A proposed policy change with low support among economically-elite Americans (one out of five in favor) is adopted only about 18 percent of the time," they write, "while a proposed change with high support (four out of five in favor) is adopted about 45 percent of the time."[48]

Okay, that's not fully depressing. They don't get everything they want every single time. But if they really don't like something, there's an excellent chance they will kill it. And while 90 percent of voters had about zero effect on policy, if the economic elites wanted something they got it 45 percent of the time. I did the math, and 45 percent is much higher than 0 percent. This is what an oligarchy looks like. This is what rule by the economic elites looks like. This is what government run by corporate machines looks like.

Now that you know what a difference money makes, you won't be surprised to find out how much money poured into politics as soon as it was allowed in 1978 by *Buckley* and *Bellotti*.

Let's look at what happened after the *Bellotti* decision. The results were soon apparent. In 1976, the total spending by candidates in the presidential election was $66.9 million. By 1980, it was $92.3 million, nearly one-third more.[49] You get the results you build for. Once the Supreme Court built a system that allowed corporations to capture politicians through donations, it was inevitable that more corporate money would capture politicians. This is not about personal corruption, this is what systemic corruption looks like. We created a new system with corruption built into it. Lewis Powell strategized to have corporations buy our government, then he executed his own plan—and it worked brilliantly.

By 1988, total spending by presidential candidates was more than $210 million. In 2016, it was $1.4 billion.[50] In 2020, spending on the presidential election reached an astronomical $6.6 billion. Spending on all elections in 2020 was a stratospheric $14 billion. And in 2022, an astounding $17 billion was spent on midterm elections![51] This is not at all surprising. In a situation where businesses are getting enormous rates of return from any product, they will continue to pour endless money into it. It's just simple math.

The corruption has gotten so bad, now different kinds of companies are competing with each other to see who can bribe politicians more. For example, in New Jersey, back in 2014, the state legislature passed a law saying that Tesla could not sell directly to consumers. What? Well, then how the hell are they supposed to sell anything? This almost literally legislated them out of existence in New Jersey. Why would any rational government do this? I'm definitely not a fan of Elon Musk, but why is he randomly not allowed to do what everyone else does? Because, as it turns out, Tesla sold its cars through company-owned retail stores, unlike all the other car manufacturers, who sold through franchised auto dealerships. And you'll never guess who some of the largest political donors in New Jersey are. Yep, franchised auto dealerships.

Jim Appleton, the president of the New Jersey Coalition of Automobile Retailers, said afterward, "Tesla is operating illegally, and as of April 1, they will be out of business unless they decide to open a franchise."[52] He wasn't very subtle, was he? They wanted more business for themselves, period. This had nothing to do with the public interest. If you use bribes like the mob, you can openly threaten people like the mob. Before you think this is unique to my beloved home state of New Jersey because you saw one too many *Sopranos* episodes, the same law passed in Texas, Arizona, Michigan, and Virginia. It turns out bribery works everywhere.

They used corruption to try to kill off their competition. And for a while, it totally worked (the law was reversed in 2015 because a billionaire like Elon Musk, unlike the average American citizen, has the power to fight back). Because politicians will do anything for money. Does this look like a free market to you? No, once you capture the government, you don't have to compete at all, let alone make quality products. You just make it illegal to compete against you. Once you allow for bribery, crony capitalism is inevitable.

Just look at the unbelievable scale of the problem. Let's do an apples-to-apples comparison. The last presidential election where bribery was still illegal was 1976, when candidates spent $66.9 million. Forty-four years later, they spent $6.6 billion! That's not twice as high or even ten times as high, which with inflation would still be outrageous, but somewhat understandable. No, they're now spending one hundred times the amount they spent before! Once the corporate machines ran the numbers, they saw the same thing I'm showing you here. There is no better way to make money than to purchase the government. When a business has a successful product, in this case politicians, they invest in it. When you have a product this good, you logically put a hundred times more money into it. If you think corruption doesn't pay, you're not very good at math.

Seriously, people who are naïve about how corporations work—i.e., the mainstream media in their entirety—just don't understand how businesses make decisions. I've been running a business for twenty years now, so I know this with great certainty: if you don't make money at something, you don't have a choice, you must shut it down. Sometimes progressives also have a naïve view of this fact. They think businesses should keep operating at a loss, especially in fields like journalism. That's not a thing. If you don't get to sustainability, you're done. Period. You literally run out of money. That's the real world. But at the same time, if you're making money doing something—and a lot of it—you must invest more in that direction. It would be negligent not to. You'd be fired if you voluntarily didn't do the thing that makes a lot of money. The rest of the business community wouldn't even understand what you're saying. Why would anyone choose not to make money? Earlier we showed that companies sometimes make a nearly 100,000 percent return on their investment in politicians through specific laws they pass. If you choose not to make that kind of gigantic profit margin, of course you're going to get fired. What I'm trying to tell you is that in this system, corruption is not optional, it is absolutely inevitable.

This is why I call them machines. Yes, the system also makes it more likely that the most ruthless will rise to the top at a public corporation, but it doesn't really matter who the driver is. If the CEO—i.e., the driver—is not being efficient at maximizing profits, they will be replaced by another driver. The system has certain inevitable incentives and disincentives. Arguing against them is silly. They're stone-cold facts. Beseeching a corporation to do the right thing is hilarious. Anyone who does that is being ridiculous. They have no earthly idea how business works. That's why when sometimes politicians or pundits say they are outraged that companies are not being more patriotic, they're declaring themselves to be utter fools. It's not a person, you thick-headed clowns! It's a machine! A machine can only do what it is designed to do. That is why these machines will roll over all of us and crush our wages and our souls to maximize profit—because that's what we programmed them to do!

The only possible answer to this corporate takeover of our government is to rewrite the code. Everything else is silliness and doomed to certain failure. The good news is ironic, however. Since we wrote their code in the first place, we can rewrite it. Later in the book, I'm going to tell you how we're going to rewrite the code so that we can free ourselves and humans can reign again. If we don't change the code, and hence the system, our defeat to these machines is not likely, it is guaranteed.

Now, do you want to know why it feels like nearly all the politicians are crooks and we have no good choices left? It's because this system also produces the very worst politicians. Why? Well, let's think about it. If money wins elections 97 percent of the time, what will logical people do if they're running for office? They'll go for the cash. They'd be crazy not to. And it doesn't really matter if they choose not to pursue the money out of principle, because then they'll lose—and the guy with no principles will win. Ninety-seven percent of the time.

Eventually, when you repeat that process enough, you will be left with only politicians who take the money. In fact, the ones who are most brazenly corrupt are the ones who are likely to be the most successful. Here's a fun example. While they were running for president against each other, Donald Trump called Ted Cruz's wife ugly and his father a murderer. So, Cruz refused to endorse him at the 2016 Republican National Convention. But he quickly turned around right after the convention and started groveling to Trump. Did you ever hear why he had such a sudden change of "heart"? It was because Robert and Rebekah Mercer were Ted Cruz's top financial donors. Robert Mercer is a billionaire hedge fund manager and Rebekah is his heiress daughter. They had given Cruz thirteen million dollars in that 2016 primary. When he went up to their suite at the convention after giving his speech, they slammed the door in his face. He was scolded and upbraided, like a little child. He had not followed orders!

What do you think he did after that? Kept his dignity and continued to defy his donors and Trump? Of course not! It's Ted Cruz. He volunteered for Trump, he phone-banked for him, and then he cleaned Trump's boots with his tongue. Ok, licking the boots was not literal, but you weren't sure, were you? Cruz allowed himself to be humiliated by Trump in every way imaginable.

But when Ted Cruz subjugates himself to the Mercers, he is doing something that is logical. He has deduced that whoever serves the donors best gets the most money, and eventually has the most power. So when he crawls around on the floor like the most servile, pathetic servant you've ever seen, he is just being a good politician. And remember, he was right in his calculation. After he debased himself by publicly fluffing the man who called his wife ugly, the donors came back into the fold for Senator Cruz, and he returned to being one of the most famous and powerful politicians in America.

Of course, his power is illusory. It disappears the moment he disagrees with his benefactors. It isn't really his power, it's theirs. He's just a sad little servant boy. But it satiates his greed for fame, faux power, status, and wealth. He gets to preen like a lord in the Capitol. It comes at the price of his dignity, but for people like Ted Cruz, that is a small price to pay. There wasn't much to lose to begin with.

As you can see, the system rewards the worst kind of people, and hence, that is who you get. If your gut was screaming that these politicians are frauds—no matter how many times the mainstream media told you they weren't—you were right! You weren't reacting out of emotion or ignorance; your instinct that they're all liars serving their own interest was absolutely correct. In fact, that's what the system was designed to produce!

The powerful weren't ever going to build a system that gives away their power. They were going to build a system that enhances their power. That is why the system rewards candidates who say things like "Nothing will fundamentally change." They love that! Music to their ears. If you're on top, the very last thing you want is change.

THE CAPITULATION OF THE DEMOCRATIC PARTY

The explosion of funds corrupting the political system that began in the seventies also helps explain the rise and dominance of Republicans that commenced in the same period. They were always the party of business interests. This couldn't have worked out better for them. They went from hopelessly defeated, as you saw in the Powell memo, to absolutely dominant. So the Republican Party became nearly 100 percent corrupt. There were a couple of antiquated stragglers like Ron Paul, who marched to his own beat, but now pretty much none of those exist anymore. The system has weeded them all out over the last forty years. The ones left are the thoroughly corrupted.

The GOP ran willingly into the friendly arms of their corporate suitors. They always wanted the money, Lebowski. The modern Republican

Party was built to be the political arm of the Chamber of Commerce. But how about the Democrats? How exactly did they get corrupted?

Now, I'm not afraid to admit I love Jimmy Carter. The most underrated political achievement of my lifetime was the Israeli-Egyptian peace deal, known as the Camp David Accords. Everyone always says that peace in the Middle East is impossible. They've forgotten that not only is it possible, it already happened. Egypt and Israel were mortal enemies, and now they have been steadfast allies for the last forty years. President Carter did heroic work to put that together. No president since has been able to pull it off (the so-called peace deals Trump presided over were with Israel's de facto allies, not opponents, in the Middle East). President Carter did something so hard people still mistakenly think it's impossible. In other words, they literally can't believe what he got done. Isn't it interesting how little credit he gets for that?

After he left office, President Carter went on to create more miracles. After his term in office, he created the Carter Center to tackle some of the toughest health issues in the world. The Carter Center wound up doing something that has almost never been done before: They eradicated a horrible disease from the planet. Wiped it out! Saved millions of people from suffering.

In our society, we don't look at Carter's achievement as positively as we do the achievement of making the Forbes 400 list. We view it as a nice side thing to do. But no one thinks Jimmy Carter is more successful than Jeff Bezos. So let me tell you what Guinea worm disease used to do, and we'll see if we view success a little differently.

It was a disease that mainly affected Asia and Africa. In 1986, it was a parasitic infection that was *in* 3.5 million people across the globe. It would start with someone drinking water that had water fleas in it. And those water fleas were infected with guinea worm larvae. Already you're trying to figure out how to skip this part of the book. Yes, this could even be triggering. But I tell you this because whether we knew about it or not, this was happening to our fellow human beings all across the world. Then the worm larvae would be inside the person and would gestate for about a year. At the end of that year a white blister would emerge on the skin and then slowly, incredibly painfully, a very long worm would emerge from inside the skin and exit the body . . . over the course of several weeks!

You had to just wait for the worm to come completely out of your body.

The pain was debilitating. Sometimes it would lead to ulcers and infections, which could kill you. The Carters said that when they saw children with the worms coming out of their bodies, they had to do something!

But you want to know the most incredible part? Before the Carter Center took on the project, almost no one was doing anything to eradicate Guinea worm disease. If it weren't for Jimmy Carter, no one was going to come to the rescue. I was lucky enough to interview the former president about this. When I asked him why no one else was working on it, he explained that it was very difficult to combat, and once you eradicated it, there'd be no money to make in treating it. Without a profit motive, everyone had left those folks behind.

The Carter Center has basically ended that disease. Incidents of it are down by 99.99 percent, and there are only thirteen cases of it left in the world (down from 3.5 million). It is very rare for us to ever wipe a disease off the planet, let alone one this atrocious. Had you heard about it? Do you get the sense that Jimmy Carter has gotten the proper credit for that incredibly heroic act? Or do you think society is much more obsessed with how much money Elon Musk has made in the last year? "How much did Musk make or lose on Twitter?" they ask breathlessly.

When I asked President Carter why he chose to spend his time on this disease instead of any other one, he said that if he didn't do it, no one else was going to, and he just couldn't bear the thought of all that suffering. That's the kind of man we should be celebrating.

But despite all that, since my job is to level with you, I'm still going to be honest about Jimmy Carter's role in our saga as well. Unfortunately, he was vital in dismantling the guardrails separating democracy (government for all people) from plutocracy (government by the wealthy).

A little-known governor when he ran for president—a famous headline when he announced his candidacy was "Jimmy Who Is Running for What?"—Carter marked the Democratic Party's transition from progressive to corporate. Instead of working for economic fairness, government programs, and equality, he gave needless odes to balanced budgets, limited ambitions, and being business friendly. "Carter, though indubitably a Democrat, marketed himself as a new kind of Democrat," two scholars wrote in their book *The Carter Presidency*. "Carter appealed to economic conservatives by economic deregulation, balanced budgets, and inflation fighting, positions traditionally championed by Republicans."[53] As president, he fulfilled his promises to slash badly needed government programs, kill legislation that would help working people, and resist movements toward universal health care.

The pendulum had begun to swing. Whereas Nixon was catering to Nader's Raiders and the progressives, Carter started catering to Big Business. The era of corporate cash—and its influence—had begun. And it had begun even under the most decent man in politics. Because it was inevitable.

Carter was the first one to fall into the trap Republicans had set. Get Democrats to do your dirty work for you by slashing spending and services—that way the economy will turn south—and then blame them for it. Unfortunately, President Carter was the poster child for this political strategy.

Massachusetts Senator Ted Kennedy said that Carter "asks the poor, the black, the sick, the young, the cities and the unemployed to bear a disproportionate share for the billions of dollars in reductions in federal spending."[54] Kennedy ran in the 1980 Democratic Party primary against Carter, but he lost. Remember, at the time Kennedy was mounting a left-wing challenge to a conservative Democrat in Jimmy Carter. Now the media paints Jimmy Carter as a huge lefty. But that's not at all true on economic issues, and Kennedy's primary challenge proves it. Progressives at the time thought he was so economically conservative that they needed to Bernie Sanders him.

However, Kennedy's loss in the primary reinforced the rising belief among party bigwigs that centrism was the way of the future. Throughout the 1980s, party leaders and ambitious would-be leaders flocked to the title of "New Democrat." That designation meant, more than anything else, deprioritizing working people and favoring corporations. Carter had helped unleash a demon—liberalism—that would eventually engulf virtually the entire party. Right-wingers couldn't believe their luck. "We used to be the kooks," said a staffer at the American Conservative Union. "Now we're the moderates."[55]

Important side note here on terminology. If you're confused by the word "liberal" being used to describe someone on the very left and at the same time being used to describe the economically conservative wing of the Democratic Party, you are not alone. Most people are confused by that. You know why? Because it's really confusing. Different people use that word to mean completely different things. Even I sometimes use the word "liberal" as a replacement for "progressive," including in this book. The old guard of American politics thought the word "liberal" meant "very left." But that is not how it is most often used these days.

I'll oversimplify here by saying that the word "liberal," or, more accurately, "neoliberal," is often used to describe an economic policy that largely agrees with conservative economics. It trusts that the powers that be are on the level and doing things on your behalf. It sounds funny even writing it. Really, people believe that? But the neoliberals really believe, or it is in their economic interest to believe, that these grand pooh-bahs of the economic system know best. And their judgment, unsurprisingly, is often that the money and power should flow to the very top (what a stunning coincidence) and that it should then be distributed wisely and very slowly to the bottom, with conditions attached! Those conditions— again, just coincidentally—usually involve those in power milking as much of the resources of the host country as they possibly can, until the worm slowly leaves the body. Except, unlike Guinea worm disease, no one has eradicated this noxious ideology.

Now, I'm sure the neoliberals would disagree. Smiling emoji. But it definitely is a top-down model and eschews populist solutions religiously. In other words, neoliberals don't like to do things that are . . . popular. Because, as it turns out, the average person doesn't like all the money and power going to the very top and the masses having to pay for it. That is why you have to defend and explain those principles as if they carry secret wisdom that is hard for a regular Joe to understand. And the mainstream media do that religiously as well. They'll explain to us that it is very hard to understand why global organizations, like the International Monetary Fund, need to direct all the money to the top and squeeze the locals for more taxes and fewer services. That's true—that is very hard to explain. They also explain that understanding how the Federal Reserve could print trillions of dollars and just give it to the top banks is very hard. No, that one is easy. They do that because those same banks *run* the Federal Reserve and would prefer to have trillions of dollars that they can access for their own profit. There, I just explained it!

What is hard is figuring out which meaning of the word "liberal" people intend these days. So, often in online discourse you will hear people talking about the liberal wing of the party—establishment types, like Hillary Clinton—and the progressive wing, which is the wing that used to be called "liberal" when I was growing up. So, be careful with the word "liberal." But what "progressive" means is clear because we have always been the empathetic, forward-looking left in this country. Plus, I spent a whole chapter defining it earlier in the book, so it couldn't be any clearer. Grinning emoji. Sunglasses emoji.

So how did Jimmy Carter do when he ran on neoliberal principles? Well, as you all probably know, he was annihilated. Reagan won 489 electoral votes, Carter just 49. An epic landslide. What lesson did Democratic leaders learn from this election? Go further right wing. Before we started going right wing, we were dominating! Once we started appeasing business interests, we immediately got slaughtered. And the lesson Democrats learned was to abandon their core and become the economically conservative party—you know, like the other party, the one that hadn't been in power for forty years straight. Remember that line from Upton Sinclair, "It is difficult to get a man to understand something, when his salary depends on his not understanding it"? Beginning with Jimmy Carter, the Democrats' economic interests had begun to depend on their not understanding American political history. And they still don't.

PATIENT ZERO

President Carter, however, was not patient zero. That honor belongs to the guy Nader had fingered as the primary culprit, Tony Coelho. Coelho pushed Carter and all the Democrats to understand how appealing corporate donations were. Ironically, after Carter lost with this strategy, Coelho only gained more power. Because he offered irresistible short-term cash whenever Democrats needed it, and they got hooked.

In 1979, Coelho was just an obscure California congressman with no experience organizing anything. Then he became head of the Democratic Congressional Campaign Committee (DCCC), which raises money for party members in the House.

Coelho took the helm just as the Reagan revolution was about to begin. After 1980, conservatives looked unstoppable all of a sudden. It wasn't just that the conservative icon had swept into power with a GOP-controlled Senate. It was the money. The DCCC raised only $1.8 million for the 1980 elections. The National Republican Campaign Committee took in more than ten times as much. There was one obvious source of funds for the Democrats to tap, however. "In the years building up to their 1980 defeat the Democrats seemed to write off the business community," *The Atlantic*'s Gregg Easterbrook reported.[56]

So Coelho made a deal with the devil: he started courting Big Business as donors for the Democratic Party. "What I wanted was to make the DCCC like a business," he later told Easterbrook.[57] He wined and dined the leaders of giant corporations and midsized businesses, explaining to them that they would be in the best shape by contributing funds to both major parties. Democrats would not be in the political wilderness forever, after all, and it would behoove businesses to get on the party's good side. "I've never seen anybody work the business community like Tony has," said Al Abrams, chief lobbyist for the National Association of Realtors, the country's largest business PAC at the time.[58]

Coelho led the DCCC for six years. Whatever else can be said, he achieved astonishing financial results. By 1986, the DCCC had cut the NRCC's fundraising advantage in half. "The business of politics is what I'm all about," Coelho said.[59] The Democrats did far better in the 1982 and 1986 midterm elections than many people had anticipated. Conventional wisdom in D.C. did not attribute that to the opposition party winning in midterm elections (which happens nearly every time); instead it was attributed to corporate money. Funnily enough, whenever the Democrats lost running business-friendly campaigns, it was attributed to other reasons. But whenever they won by taking loads of corporate cash, Democratic leaders and the press said it was because they were savvy enough to go "center-right" and be "business friendly."

But to be fair, in the short term the money usually did make the difference. In the long term, though, it cost Democrats everything. They could greatly improve their chances of winning the next election if they took the corporate cash, but it would come at the cost of the party's soul. Over the decades, they didn't notice as their brand was destroyed and they started to compete on Republican ground—over who could serve business interests better.

If you were a Democratic voter, did you care whether Democrats won their next election, if they did it by promising loyalty to their corporate donors? It might have helped those Democratic politicians to accrue more personal power, but it meant that both parties were now serving the oligarchy. And that didn't help the voters at all. If by the "Democratic Party" you mean Democratic politicians, then yes, the corporate cash helped some of them. But if by the "Democratic Party" you mean Democratic voters, then taking the corporate cash was catastrophic.

Just as the Republicans of today are not the Party of Lincoln, the Democrats of today are not the Party of FDR.

In fact, Coelho admitted that he copied his methods from Republicans. And he was very good at it. Robert Kuttner wrote for *The New Republic* back in 1985 that Coelho taught Democrats that they could basically demand money of corporations like the GOP did. He said part of Coelho's strategy back then was to say to corporate donors, "You might not like us, but we've got our hands on the levers right now; you have to give to us."[60] The corruption acknowledged in that statement is not subtle. Coelho was, in many ways, a blunt instrument.

During the Coelho era, the DCCC started accepting "soft money" donations from corporations for the first time. That was a nakedly transparent way to get around the normal limits on donations that corporations could give to candidates directly. Coelho then started the "Speaker's Club" that allowed corporations to contribute fifteen thousand dollars through their business PACs, so they could "serve as trusted, informal advisers to the Democratic Members of Congress."[61] Yes, he actually said that. Blunt instrument.

Former DCCC staffer and Coelho acolyte Thomas Nides explained that his boss believed that "if a member deserved business support, that there's no reason just because they happen to be a Democrat that they shouldn't receive it."[62] Fun side fact: Joe Biden made Tom Nides ambassador to Israel in 2021. Coelho's influence still rings through the corridors of Democratic power.

Yes, but did the Democrats do favors for Big Business in return? That's a hilariously naïve question only a Washington reporter would ask skeptically, but nonetheless, let's answer it. Ellen Miller, executive director of the Center for Responsive Politics, explained back in the 1990s, "[Coelho] was the mastermind of the candidates' appeal . . . to the corporate world, through their business PACs. What that has meant, pretty clearly, is a kind of stifling of what had been the predictable Democratic response on a whole host of issues."[63]

In other words, the Democrats were neutered. In return for the corporate cash, they agreed to surrender.

In her brilliant write-up on Tony Coelho for *The Washington Post* back in 1995, "The Fall of the House of Coelho," Marjorie Williams summarized Coelho's tactics this way:

> This was, in short, access-peddling. Republicans had pioneered many of these tactics, but for them, cozying up to business posed no conflict with the party's ideology; for Democrats, on the other hand, reliance on business money challenged the party's basic identity. For the first time, Coelho had explicitly severed the connection between the party's goals and the sources of its funding.[64]

Unfortunately, that tie between the party's ostensible goals and its funding would not be restored for decades, until Bernie Sanders and the Justice Democrats popularized grassroots funding of their campaigns.

Williams further explained how Washington players justified this corruption:

> In Washington, a conversation about political money is conducted in cliches. It is a conversation dominated by pragmatists like Coelho, who say that political contributions are just a means to an end; that you have to play by the rules that are on the ground, whether you like them or not; that you can't unilaterally disarm while your opponent is socking away PAC money.[65]

Coelho didn't just create a new financing system for the Democrats, he remade their culture and their personnel. Notorious insider Terry McAullife, who later also ran the DNC and was a top Clinton adviser, governor of Virginia, and top Joe Biden surrogate in 2020, started out as . . . Coelho's finance director at the DCCC.

You're not going to be surprised to find out that former Obama chief of staff and current ambassador to Japan Rahm Emanuel also got his start with Coelho. When Emanuel became the national political director of the DCCC, Coelho explained, "I had to convince him to move from cause-oriented politics to system-oriented politics."[66] That worked. And it left a mark. From then on, Emanuel became famous for "system-oriented politics," i.e., corruption.

But Coelho didn't just influence the Democratic Party, he eventually became so successful at wooing corporate donors that the Republicans started copying his tactics! When Tom DeLay was the House Majority Whip for the Republicans, he started something called the "K Street Project." K Street is where many lobbyists' offices are located, so it has become a synonym in Washington for lobbying. Naming the project after lobbyists was brazen. It was the Republicans declaring they were openly corrupt and ready to sell any remaining conservative principles for a price. Former Republican Vin Weber explained, "It's not an overstatement to say that the K Street Project was a very direct attempt to replicate what Coelho had done in the mid-80s. Republicans were frustrated with the Democrats' success in extracting substantial amounts of money from the business community."[67]

Tony Coelho was a lot of things, but he definitely wasn't a progressive. Coelho was basically nonideological. He was responsible for passing very little legislation and worked hard for very few causes other than money-making. That made for great fundraising. And it undoubtedly solved the Democrats' cash problem in the short term.

But it was devastating in the long term. Coelho attached the party's future to corporate interests—and those interests demanded something in return. Of course, they received it. "Democrats as well as Republicans built the new financialized political economy, whether in new approaches to regulation and antitrust, the slew of bipartisan bills from 1980 to 1999 that collectively untied many of the restraints around financial institutions first erected during the New Deal, or housing policy that pushed credit to consumers even as their incomes stagnated," the political scientist Daniel Schlozman observed in a 2016 working paper on the relationship between Big Finance and the Democratic Party. "The rise of pro-finance Democrats emerged from particular political compromises made by a beleaguered party."[68]

The 1980s mark the era when the Democrats became the neoliberal party they largely remain today. For one thing, they abandoned unions, which had been mobilizing voters for the party since the New Deal. "Together, the Democrats and labor made a middle-class America," then–House Speaker Tip O'Neill said in 1981.[69] "We put together thirty of the greatest, fruitful and beneficial years that a democracy ever had." But unions and Big Business cannot coexist peacefully in a political coalition. As Kuttner reported, Coelho "realized that the Democrats, as the majority party in Congress, could raise bushels of money from organized business. Getting too cozy with labor undercut that strategy."[70]

The party almost entirely stopped talking about, and working toward, assisting the poor and achieving some semblance of equality. They ceased talking about raising taxes on the wealthy and instead pushed to give them tax cuts. Cutting government programs and regulations on banks, keeping health care private, and of course, abandoning campaign finance reform—all this dates to the eighties. To some degree, Democrats knew they were selling out. "We Democrats have a tendency to underestimate the importance of money in politics," the party's finance chairman at the time said. "If we could simply rid ourselves of that weakness and dream a bigger dream, our job would be so much easier."[71] Yes, their jobs would be easier. The progressive cause would be harder, however. And the American people? Well, who cares about them? Not corporate Democrats. "Today, liberalism is the philosophy not of the sons of toil but of the 'knowledge economy' and, specifically, of the knowledge economy's winners: the Silicon Valley chieftains, the big university systems, and the Wall Street titans who gave so much to Barack Obama's 2008 campaign," writes Thomas Frank in his book *Listen, Liberal*.[72] That drift rightward started in the 1970s after *Buckley* and *Bellotti*.

That is the message millions of Americas heard when Democrats climbed in bed with Big Business. The party that was seen as the home of the working man now became known as the home of middle managers. And the thing is, warmed-over conservatism doesn't actually appeal to anyone—voters who like corporate-friendly positions will just opt for the real thing in the GOP. The Democratic presidential candidates who garnered more votes than their opponents—Bill Clinton, Al Gore, Barack Obama, Hillary Clinton, and Joe Biden—held economic positions unimaginable to any Democratic leader before Carter. Those Democratic candidates were far more economically conservative than *Republican* candidates before the corporate money takeover. It's no wonder that voters have chosen Republicans for president in 1980, 1984, 1988, and 2004—not to mention as members of the House and often the Senate, plus most state legislatures and governor's offices around the country. Why vote for conservatism lite when you can have the real thing? By embracing Wall Street, Democrats lost Main Street.

Think about what a terrible strategy this is in the long term. You give up your biggest asset—being the people's party, the thing that won you decades of political dominance. And in return you get half as much corporate money as Republicans get. You argue for their positions instead of your own, and you are relegated to permanent loser status. Even if you have positions that are wildly popular, as Democrats do, you never talk about them in elections and you never fight for them, so no one even knows you have them! All they hear is what you're saying: probusiness, conservative positions are wonderful. No wonder they started voting for Republicans—you told them to.

There is an interesting irony that I want to explain in these numbers. You see Democrats getting destroyed at almost every level, losing over a thousand seats nationwide and forfeiting their long-held political dominance, but, on the other hand, Republicans have won only one popular vote at the presidential level since 1988. There is a logical explanation for that. At the presidential level, there is a ton of media coverage that allows people to eventually understand where the candidates roughly stand on important issues. Since Americans are very progressive, they vote for Democrats in these highly publicized races. The rest of the elections in this country, unfortunately, receive very little press coverage. The smaller the race, the smaller the coverage. In those races, paid media dominates over free media. In other words, almost the only place people get information is in political ads. That's why money in politics dominates everywhere, except ironically in the most visible contest—the presidential one. Even in that race, of course, money makes a big difference, but Donald Trump got enough votes to win the Electoral College in 2016, even though he had raised a fraction of the money Hillary Clinton had. That's because he received so much free media. The more you have to pay for media, the more corruption there will be. That's why the presidential contests create a downpour of legalized bribes, but everywhere else it's much worse. Corruption is a Category 5 hurricane that has consumed our democracy throughout the country.

So, I know why Coelho did what he did, and there was some short-term logic to it, but he doomed the Democratic Party with the decision to sell out to corporate interests. He bled out the principles and the passion of the party, and in return chose to fight on a battlefield—money—that was permanently rigged against it.

What was the conclusion to this dynamic of helping Democratic candidates with corporate cash in the short term at the expense of the long-term health of the party? Well, in 1994, Coelho was put in charge of the DNC as its chief strategist. He strategized it into the worst defeat of our lifetimes. For the first time in decades, the Democrats lost both the Senate and the House. It was a historic failure.

FRANKLY, MY DEAR, THEY DON'T GIVE A DAMN

That historic failure continued for decades, all the way through to the epic defeat of Hillary Clinton at the small, boorish hands of Donald Trump. In 2016, former congressman Barney Frank, who had been chairman of the House Financial Services Committee for the Democrats, was one of Hillary Clinton's top surrogates. A *TYT* reporter caught up with him in late 2015 and asked him about both the huge campaign donations and direct payments Hillary Clinton had taken from the big banks (in the form of millions of dollars in paid speeches). Frank was adamant in his defense not only of Secretary Clinton but also of the idea of taking giant amounts of money from financial institutions. "I get big donations from banks. I don't believe that people on the left should engage in unilateral disarmament. Is it really your goal to have us all lose?"[73] Those words were nearly identical to how Marjorie Williams described Tony Coelho's statements twenty years before. She explained that Coelho had said Democrats "can't unilaterally disarm."[74] Same talking points, same losses.

The cancer that had begun in the late 1970s had enveloped the whole Democratic Party by the 2016 election. Democratic leaders were positive that if they kicked their habit of taking money from giant corporations, they would all instantly lose. They couldn't see the irony right in front of them: this way of thinking is why they were losing in the first place!

But it got worse. Former representative Frank continued, "Not only did I take a lot of donations from financial institutions when I was chairman of the committee, where I was passing the Volcker rule and Consumer Bureau, but I tried to get them to give to other Democrats." First, let's get the facts straight on what he bragged about getting accomplished despite taking money from the banks.

The Consumer Financial Protection Bureau was created after President Obama and Democratic leadership fought it tooth and nail behind the scenes. After Elizabeth Warren, to her lasting credit, embarrassed them publicly enough that they finally agreed to pass the bill creating it—and as you can see here, they later shamelessly took credit for it.

The Volcker rule was named after the former head of the Federal Reserve, who was considered very conservative back when he ran the Fed in the 1980s, but by 2010 was considered an advocate for progressive regulation of the big banks. By the way, he hadn't moved his positions at all;

Washington moved around him and became completely captured by the companies they were supposed to be regulating. So now he was considered a reformer because Washington had gotten so corrupted. The Democrats named a portion of the Dodd-Frank financial regulation bill after him. Volcker himself explained what it was supposed to do: "I'd love to see a four-page bill that bans proprietary trading and makes the board and chief executive responsible for compliance."[75] That would have prevented the big banks from gambling with your money (they were using your deposits to do "proprietary trading," and they took home the profits for themselves).

Instead, the Democrats gutted it. It became so weak that Volcker wanted his name taken off it. He said, "I don't like it. . . . I'd have strong regulators. If the banks didn't comply with the spirit of the bill, they'd go after them."[76] So Representative Frank was bragging about something so weak and neutered that the former head of the Fed was saying it was embarrassing to be associated with it. They used his name for marketing purposes to pretend it was historic reform and instead passed a bill that had extraordinarily weak regulations of the big banks. Remember, Frank thought this bill was so great, he used it as an example of not only his accomplishments, but why other Democrats should take banker money, too!

To be fair to Frank, this way of thinking was so thoroughly aided and abetted by the mainstream press that it was considered conventional wisdom in Washington. He was just saying what everyone else was saying. Whenever Democrats passed incredibly weak legislation, brazenly watered down by industry lobbyists, corporate media would immediately declare it a "historic" achievement. Almost every article on the Dodd-Frank bill called it "historic." Recently, the Democrats put in a provision in the Inflation Reduction Act that supposedly regulates drug prices. It does no such thing. It regulates prices on just ten drugs out of thousands and doesn't even start doing that until 2026. It's a fraud perpetrated on the American people that actually prevents price negotiations on 99 percent of drugs. Guess what the press called it? "Historic."

But isn't it amazing that a Democratic leader in the year 2015 thought nothing of bragging that he tried to get other Democrats to take as much corporate cash as possible? He didn't think this was remotely a controversial opinion. And neither did the press. No one else made note of this interview. Washington reporters didn't think it was an interesting revelation. And again, to be fair to them, it really was business as usual. It was perfectly normal to everyone now that Democrats would be legally bribed by the big banks—and brag about it in public!

Then Frank added this doozy: "Do you think it would really be better for liberals, regulators, if all the money from the banks went to Republicans as opposed to just 80 percent?" Yes! For God's sake, yes! How could you not see that if you agree to let corporate money be the metric that determines if you win—and you only get 20 percent of it—you are destined to fail? You're agreeing to a game rigged against you!

Taking zero percent of the banker money and instead being a populist and popular party that represents the voters not only is a better idea, but we know with absolute certainty that it led to political dominance before. The Democrats convinced themselves that getting crumbs off the table of corporate donors was a brilliant idea when it is, by definition, a losing strategy. How can you possibly win a game centered around money when you only have one-fifth the money the other guys have? Yet this had become such conventional wisdom that Barney Frank stated it boldly and confidently in a room full of reporters as if he were stating something obvious. Forget the voters, obviously you take the money, Democratic leaders were screaming! Even if it means you set yourself up at a permanent political disadvantage. They still want the money, Lebowski!

Later in the same interview, when asked about Donald Trump, Barney Frank concluded, "I don't believe there is any remote chance of him being elected president." Oops.

How could the Clinton team lose? They had taken so much corporate money! She had raised twice as much money as Trump![77] It never occurred to them that they had lost track of the means and the ends. Corporate cash was supposed to be a means to getting elected. Now they couldn't kick the habit, even when it was obviously costing them elections. The means had become the ends. The Democratic Party had completely adapted "system-oriented politics." And the system was corruption, for its own sake.

When Tony Coehlo was hired to be a "senior adviser" to the DNC in the middle of Bill Clinton's first term, Barney Frank jubilantly responded, "My reaction to Tony being there was, 'Hey, great, the adults are back.'"[78] That was right before the catastrophic 1994 results. Two decades later Barney Frank had learned nothing.

It's not that Coelho and Frank are particularly unintelligent or craven, it's that they can't see straight because they're obsessed with the carrot being dangled right in front of their noses. Once you write a certain line of code into our system, the rest becomes inevitable. The Democratic Party never had the courage to say it would refuse any of the corporate money and choose to fight for its voters, the average American workers. That would have been a winning political strategy, as it had been for decades. And in 2018, it *was* the winning strategy for Justice Democrats, and it fueled Bernie Sanders's shockingly effective campaigns against Hillary Clinton and Joe Biden. No one in Washington thought these progressives could be competitive without corporate cash, but they were wrong, as usual.

Perhaps most important, the decision of Coelho and other corporate Democrats to prioritize business interests allowed inequality to run rampant. Without even one major party committed to economic fairness, the subsequent forty years were a repeat of the forty years before the Progressive Era: a new Gilded Age. We have income inequality because we let corporations and the wealthy bribe politicians. It's that simple. It wasn't an accident of fate; the system was redesigned to achieve that specific objective. That's why making America work for all its citizens absolutely, positively requires getting money out of politics. You can rail about income inequality all you want, but nothing will change unless legal corruption is exorcised from the political system. Until you end the private financing of elections, there will continue to be ten or twenty Barney Franks for every Bernie Sanders.

It's human nature to fall victim to the allure of the money. Harvard Law professor Lawrence Lessig says politicians in this system "lean to the green."[79] You can't change human nature, but you can change the rules. If you make it illegal to take the money, then fewer people will take it. If you make it perfectly legal, unfortunately, the great majority of politicians, including Democrats, will take it. And they'll keep taking it, no matter how much it destroys their own party.

So what was the result of both parties serving corporate interests for the last forty years? CEOs have seen their pay grow by 1,460 percent since 1978, and the average American worker has only seen their salary go up by an anemic 18.1 percent over all those decades.[80] The people in charge of the corporate machines decided to give themselves almost a hundred times more than what they gave you once they captured your government. There were no more representatives to fight for you. It wasn't your government anymore, it was theirs. The machines had won.

5

THE MATRIX

EVERY SPORTS FAN KNOWS THAT THE MOST IMPORTANT THING YOU NEED FOR a fair game is an unbiased referee. A study showed that home teams have an advantage in football not because of the field or the fans but because referees are influenced to call fewer penalties for the home team.[1] This could make a giant difference in a game. Even worse, if the refs are bought, then the game is useless, of course.

If the refs had cheated during the Michael Jordan era, then Jordan wouldn't have been the greatest player of all time. He would probably have been a lovable loser who never made it. Why? If the refs aren't going to call any fouls, the first thing any rational opponent would do is foul Jordan so badly that they hurt him. You don't want that guy in the game. You know he's going to beat you. And you know the refs aren't calling any fouls. You gotta make sure Jordan can't play.

In politics, the media are the refs. If they are being fair, the citizens in a democracy will get the information they need to make the right decisions. If they're not fair, then the game is rigged. The bad guys will foul anyone they like with impunity—and it'll never get called. It completely ruins the game. Not only that, but it makes the worst guys—the ones most likely to foul—the most likely to win.

Conservatives have been calling the media liberal for years (this is called working the refs). But you've seen in this book that oftentimes the media do the opposite. They frame issues in a completely conservative way, especially on economic issues.

And as we talked about earlier, the corporate media are both mainstream media and right-wing media. Like the Democrats and Republicans, they also play good cop–bad cop. MSNBC is the good cop saying you should treat everyone equally, and Fox News is the bad cop saying you should hate the others. But interestingly enough, when it comes to economic issues, you find out they're on the same team. The culture wars are the soap opera they use to keep you engaged—without actually ever solving anything!

In 2003, the journalist Eric Alterman wrote a book called *What Liberal Media?* It became a bestseller, which, again, surprised people in the media and politics who assumed that everyone thought like them—that everyone just knew that the media is liberal. But they only knew it because Republicans kept saying it. "Conservatives have successfully cowed journalists into repeating their endless accusations of liberal bias by virtue of their willingness to repeat them . . . endlessly," wrote Alterman. But the reality was that corporate media moguls owned the playing field—and they got to set the rules and hire the players. "You're only as liberal as the man who owns you," as Alterman put it.[2]

Does that mean the media are exclusively right wing? No, they're generally left wing on social issues. They usually think minorities and gay Americans should be treated equally to all other Americans. And boy, did they hate Trump!

But wait a minute, they also hated Bernie. Hmm.

Well, who do they like? Nancy Pelosi is their absolute favorite. She is consistently called a "master legislator" in the national press. They also have respect for George W. Bush and have hired his former officials all over the media. Nicolle Wallace was his communications director, and she's now a host on . . . MSNBC. Now, with Liz Cheney attacking Trump, even Dick Cheney is being celebrated on MSNBC and CNN.

This looks like a hodgepodge of Democrats and Republicans that you can't make heads or tails of, right? Nope. There is actually a perfectly consistent explanation. The mainstream media are not liberal or conservative, they're corporate. Both literally and politically.

Almost all the mainstream outlets are giant multibillion-dollar corporations. And most of their revenue comes from other giant multibillion-dollar corporations that are their advertisers. Any rational person would instantly understand that they have all the reason in the world to support giant multibillion-dollar corporations. In fact, their very existence, and all their profits, depend on it.

When you put on this decoder ring, you instantly realize that the media are very consistent. They always support corporate politicians. Both Republicans and Democrats who take corporate donations are their favorites. They are always painted in a glowing light. "They are moderates! They are wonderfully bipartisan!"

And outsiders, both on the right and left, are always painted as illegitimate radicals.

Pelosi loves corporate donations—she's raised over a billion dollars in her career. Mitch McConnell also loves corporate donations—and he's raised about a billion dollars as well. They are always referred to as serious politicians who are great at what they do. That has an element of truth to it, because they are both great at corruption. But that's not what you hear on TV.

You hear that bipartisanship is the greatest thing of all. That's why when Lindsey Graham and Joe Lieberman agree on starting a war that will make defense contractors and oil companies rich, you hear that they have reached bipartisan agreement! The holy grail of Washington politics. What they don't tell you is that when the fake corporate politicians from both sides agree on something, watch your wallet! That's why decade after decade, since we have been living under corporate rule, the only thing that passes consistently is tax cuts for the rich and for . . . corporations.

Think about it. Why is supporting bipartisanship the objective position? Isn't it, by definition, not objective? When the media celebrate it, they're picking a side—not between the parties but among different policy positions. If there is bipartisan agreement to create a carried interest loophole that cuts taxes for hedge funds—and the media celebrates that as positive since it involved politicians from both parties—they are writing positively about a policy position that very few Americans actually agree with. In reality, there is bipartisan agreement among the voters *against* that policy. But that is not how it is portrayed by the corporate press. It is portrayed in the exact opposite way. "Washington has found bipartisan compromise—everyone celebrate! They're so moderate!"

The implication is that these are reasonable legislators who have come together because they care about the country. What the media don't tell you is that these politicians are actually united in how much they care about their donors. Because that doesn't sound nearly as good.

So why did the press create this enormous bias and call it objective? Because it protected the status quo. The positions that actually represent the country are called radical left (and sometimes, though very rarely, radical right). We have the polling to prove it, as you saw in chapter 1. But the positions that are unpopular and represent corporate interests are called "moderate" and "bipartisan."

If you go along with corporate rule, the press will have glowing things to say about you. And they will call that position objective. If you challenge the system, they will call you biased.

How about outsiders? How do they get treated in the press? Well, you see what happened to Trump. To be fair, he more than earned it. But his corruption, all of a sudden, was not acceptable. Why was his corruption worse than McConnell's? Because McConnell works for corporate donors. Trump works only for himself.

This is part of why Trump supporters ignore mainstream media critiques of Trump—because they notice the wild disparity between the treatment of his corruption and the corruption of all the other politicians. That's corporate media attacking an outsider (correctly so, in this case) but leaving the corruption of corporate politicians completely unaddressed. They might not articulate it exactly like this, but that's the gnawing hypocrisy that makes every right-winger despise the mainstream press. They're not completely wrong. Trump is a con man, but he is a bit of an amateur compared to corporate media. They run the most sophisticated con job in the country.

Remember, mainstream media also hated Bernie Sanders. If you want to challenge the status quo, your biggest opponent by far will be the corporate media. They will bury you.

I'm not breaking new ground here. Noam Chomsky wrote about this brilliantly decades ago in *Manufacturing Consent*. The media don't manufacture news, they manufacture compliance. Compliance with corporate rule. So the status quo is always great. Change is always radical. Corporate politicians are well-meaning, honorable legislators having earnest debates about policy. Right-wing and left-wing populists are illegitimate radicals.

Good news—the American people are onto them. An October 2022 *New York Times*/Siena College poll asked people what they think are threats to democracy. As expected, Donald Trump came in very high, with 45 percent of Americans saying he is a major threat to democracy (they are correct). But Joe Biden finished surprisingly high, too. Thirty-eight percent of Americans said he might end democracy (if by democracy, you mean the current system, they are incorrect; corporate politicians like Biden love this system and would never change it). But that wasn't the big surprise. What came in first was the shocker to the media—it was them! They came in first! Fifty-nine percent of Americans said mainstream media are a major threat to American democracy.[3]

Every time the national media see something like this, they don't believe it. They think that's the craziest thing in the world. They're not the villains. They are the honorable fourth estate. Are they? Let's find out.

INVISIBLE HAND OF THE MARKET

Well, that's the thing—the individuals within the press are not exactly wrong. Personally, they're not really villains. I've met many of them. Generally speaking, they're lovely people. But what kind of person would create a conspiracy to rig the game in favor of the richest corporations in the world and ruin our democracy? The kind who have no idea that they're involved in that plot.

You see, there is no conspiracy. There is no smoke-filled room where they make these decisions. There are no memos they write to all the reporters, editors, and producers telling them to support corporate politicians. They don't have to. That's the beauty of the invisible hand of the market.

Here's how that works. The CEOs of the media companies hire executives who think just like them: This system that put us at the top is awesome! They then hire publishers and executive producers who think . . . just like them. They then hire editors, reporters, producers, and anchors who think . . . just like them.

Do you think those corporate executives are going to hire radicals? Outsiders? How about progressives who challenge corporate corruption? Hell, no! Those are the last guys in the world you'd want to hire. Look around the media. None of them got hired. Mission accomplished.

Half of MSNBC's lineup are "former" Republicans. And they're supposed to be the left-wing channel. Hilarious. There's not a progressive in the building. How about Rachel Maddow, you say? When was the last time you heard her criticize Democratic leadership? I'll give you a minute with that one. Yes, she and all other MSNBC hosts love Democrats, but do they like progressives challenging the system? If they do, they have a funny way of showing it.

The elegance of the invisible hand is that no one has to tell the reporters what to do. They were preselected to already have the kind of ideas, or groupthink, that were needed. The reason they genuinely don't know that they're in on a plot to do corporate propaganda is because no one told them! Their bosses just hired them for who they were.

If you had gotten a great multimillion-dollar job on cable news, would you think that you got hired because you're a terrific journalist or because you were the most compliant to corporate rule? Of course, you'd think it was because you were Walter Fucking Cronkite. No one wants to think of themselves as a stooge. Plus, remember, they have no idea this is happening. The elegance of this machine is that the system naturally selected them because of how much they believed in maintaining the status quo, so it never had to give them orders to maintain the status quo. That ideology came baked in for each hire.

Now, what happens if you are a real reporter and not compliant? We'll get to that in a second. Suffice it to say, it doesn't end well.

If this sounds like a foreign or novel concept to you, it shouldn't. Adam Smith, arguably the godfather of capitalism, wrote about it all the way back in 1759. He explained that the invisible hand of the market is a collection of people acting in their own interest that winds up creating the right price or market conditions in the long run. This concept is one of the core pillars of capitalism.

The problem that Smith anticipated is that if corporations got too powerful, for example in monopolies or oligopolies, they could short-circuit competition and free markets. And that's exactly what corporations in America have done. Once they moved their political and media pawns into place, there was no one to resist them on behalf of the people and no one to hold them accountable in the press.

So what happened after that? The establishment created a system where student debt would weigh you down so much that you would have to work for a corporation to pay it back. Then health care tied to employers would make you beholden to any company you work for because you might literally die if you leave them. Then the system would make housing unaffordable, so that you are not accumulating wealth anymore but having your wealth extracted in rent. This way they could turn almost all of us into indentured servants without having to say it! The illusion of freedom, with servitude that lasts a lifetime.

If this sounds like a nefarious plot, it is and it isn't. Unlike Lewis Powell's memo, a literal plan to take over the government, this one had no central coordination. Again, the market forces moved in concert with their own self-interest. The market guides companies into a position where they would have a vise grip on their customers and employees. And they would use that vise to squeeze out every last penny of profit, not just from their customers but also from their employees. The invisible hand of the market in this context naturally leads to a political order where we humans serve the corporate entities, which were machines of our own making.

And what would be critical to this system is the illusion of choice. So the corporate Democrats and Republicans give you the illusion of choice with their good cop–bad cop routine. But so do mainstream media and right-wing media. It sounds like they are disagreeing at a feverish pace. But when you look below the surface, it's all on minuscule culture issues, like if trans teenagers are playing on the right team in high school sports. Why make an enormous national issue out of something that affects only a handful of people in the country? My cohost on *The Young Turks*, Ana Kasparian, explains this best—these culture wars are a perfect distraction from the corporate oppression you're living under.

But notice that Fox News, CNN, and MSNBC were all against Medicare for All. As you might remember, from 2016 to 2020, the great majority of these networks' anchors and pundits spoke skeptically and critically of that proposal.[4] It's hard to remember a single pundit on cable news who was in favor of the proposal that 70 percent of Americans say they want. When it's an economic issue, they close ranks immediately! Because they too are playing good cop–bad cop. They are the Matrix of our lives that puts us back to sleep so that we don't realize we are living under corporate rule.

How many stories have you seen about corporations squeezing the life out of their employees by keeping wages low and their workers chained to their employers? None. Where are the so-called populists of Fox News? Nowhere to be found. And this doesn't affect a small number of people in the country. This affects us all!

But if right-wing and left-wing voters knew they were being oppressed by the same machine, they might rise up in their wrath and take control back. On the other hand, if you can get the masses to rip each other apart on social issues, that would be a perfect way of distracting them and getting them to fight each other instead of the people at the top. The invisible hand of the market is a hell of a beast.

Do you keep thinking, "Jesus, this makes so much sense. And it's embedded in logical market forces that are indisputable. So how come I've never heard of this before?" Well, that's because you live inside the Matrix. The media have a cord tied to the back of your modem or cable box (instead of your neck) that is constantly feeding you propaganda that the status quo is great and that your only problem is the worker right next to you. But whatever you do, do not look up!

In order to maintain that hypnosis over the American people, what else would you do? You'd have to set up a perimeter defense. What would you be defending against? Outsiders who are going to tell people about what's wrong with the system. The radical right are outsiders for a couple of reasons. One is that they are against multiculturalism. Wait, why is that a problem? Because Coke and Nike have to sell to everyone on the planet, and there are a lot of Muslim, Black, gay, and Asian customers in the world. They naturally want to sell to all of them. So they don't like the antidiversity talk that comes from the right. But more important, a guy like Trump is a real threat to the system. And the status quo must be protected!

Now, is Trump a healthy challenge to the system? No, of course not. He is not doing it for some altruistic goal, he just wants all the power (and money) for himself. It's the worst kind of populism. He's a Rebel with His Own Cause. But a rebel, nonetheless. That's what his fans love about him. And that's what the establishment hates about him.

But if you thought that was rough treatment by the press, wait until you get a load of how they treat progressives, who are an actual, logical threat to the system. And one that is harder to control.

We get the worst fate of all: the silent treatment. Progressives are allowed almost nowhere in corporate media. The right-wing media only allow fake leftists, like Tulsi Gabbard, on their air. And their role is to pretend they are on the left but agree with right-wing policies. These appearances look like pathetic hostage videos. Watching former progressives dancing for the amusement of Tucker Carlson is one of the most stomach-churning experiences of my life. And mainstream media hate progressives even more. If you're skeptical about that, wait until you hear the stories from behind the scenes later in this chapter.

THE CREDIBLES

Progressives are invisible to the mainstream media. Why? First, the media is obsessed with power. Progressives have been out of power for a long time. But what was interesting is how many times I and my cohost, Ana Kasparian, were on CNN when Bernie Sanders was leading the race in 2020. We were almost never on before then. We were on about a dozen times when Bernie was in the lead. And we haven't been asked on once since Bernie lost Super Tuesday. They adore power.

Second, progressives are a real threat to the system. Right-wing populists are genuinely populist on cultural issues (unfortunately), but they are utterly full of crap on economic issues. They have no economic populist policies at all. In a lot of ways, they accidentally back corporate rule. So, while Trump is bashed by the media, he's still allowed on—a lot. And his advisers and supporters are all over television. That's because they're not that big a threat to the system (or at least they weren't until January 6).

But progressives mean what they say. We are desperate for change. We want to stick up for the average American, and we're against corporate rule. That is anathema to corporate media. So they use a much more potent weapon against us—the sound of silence. They just never let us on air, so no one ever hears our ideas. They then lie about all our policy positions and say that we are unpopular. None of that is true, but how would you know? You never get to hear from us.

But there is one other reason why there are almost no progressives in establishment media. Since almost no one can see past their own perspective, the media can't relate to us. And since they can't relate, we occupy no head space for them. Not only do they not know about us, but they don't even realize there is something else to know. And for the ones on TV, they think they're so smart (remember, to be fair to them, people are kissing their ass 24/7, so it's hard not to think you're the greatest thing since sliced bread if that's what everyone is constantly telling you) that the idea that an outsider could educate them about the news or politics would be laughable to them. Absolutely riotous. What would they know? We are the credible professionals.

In their minds, they're the superheroes, The Credibles!

If you're poor or sick, and you need big change, giant change—you're not credible. You're a radical. Credible people know what is possible and not possible. You're going to be shocked to find out that almost nothing is possible. Unless, of course, it helps the already wealthy and powerful. Don't worry, The Credibles say it will trickle down on us one day.

It's been forty years of stagnant wages and corporatist oppression, and if anything has trickled on us, it ain't wealth.

So when The Credibles see progressives, do you know what they see? Nothing. Absolutely nothing. We're invisible to them.

Until there is an intruder alert. Then they attack.

THE CLOSET

When I was a host on MSNBC, I challenged nearly everyone in power. I'm a progressive, so I critiqued the Obama administration and the Democratic Party from the left, and I ripped into Republicans. At the time, MSNBC didn't mind hitting Republicans (but not too hard: I was admonished for yelling at a former Republican congressman who wanted to cut Social Security). But Phil Griffin, who was the head of the network at the time, pulled me into his office one day and literally said, "I was just in D.C., and they are not happy with your tone." How is that for heavy handed? It gets worse. He also told me, "Outsiders are cool. They wear leather jackets and ride motorcycles. But we're NBC. We're not outsiders, we're insiders." It was a stunning speech. It was so over the top I'd think it was too outlandish if it was in a movie. The critics would say it was "too on the nose."

Phil Griffin told *The New York Times* that he denies my assertions, but I had the advantage of being in the room at the time, so I know exactly what happened. Even Griffin acknowledged that one of their problems with me was that I was "making it harder to book guests."[5] I'm not sure he realized that was a direct admission that they tell their hosts to tone down critique of the powerful so they can have better access to them.

My executive producer at the time would say, "Cenk, remember who the home team is." I thought it was the audience, but that's not what they meant. They meant it's the Democratic Party, and your job is to kiss the party's ass. Another time, I criticized President Obama for taking both sides of the Egyptian revolution, because he very clearly did in an absurd speech where he said he was thankful for our ally Hosni Mubarak and was encouraged by the revolution against him. I was told that you can't criticize the president right after his speech. I asked, "How long do we have to wait before we tell the truth?" And I was told at least twenty-four hours, but a couple of days was preferable. In other words, until it was out of the news cycle.

They must have thought I was the slowest guy in television. When is this knucklehead going to get it? *Don't criticize the Democrats!* And of course, by Democrats, they meant the establishment Democrats. You could criticize progressives until the cows came home. But this story isn't about me. It's about the system and what's wrong with it. And how you are lied to as a matter of course. So let me tell you the publicly documented stories of other anchors at MSNBC.

In the great majority of cases, they never have to give cable news anchors the speech that Griffin gave me. The memo is usually delivered in their actions, in what they reward and punish. When I was eventually asked to go to the weekends instead of the coveted 6:00 P.M. hour I was already in, everyone in the building got the memo: That guy was tough on corporate Democrats—*don't do that!* You'll lose your multimillion-dollar job (and status and fame and respect and all the things you care about). They almost never have to *write* the memo, just like with donors giving funding to politicians who are good boys and girls and denying money to those who don't play ball.

I turned down their multiyear, seven-figure offer to move to the weekends because I couldn't live with being inside that system. I had gone to cable news to spread the word about what was actually happening in our politics. If they weren't going to let me do that, then there was no point in staying. But my story isn't the most brazen case of mainstream media's corporate agenda. That honor belongs to Ashleigh Banfield.

Banfield was a rising star on TV, and back in the early 2000s there was a bit of a bidding contest to get her. MSNBC won that contest, and they proudly featured her all over their network. Then one day, she disappeared. At the time, I didn't know what had happened behind the scenes, but it was weird—she was gone. You couldn't find her anywhere anymore.

It turns out she had given a speech at Kansas State University explaining why the Iraq War was problematic. Now, were the facts in her speech inaccurate? No, they were stunningly accurate. And that was the problem. At the time, MSNBC was not the neoliberal shill for the Democratic Party that it is now, it was just flat-out conservative. Keith Olbermann had not led the revolution there yet. So, in the lead-up to the Iraq War, the network bosses fired everyone on air who disagreed with the war. They even fired their top-rated host at the time, Phil Donahue.

Later, a memo from one of the network executives leaked that explained why they fired Donahue. It said that he was a "difficult public face for NBC in a time of war. . . . He seems to delight in presenting guests who are anti-war, anti-Bush and skeptical of the administration's motives."[6]

Think about that: no one who was against the war was allowed on TV. They were a problem because they "seemed to delight" in having an opinion that was contrary to the business interests of GE, which owned MSNBC at the time. It might be relevant for you to know that GE was a massive defense contractor that stood to make billions from the war. So, at this point, you're not going to be surprised that "news" anchors who were delighted at the thought of war were very much welcome on air. All over their air, literally 24/7.

Notice that the executive also chastised the journalist for being opposed to the powerful. Donahue had the temerity to challenge the president. Wait, isn't that what journalists are supposed to do? Well, at least that's the fairy tale we've all been told. The reality, as you can see in their internal memos, is very, very different. Challenge the powerful and you will be instantly fired from mainstream media.

But that was just MSNBC, right? Well, let's read the rest of the memo. The internal message warned that Donahue's show could become "a home for the liberal anti-war agenda at the same time that our competitors are waving the flag at every opportunity."[7] Oh, so literally every channel was waving the flag enthusiastically at the chance of bloody war. MSNBC was worried that it was going to miss out on the feeding frenzy. MSNBC was a particularly egregious example of this kind of greedy bloodlust, as you'll see in a minute, but almost all the channels had defense contractors as advertisers. Everybody was going to make a killing! Unfortunately, that was also pretty close to literal.

Jesse Ventura later told me that at that time, MSNBC had signed him to a huge contract, but they found out right before he went on air that he was against the war, so they told him to go home. They'd pay him anyway—they didn't want a kerfuffle—but he was not to go on air! Now, Jesse says some stuff I believe and some stuff that's harder to believe. But in this case, I knew he was telling the truth for sure. Why? Because his cohost in the MSNBC auditions was . . . Ben Mankiewicz.

In a stunning and actual coincidence, MSNBC had asked Ben, my *TYT* cohost at the time, to play the role of Ventura's cohost. I don't think they were considering hiring Ben, but they needed a smart guy to bounce things off Jesse to see how he did. And they thought Ventura did great! Good thing for Jesse that Ben never asked about Iraq in those practice runs. Ventura told me that they paid him *millions* and never once used him on air after they realized he was against the war.

All of that is background so you know that what happened to Banfield was not at all a fluke. Not only did they upbraid her after the Kansas speech, they took her off the air! But this is where it gets weird and reveals the game. She naturally asked to be let out of her contract. They said no. Wait a minute, why? Okay, they want to wave the flag, but why would you pay her all that money to not work? Why don't you just let her out of her contract and let her say the things you think are unpopular somewhere else? That's a win-win—you save a lot of money and she'll bring bad ratings to your competitors if you're right that Americans love war. Of course, you wouldn't do that if you thought what she was saying would actually be really, really popular. You'd want to make sure she couldn't say it anywhere else.

But it gets worse (doesn't it always). You're not going to believe this, either, until I show you the actual quotes. Because truth is stranger than fiction. MSNBC executives told her that they were moving her office. Why would you even bother? You canceled her show, so what difference does it make where she sits? The only way it would make a difference is if you were trying to send a message. And not to her, because she already got her message—you're banished. The message was meant for everyone else in the building.

They moved her office into a closet!

Not joking, not exaggerating. They moved her into a tape closet. It's so literal and so metaphorical at the same time. Mainstream media wanted unsanctioned (and correct) analysis stuffed into a closet where no one could see it. Out of sight, out of mind. Whatever you do, if you're a progressive, or just an honest journalist, do not come out of the closet!

Banfield explained, "For ten months I had to report to work every day and ask where I could sit. If somebody was away I could use their desk. Eventually, after ten months of this, I was given an office that was a tape closet. They cleared the tapes out and put a desk and a TV in there, and a computer and phone. It was pretty blatant. The message was crystal clear."[8]

Neal Shapiro, who was NBC News president at the time, said the move to cancel her show and "reduce her visibility," as *The New York Times* described it, was done solely because everyone would be better served if she made NBC News appearances that were more . . . sporadic. *The New York Times* added that "several people at NBC said, Ms. Banfield alienated bosses and colleagues."[9] Apparently, they wanted the message to be so clear that they leaked to the paper of record that her transgression was alienating her bosses. And what did her bosses' bosses want? On top of the ample defense contracts, GE also got $3 billion and $15 billion contracts from the Iraqi government to develop power stations.[10] That's the kind of money you don't want to "alienate."

This is how the invisible hand of the market works. Number one, you only hire people who agree with you. And number two, if you make a mistake and you accidentally hire a real journalist, then you shut them up and stuff them into a small, dark room—and make sure everyone else in the building sees you doing it. Then you never have to write a memo telling people what to say. The closet is the memo.

That is exactly how we get groupthink and exactly how we got the compliant press we have now.

This is also how we got Donald Trump.

When people stop believing the press, they go looking for answers and often wind up in all the wrong places. How did all those voters, including independents, come to believe the insane things Trump says? Well, they knew what the people in power were saying was not true, so when a big, confident celebrity came in and said things that had the air of honesty to them (because the comments were so clearly not scripted), they thought, "Maybe he's got it right."

And remember, the media had bottled up Bernie Sanders so much in 2015 (in the lead-up to the primaries in 2016), people who were not neck deep in politics had barely heard of him. So they only had two options for what was true. They had already eliminated one as a possibility—that the media was telling the truth about how wonderful corporate politicians like Marco Rubio and Hillary Clinton were—so that only left them one other option: Trump.

Because Democratic leadership and the mainstream media had so effectively kept progressives in the closet, if America wanted to go populist— and they definitely did—they thought they had only one option. So they jumped on it. That's how sick America was of the establishment.

I remember seeing a bumper sticker back then. It looked like a standard campaign sticker, but instead of the candidate's name, it said: "Meteor 2016."

Ask and ye shall receive.

The pressure in the country keeps building up as the press keeps lying and lying on behalf of the powerful. This thing is going to blow. If it goes populist right, we might very well have fascism in America. I know that the mainstream press, living in its comfortable elitist bubble, thinks that's not possible. But it definitely is. If the country goes populist left, we can actually defeat the machines and restore democracy.

But this is not strictly a progressive issue. We must band together at some point with honest people on the right to take on the corporate machines. We can't win just on our own. And they can't win on their own. We need most of the country united to rewrite the code of this system, as I'll explain in a little bit. We must form a rebel alliance against the machines. Otherwise, our democracy, and any remaining honest members of the press, will be stuffed into a dark closet, never to be heard from again.

HARDBALL

One of the reasons I sometimes get angry on a personal level about this shell game that the media play is because I was duped. I grew up on television and believed the mainstream media. Brainwashing sounds like a harsh word, but that does accurately describe what is happening to all of us. I know it happened to me.

When I was a kid, I watched *Meet the Press, This Week with David Brinkley,* and my personal favorite, *The McLaughlin Group.* Yes, I was a nerd. I watched those shows from the time I was ten years old. And I believed what they were saying. I thought the politicians were having real debates about public policy.

And what did they do once they had me locked in? They walked me straight over to the Republican Party. Remember, I came in as a blank slate and didn't know anything about the two parties when we moved to America (I was eight years old at the time). I genuinely believed in "morning in America." If you were watching TV in the 1980s, Reagan seemed like a natural choice if you believed in and loved America. The corporate media made his message sound so alluring. To this day, I still think we can be that shining city on a hill. But Ronald Reagan took that dream of mine and used it to trick me into believing in tax cuts for the rich. And the media helped him do it!

How did they help? First of all, they never busted the myths. The guy was an actor dressed as a cowboy—and the media took him seriously. They never told us definitively, remember, this guy is a fucking actor! This is all an act. I'll give you a perfect example from another actor in politics. Fred Thompson was another literal actor. He is probably best known for being in the NBC hit *Law & Order* (ironic, given where the Republican Party wound up). He had worked in politics earlier in his life, including as a lobbyist, but he was predominantly known for his roles as high-ranking government officials or military figures in a number of blockbusters he appeared in, like *The Hunt for Red October* and *In the Line of Fire*. He eventually became a senator from Tennessee. Fine, actors are allowed to run for office, too, like any other profession. But he continued the act and the press let him.

Thompson had this old beat-up red pickup truck that he used on the campaign trail. It made him look folksy and down to earth. It was the perfect prop. But here comes the fun part—he would drive up to campaign events in his limo, then get into the pickup truck, drive around, and when it was over, get back in his limo to drive back to his mansion. In full sight of the press! And the press never told the good people of Tennessee about the limo! They dutifully reported Thompson in the pickup truck, as if that's what he regularly drove.

Remember, the press is supposed to challenge power. There's a great line from Finley Peter Dunne, an early twentieth-century writer, where his character Mr. Dooley explains that the press is supposed to "comfort the afflicted and afflict the comfortable." Well, that's not how it turned out. Why wouldn't you expose the fraud that Fred Thompson was? Why would you let him play that trick on people and laugh at them behind their backs? Because you didn't want to make the powerful uncomfortable, that's why.

Chris Matthews, former pillar of cable news and one of the most respected television anchors of my lifetime, was ground zero for the media's obsession with how politicians looked and not what they did. Don't tell people the truth, help the politicians tell them fairy tales. Be a fawning, obsequious fanboy of the phonies and you will get to be a really well-paid television host for decades! And everyone will pretend you're a journalist. It's almost as if the news anchors on television are also actors.

If you think I'm being overly tough on Matthews now, you won't by the end. You'll think I wasn't tough enough, and you'll be shocked that this is what everyone pretended was journalism for all these years.

First of all, remember when George W. Bush landed on the aircraft carrier and pretended that he had won the Iraq War right around when it had just gotten started? They hung that fateful "Mission Accomplished" banner behind him. That proved to be an embarrassment for the rest of Bush's career, and it was one of the rare things he said he regretted. He didn't regret the torture he authorized, but he regretted that aircraft carrier speech because of how poorly it went.

You wouldn't have known any of that if you had turned to MSNBC on the day of the speech. You would have thought that it went spectacularly well. Now, before I tell you what Matthews said, remember that this was not on Fox News, it was on MSNBC—and Matthews is considered left wing in Washington (I chuckle every time I think about that—this is the same guy who said he was worried that socialists like Bernie Sanders would bring on an era of executions in Central Park[11]).

Here is what Chris Matthews said on that day about George Bush:

> He looks great in a military uniform. He looks great in that cowboy costume he wears when he goes west. We're proud of our president. Americans love having a guy as president, a guy who has a little swagger, who's physical, who's not a complicated guy like Clinton. . . . Women like a guy who's president. Check it out.[12]

First of all, fuck off. Second of all, what the hell would you know about what women like? Third, it appears that's what *you* like, not women. It's called projection, look into it. But most important, he actually applauds Bush for playing dress-up! He looks good in different costumes!

He never mentioned that the mission was not in fact accomplished. There was no talk of substance. And of course, there was no talk of Iraqi civilians killed and maimed at the business end of our pretty bombs that Matthews liked so much. Many years later, Brian Williams, on that same MSNBC channel, would say, about fifty-nine Tomahawk missiles that Trump had launched at Syria, "We see these beautiful pictures at night from the decks of these two navy vessels in the eastern Mediterranean. I am tempted to quote the great Leonard Cohen: 'I'm guided by the beauty of our weapons.' And they are beautiful pictures."

Back on the aircraft carrier, when Bush made what he thought was the biggest strategic error of his career, the "news" story of the day was how great he looked! And that was on MSNBC!

This was not at all an aberration. How well politicians played dress-up was a constant source of discussion on Matthews's show, ironically called . . . *Hardball*. Here is what he said about the loathsome Rudy Giuliani: "[He is] the one tough cop who was standing on the beat when we got hit last time and stood up and took it." Reagan was a cowboy, Bush was a fighter pilot, and Rudy was a tough cop. Matthews went on to say Rudy was the "perfect candidate." Oops. And then the most important thing for Matthews—he "looks like a president," he "acts and talks like a president." He literally applauded him for "acting" like a president.[13]

I don't know if Matthews is equally enamored of how Rudy these days is "acting" like a lawyer.

Let's go back to Bush, because, unfortunately, there's a lot more fawning I have to tell you about. How can it get worse? Buckle up and brace for impact.

Even before the aircraft carrier speech, Bush had gone to Yankee Stadium to throw out the first pitch sometime after 9/11. It was admittedly a nice moment because it was signaling to the country—let's get back to normal, let's not let this attack shake us. No one would have begrudged anyone stating that at the time. But you know Matthews isn't going to leave it at that. So here was his hardball about Bush the next day:

> There are some things you can't fake. Either you can throw a strike from sixty feet or you can't. Either you can rise to the occasion on the mound at Yankee Stadium with 56,000 people watching or you can't. On Tuesday night, George W. Bush hit the strike zone in the House that Ruth Built. . . . This is about knowing what to do at the moment you have to do it—and then doing it. It's about that "grace under pressure" that Hemingway gave as his very definition of courage.[14]

Hemingway? George W. Bush reminded him of Ernest Hemingway? Throwing a baseball sixty feet was the "very definition of courage." And as Bush was faking being presidential—remember, Bush ignored his Presidential Daily Briefing that warned a month before 9/11 that Osama bin Laden was determined to attack inside the United States—Matthews told people that Bush's authenticity couldn't be faked! Because he threw a baseball sixty feet.

Remember, the news actors on television are all saying Chris Matthews is a lifelong Democrat. So his validating Bush's optics makes the whole country think, "Well, I guess the Republicans must be right. Even the left agrees how courageous he is and what a wonderful fighter pilot he is. God, I hope that great cop, Rudy, also joins him in protecting us all."

We had the cop, the cowboy, and the soldier. It's unclear if Matthews ever broke out in a rendition of "YMCA" to accompany his ode to the near complete cast of the Village People.

Wait, I'm not done with Matthews. If you thought all of that was bad . . . oh, no, not more . . . here is what Matthews said about a trip to the White House he had where he got to meet the legendary cowboy/fighter pilot/baseball hero.

First, he explained on air that Bush might belong on Mount Rushmore. Really? Here is the direct quote: "If his gamble that he can create a democracy in the middle of the Arab world and he does it, he belongs on Mount Rushmore."[15]

Remember that when Trump suggested he might belong on Mount Rushmore, everyone was aghast. In this case, Matthews was suggesting it for Bush—and everyone thought it was perfectly normal.

Why was he so excited about the president? It turns out he had visited him the night before at the White House. Must be nice. Here is what he said:

> You know, I felt sensitive. I was with him last night, the president. We all went to see the president. You were there—went to see the president for our Christmas. You get your picture taken with him. It's like Santa Claus, and he's always very generous and friendly.

Santa Fucking Claus? Are there no bounds? He went to sit on his lap for Christmas. And he felt "sensitive" about it. For younger people, yes, believe it or not, this is what passed for serious journalism on television for decades!

The man who got hundreds of thousands of civilians killed in Iraq—grandmothers, babies, aunts, uncles, moms, all dead, with their skulls crushed under the cement that fell on them when we bombed their buildings.

The man who brought torture back into vogue. The man who spied on all Americans and brazenly lied about it. The man who left people in New Orleans to drown without assistance during Hurricane Katrina because of his incompetence and indifference. That man was "generous and friendly" to a television anchor, so he became Santa Claus. This is exactly how mythmaking works.

Wait, I'm still not done wrecking this absurd belief that people on television are journalists who are accurately covering the news. In that same show, Matthews went on to say something even more vomitous.

> I was wearing a red scarf. And I wanted to look a little bit festive for the occasion, look a little preppy. And he came up to me and said, "Matthews, I didn't know you were that preppy." This is the president of the United States after his biggest victory, and he goes, "I didn't know you were that preppy." And I said, "Well, you know, I went to Holy Cross, but you guys started with all this stuff—the old guys started with all this stuff," and then he started kidding around. I felt like I was too towel-snappy with him. I felt he deserves a little—I mean, he deserves a lot of respect for this bet he's making.

Too towel-snappy? George W. Bush deserves more respect? You did all but blow the guy on national television. How much more could you have respected him?

The official transcript doesn't have it, but we covered it on *The Young Turks* at the time. I remember Matthews clearly saying they "started with all this stuff at Yale." That's why he was referring to how he wasn't worthy since he was just from Holy Cross. This is exactly what I'm talking about when I often refer to The Club on air. These guys still have the mindset that Skull and Bones runs the country and a guy like Matthews from Holy Cross is lucky to have made it into this club. He doesn't get that his role in the play is to be their goddamn butler and make sure their pillows are fluffed properly.

It wasn't just that Matthews happened to have a schoolboy crush on George Bush. He had a crush on all politicians. MSNBC didn't have him on air for decades *despite* his ridiculous fawning coverage of people in power; they put him on air precisely *for that reason*.

Which leads us back to Fred Thompson. So, did Matthews expose his red pickup truck bullshit and tell people what a fraud he was? If you think he did, you really haven't been paying attention, or you still can't get yourself to believe that this has all been a show. And that you were the audience in this play. Here is what Matthews said about Thompson:

> Gene, do you think there's a sex appeal for this guy, this sort of mature, older man, you know? He looks sort of seasoned and in charge of himself. What is this appeal? Because I keep [seeing] star quality. You were throwing the word out, shining star, Ana Marie, before I checked you on it . . .
>
> Can you smell the English Leather on this guy, the Aqua Velva, the sort of mature man's shaving cream, or whatever, you know, after he shaved? Do you smell that sort of—a little bit of cigar smoke?[16]

Shining star. Sex appeal. Aqua Velva. English Leather.

Now we had the leather man, too. The Village People cast was nearly complete.

You might be thinking, Wait a minute, I thought Matthews was a Democrat. That's right. He was actually the Chief of Staff to legendary Democratic Speaker of the House Tip O'Neill. And they used that as a marketing gimmick to get everyone to believe that the awful Republicans doing the Southern Strategy, etc., were backed by even the most stalwart Democrats, like hardball-throwing Chris Matthews. That's what a clever playwright would do. They wouldn't get the right-wing news actor to deliver this type of complementary commentary, they'd get the left-wing news actor to do it. So that it's more believable!

You also remember Matthews is a Democrat because you remember one of his most famous lines. He said about Barack Obama, "I have to tell you, you know, it's part of reporting this case, this election, the feeling most people get when they hear Barack Obama's speech. My, I felt this thrill going up my leg. I mean, I don't have that too often."[17]

Of course, the biggest lie in that statement is that he doesn't have that feeling too often. He has it nonstop, about anyone in power. It's not that Matthews is secretly a Republican, it's that he is in love with power. The invisible hand had found the perfect cable news actor.

So that leads to my very ironic defense of Chris Matthews. I know Chris personally. We're not fishing buddies or anything, but I worked with him at MSNBC when we were both anchors there. I guest-hosted his show. I had frank conversations with him before and after I worked at MSNBC.

We had a very friendly exchange as late as the 2020 campaign, when we saw each other in the middle of a spin room after one of the presidential debates. At the next debate, when he was seated at his MSNBC chair, he shouted when he saw me in the middle of the whole place, "Young Turks!"

Am I about to tell you that because of that personal relationship I'm cutting him a break? Does it sound like I've cut him a break so far? This passage will probably be one of the parts of the book that The Club will be most scandalized by. A lot of them know and really like Chris, so they won't be happy about this passage. Because the number-one rule of The Club is that you don't fight other people in The Club. You can be vicious to others. You can take away their rights, their dignity, and even their lives, but you must never break the cardinal rule—do not be impolite to anyone inside The Club.

Then why do I not think so harshly of Matthews personally? Because I don't think he has bad intent. I think he genuinely loves politics, and everyone who meets him can feel that. He has so much enthusiasm for what he does that it's infectious. The problem is that while he loves the play that is politics, he doesn't love the substance. The unvarnished truth is ugly and discomforting. He loves the red scarf and the red pickup truck. The show-and-tell version of politics.

And that gets to the core of the problem. There are 330 million people in the country. Television executives could have picked anyone to cover the news. They picked Chris on purpose. In a sense, it's not his fault. He didn't know he was auditioning for a role. The director who cast that play is a thousand times more culpable than any one actor in the play.

I know an acquaintance who was auditioning for Don Lemon's job at CNN before Lemon landed the job. This person is Black, gay, and attractive. Just like Don Lemon. They were casting a role. They didn't pick Lemon because he was the best journalist available for the job. They picked him because he was the best news actor for the part they were casting.

I've also met Don, and as you might suspect, he is a wonderfully friendly guy. So, in a sense, I feel terrible telling you guys about the play. These are real people with real feelings. And it's not going to feel good reading any of this. But you have to know! If I kept it secret, like everyone else does, because it would help my relationships with these important and powerful people—or just because it doesn't feel good to tell you something unpleasant about people I know in real life—then I would be doing you a grave injustice. It's imperative that you know.

And the good news is once you see the Matrix, you can't unsee it. From now on, you will be able to spot the media doing all the things I have described here. I had to tell you so that you could see it for yourself.

At the end of the day, I don't begrudge Chris Matthews any of this, because if it weren't him, it would have been someone just like him. They would have cast a different news actor to play that role, but it would have led to the same exact result. Chris kept his job on air for decades because he was a particularly enthusiastic actor who was really right for that part, but to this day, I don't think he knew that he had been cast and what role he was meant to play.

It's not about him. It's not personal. It's about the system. It's about the play.

The play is the illusion the Matrix creates to get you to believe that you live in a democracy, when in reality, as we showed you in chapter 4, 90 percent of us have absolutely no effect on public policy. Our voices don't matter at all. If everyone knew that, they might be really pissed. That's why you need quality news actors who can lull everyone back to sleep and tell them pretty stories about cowboys and soldiers. Don't worry, the sexy men who smell like English Leather have your best interests in mind!

That's why the corporate media are the most important tool in the corporate machines' arsenal. Because it's the one that gets you to sit back down and not challenge the machines! As long as you are plugged into the Matrix, you won't even know you're supposed to fight back. It's essential that media create this illusion, otherwise they'll have a rebellion on their hands. That's why mainstream media are not really in the news business. They are in the marketing business. But instead of doing marketing for cars or jeans, they do marketing for corporate politicians and corporate rule. And they're really good at their jobs.

6

HERE COMES
THE REVOLUTION

IT IS UNSURPRISING THAT IN A SYSTEM RIGGED AGAINST US, PROGRESSIVES, or all thinking people, would want change. If the corporate machines have taken over in the way that I've described—and it is indisputable that they have—then how do we fight back? How do we create structural change in the system so that humans can rule again?

How do we fight and defeat a system that is structured around crushing our wages, our dignity, and our very humanity at the altar of corporate profits? How do we defeat this colossus? Most important, how do we regain our power and sovereignty as people and citizens?

The good news is that we can all go on this mission together (except the servants of the corporate class, unfortunately). But this mission can and should unite conservatives and progressives. In fact, let me give conservatives some rare credit here. They figured out the system was rigged against them before most Democrats did. They were positive that the mainstream media were full of shit when they celebrated and venerated obviously corrupt politicians. You were right, my conservative brothers and sisters. You had this gut instinct that the game had been rigged and that was why you were being screwed. You just had the wrong targets. Ironically, corporations used outlets like Fox News—a multibillion-dollar corporation that serves other multibillion-dollar corporations—to misdirect your justifiable anger at all the wrong people.

If you want to know who rigged any game, you should always start with who runs and controls the game. Poor immigrants or middle-class Black folks don't have anywhere near enough power to rig anything. They're lucky to survive, just like you. No, the people who set the rules are at the very top. As I've explained before, they are not wedded to any one religion or ethnicity. That's a red herring meant to distract and divide us. No, in this system, it isn't any one group of people that sets the rules. It isn't even people. It's corporations that took over the body politic, as I've outlined. So we must unite and fight back against the corporate machines.

We have to once again be their boss, rather than the other way around. We need a human revolution against the machines.

That is why the very first political group I set up was nonpartisan and aimed at the core of the problem—money in politics. That is how corporations were able to seize power, through the use of unlimited money to buy off our government. If you can turn off that spigot, or firehose, of money, then you might be able to regain your government of the people, by the people, for the people. Our representatives must serve the public interest—our interests, not private interests.

In a system built on private financing of politicians, you will always have politicians serving private interests. If, instead, you built a system on public financing of elections, then you might, and likely would, have politicians serving the public interest.

Although the press likes to pretend otherwise, politicians don't usually get into the profession because they can't wait to do good in the world. They largely do it to attain power. It's a turn-on for them. Let's be honest about it. Generally speaking, you don't seek power because you don't want it. So the critical question for our democracy is: Where do politicians get their power?

Because that is what they will serve. They are seekers of power. If you put structural power in the hands of money, then the politicians will serve money. If you put power in the hands of corporations, then the politicians will serve corporations. These are immutable facts of human nature and politics.

That is why my first effort at achieving fundamental change was to reset the system so that it serves the public—i.e., us. If politicians get their power from the public, they will serve the public. We can't afford to be idealistic and naïve and assume that power will voluntarily submit itself to reform. We must take action to change the rules of the game so that power is forced to serve us. That is exactly what democracy was supposed to do—give *power* to the people.

First, the good news—we're going to win. That seems like a pretty significant plot twist after I showed you how thoroughly the machines have taken over. But you'll see that there is a very good reason for my optimism.

Most important, time is on our side. The young are progressive, very progressive. Let me prove it to you in the numbers and then you'll see—holy cow, we're not the underdogs, we're the favorites!

THE TIDE OF HISTORY

Frank Luntz has been the top Republican pollster nearly all my life. He did a poll of young voters in 2016 and came to the conclusion that they were frighteningly liberal! If the top GOP pollster is that afraid of younger voters, that means we're in really good shape. But let me show you how stark the difference is between the different generations of Americans.

Luntz polled eighteen-to-twenty-six-year-olds in 2016, and the numbers were startling. When asked which system of government is most compassionate, 58 percent said socialism! Another 9 percent said communism. Only 33 percent said capitalism.[1] That's two-thirds of younger voters saying they think capitalism sucks. Now, you never see that kind of talk on television because it's run by old people. But if you call yourself a capitalist online, the younger people who are focused there think you're probably a bad person. I should know because I call myself a capitalist. In fact, earlier in the book I made the case for democratic capitalism. But every time I use the word on air now, I have to explain what I mean so younger viewers don't think I'm a monster.

On a more practical level, what party do they identify with? As you might suspect, it is overwhelmingly the Democratic Party. Forty-four percent say they are Democrats. Only 15 percent identify as Republican! Well, what about the rest? Here's how Luntz described it: "The remaining 42% say they're independent, but on issue after issue they lean toward the Democrats."[2]

Oh, my God, about 85 percent of young voters are either Democrats or lean Democratic. Good night, Irene. This thing is over. And it appears it's not even going to be close. I told you, we're the favorites.

Yes, but are they progressive Democrats? Of course! More progressive than any generation before them (also larger than any other generation before them). Who was the politician they liked and respected the most? Bernie Sanders. By a lot. Thirty-one percent of young Americans Luntz polled said they liked him the most. Barack Obama got 18 percent support.[3] Senator Sanders was more popular than every Republican combined!

This is not just theoretical; it translates into real votes in elections. You remember that miracle in Michigan in the 2016 primaries? Bernie was supposed to lose by 21.4 points, according to the average of the polls, but instead he won by 1.4 percent. That's nearly a 23 percent difference. That's gigantic. Do you know how he did that? He got 81 percent of voters aged eighteen to twenty-nine. The progressive Democrat beat the establishment Democrat by a margin of four to one among younger voters!

Luntz is a hard-core, lifelong Republican, and, of course, a capitalist. He was unnerved by the numbers. He explained it this way: "The hostility of young Americans to the underpinnings of the American economy and the American government ought to frighten every business and political leader" and "excite activists for Sanders."[4]

Yep, you should be excited. That's not what just progressives like me think, that's what the top Republican pollster in the country thinks! He thinks Republicans are screwed and progressives are going to dominate American politics for years to come. He explained, "This isn't just a slant toward the Democrats; it's a chasm of disconnection that renders every prominent national Republican irrelevant with the voting bloc that could control campaigns for the next 30 years."[5]

By the way, in that same poll, bankers scored a whopping 2 percent approval rating, elected officials got 4 percent, business leaders got 6 percent, and the media got 7 percent.[6] I know it's hard for them to accept, but for older political and media stalwarts, you have to understand that younger generations are just not that into you. In fact, they think you're pricks who ruined the country.

Have you ever seen these poll numbers in the press? Is it part of conventional wisdom? Probably most of you have never even heard of these startling numbers. Think about it. You think mainstream media are going to tell you that 93 percent of the younger generation hates them and thinks they're full of shit? Of course, they immediately stopped talking about it. My guess is that it is so outside of their experience that they probably didn't even believe it. In their D.C. bubble, the powerful people ruining everything are so revered that it seems unthinkable to them that they are hated by the rest of the country, and particularly the young.

But whether they report it or not, it's still real. And it's still headed in their direction, like a freight train.

Luntz, on the other hand, is a pollster, and part of his job is to warn his side of icebergs. So he would not stop saying how screwed the right wing was:

> The Republican Party doesn't have a problem with younger voters. Younger voters have a problem with the Republican Party, and it is rapidly becoming a long-term electoral crisis. . . .
>
> So while Republicans sling mud and shove their heads in the sand of whatever primary is next, America itself is changing beneath their feet. The younger generation and the Republican Party simply see the world, and America, very differently. . . .
>
> Republicans, ignore this generation at your own peril, because they sure as hell are ignoring you.[7]

Of course, nearly every poll on the issues confirms these findings. When Medicare for All was polled in 2020, 75 percent of eighteen- to thirty-four-year-olds said they wanted it. Though, to be fair, 83 percent of thirty-four- to forty-nine-year-olds also said they wanted it.[8] The age for what is considered a young progressive keeps creeping up every year. In 2020, Bernie Sanders started winning the "under forty-five" category solidly. For example, in the 2020 Michigan primary, Bernie lost the race, but he won eighteen- to forty-four-year-olds by a 22-point margin![9] Is a forty-four-year-old still young? Every year, the progressive contingent gets larger and larger. Soon, we'll have to stop calling them young and start just calling them the general population.

In a 2019 Data for Progress poll, 64 percent of millennials expressed support for the Green New Deal (even after it was pummeled in the traditional press with absurd claims that it would outlaw planes and hamburgers).[10] In a Harvard Institute of Politics poll, 70 percent of eighteen- to twenty-nine-year-old likely voters said they want stricter gun controls.[11] According to a Pew Research Center poll in 2020, 67 percent of eighteen- to twenty-nine-year-olds want universal basic income.[12] That number is only 26 percent for voters above sixty-five years old. Look at that chasm of political ideology. That's a whopping 41-point difference between older and younger voters.

In fact, I think the largest cultural gap in America is not between races, religions, or ethnicities. It's between the old and the young. That's why you're seeing these gigantic differences in how they view the world. And these days forty-five years old is probably a good cutoff for that divide. There's a reason for it—we grew up on different media, so we have completely different cultures. Older generations grew up on television, which is largely pulp. I'm not just being gratuitously insulting, it's the nature of the beast—TV news outlets do very generalized discussions because they're trying to reach a broad cross section of Americans. The younger generation grew up on the internet, where they were constantly looking things up. They're used to googling anything they want. They have access to much more specific information. I guarantee you that the younger generation has much more information about Medicare for All or the Green New Deal than does the older generation, who heard on TV that these programs are scary and are going to cost a lot.

TV talks down to you from the mountaintop. Online communities share information and build engagement with one another. Hence, TV creates a culture that generates reverence for established norms and authority figures. Online media create a culture of independence, self-reliance, and a more egalitarian mindset.

TV also avoids policy discussions because the networks don't want to alienate any of their audience. Online you can get the details of every policy, anytime you want. When they learn the details, no one wants to turn down free health care when it's better coverage and costs the government less. Of course, whenever we talk about generations, we talk in broad strokes. Some of the most progressive people in the country are in the older generations. But generally speaking, if you're an older American getting your news from television, you are likely to be a lot less educated about the issues. Younger generations are more progressive because they have more facts at their disposal.

Also, they didn't get brainwashed by corporate media constantly telling them how great the status quo is. If you take away that gaslighting, no one wants to vote for corporate rule. That's also why the right wing, who also have formed communities online, are now also turning against Big Business. The internet isn't manufacturing consent. For better and for worse, it is manufacturing independent thought. That is very bad news for corporate rule.

Their biggest tool—mainstream media—is breaking down. They aren't able to brainwash people into compliance the way they used to. Change is coming. And then justice.

Yes, but do we see these differences in electoral politics? Absolutely. Here is how Ibram X. Kendi broke down the 2020 Michigan primary in *The Atlantic*:

> When younger Americans did swing to voting in the 2020 Democratic primaries, they usually cast ballots for Sanders by large margins, even in states that Sanders lost by large margins. Take Michigan, where Biden won by nearly 17 points. Sanders won 18-to-24-year-olds by 61 points; 25-to-29-year-olds by 56 points; and 30-to-39-year-olds by 19 points—while losing 40-to-49-year-olds by 6 points; 50-to-64-year-olds by 44 points and voters aged 65 or over by 52 points.[13]

That's within the Democratic Party. Look at those gigantic differences. Now, who do you think is going to win elections in the future? This is not close. We're going to rout them. At this point, conservative voters are holding on to that old canard as their fail-safe escape hatch: it's okay, they think, voters get more conservative as they get older! Do they? Let me show you what the studies say.

First, the power of media and their mythology is overwhelming. Most of you have likely heard some variation of this quote supposedly by Winston Churchill, "Any man who is under thirty, and is not a liberal, has no heart; and any man who is over thirty, and is not a conservative, has no brains." Well, it's not true, in several ways. First, Churchill didn't say it (nor did Victor Hugo or Benjamin Disraeli, to whom it is sometimes attributed). It was French monarchist statesman François Guizot who said, "Not to be a republican at twenty is proof of want of heart; to be one at thirty is proof of want of head."[14] But he was a monarchist. He was also wrong. Studies show that people do not change their political views, in either direction, as they get older.

A fifty-year study of Bennington women showed that "through late childhood and early adolescence, attitudes are relatively malleable . . . with the potential for dramatic change possible in late adolescence or early adulthood. [B]ut greater stability sets in at some early point, and attitudes tend to be increasingly persistent as people age."[15] Two Columbia researchers, Yair Ghitza and Andrew Gelman, conducted a study of generational voting patterns and concluded, "[The perspectives of] generations appear to be formed through a prolonged period of presidential excellence. FDR and the New Deal, Eisenhower, Kennedy and Johnson's Great Society, the Reagan/Bush conservative revolution, and the Clinton years are all characterized by long periods of high approval ratings, each of which steadily pushed the cumulative voting preferences of a generation in one direction or another."[16] Once the political leanings of members of a generation were cemented between the ages of fourteen and twenty-four, they stayed that way throughout their lives. Pew Research Center surveys over the past two decades also have found compelling evidence that generations carry with them the imprint of early political experiences.[17]

Oops. There goes conservatives' only hope for the future. It turns out every study confirms that people do not get more conservative as they get older, they stay with the political ideology they were imprinted with when they were younger. Did you know that a majority of young Americans voted for Republicans in 1988? That was the Alex Keaton generation, and they stayed conservative. Generations that start right wing stay right wing. And ones that start left wing stay left wing. Another fun fact: In a 2011 study, people over sixty-five were the most consistent Republican voters, but people over eighty-five tended to vote Democratic![18] Why? Because they grew up on FDR. And that imprint lasted all the way to 2011!

Funnily enough, there is one other guy who agrees with Frank Luntz—Noam Chomsky.

I interviewed Chomsky in 2020 and found him to be surprisingly upbeat. I asked him both on and off air why he was so seemingly optimistic, a trait he is not well known for. He explained to me that he thought we had moved the ground out from underneath the establishment. He said the younger generations were so progressive that the handwriting was on the wall. He reverted to his trademark pessimism when talking about the current generation in charge. Chomsky said they're hopeless because once their way of thinking is set, it is nearly impossible to move. They are not going to voluntarily cede power or change their minds. But the good news is that now we don't need them to! Because we have already won over the next generation of leaders. That's what four-dimensional chess looks like.

Honestly, that's what I've been preaching on air for a long time, but to have him confirm that notion was like having a weight lifted off my shoulders. Because the establishment gaslights you so much (and I grew up watching television!). You saw poll after poll showing Trump winning the Republican primary in 2016, and the media said he was not going to win. You see politicians take millions of dollars in donations and do exactly what their donors tell them to, and the media tell you that it is not corruption. You see endless polls showing the young are overwhelmingly progressive, and the media tell you it's irrelevant and the progressives will never have power. The gaslighting is so thick you can cut it with a knife.

But now the top Republican pollster *and* probably the smartest man alive are telling you the same thing! You're not the one who took the crazy pill; the younger generations are progressive, and of course they'll take over the country. See, doesn't that feel amazing when you can actually take off the oppressive cloak of misinformation that corporate media surround you in? That's why Public Enemy said, "Don't believe the hype." The people in power now are trying to brainwash you into your own defeat. Because the only way you can lose at this point is if you give up right before victory.

Doesn't it feel good to know you're finally the favorite? It's charming to be the underdog, but at some point, if we don't gain power, we're never going to be able to improve people's lives. Well, it looks like justice is coming. We are going to make people's lives better with higher wages, better health care, and a better planet, and we're going to bring democracy back to this country! And there's nothing the establishment politicians or media can do about it. It's already over, they just don't know it.

TYT—NEW MEDIA

In this book, you have seen over and over again that the media have made all the difference in politics. If the media frame something or somebody in a certain way, that is how they will be perceived—and the contest is lost before it even begins. Because no one can know the facts without the filter of the media. That's where they get their facts, or at least where they get what they think are facts.

All the advantages in the world—having huge name recognition, the voters agreeing with him on nearly all the issues, an energized volunteer base—couldn't help Bernie once mainstream media turned on him with all their fury. Cable news killed progressives in 2020. Sanders had won the first three states in the Democratic primary that year. Normally, this would lead to a massive amount of positive press coverage. Instead, this time, it led to a host of cable news anchors warning of a socialist take-over. But when Biden won his first state, South Carolina, it was a completely different story in the media.

As Caleb Ecarma explained in *Vanity Fair*:

> During the time between polls closing in South Carolina on Saturday and the first poll closures on Super Tuesday, Biden had received nearly $72 million in earned national media coverage, according to data published by the media-tracking service Critical Mention. That Goliath figure did not factor in coverage from local news networks; so his campaign's earned, or free, media could have reached at least $100 million.[19]

Biden only had to spend $2.2 million in Super Tuesday ads because mainstream media gave him a free $100 million in positive coverage. But they claim that they are unbiased! Hilarious.

But wait, let's be fair. How did a mainstream media outlet like CNN treat Senator Sanders after his resounding victory in Nevada? An analysis by *In These Times* revealed, "In the 24 hours following his massive win in Nevada, Sanders received 3.26 times the proportion of negative CNN coverage than Biden did following the latter's South Carolina win—despite the two wins being by similar margins."[20]

CNN then had Democratic House Whip James Clyburn on to say this about Bernie after his Nevada win: "On Super Tuesday, people are concerned about this whole self-proclaimed democratic socialist. Socialism since I was a student in grade school was something that engendered a kind of vociferous reaction among people of a negative nature."[21]

Then, in the same twenty-four-hour period, the blitzkrieg against the outsider continued. Red alert. There is an intruder who has not agreed to corporate rule. We must fight this virus. CNN brought on former Reagan administration official Linda Chavez to say, "But the problem is, the real winner last night I believe was Putin. I mean, we are going to have the most divisive election if Bernie is the nominee."[22] Did they have that talking point ready to go if anyone but Biden won? Trump or Bernie win and you get pundits saying that our enemies are rejoicing. Biden wins and they say America is rejoicing. And none of these opinions by establishment pundits are ever backed up by polling or any other facts—it's just pundits declaring how much Americans love corporate candidates and hate outsiders.

This one is my favorite. CNN's White House correspondent Jeff Zeleny landed an interview with Joe Biden in this same window of time. He asked Biden this hardball question, "[Would] Senator Sanders as the nominee be a McGovern-like mistake for this party?"[23] Don't hurt him, Jeff! Instead of asking a challenging question of Biden, he planted a question so biased against Sanders that Biden didn't have to say anything negative about his opponent. The "unbiased" reporter had already done it for him.

This is not an aberration. Every progressive candidate is painted as an unacceptable, unelectable radical. Every establishment candidate is painted as our savior, who is the only one who can win an election (even though they lose an astounding amount of the time). If you listened to the pundits on cable news saying that only the establishment candidate could beat Trump in 2020, you might have thought Hillary Clinton had won in 2016. Every cable news network from Fox News to MSNBC agrees on one thing—the progressive must not be allowed to win!

If you don't believe me, just tune in the day after any election in America. You will hear all of the anchors/actors blaming progressives, no matter what actually happened. In 2021, they comically did it even after the most establishment candidate of our lifetime, Terry McAuliffe (the protégé of Tony Coelho), lost the governor's race in Virginia. Every network, and especially MSNBC, blamed progressives for the loss. The exact opposite of reality. Their beloved corporate Democrats had to be protected!

Unfortunately, these days, cable news still sets the agenda for the issues everyone else talks about. Now pause for a second to think of a wondrous land where that isn't the case. A place where people get the actual news without a pro-corporate lens to filter it through. A place where they get actual facts, not a mirage that maintains the status quo.

For example, a place where people in news explain that even though Medicare for All costs thirty-two trillion dollars . . . it saves thirty-four trillion dollars. In the land where you only hear the first half of the sentence (America under mainstream media hegemony), you'll vote against Medicare for All even though you would love universal health care. In a land where you hear the whole sentence, the overwhelming majority of the voters would think, "Wait, we all get free health care—better than the coverage we have now—and the country saves two trillion dollars? Where's the question? We should do that right now."

Good news, we're on the road to that new land. Let me show you why.

The average age of a person in America is thirty-eight. You want to know what the average age of a CNN viewer is? Well, that might be a little higher, right? Maybe even a decade older than the average. How about two decades? As they used to yell in the old game shows—higher, higher! It's sixty-four! The average Fox News viewer is sixty-eight! Well, MSNBC is left wing (according to Washington), so it's going to have the younger, hipper audience, right? Wrong. Sixty-eight![24] They're more likely to need hip replacement surgery than actually be hip. The cable news stations are basically doing their shows from senior citizens' centers. The only thing missing is Joe Scarborough yelling, "Bingo!" These audiences are not magically going to get younger. It looks like this thing is over. It's just a matter of time.

Now, do you think young people are going to, all of a sudden, discover the *CBS Evening News* and start watching mainstream media? Everyone reading this, even the old guard in D.C., knows there is approximately zero percent chance of that happening. Quick, who is the *CBS Evening News* anchor? My guess is the great majority of you, if not all of you, are scratching your heads wondering who it is. I don't know, either. And I didn't even bother looking it up because it's so irrelevant.

Remember when the *CBS Evening News* anchor was Dan Rather? Everyone knew the answer immediately back then. Now, if you're wondering which is the last news network Dan Rather worked for, you might be surprised to find out it was TYT. We not only have all the dynamic new anchors, we even got the best of the old school. All the real journalists are now in independent media; only the actors are left on network and cable news.

If you think that's too harsh, quick, name the last story any prominent news anchor broke on television. A story that challenged people in power. I can show you dozens we broke at *TYT* and David Sirota broke at *The Lever* and Ryan Grim broke at *The Intercept*. Tons of stories challenging the powerful and showing their wrongdoing. Why do you think they don't break that kind of story on cable news when they have all the resources in the world? Because they don't want to challenge the powerful. They are the powerful.

But now they're screwed. New media has all the younger viewers. The idea that my kids would watch cable news is hilarious. They have never heard of the letters M-S-N-B-C in that sequence. They were babies when

I worked there, and now, when would they have occasion to watch it? Since we cut the cord, the only place they could find MSNBC is on the YouTube TV app. But why on God's green earth would they go there to watch a bunch of old people talk about politics when they could just look up any fact they want online? I just asked them the other day about the broadcast networks, and they had no idea what a CBS was. They asked if it was a pharmacy.

Now, who do you think owns the future? I showed you how progressive the younger generations are in the political context. This is also true in the media context. Younger generations watch progressive programming. And that's not a coincidence. You are what you watch. If you watch Fox News, you become a cantankerous old man (happened to a couple of family friends, which was a sad sight to see). If you watch YouTube and TikTok, you're likely to be a progressive. And you're very unlikely to hate gay people or minorities.

I know conservatives can't stand that. So they launched a number of well-funded shows on the social media platforms, but they are swimming against an enormous tide. Yes, they now have a handful of popular right-wing shows that prominently spit out hate on a regular basis. But overall, the blue wave in digital media is so gigantic that they just can't get people to hate each other based on race anymore. It's deeply frustrating to them. How will they convince young people to vote for tax cuts for the rich now?!

Well, they won't be able to. In fact, young people aren't just progressive, they are socialists. And they hate corporate rule! Who could blame them? It's ruined their lives.

In 2019, YouGov/Victims of Communism Memorial Foundation conducted a poll about different economic models. Given the name of the organization that worked with YouGov on this poll, I don't know what their expectations were, but they were likely very disappointed in the results. It turns out that 70 percent of millennials said they would be somewhat or extremely likely to vote for a socialist.[25] That was 30 to 40 points higher than older generations! That's not a little difference. That's a tsunami.

Axios explained, "50% of millennials and 51% of Generation Z have a somewhat or very unfavorable view of capitalism—increases of 8 and 6 percentage points from last year. Meanwhile, the share of millennials who say they are 'extremely likely' to vote for a candidate who identifies as a socialist doubled."[26]

How does it feel to be the favorites? All my life, mainstream media told me that capitalism was God's gift to humanity. I still don't call myself a socialist, but I'm not in the younger generation. I grew up on television and *The New York Times.* As I said earlier, I was "programmed" to believe in the established system. But the younger generation didn't grow up with those media! They grew up with us.

The Young Turks has been around for twenty-one years. We are the longest-running daily live show in internet history. We were the first partner channel for YouTube, in 2006. We are the original YouTubers. And we were among the first partners for Facebook as well. We average three hundred million to five hundred million views a month. We have twenty-one million subscribers and have amassed twenty-two billion views over the lifetime of the network.

I don't know if we had a significant role in helping those younger generations become progressive or if we just rode an existing wave. Probably a little bit of both. When you have views approaching three times the global population, you probably had an impact. We hit the establishment hard enough to leave a mark.

But whether it was partly us or just the tide of history, the result is the same either way. With this kind of progressive media dominating in viewership among millennials and Gen Z, corporate rule is toast. Go ahead, try to get them to vote for corporate tax cuts or deregulation of the oil industry. Good luck to you, you're going to need it.

As hard as it is for progressives to move the older generations, it will be just as hard for conservatives or corporate goons to move the younger generations.

We're not out of the woods yet. The problem is that the only people left who still trust mainstream media are the exact people we need to finish the revolution against our corporate overlords—Democratic primary voters. Progressives could shred Republicans if we could just get past the corporate Democrats. I'll explain why in a little bit. But corporate media still have a headlock on those older Democratic voters. Only 14 percent of Republicans have a fair or great deal of confidence in mainstream media. Only 27 percent of independents do. But 70 percent of Democrats still believe in mainstream media.[27] And those voters bottle up the one political force in the country we need most—progressives. Once younger voters breach that wall, this whole thing is over. Progressives are coming. And so is justice.

I have to thank mainstream media, though; if they had not left this giant part of the population unaddressed, we never could have had the success we did at *TYT*. They never believed in serving progressive viewers. There was this hilarious mythology when I first got started in media that liberals weren't successful on air because they didn't know how to be entertaining. Yes, they said this at the same time they said all of Hollywood is liberal. Remember, conservative talking points go completely unchecked in mainstream media. You want to know the real reason there were no big progressive talk shows at the time? Because they didn't let us on the air!

Conservatives now complain about being shadow-banned by social media platforms. That's more whining to the refs, and they have never proven one instance of it. Meanwhile, progressives have been shadow-banned from traditional media for decades. Yet no one talks about that phenomenon. You never heard about the ban because the people who were banned were never allowed on air to tell you about it. In fact, I have been told by several producers and bookers that I'm personally banned right now from CNN and MSNBC. That isn't some esoteric shadow ban. That's corporate executives making a willful decision that they won't let me on their air. These cable news stations are bureaucratic labyrinths, so I don't know if it's a hard ban from those networks, but I do know for a fact that bookers at several shows on both networks have said recently that when they tried to book me, management prevented it. Why? Intruder alert. A strong progressive is a real danger to the system.

And remember, when I was on MSNBC, they wanted to move me out of prime time because I was criticizing the establishment too much. Again, not a shadow ban but a real one. Progressives are an actual danger to the system. Not because we hate democracy, but because we love it.

But when digital media came along, there were no gatekeepers. There was no one to ban us. So progressives stormed the castle. Shows like ours got an enormous market share of viewers because the field was wide open. In a lot of ways, it still is. There are tons of organic, online shows that are progressive, including one of the most popular shows on Twitch, run by my nephew and former *TYT* host, Hasan Piker. But outside of TYT, there are still no major companies that carry an authentic progressive message. Why? Because corporations can't help themselves. They immediately rush to serve other corporations (advertisers and sponsors) and immediately lose all credibility with younger viewers. The internet—where corporate propaganda goes to die.

For example, *TYT* did thirty-four videos about Alexandria Ocasio-Cortez before she won her primary. At that point, she hadn't yet defeated Joe Crowley in one of the most stunning upsets in American history. So mainstream media had done almost no stories on her. We did more segments on her than the rest of media combined—and tripled. I did a segment called "Alexandria the Great." At that point, she was a bartender and everyone in D.C. thought she had absolutely no chance of winning. How did we know? Because when we say we are connected to younger viewers and voters, we aren't bluffing. Digital media are so much more interactive than traditional media. We hear from our audience all the time—and we actually listen. So we have an enormous advantage in being able to know what they think before the elections come around.

In fact, I predicted on air in 2013 that Bernie Sanders could beat Hillary Clinton in 2016. At the time, everyone thought that was just nuts. Again, how did I know? How could I have known Bernie was going to run a great campaign that nearly pulled off the impossible? Because it didn't depend on whether he ran a great campaign. I knew that all a progressive had to do was raise their hand and people would flock to them. That's because I had already read all the polls showing how progressive the country was, and I knew that younger voters were just waiting for a progressive candidate to be their champion.

If you remember, in 2016, Bernie wasn't the only one running against Clinton. There was a smooth-talking corporate politician named Martin O'Malley. Mainstream media thought he had a much better chance than Sanders. Oops. He was younger, good looking, and had all the other superficial attributes that mainstream media think are important. It was unclear whether he used English Leather, but he might have! So why didn't young people flock to him? Because they didn't want another corporate phony, they wanted a progressive! If you were in old media, you would have never seen that coming—and they didn't. But if you live in new media, you could see it coming from a mile away, or perhaps three years away.

Frank Luntz is right. Noam Chomsky is right. We were right when we predicted the rise of AOC, Bernie Sanders, and the Justice Democrats. In fact, I don't even know how corporate media can turn it around. How is Wolf Blitzer going to convince younger voters who love socialism that corporate rule is in their best interests? I'll let you take a minute with that one, too. Good luck, Wolf.

Go ahead, tell younger voters that they should vote for older, corporate-funded politicians because they smell like Aqua Velva and women find that sexy. I dare you.

Corporate media have no idea what's about to hit them. With progressive networks like TYT, progressive shows like *The Young Turks, The Damage Report, Indisputable,* and thousands of young progressives broadcasting from their own homes on social media, the future is all ours.

TYT now has everything from a twenty-four-hour channel on platforms like Roku, Pluto, Xumo, Samsung, and YouTube TV to one-minute videos on TikTok, Snapchat, and Instagram. Not to mention our dominance on YouTube and Facebook, which we have maintained for about a decade and a half now. It'll take corporate media executives years, if not decades, to learn what we already know about digital media. And by that point, they'll have run out of time.

There is one last nail in corporate media's coffin. Traditional media talk down to their audience. They are on the mountaintop, and their job is to push the information down to you. But in new media, people pull the information toward them. They don't tune in, they look up. They look up information. They browse shows until they find one that makes sense for them. Two-thirds of the country is progressive, so now when they have an opportunity to watch anything they like, they watch progressives. Before, the box in the corner of your living room spoon-fed you corporate marketing. But now the screen in front of you has liberated you rather than trapped you.

Yes, sometimes that liberation has led to madness. QAnon also flourished in this environment. But what you never heard in traditional media—because they despise their competitors in digital media—is that a giant community of progressives has also flourished. Since mainstream media have banished us, they don't realize that we are the new silent majority. We're not at all silent online, but we are silent in establishment media because they purposely shut down our voices. While they were adamantly not paying attention, we built an armada in their backyard. Since progressives are invisible to them, they're never going to see us coming.

TYT understood this dynamic from day one. We have always told our audience, "We're not The Young Turks. You're The Young Turks." Without their support, we would have never existed in the first place. We had no money, no marketing, and no infrastructure to support us. We would have collapsed if the audience didn't carry us on their shoulders. So, we don't represent ourselves, we represent them. And in new media, if we stop representing them, they'll stop watching. That's exactly how it should be.

Now, how are you going to stop a media organization that based its whole model on what the audience wanted? We even hire from our audience. Half our hosts and dozens of our employees are from our audience. We *are* our audience. That's unstoppable.

When we needed to build a studio, we asked our audience for money for construction. They gave us $400,000. When we wanted to hire reporters, they gave us $2 million. When we told them about a new political group called Justice Democrats, they gave them $2.5 million. When we needed money to keep all our employees at the beginning of Covid, they gave us another $2 million.

How are you going to stop a network that is of the audience, by the audience, and for the audience? You're not. We're coming and we're bringing justice with us.

PAC ATTACK

Yes, we have the future on our side. But how about today? We still have to win elections now. I mentioned earlier that progressives could beat Republicans if we could get into general-election matchups with them. How? Because we're willing to fight fire with fire. And fight money with money.

Money has the same exact role in politics as it does in life. It is an essential tool, but people forget that money is supposed to be a means to accomplish an end, not an end in itself. As you saw in chapter 4, this is exactly what happened to the Democratic Party. Its leaders started by taking corporate money so that they could win elections. Then they became so obsessed with raising money that they didn't notice that they were losing a lot more elections in this system than they had in the past. They had agreed to a rigged game against themselves without realizing it. Why? They became obsessed with corporate money and forgot the original goal—winning elections and passing progressive laws.

But if you know that lesson and you're careful not to be seduced by money, then you can use money as the powerful tool it was intended to be, rather than being used by it. What does it mean to be careful? You can't just hope that people remember not to get infatuated with money—that would be a very poor strategy. No, you have to build it into your systems. At Justice Democrats (JD), the most important decision we made was to say that none of our candidates were allowed to take corporate money. That doesn't mean you run elections on no money—that would be impossible. You couldn't hire any staff; you couldn't let anyone know what your positions are. So of course it's okay to take small-dollar donations— those donors are the people you're supposed to be representing anyway.

By getting the right amount of attention to our candidates, we wound up raising millions for the first cycle for Justice Democrats. That was enough seed money to get four wins out of seventy-eight campaigns. Doesn't sound like much, but that was a hell of a four who won: Alexandria Ocasio-Cortez, Rashida Tlaib, Ilhan Omar, and Ayanna Pressley. We also saw three sitting members of Congress declare themselves as Justice Democrats, who subsequently won their races: Ro Khanna, Raúl Grijalva, and Pramila Jayapal. In the 2020 cycle, we added Cori Bush and Jamaal Bowman. In 2022, Summer Lee and Greg Casar joined their forces. Those are some of the most forceful voices in American politics today. Why were the Justice Democrats so strong compared to other Democratic politicians? Because they didn't have to check with lobbyists every time they made a statement. It's not hard to fight for the people if no one is stopping you. The whole point of corporate cash is to stop you.

This grassroots funding has changed the whole pay-to-play dynamic. Bernie Sanders's two presidential campaigns proved that small-dollar fundraising could bring in enough money to make you competitive in American politics. In 2016, he raised a stunning $228 million. And he famously raised it $27 at a time. In 2020, he raised an even more stunning $211 million—even though there were twenty-seven other candidates in the race! This ability to raise record numbers from the grass roots— without needing corporate money—changes the whole game.

Now, a giant number of small donations can beat a small number of giant donations. In fact, in the Democratic primary, Bernie outraised everyone in 2020. The trick is to be able to congregate all those small-dollar donors effectively in one place. When you have a presidential contest, that's easier. Why? Because presidential campaigns give progressives what they have needed and been missing the most—media coverage. That's our number-one problem. Since the mainstream media almost never legitimize or cover progressives, voters who would have supported progressive candidates never even get to find out about them. This is especially true in local and state races, where media tend to favor incumbents and the status quo. That's also why new-media outlets like TYT are so important. We let people know about Bernie and Justice Democrats, and they raised millions from our audience. If we still only had traditional media, that would have been a lot less coverage and a lot less money for progressive candidates.

Also, in presidential contests, there is usually one unifying candidate—so you know who to give the money to. In other races, before Justice Democrats came along, how did anyone ever find out who was the progressive in the race? Well, they had to do painstaking online research and hope that the source they found was credible and had led them to the right candidate. That makes it much harder to give and less likely that people will fork over their hard-earned money to a candidate they never heard of and are not completely sure is on their side.

This is why the new progressive PACs are so important. When we started Justice Democrats, nobody had ever heard of it, of course. But now it has received hundreds of millions of dollars in free media because of our spectacular wins—and the impact those legislators have made. Now it has momentum of its own. If someone is a Justice Democrat, you know they have been vetted—they're a real progressive and they're clean! Since they don't take corporate money, the small donor has more peace of mind that the candidate is not going to turn around and screw them like a regular politician. There have only been a couple of electoral cycles since its founding, but needless to say, JD's fundraising has gotten significantly better in each cycle. In politics, branding is everything. They can't vote for you if they don't know your name. They can't support a political group if they've never heard of it. Now we're in much better shape on this count, because not only do we have our own media, but we have also hacked into the mainstream media through our electoral successes and political showdowns.

For example, on *The View,* Whoopi Goldberg was mad about the sit-in that AOC had done in Nancy Pelosi's office on her first day in Congress to draw attention to the Green New Deal. Whoopi loves establishment Democrats, and to be fair to her, she is very wealthy, so she probably doesn't want any change. She said about the sit-in, "You can't come in and pee all over everything."[28] That basically compares us to wild animals. Imagine if a progressive had said that about Nancy Pelosi or Joe Biden or Barack Obama. All of media would have talked about it for years. But you can say anything you want about progressives on TV.

But that's not why I bring this up. Whoopi also had my favorite line about Justice Democrats in that same episode. She said, "Are you saying that other Democrats, who've been fighting for twenty-five, thirty years, aren't Justice Democrats?" Yes, that's exactly what I'm saying. Because as I showed you in chapter 4, the other Democrats have not been fighting for justice at all for the last thirty years. But I loved the branding! Say it loud, say it proud. I gave Justice Democrats that name because we are for social justice, economic justice, legal justice, and political justice. Every time someone in mainstream media says the name of the group, it reinforces that progressives are the ones fighting for all that justice.

Then there are right-wing media. I remember one segment on Fox News where Sean Hannity put up a list of priorities for Justice Democrats. He was trying to make fun of us, but God, it looked good! He was telling everyone how we were trying to raise their wages and give them better health care. Even conservative media are now accidentally doing free publicity for us. One conservative video "charged" that I was the mastermind behind trying to get everyone free health care! I've never been prouder. Who needs a publicist when you have the other side marketing you that well?

Even with the sneering mainstream media, every time they say that we can't afford another program that Justice Democrats are proposing in Congress, they are doing us a favor. Every time Jake Tapper tells you that we can't afford higher wages for you, but we can afford every imaginable war, he gets us another voter.

Can PACs make a difference? Hell, yes. Can we really win? Remember, we already did! Everyone in the establishment was enormously skeptical when we first started JD. When AOC was running against Joe Crowley, one of his aides, Lauren French, was asked if AOC could beat her boss. French said with a sneer, "She'll get ten percent and get a job with *The Young Turks*."[29] I'm happy to report that AOC does not have a job with *The Young Turks,* because she took Crowley's job. We have already had spectacular wins. We have already pulled off some of the most stunning upsets in American history. This is not theoretical, they're in Congress right now. There are already eleven Justice Democrats in the House in 2022. And more are on the way.

Well, can these PACs stay true? Yes, but only if you set the right rules. If you were a purist who said we shouldn't have set up Justice Democrats because it required a PAC, you would have cost us absolutely critical victories. If you say our side shouldn't take corporate money because it corrupts, that is exactly right. But if you say our side shouldn't take any money, that doesn't make any sense. How would we have the resources to run campaigns? In fact, the people who tell you progressives shouldn't take any money are either incredibly naïve or right-wingers who are trying to trick you into giving away all your power.

Money is just a tool. But it is an important tool, especially if you want to win elections.

Now, progressives have one more advantage here. We can pool our resources for a smaller number of candidates. ExxonMobil has to spend its money on hundreds of corrupt corporate politicians. For progressives, there aren't that many of us running for national office (at least for now). There were only eight JD candidates for national office in 2020. It is easier to support that number with the financial resources at our disposal. It was so doable, nearly half won. And, of course, the best example was Bernie Sanders. There were over twenty corporate candidates in 2020, but there was only one Bernie. That is the main reason why he outraised them all. Corporations and the wealthy had to spread their money around and cover their bets; we just had to give to our one true champion.

I hope this won't last. Soon there will be a tsunami of progressive candidates. Some will be backed by JD and many others won't. That's part of the reason I started Rebellion PAC.

Justice Democrats is meant to save the Democratic Party. Rebellion PAC is meant to save progressives. Wolf-PAC is meant to save democracy. That's why Wolf-PAC is the most important, but it's nonpartisan, so let's discuss it last. Justice Democrats is the pirate ship that was meant to board the Democratic aircraft carrier and take it over at the national level. So far, so good. Rebellion PAC was founded to make sure excellent progressive candidates throughout the country have a fighting chance.

Now, of course, even Rebellion PAC (RP) can't give to every progressive running everywhere, but there are many other things we can do. Because we are not connected to any particular legislator, we can run any damn ad we like. Candidates don't just get JD's endorsement, they become Justice Democrats. That has an enormous upside in building the brand, but it has the downside of making the group a tad more cautious. People in

Washington don't think JD is playing it safe; it's already more aggressive than any other PAC. But wait till they get a load of the Rebellion.

In any given campaign, RP will have no qualms about running the most vicious ads you've ever seen. We have no reason to hold back in calling out corporate Democrats for the corrupt toadies that they are. They're not our colleagues. They are our primary opponents. Literally. That's who we face off against in primaries. We have to get through the corporate Democrats to get to the Republicans. If they're standing in our way, we will rip them down.

This is when the genteel crowd in Washington cries, "That's not civil!" I'm amused by their crocodile tears. They will use corporate media to viciously tear down any opponent, especially progressives. They are the masters of character assassination and dirty tricks. But the minute anyone fights back, they'll use their buddies in the mainstream press to cry and cry. Let those tears pour out, we need to fill our cup tonight. If you're going to work for the corporations shredding our democracy and ruining our country, then you'll excuse us if we don't give a fuck about your feelings.

A giant difference between us and establishment candidates is that we don't lie. They lie with reckless abandon about their opponents. In 2020, Democrat Richard Neal's campaign mounted a vicious slander campaign against his JD opponent in the primary, Alex Morse. They had a former staffer intimate that Alex was trying to pick up young men from college. It was a horribly homophobic line of attack without a shred of truth to it. *The Intercept* uncovered the messages that showed that these former staffers planned the character assassination and how they got the mainstream media to play along. If Rebellion PAC has enough money next time there's a progressive running against him, we will run literally dozens of ads telling you about how Representative Neal, when he was chairman of the House Ways and Means committee, sold out his own voters on behalf of his donors because he is one of the most corrupt men in American politics. And the upside of all those ads will be that they are true!

Isn't it amazing that you've probably never seen a political ad in your life calling out the corruption of politicians when we live in a country that has systematically legalized and industrialized corruption? That's because there are no corporate donors willing to fund ads about the corruption of other corporate candidates. You might think that's obvious, but remember that these would have been the best ads for Democrats to run against Republicans in general elections. Your whole life you've seen Democrats run incredibly weak campaigns when they could have eviscerated the GOP on its corruption. Republicans obviously work for Big Business. But Democrats never said it because they also took money from Big Business!

The genius of corporate donations is that they not only corrupt Democrats but also get them to disarm and not use their best weapon against Republicans. When you fund really strong Republicans and tell the Democrats they're not allowed to fight back, you'll have a government completely controlled by corporate interests. And that's exactly what happened.

Well, we don't take money from corporations, so we're going to say it. We're going to talk about the issue that resonates most with the American people—and that a government and media completely owned by Big Business kept from you for all these years—corruption!

And we're not just going to say it in Democratic primaries, we're going to say it very loudly in general elections against Republicans! Finally, you'll have Democrats who are not afraid to call out the other side, very, very forcefully. No more Joe Donnellys and Claire McCaskills playing patty-cake with the other side as we get handed one loss after another. This time we rip their face off. We do that politically, of course, not physically. We're not right-wingers.

If you're a mainstream media reporter reading this, you're weeping right now. You are ready to write a scathing column about how uncivil we progressives are. What do you think Republicans have been doing to us for our whole lives? They have said the most vicious things about the left while the press did nothing. You gave them a free ride as they called us baby killers, Castro/Stalin/Mao, satanic, and everything else they could imagine. So you'll excuse me if I don't give a shit about your delicate sensibilities.

And remember the mainstream media are liars—they don't actually care about civility. Again, they take for granted that Republicans will bash Democrats viciously. The media never called them out as the monsters they are for saying all these outrageous things. They made it seem normal. They only pretend to care about civility if anyone on the left ever fights back.

I'll give you an example of how feckless Democrats have been since they put the corporate shackles on. Rick Scott oversaw the largest Medicare fraud in American history when he ran Columbia/HCA. He had a lame excuse that as CEO he didn't know anything that was happening in his company, including billions it had stolen from the American government. Yes, billions. The company had to pay a $1.7 billion fine, which is likely to be a small fraction of what it made robbing us. You can tell how much it had left over after the robbery because Scott got a $10 million golden parachute over five years and $300 million in stock and options.[30] That was for a robbery well done!

Mind you, these are facts. The company was found guilty of fourteen felony counts of fraud. The company's leaders definitely did it. They had two different sets of books—so they knew exactly what they were doing. They targeted American taxpayers as suckers they could easily steal from. But comically, in our system, there was no one person who was held responsible. It was as if the machine ran itself. If that's true, that's even more scary. But either way, someone had to program the machine to rob us. Obviously, the CEO would be the main culprit. Rick Scott says he didn't know what was happening inside his own company—is that why they paid him over $300 million? As you can clearly tell, I think Senator Scott is a degenerate crook, but my editors would like me to remind you for the third time that he was not technically convicted of this crime. So, the company is guilty, but theoretically no one at the company did it. The machines are almost laughing at us now.

Why in the world would the Democrats not make a big deal out of this when Scott was running for office? Rick Scott won the governor's office in Florida—twice! Now he's a senator, and in 2022 he was the head of the National Republican Senatorial Committee, the primary campaign funding and organizational center for Republican senatorial candidates. Jesus, establishment Democrats suck! They couldn't fight a Republican if their life depended on it. And their political life actually does. They still get slaughtered.

Why didn't they hammer Scott on being a giant crook? Because it would have offended their own corporate donors. In a sense, Democrats are paid to lose. That's their role under corporate rule. And unfortunately, they play it well.

So what would Rebellion PAC have done differently if we were involved in those campaigns (as we just might be when Scott runs for a second term)? We would have run endless ads calling Scott *the biggest crook in American history*. Since he was the head of the company that literally did the largest Medicare fraud in history, there is excellent proof for our claim. The amount of money he has stolen would make Al Capone blush.

He is not rich because he's smart or accomplished. He's rich because his company stole from you, and he used the hundreds of millions he got from them to evade justice. He is literally one of the most immoral people in the whole country. Every time you see his face, you should think of a dirty crook who robbed your grandmother in the middle of the night. Because that's who this lowlife is.

We would have repeated that so often that the voters of Florida would have asked us to please stop telling us about how big a crook Scott is; they would have said, "Please, we get it! He is the biggest crook there ever was. We can't take it anymore. You've bludgeoned this guy. Of course, no one is going to vote for him, just please stop hurting him already." Good, mission accomplished.

This is when some loser Democratic consultant will tell you that is not a good strategy because voters don't like candidates who are mean. Really? Because I could swear Donald Trump was president.

Secondly, Rebellion PAC isn't a candidate. We're going to run those ads no matter what. Our job is to destroy Republican candidates, whether the weaklings in the Democratic Party like it or not. Nominate a progressive and I guarantee you Rebellion will pulverize their opponent.

I look forward to Republicans crying about how we're too mean to them. For that alone, you should go donate to rebellionpac.com right now. Rebellion PAC—we make Republicans cry.

That's supposed to be normal politics, and it is what Republicans do all the time. But if you're a Democrat who grew up on the gentle whispers of NPR, you're probably aghast right now. "We're the good guys, we're supposed to lose gently and politely," the *New York Times* reader mumbles to himself. Yeah, agree to disagree.

Remember, all our lives depend on the outcomes of these elections. Forty-five thousand people a year die because they don't have health insurance.[31] The feelings of Republican politicians are far lower on my priority list.

But that's not all Rebellion is going to do. We're also going to meticulously study digital ads. We're going to be smarter than the other guys and absolutely master digital advertising. Our executive director is Brianna Wu, who is a nationally recognized software engineer and a professional tech commentator for over a decade on 5by5, Relay FM, and TWiT. I started a digital media company that knows a thing or two about how to win online. The political world is still slow to adapt to the online world. There is a reason for that: consultants usually get paid 15 percent of the "ad buy" of a candidate. When you have corrupt consultants advising you, they tell you that you should do a lot of expensive television advertising and as much mainstream media as you can. Why? Precisely because it's expensive! They're getting 15 percent of every dollar your campaign spends on ads, so they want you to spend as much money as possible on expensive ads.

Without those constraints, we are going to be hyper efficient in how we spend our money. Our job is to find the most efficacious ways to utilize resources for the maximum number of wins. Progressives don't have enough money to waste any of it. We don't allow corruption. And we're on a mission. If we raise enough money to be able to solve online advertising—a very solvable equation—we're going to mercilessly use that advantage. Supreme Court decisions have allowed endless money into politics. So, we're going to use the weakness that corruption naturally creates against itself.

Once word gets out that Rebellion PAC runs devastating campaigns against crooked, corporate politicians, my guess is that we're going to raise a lot of money. Imagine what we could do if we attracted the giant number of small-dollar donors that Bernie found, but used it to win dozens, and maybe hundreds, of races across the country instead of using it on just one presidential race. I guarantee you that if Rebellion had the $211 million that Bernie raised in 2020, we would have literally dozens more progressives in Congress.

Don't get me wrong, that doesn't mean you shouldn't give in presidential races or to an amazing, transformational campaign like Bernie's. It just means that you'd be amazed and thrilled to know what that money could do in other contexts. If you're skeptical that a new group can make that much of a difference, well, that's exactly what people said about Justice Democrats just five years ago.

If we do this right, when a corrupt candidate sees the headline THE REBELLION HAS JOINED THE RACE, they're going to shake in their boots. Imagine you're a Republican and you were planning to run against a soft establishment Democrat—and knew that they were barely going to lay a glove on you—and instead you get a populist progressive who is pledging to fight for the people and they're backed by the toughest PAC in the world. Trust me, they're going to be concerned. They'd much rather go against the patsies. Instead, now they have to brace for impact. For the

first time in their political lives, they know they're going to get brutalized by the other side. Imagine Republicans being scared of Democrats!

By the end, they're going to say that it's not fair. Our ads are too hard
hitting. We're too good at targeting voters. We're too good at tech. They'll
even wonder if they can shut us down because we have too many unfair
advantages. And best of all, by the end, they're going to try to get money
out of politics just so they can get *our* money out of politics.

Which leads us to Wolf-PAC.

BEST FOR LAST

Wolf-PAC doesn't lead to progressive dominance, it leads to something
better—a combined nation, once again. The value of conservatives and
progressives working together is immeasurable. It doesn't just fix our
most important political problem, it begins to fix our culture. Because
for the first time in a long time, we will be genuinely working with each
other instead of against each other.

Wait a minute! You just read a minute ago that I started a PAC to kick
Republican ass. Why would you believe that I want to work with Republicans? There are several excellent answers to that question.

First, remember that the objective is not some partisan bullshit where
one team wins and the other one loses. I don't care about the teams. And
establishment Democrats probably hate me more than Republicans do.
The groups I've set up affect Democratic incumbents more than anyone
else. As I just explained, in order for Rebellion PAC to defeat Republicans,
it first has to defeat Democratic incumbents in primaries. We're equal-
opportunity ass kickers. I don't care what logo is on your helmet. In fact,
if the parties switched brands and Republicans became the clean, uncor-
rupted party, I would vote for them. For partisans, that's heresy! Who
cares about the fricking names? What a silly, insubstantial thing to stake
your life and career on.

Also, remember that the parties have switched positions completely
before. The Republicans were the ones who fought against slavery and
the Democrats used to be the racist party. When they switched positions
after the Southern Strategy, were people supposed to stay in the Republican Party out of loyalty even though they made an active decision to be
the racist party? So, it's obvious that party loyalty is ridiculous. It's for

children who don't care about policy. Progressives definitely care about policy!

Now, is there any hint that Republicans are becoming the better party or the less corrupted party? Hell, no. Not even close. That's why I'm against them now. But I'm also against the 90 percent of the Democratic Party who are just as corrupt as they are. This is part of why some conservatives trust me more—I'm clearly not bullshitting them, and I really hate corruption in *both* parties.

If you think Wolf-PAC is a trick just to help Democrats, just ask Democratic leadership what they think of it. They'll tell you that they hate us. And then they'll prove it by spending money against us and using their buddies in the corporate press to attack us. It's not theoretical, it's already happened many times.

Wolf-PAC has twenty-five thousand volunteers and two very poorly paid full-time employees. The leaders of Wolf-PAC are literally mechanics and electrical company workers and nurses. None of them ever worked in politics before. They are desperately trying to end corruption and bring Republican and Democratic voters together, in an incredibly noble way. Have you ever read one positive piece about them?

Well, maybe that's because they are ineffective? No, they've already had their resolution pass in three states. The Wolf-PAC resolution calls for a convention to get money out of politics. They've also passed this resolution in twenty different statehouses, three of which were Republican controlled. How many other resolutions in the last decade have passed in both blue and red legislatures? Very, very few. The cause of ending corruption is the one thing that brings everyone together. And when the grass roots from both sides put pressure on, their state legislators listen.

In fact, there are 7,383 state legislators in the country. Over 1,100 of them have indicated that they are committed or lean toward supporting Wolf-PAC's resolution. Of those, 833 are Democrats, but 303 of them are Republicans. That's actual bipartisanship. Lately, Republican legislators are signing up at a quicker rate than Democrats. I'm not sure I've ever seen state legislators working together across party lines as well as this.

In all that time, the only articles written about Wolf-PAC were almost all negative. Gee, I wonder which side the press is on? Remember, it isn't about Republicans or Democrats, it's about corporate or noncorporate. I have seen the establishment press write endless glowing pieces about Republican politicians—but only if they are corporate Republicans. If a Republican is a populist, they'll get shredded. If there is anything the American press despises, it's a populist.

So, if Wolf-PAC is working in a bipartisan way, then why am I so adamantly against the Republican Party? As I explained in chapter 3, there are social issues that are nonnegotiable, and I am 100 percent opposed to Republicans' positions on them. I'm not going to agree to be discriminated against, or to have others discriminated against. But just as important, the Republican Party right now is even more corrupt than the Democratic Party. If you're a Republican and you're skeptical, go ahead, ask any national politician on your side if they'll turn down corporate PAC money so they can represent only your interests, and they'll throw you out of their office. They pleasure corporations for a living. At the national level, the GOP is nearly 100 percent corrupt.

Ironically, a guy I disagree with on almost all the issues, and one I recently had an on-air shouting match with, is the one guy on the other side who prevents me from saying *all* Republican politicians on the national level are corrupt. The Republican who doesn't take any PAC money is . . . Matt Gaetz.

And guess what he proposed after the Republicans won the House back in 2022? Four anticorruption bills, including a lifetime ban on national politicians becoming lobbyists. I completely agree with that! We can disagree on everything else, but if someone doesn't take corporate PAC money, they're honest. They might be honestly awful, but at least they're honest. And wouldn't it be amazing if we agreed to fight corruption together?

I know that a lot of Democrats who just read that threw up in their mouths a little. And tons of people on the left will say they wouldn't work with someone like Gaetz on principle. But you'd work with sellout corporate politicians who pretend to be on our side and then kill off all our policies in the middle of the night? When you say you won't work with people on the other side—*even if they agree with you*—you're saying that the divide-and-conquer strategy of the establishment worked.

In a democracy, you're supposed to disagree. So let's get our democracy back and then beat Matt Gaetz in a fair fight.

The great majority of Republican politicians take tons of corporate cash and are deeply corrupt. But remember, their voters aren't! Yes, I have massive disagreements with their voters, too, but at least they're not crooks. They have no incentive to be. Nobody is bothering to bribe them, and they're getting screwed as hard as we are. And, as I said earlier, Republican voters seem to hate corruption even more than Democratic voters (probably because they listen to mainstream media less).

So, no matter how much I disagree with you on other things, if you're clean, I'm willing to work with you to end corruption and bring our democracy back. We're not going to resolve culture war issues overnight, but we can easily have bipartisan agreement against corruption. And by bipartisan, I don't mean the Washington definition, where corporate Republicans and corporate Democrats agree to screw over the rest of us. I mean actual bipartisan voter agreement. Every poll indicates we already agree on this issue! Polls show that over three-quarters of the country thinks money corrupts politicians and we should get it out of politics! Real people on the left and the right already agree, they just don't know it because of the oppressive cloak of corporate media. We just have to get past the culture war issues that the media engage in to distract us from the political issues that matter most. The last thing they want is for us to realize that we can work together on this.

Here the right-wing media are more guilty than even the corporate media. Why do conservative media try so hard to get you to care about the tiny number of trans students who are participating in high school sports? Even if you're outraged by that, it's a minuscule issue that affects a relative handful of people in the whole country. They want their audience to concentrate on that tiny issue because they desperately need to distract right-wing voters from the thing they care most about—draining the swamp. They know how much their own viewers care about that, and they also know that almost every Republican politician is corrupt, so they have to distract you!

Ted Cruz took thirteen million dollars from a Wall Street banker in the 2016 election. Isn't it weird that faux-populist Fox News never told you that? Has any Fox News anchor ever talked about the hundreds of millions that Trump took from Sheldon Adelson? Of course not. Never. Trump's crowds were all chanting "Drain the swamp," yet not a single Fox News anchor told you about the billions of dollars that Republican politicians were taking from Big Business. And how they were voting with them—and against you—every time. Of course, Fox News is also a multibillion-dollar corporation. The people who run it don't have *your* best interest in mind, they have *their* best interest in mind.

But I do have good news even about Republican politicians. Yes, at the national level they are a disaster. There is no one in the world better at servicing corporate executives than Mitch McConnell. Like Nancy Pelosi, he didn't get to be a leader of his party because he doesn't take corporate money, he got to be a leader because he takes the *most* corporate money! But at the state level, there are still honest Republican legislators!

In fact, there are many Republicans in state legislatures who still love this country and think it should not be sold to the highest corporate bidder. They still believe in their voters and our Constitution. No, they do not agree with me on social issues at all!

In fact, I guarantee you there will be a corporate media hit piece on me and Wolf-PAC one day that says that we are secretly Republicans and that we help Republican politicians who are terrible on social issues. For our whole lives, the mainstream media has been celebrating the idea of bipartisanship, but that was only if politicians agreed to sell us out to corporate interests. The minute Wolf-PAC creates actual bipartisanship in the country against corruption, the media will launch endless attacks against . . . bipartisanship. Their hypocrisy knows no bounds.

How do I know some Republican politicians at the state level are honest about this issue? They already voted for Wolf-PAC's resolution, that's how. What's a good sign that you want to end corruption? When you vote to end corruption!

Wolf-PAC also works with Republicans because there is literally no other way to win. In order to get permanent change—to fix democracy once and for all—Democrats and Republicans must work together. They don't have a choice. That's how the U.S. Constitution is set up—you have to have nearly universal agreement to pass an amendment.

If you're trying to get free and fair elections, the Supreme Court will block you every time. This is exactly what Big Business planned in the Powell memo, as I explained in chapter 4. This is how they planned to take over our government—and it worked! And now both Republican and Democratic voters have seen the Supreme Court work against their interests. Isn't that weird? You are told that the court is either conservative or liberal all the time. But they are not united in those political camps. The one thing that unites court justices is that they almost always rule in favor of Big Business.

As a federal judge, Neil Gorsuch ruled that if an employer orders an employee to freeze to death, he must do it, otherwise they're right to fire him.[32] It was an extraordinary decision that no other judge that heard the case agreed with. And it got him a one-way ticket to the Supreme Court. Brett Kavanaugh ruled that SeaWorld didn't owe anything to an employee who was drowned by a killer whale.[33] And he got a one-way ticket to the Supreme Court. If you're extreme enough to say corporations can get away with killing their workers, you instantly become a candidate for the Supreme Court! Gorsuch and Kavanaugh didn't get on the Supreme Court because they were looking out for the average American, they got on there because they raised their hands and said they would *not* look out for the average American.

So if you're waiting for the Supreme Court to clean up corruption, I have really bad news for you. They're the ones who started the corruption in the first place. No legislature legalized bribery; that's what the court did. As I explained earlier, Powell's plan was to plant "activist" judges on the court in order to help corporations take over. The people who started corporate rule are not going to be the ones that end it. You have to go above their head!

The only thing above the Supreme Court in our system is the U.S. Constitution. If we pass an amendment outlawing bribery, saying that you cannot give giant amounts of money to politicians, then there's nothing the court can do about it! In fact, we can pass any amendment to clean up our elections.

If you're a Republican who was furious about the 2020 elections, how many of your politicians told you how to fix it? Did they ever talk to you about an amendment to fix it? Did they ever mention that you could call for a state's constitutional convention to get that amendment without ever going through Washington? Funny how they didn't mention that, right? It's almost like they want you to get angry and send them more money, but not actually fix the problem. That's because they are the problem!

Now, I'm not going to agree that Trump won in 2020 (because he definitely didn't), and I'm not going to agree that we should redo that election. But if Republican voters were adamant about a legitimate way to independently verify the results of elections, I'd be thrilled with that. That's what progressives have been trying to do for decades. But even if they proposed amendments I didn't agree with, that's still okay. It's called democracy. You propose amendments at a convention, but nothing can pass without three-quarters of the states ratifying it.

That is an incredibly high bar. That's what I mean by needing near universal agreement in order to get this done. Here's how it works. You need two-thirds of the states to authorize a convention to propose amendments on this issue. But that's just the first step. In the convention, we'll hammer out several proposals, some of which will likely skew conservative and some of which will skew progressive, but only the ones we both agree to will have any chance of getting three-quarters of the states to agree. That's thirty-eight states. You need just thirteen states to block any idea.

So if Republicans propose that the remedy to fix elections is not to have them and declare Trump dictator for life, I'm pretty sure we can muster up thirteen blue states to block that. Although I'm using the most extreme example, Democrats will actually worry about that. It's so easy to scare Democratic voters. Corrupt politicians and their minions use this all the time. Whenever you say we should do a convention to end corruption, they say that Republicans will use it to end abortion, gay rights, Black people, life itself. There's no end to the fearmongering Democratic politicians will use to scare you away from the one thing that could actually solve the problem. While establishment Democrats were busy scaring their voters away from a convention because it might end the right to an abortion, the Supreme Court ended that right itself. Everything keeps getting worse as Democratic leaders keep telling you that we shouldn't change anything.

Is there any chance that Rhode Island and Hawaii are going to ratify an amendment to treat gay people as subhuman or to make Trump President for Life? Of course not. It's absolutely ridiculous. And yet politicians say it with a straight face. We live in a very divided country; there are far more than thirteen blue states and far more than thirteen red states. No polarizing amendment is going to pass. Anyone telling you otherwise is probably lying to you on purpose.

By the way, that also applies to any progressive amendment. On the Republican side, they also have their conspiracy theories that were specifically hatched to protect this corrupt system. They claim Democrats want a convention so they can secretly give women equal rights. Well, that's not a secret, we did try that. It was called the Equal Rights Amendment. And even that didn't pass! So when they tell you Democrats are going to pass an amendment that demands that every other president be Black or bisexual, remember that we couldn't even pass an amendment that suggested women be considered equal to men. How the hell would we pass any amendment that is further left than that? No, whether we like it or not, Republicans can block any amendment.

In essence, we both have veto power here. If both sides don't fully agree, it will be very easy to defeat an amendment.

We have to rewrite the code of our government—the Constitution. Not all of it, just the part that's broken. That's what amendments are for. That's why the founders created the process for amendments and used it themselves! They believed in fixing the Constitution so much that they proposed and passed the first ten amendments. Remember, some of the best parts of the Constitution are the amendments themselves, like the First Amendment. Anyone telling you that you shouldn't amend the Constitution missed the whole point of the document. We, the American citizens, are supposed to be part of the process of perfecting the union.

The irony here is that there was nothing wrong with the Constitution to begin with on this issue, it was activist judges who pretended that the Constitution allowed bribery. We have to write a new line of code clarifying that it doesn't. We have to be very clear—this country, this government, this democracy is not for sale! And in order to do that, we *must* work together.

This is the point when you ask, "Then what the hell is the point? We're never going to agree with each other. We practically hate each other!" Do we? Or did corporate interests, through their politicians and their media, get us to hate each other? And was part of the point of that to distract us from their main goal—the great American robbery? They're using their nearly complete control of national politicians in both parties to redistribute the wealth to themselves while we're busy fighting each other.

You see in movies how the robbers plan elaborate distractions to get the police to go somewhere else while they rob the bank—that's exactly what the culture wars are. The robbers—the donors—had already paid off the cops—the politicians. They then set up the world's largest distraction—an endless food fight about social issues carried 24/7 by both mainstream media and right-wing media.

If you're looking for who redistributed the wealth, don't look down, look up. People with no power can't do that; people with a lot of power can. And who do you think the rich are going to say should get the money, you or themselves? Trust me that they are going to find any excuse to say that they should get the money, including your money. Why do you think they're always cutting corporate taxes, but you feel like you're paying more? That's because you are! They rigged the rules through legalized bribery to give themselves all the advantages and screw you over the in the process.

Can we unite around that, at least? Yes, but it's going to be difficult. We're going to have to get past a wall of corporate deception that the mainstream press will hit us with. There is a zero percent chance that the national media will think a convention is a good idea. It's the most populist thing you can do. They'll hate it! The elites don't want you in charge. Guess who they think should make all of the important decisions? Them! What a surprise! And despite the marketing that they do for themselves, the mainstream media are one giant factory that produces consent for the ruling elite. And the rulers do not want you to change the rules under any circumstance.

The mainstream media do not work for you, they work for the rulers. They are the marketing arm for corporate rule. So they will be our fiercest opponents. There will be a wall of lies about why it's a bad idea for people to seize power in a democracy. Yes, they'll say that as if it isn't hilariously ironic. Don't listen to them. You're obviously supposed to have the power in a democracy, and that's exactly what a convention does. It at least gives you the power to *propose* a change. And then you can reflect afterward and see if you like it enough to ratify it, on both sides!

We'll also have to get past our own politicians on both sides. Luckily, state politicians are more honest and more accountable. But in the beginning their leaders will get their marching orders from the national guys telling them to stand down. This has already happened on the Democratic side. I guarantee that it will also happen on the Republican side. The very last thing McConnell wants to do is clean up corruption. No one has taken more bribes than him. He's taken so many bribes it would make Nancy Pelosi blush. So he will inevitably give the order to kill this movement. We promise not to listen to Pelosi if you promise not to listen to McConnell.

Imagine if it worked! Imagine if we put aside our (significant) differences to work on this together. If we mobilized in the face of a national emergency and retook our government, even though the whole national government and national media were against us. It's almost like a revolution. Oh, yeah, that's what amendments are—they are political revolutions!

If you think that's impossible, that's exactly what they told Washington, Jefferson, Madison, Franklin, and the other founders. Where do you guys get off thinking that you could defeat the mighty British Empire? The British didn't just rule a country, they ruled the world. And we beat them anyway! Yes, the corruption has taken root here, and yes, the forces against us will have infinite money and power—and yes, in a sense, corporations are the new rulers of the world—but I think we can rise up against the machines. I think humans can win. We created the machines in the first place, and we can defeat them.

But we can and we must work together. Otherwise, our wages will never go up, our politicians will never represent us, and we will never be able to get out from underneath this corporate oppression. And that's why Wolf-PAC is nonpartisan (check it out for yourself at wolf-pac.com). If, for once, we can come together in one pack, we can have enough strength to topple our new rulers. And bring democracy back!

7

WHAT HAPPENS WHEN PROGRESSIVES WIN

FIRST, IT SHOULD BE NOTED THAT IF PROGRESSIVES WIN AND WE ARE IN CHARGE, at least conservatives still get something out of it. Our victory will mean we defeated corporate rule. There's no way corporations are going to let us be in charge if they can help it. They can live with even populist Republicans, as long as you guys leave their tax cuts alone and let them do anything they want to their workers. But if we're in charge, there's no way we're going to let them do that—and they know it. That's why the only people the media fight harder than conservatives are progressives. They might love Democrats, but they can't stand us.

If we win our democracy back, there's even more good news for conservatives. We can go back to fighting about the stuff you love—nonsense cultural issues. We can go back to fighting the War on Christmas! Will people continue to say "Happy Holidays," or can we force everyone to say "Merry Christmas" instead? Wow, that does sound important. Wink emoji. But don't worry, in a democracy, you'll at least be fighting on even ground. So, if the American people think we should force merriment on people during Christmas time, then you'll win.

Once you unrig the game, then there is nothing stopping you from winning on any issue. I think the question of Mr. Potato Head's gender is an absurd, manufactured issue that is meant to make you angry and distract you from your real problems. But once we have our democracy back, have at it, hoss! We'll meet you on that battlefield and see who comes out on top. I've got Mr. Potato Head at nonbinary because he's a fucking potato. But to each his own. At least the game won't be fixed.

I think progressives are the great majority of this country, and that's the argument of this book. But if you're conservative and you're positive that America is a center-right country and that you guys are the real Americans, then great, you'll win. Let's end corruption and corporate rule and see who actually wins in a democracy. Wouldn't that be great? Wasn't that supposed to be the whole point of this country?

Sounds like freedom to me.

TAX AND YE SHALL RECEIVE

What is the one thing that the media uses the most to scare you about progressive rule? They go to the most overused well in American politics: They'll raise taxes! Ahhhh!

This is supposed to be our biggest downside. Our Achilles' heel. Once people find out that progressives will raise taxes on the wealthy, progressives will become unpopular. Will we? As I showed you in chapter 1, in reality, polling shows the American people can't wait to raise taxes on the rich. Eighty-two percent of Americans think the wealthy have too much money and power—doesn't sound like they're worried that the rich don't have enough goodies. And 76 percent want to raise taxes on the rich. Only someone working in mainstream media could say with a straight face that a policy supported by three-quarters of the country is unpopular.

Elizabeth Warren surged to number one in the Democratic field in 2020 when she was championing the wealth tax. After the media harshly criticized her for that populist idea, she stopped talking about it, and her numbers fell off a cliff. Both Sanders and Warren did their best when they were taking on the powerful and the wealthy. If we could just get one progressive presidential candidate to ignore the jackals in the mainstream media, we might be able to not just start ahead but finish ahead. You know why? Because people have a sense that the wealthy aren't paying *enough* taxes, and they can't wait for a politician who's going to make them pay it!

Think about when we had our golden years in America. From the 1950s through the '70s, we had the best growth the world has ever seen. And even conservatives look back at those years longingly as the good old days. When they say "Make America Great Again," this is the era they're referring to. That's when we had taxes as high as 91 percent. Yes, we taxed the top bracket a marginal rate of 91 percent! And the economy kicked ass! That's a fact.

A new progressive tax rate doesn't have to be that large, and it won't even apply to much of the wealthiest people's money, let alone yours. Remember, it's a marginal tax rate; that means the higher rate only applies for income above a huge number like ten million dollars a year. In a scenario like that, if you're not making over ten million bucks a year, it won't affect you at all. This is when they'll say they can't afford it and we'll laugh and laugh. Billionaires have literally cried on television, telling us that they can't afford any increase in taxes. Of course they can afford it, they're fucking billionaires!

So, you see, even the perceived downsides of the Progressive Era are actually upsides. The only reason you perceive them to be downsides is because of our old friend . . . media mythology. Corporate media has been demagoguing about higher taxes as if it were the greatest evil the world had ever seen. I wonder if those same companies being multibillion-dollar corporations had something to do with that (and all the anchors at those networks being multimillionaires themselves). As usual, when you lift the veil of corporate propaganda, you find that the truth is the opposite of what they have been telling you. Again, these are facts you can look up. They can call me all sorts of names, but it doesn't change the numbers. We are right and they are wrong.

So, when progressives are in charge, yes, the majority of the country will get what they want—higher taxes on giant corporations and the absurdly wealthy. You want these things because you have a sense that the rich are not paying their fair share. The numbers back you up. You were right all along. The only reason you didn't get what you wanted—and what would help the country economically—is because of the greed of corporate media and corporate politicians (and, of course, the people who fund them). We are going to end that and bring justice back for all of us.

POWER AND JUSTICE

Power is self-defining. You have it by having it. You can't ask for power with a please. You must take it. It is not in its nature to voluntarily surrender itself. Money is an inanimate object. It can be given, taken, transferred.

It has no force of its own. It's just a tool. Power resides in people, so it is a living, breathing force. To ask for power is to misunderstand its nature.

I have great news for the nonwhite people of this land. It's our time. You no longer have to ask permission from a white person to do something. You can just do it. You have every bit as much right to it as anyone does. If you're white, you must be wondering what I'm talking about. You don't ever remember giving anyone permission to do something or any minority ever asking you for permission. But you're wrong—we did have to ask, and you did have to grant it.

For example, when we apply for a job, we're asking for permission to do our profession. We have studied it, maybe even excelled at it, but we require your permission to join the company or the firm or any enterprise. Yes, there were some minorities in some positions of power at some institutions before. But they were small enough in numbers that they too required permission. They all knew it, even if you didn't. We all knew that if we stepped out of line from "what was expected," we would no longer have permission.

There was someone setting the rules—and it definitely wasn't us. In the beginning, it was all white males setting the rules in every context. They literally set the rules of government. Then business, media, culture, and even nonprofits. And even if you weren't white, you were such a figurative, as well as literal, minority that you knew you had to conform to white culture. White identity ruled without even knowing it was ruling.

White people didn't even consider including others—because that is the nature of power. The founding fathers are an excellent example. They knew slavery was wrong—several of them even wrote screeds against it. But they still held on to their slaves! Because that is the nature of power. It does not surrender. It must be taken.

Power doesn't care about justice. It thinks justice is silly. Why would I give you my power in exchange for your justice? What do I get out of it? Well, as you might have seen in the slogans, what you get is peace.

No justice, no peace.

And this is as it should be. One more time, my hero, Frederick Douglass: "Power concedes nothing without a demand. It never did and it never will." We have been fighting the same battle from time immemorial.

Remember, the whole system is built by the powerful, of the powerful, and for the powerful. That is why one of the familiar refrains of progressives is "the struggle continues." Because the struggle for power is consistent through all of time.

Power is greedy. We make a demand. We fight. Power must concede some portion of itself if our demand is strong enough. We have peace. Then another demand. History is a cycle of these demands and struggles, until we have balance. Until we have justice. So you see, justice is, in fact, coming. It is the nature of things. It is how we achieve balance.

Now, some white folks are thinking, "Wait, does that mean they're taking some of our power?" Yes, it does. Democracy means we share power based on our voting, not based on race. So, as the number of minorities in America rises, their share of power will rise. Yes, that share of power will largely come from the white majority, but it doesn't mean it's against the interests of white people. It just means we live in a democracy with a more diverse electorate now.

But that is why a huge portion of the right wing fights us, vigorously and sometimes viciously. They don't want to give up their power. This by itself explains the whole Trump era. That's what it was all about. No one cared about policy; no one cared about the issues or really anything else. It was nothing but a titanic struggle for power among the different identities of America.

Does that mean white people are screwed now? Yes, we got 'em! No, I'm kidding. But I think that many white people, whether Republican or Democrat or independent, of all genders and classes and walks of life, genuinely do worry about that. I'll show you in a minute why you don't have to be worried. But some people are concerned because they assume subconsciously that minorities will be just as vicious to them as white people have been to minorities throughout the history of this country.

Pause here to debate whether it's fair to call white people historically vicious in this country. First, good news, as I stated above, I don't need your permission. I can say it even if it offends you. Minorities are always worried about walking on eggshells to not offend the whites. They are a very sensitive people. If you accuse not just them but also their ancestors of ever doing anything wrong, they get super touchy, super quick. Not all white people might know this, but every minority in the country knows it.

So, we had to tiptoe in the past and say things like, "Yeah, maybe that slavery thing wasn't so great. And Jim Crow was kind of a bummer. And it's still kind of going on with this criminal justice system . . . Sorry, sorry, sorry, we didn't mean it's your fault! And we know you mean well with your criminal justice system that locks us all up, and we are largely at fault, but we were wondering if we could just tweak it a little bit? And we're so sorry for the language we used. We'll call it whatever you like. Could you please ask your hired security (cops) to stop cracking our skulls?"

Second, of course slavery was vicious, the thousands of lynchings were vicious, the attacks on young Black kids integrating schools were vicious, the ethnic cleansing of Native Americans via scorched-earth war, diseased blankets, and mass dispossession was vicious, the police shootings and beatings of Black adults and children are vicious, the endless discrimination in housing, health care, education, voting, and employment opportunity is vicious. Historically, white people told minorities that they were *inferior* because of who they were. That they had to be discriminated against—and sometimes killed—just because of the color of their skin. That they were by nature lower than everyone else. It's painful to write. It's painful to read. But it's really important that you know it was, and still is, done.

The median Black family now has $24,100 in wealth, and the median white family has $188,200.[1] That is a gigantic, life-altering difference. That kind of advantage or disadvantage can change the whole trajectory of your life. That means the average white kid is born into a family with about eight times the wealth of an average Black kid. There is nothing you can do about what you were born into. To say that discrimination did not cause that is absurd. Do you think it matters whether you were born into a poor or rich family? Do you think it might affect your chances of being wealthy yourself? Of course!

This is part of what white privilege is. Does it mean every white kid is rich? Of course not. But it does mean, on average, whites have it eight times better—and you don't know it. No one is accusing you of doing anything wrong; we're just saying that you were born into a privilege you're not aware of. Knowing where that came from is important. It wasn't an accident. It was the deliberate actions of past generations that systemically robbed African Americans and others in this country. History rains down on us through the generations.

That's exactly how the past has affected the present. Just ask any poor white person if it's their fault that they aren't already rich like the people in Beverly Hills. They know it isn't their fault. It's terribly unfair to tell anyone that they are to blame for being born poor. It's also not the fault of African Americans for being put in a hole it takes so long to climb out of. But when progressives point that out, the other side says we just want a handout. You know what was a handout? When Black people did all your work in the South for free for hundreds of years.

And when Black people had their property seized, so it couldn't be inherited or its potential value accumulated, that was also redistribution of wealth. And when white people could buy a house in the nice part of town and Black people weren't allowed to, it allowed white people to accumulate wealth in the value of their homes, but not Black people. All of these were giant handouts to white people everywhere, not just in the South.

Again, it's not just in the past. Think about how absurd the right-wing claim is that there isn't racism in America anymore. In order to believe that, you have to believe that nearly every Black person in the country is lying. That they are all either delusional or purposely making up stories in their lives that never happened. That millions of Black people are doing this en masse. Yet we're all so used to that meta-racism that those right-wing claims seem perfectly normal to us. We might disagree, but society has trained us to believe they're not extraordinary—that it is debatable whether all African Americans are lying about their experience of being discriminated against.

So when people claim that police are not abusing Blacks in this country, contrary to the testimony of nearly every Black person in America, a lot of white people generally find that believable. In fact, until recently, the police were believed almost every time. White juries almost always assumed police were angels who would never lie on the stand and that *all* Black people must be lying. How is that for an oppressive assumption? You start out in a hole of assumed guilt, no matter what you've done, and then see if you can perform the impossible task of climbing out of it.

And the assumed guilt is not just in a court of law. That's why Black people complain about being followed in stores, and oftentimes even in their own neighborhoods, or just while having a barbeque in the local park. And white America says, almost in unison, "We don't believe you!"

And all those assumptions are literally on your skin. You can't shake it. It follows you everywhere. When people see you, it triggers their awful assumptions. Jesus, I have trouble breathing just thinking about it.

Even though I am an immigrant and grew up a Muslim in this society, I never had it that tough. Can you please begin to see it from Black people's point of view and empathize a little? How can we redefine power so that justice is part of it, rather than always having to fight against it? Isn't

America supposed to be all about justice? In fact, isn't it supposed to be justice *for all*? Wouldn't it be amazing if progressives got us some of that long-overdue justice?

Inequality doesn't just hurt minorities, it hurts our culture and our shared identity. We all want to be proud to be Americans. Imagine if we were all truly equal and we shared power in a fair way actually determined through democracy. Wouldn't that be exactly what America was meant to be?

The great majority of us want justice. We want equality. It might be naïveté or it might just be hope, but we secretly believe in the idea of America. It might not yet be true, but we really want it to be.

So, what will progressives do with white people once we have the power? Nothing! We, at that point, will be truly—we. That doesn't exclude white people, it just *includes* minorities. Historically, minorities have been so far removed from power in America that the idea of using our power to oppress others hasn't even dawned on us. We have never had the opportunity to even imagine doing so.

Do minorities plan to misuse power on religious, cultural, or racial issues? No, of course not. We didn't strive for justice all this time to turn around and betray our own principles.

Now, here comes the really good news, because the search for justice has so thoroughly defined the culture of minorities in the country that justice is ingrained in our psyche as the ultimate goal of society. Our objective is not domination, it's just equal treatment.

One, we'd be super lucky to get it, so it has been the outer edge of our hope and imagination. Two, we have internalized it as the golden object. There are no people on earth who want equality and justice more than minorities in America. So that means minority Americans are, in a sense, the most American. Because we are seeking *exactly* what our founding documents said was the moral core of this country. We are not Americans as an accident of geography, we are Americans by pursuit and longing. We are Americans in our hearts and in our culture. We've always been on the road to America, we can't wait to arrive!

To us, it's obvious that we would demand fairness instead of oppression. Oppression has been an albatross around our neck for as long as anyone can remember. We can't wait to get rid of it! Not just for us, but as a concept altogether. So don't worry, white folks, you're in luck, justice is coming. And, by definition, it will also be just to you.

Also, remember that a huge percentage of progressives are also white! We're not going to choose to discriminate against ourselves. That makes no sense. For example, I might not be white, but a majority of our audience is. And we're not The Young Turks, they are. They are not going to agree to their own oppression. We didn't come all this way together to let others rip us apart on nonsense identity politics. That's the antithesis of what the progressive movement stands for.

Yes, we will need to remain ever vigilant. Is it possible that at some point, there's a new boss in town and those folks, whoever they are in the future, will also jealously guard their power? Of course! Minorities today are culturally more aligned with justice and parity, but culture can change. Minorities can become majorities. And power can be awfully attractive. It is in its nature to grow where it resides.

So we must put in the right rules, safeguards, and precautions. We must not fight for justice just for ourselves. We must fight for it for everyone through time. We must protect our white brothers and sisters in the future, but remember, the tide can turn in any direction, so we must protect all of us against the people who will want to wield power unfairly in the future. We must perfect the union in time to create—and to preserve—justice.

If you are doing this to seek advantage for yourself, then you are not a progressive. We don't fight for ourselves. We fight for someone we don't know. We fight for justice itself, not just because of its effects on us. That is what makes us progressive.

THE STARBUCKS DOCTRINE

Of course, after they're done demagoguing about race and taxes, conservatives will then turn to another classic trope. Progressives are out to control your lives! They will say this without a hint of irony while trying to control our sex lives, our reproductive choices, which bathrooms we can go into, which sports we can play, who we can adopt, and even who we can love.

So, let me start instead with what it won't look like when we win. Quick answer: anything you've ever heard in conservative media. Tucker Carlson did a segment on his show around the time of the 2020 election saying that if Joe Biden won, progressives would make everyone drink coffee! Starbucks coffee!

First, it should be noted that it's hysterical that this is something they perceive to be a significant threat. They're going to make us drink coffee! The fucking Communists! Second, why would Communists force you to buy drinks from a very capitalist company like Starbucks? That's what Marx would have wanted, I'm sure. How could they possibly believe this stuff?

But at this point you're thinking, Come on, Cenk, he didn't really say that. That's too silly even for Fox News. You're exaggerating. So here is the direct quote:

> You're happy with your corner coffee shop. They want to make you drink Starbucks every day from now until forever! No matter how it tastes! That's the future they promise. Everyone doing the same thing.[2]

You're almost done with the book now. Is that what we promised? I think if I proposed Starbucks for everyone every day, the first question I'd get is, "How are you going to pay for that?" Second question would be, "Why?"

I have my own brand of coffee—Too Strong Coffee. It's organic, fair trade, and delicious. And the brand is proudly progressive. So if we were going to make you drink coffee, it certainly wouldn't be another brand. And if we wanted uniformity, why did we start a whole new brand of coffee? Does Tucker Carlson live on the same planet as we do?

No one on the left would make you drink Too Strong Coffee, even if we love that brand (and we do! toostrongcoffee.com). It wouldn't even occur to us. Why? Why on God's green earth would I care what you drink?

How much do you think my life sucks that I'm spending my time monitoring your coffee consumption habits?

"Has he drunk the coffee yet, comandante?" said no one ever.

So why is Tucker saying certifiably deranged things on national television while pretending to be the William Wallace of corner coffee shops? You have to get people to believe that if the progressives win, they will be taking over your lives and dictating what you do. Why? Because in reality, progressives want to create reasonable regulations on Big Business—for example, making sure there is no fecal matter in your pork. But Big Pork doesn't want any regulation, so they make up lies about how no one will be allowed to eat bacon anymore! Ahhh! Run for the hills!

Anyone who knows me would tell you that I'd rather leave politics than leave bacon. But it'd be nice if Big Pork, Beef, and Chicken had safety for their workers and less hair and feces in their product. That's actually the future we promise.

This is the same argument that conservatives used to try to block Ralph Nader from putting seat belts in cars. They said it was too much regulation, against freedom, and would make us all do the same thing. Well, it partly did. It made all of us stay in our cars instead of flying out the windshield and onto the pavement. You know what that led to? Saving millions of lives. You're welcome.

To be fair, it might have driven up car prices by about five bucks. Conservatives are unsure about that trade-off. It's kind of a no-brainer for me. Would I rather save millions of American lives or pay five bucks less for my Camry? Is there a decent person in the world who thinks that's a hard question? Yet an entire political party says that regulations like that are un-American because they take away your freedom to fly out of your windshield! And people believe it. So they repeat that not letting you marry the person you love does not impinge upon your freedom, but costing General Motors five bucks does.

These are the people we're debating. And the corporate media say they can't tell who is right. Of course, they say that right before an ad for cars made by . . . General Motors.

But there is a clever second point that Tucker is making. He knows that even his populist right-wing audience hates Big Business now. That's why he threw in the line about the corner coffee shop. He knows it doesn't exist anymore. It was actually Walmart that drove it out of business, along with literally almost every mom-and-pop shop in small-town America.

He is stoking your anger at the big businesses that drove you out of your own business. You used to run a small shop in your hometown and people respected you. You weren't a millionaire, but you made it work. It was hard, but you loved it. Now you work at Walmart for $9.75 as a manager. And you have to get food stamps for your family every once in a while. You've lost your self-respect, you're angry, and you hate everyone in Big Business, Big Media, and Big Government. They all lied to you.

And here comes smooth-talking Tucker Carlson, ready to sell you a story about how big bad progressives made everyone get a Venti mocha and that's why your life sucks. No, it was his Big Business buddies and most of his advertisers that ruined your way of life. And now he wants to make sure we can't regulate them, so he turns your frustration into a weapon that is used to help the people who screwed you over in the first place.

LOVE

So, if we don't want racial superiority for ourselves and we don't want to continue the corporate oppression of all of us and we don't want to control your lives, what do we want?

Well, let's talk about love.

Now, this might be an odd thing to put in a political book, but it's really important. So get beyond the awkwardness of the topic and hear me out.

I want to talk to you about love. Because it is arguably central to the way progressives think. I believe people misunderstand what love means. It's not about attraction, butterflies, lust, or even just warm feelings. I think it has a more exact definition.

We are not our elbows or knees or arms or legs, we are our identity. Our physical body is a very small percentage of what makes up our sense of self. The rest is what you think of yourself, i.e., your identity. That is why identity politics is so strong and so pervasive. Political forces have correctly assessed that this is the most important thing to us.

By the way, this is true anywhere. You can find the most progressive Turk in the world and then ask them about Kurdish uprising and all of a sudden they'll turn into a massive conservative. Why? Because you just touched their core identity, how they view themselves. Yes, being a progressive is a big part of their identity, so they should be open to much greater Kurdish rights inside Turkey. But being Turkish, oftentimes, is a bigger part of their identity—so that trumps their progressive instincts (pun slightly intended).

You can see the same phenomenon in almost all old-country immigrants or ethnic groups. Jewish Americans are the second most reliable block of Democratic and progressive voters, until you ask them about funding of Israel's military. For a lot of older Jewish American voters, even if the most right-wing politician, like Bibi Netanyahu, is in office, Israel must be protected no matter what. Now, there's some logic, of course, to protecting Israel in a hostile region, but once you touch folks' core identity, there is no more rational balancing of interests. One interest overwhelms all the others, because it is closer to our view of ourselves, to our identity. This applies to almost every immigrant community—and, as we established earlier, it also applies to white people. That's why Trump was elected.

Obviously, the more important part of this is the larger identity wars that are being waged in this country, as we have explained throughout the book. But wait a minute, what does this have to do with love?

Loving somebody is making them a part of you, part of your identity. It can take wonderful forms like loving your lifelong romantic partner. If you share enough, your lives become intertwined. Love is when that person is no longer fully them but partly you. Arguably, the most intense form of this is the love you have for your kids. They are not just them, they are in some ways an extension of you. You love them with all your heart because they *are* you.

There are also unhealthy versions of love. In an infatuation, you make someone a part of your identity in an unhealthy way. You can't stop thinking about them, you're obsessed by them. It might not be a good thing, but they have become a part of who you are. You love them—even if it is not returned—because you have made loving them a central part of your identity.

For God's sake, Cenk, what does this have to do with politics?

Expanding the circle of liberty is expanding your identity to others. It's loving them!

Even a guy like me, who fights and often even mocks conservatives, as a progressive, loves them. So, you right-wing assholes, I still love you.

That was awkward, right? It was for me, too. But it's okay, sometimes we have to be strong to hear a message that sounds soft. The reason it feels uncomfortable is that it feels like we're opening up too much when we are still enemies. But at some point, if we're going to heal, we have to be vulnerable to each other. That first step of trust is the hardest.

Okay, fine, some of you vomited. I almost did, too. Clean up and let's keep going.

I don't want the left wing to get me wrong. There is no way in the world we should just trust conservatives now and let them keep their power. They don't exactly have a great track record of sharing that power or extending love back to us. No, we must defeat them thoroughly and then reach out to bring them into our wagons once the battle is over. During the battle, you should never be naïve or make unilateral concessions. You build trust after you win, not a second before. But as after World War II, the moral and the *smart* thing to do is to make your enemies your allies. Yes, to love them and make them your own.

I know conservatives have plenty of love in their hearts, but it's directed toward people inside the wagons. They view their family and their community as part of who they are, so they fight for them (sometimes in unhealthy ways). Progressives, on the other hand, believe that more people are part of their community. Different races, ethnicities, backgrounds, faiths, cultures, and even countries. We fight for everyone because everyone is us. We expanded not just the circle of liberty but the circle of love. We fight for them because we love them. Because they are us!

That's the thing conservatives fundamentally misunderstand. They can't help but project their feelings onto us. Their mindset is that you take care of your own. And they think everyone else is "the others." You take care of the people inside the wagons, and they view us as outside the wagons.

Even more important, they think we view them as outside *our* wagons. But they're wrong. To us, they are inside our wagons. We didn't expand liberty to exclude them, we expanded it to include us.

It's not us versus you. That's not how a progressive thinks. We've never been against you because we've always assumed that all humans were the same. That's why we wanted equality and justice.

We didn't seek justice to turn it into injustice. We sought it for all of us. So that it may set us free. As Martin Luther King Jr. said, so that "justice may flow as water and righteousness like a mighty stream."

When justice comes, it isn't for retribution. It's come for you—to bring you justice, too. Because you deserve it just as much as anyone else. Wherever this flag is flown, we protect our own. And you are our own.

If you noticed, Bernie Sanders's slogan at the end of his 2020 campaign was "Fight for someone you don't know." Exactly! Bernie's team didn't use political theory to get to that conclusion, it was just instinctual. That is what they thought progressives would like. And they were right. Every time I ask a progressive to fight for someone they don't know, they absolutely love it. Because it's who we are. In a sense, we literally love more.

And there's more good news here. Love is not a limited good. When you give out love, it doesn't make you smaller, it makes you larger. Your identity grows because it covers more people and, in a sense, makes you the bigger person.

Here, I'm trying to help our conservative brothers and sisters to see that this is not something that is being taken away from them, it's something they can add to themselves. It turns out that old cliché about giving being better than receiving is true! When you receive something, all you get is a commodity. But when you give, you do something immeasurably better: You add to yourself! You grow! You become bigger by giving love and expanding your identity. You can't grow by receiving, but you can by giving.

If you're a young conservative guy, you hate this kind of talk. It's not tough. I know, I've been there. I used to think that way. In my twenties I would have found this to be laughably mushy. But it's actually about raw power, too. The more you make people a part of *your* identity, the more powerful you are. That's a fact. If it makes you uncomfortable because you're so weak you can only think in terms of dominating others, your power will always be limited.

You might say, "No, I will choose to only care about a limited group of people. I will choose to be small because it makes me feel tougher. That's why I'm choosing to do something counterproductive—because it makes me feel better." That's sad on several levels, but it's your choice. It's a free country. While you're busy hating and fighting, we'll be busy growing and gaining more of us. That is part of why progressives always win at the end. Our power is constantly expanding, while conservatives are fighting over smaller and smaller pieces of the pie.

Now I know what Martin Luther King Jr. meant when he said, "Hate cannot drive out hate, only love can do that." Hate just adds to the conflict that separates us. If it is perpetually met with more hate, that just pours fuel on the fire. Whereas love, through inclusion of others in our identity, can actually drive out hate. Because it expands to envelop the person hating you. Then once you—and they—feel that you are one, then you have driven out hate from both of you!

So if you're wondering what happens after progressives win? No, it's not vengeance or oppression. It's reconciliation and a drive for real unity. The kind of unity that can make the *United* States of America real, too.

That's what we offer, not Starbucks coffee.

In the end, we're actually rooting for you. I know you can't believe it, but we really want you to have a better life. So what are we going to do when we win? I hope you're sitting, because this is going to be a heavy blow. We're going to give you free health care! I know, super scary. And then we're going to get you higher wages! What kind of person would do such a thing? To look out for their fellow man that way? A progressive.

ALL OF A SUDDEN

One day, when I was a teenager, my family was walking through Istanbul and we saw a remarkable sight: a little mosque tucked away on a side street with my mom's name on it. What? How was that possible, and how could we not have known about it?

Well, of course, it wasn't her full name or her married name; it was her maiden name. The surname on my mom's side of the family is unique. It's Yavasca, which means "slowly." Yes, that's a strange last name, even in Turkish. There are very few people named Yavasca in Turkey because it comes from a specific lineage. Hence the mosque.

So when we saw "Yavasca Pasa" (Commander Slowly) on the mosque, we were taken aback. We went in and inquired. We found the imam, the equivalent of the pastor of the mosque, and he told us an amazing story. One he couldn't believe we didn't know.

My mom's side of the family knows that they were granted vast properties in southeastern Turkey, so far back no one remembers how or why. They know that their ancestor was an important person in the Ottoman Empire at some point. The imam explained that our ancestor was the admiral of the Ottoman navy when the Ottomans conquered Constantinople. Holy shit! That's amazing. Constantinople was the capital of the Eastern Roman Empire and considered an unconquerable city. Until Grandpa rolled into town.

The reason it was thought to be unconquerable is because it had never been conquered. Constantine had built the capital and the Romans had never lost it.

Why? Because in order to get into the city you had to cross the Golden Horn, a waterway that's the primary inlet into the Bosphorus. Bottom line, you had to cross a narrow strait to get your ships into the Bosphorus to bomb the city. Once you were inside the Golden Horn, you were sitting in the middle of the city and it was nearly yours. But that was basically impossible.

There was a giant chain that stretched across the strait. That's where all the ships would get stuck; they'd get cannonaded from both sides and they'd be defenseless. That's why half the world's ancient navies are at the bottom of the Bosphorus.

So, how the hell did Gramps get past the chains and the cannons? Fatih Sultan Mehmet, the great Ottoman conqueror, tasked our ancestor with solving that riddle. And one day he came up with an idea. What if we passed the ships into the Golden Horn over land?

Well, how the hell would you do that? Gramps started building giant wooden planks in the forests outside Constantinople that the Ottomans did control. They then struck a deal with the Genoese who controlled a piece of property that led into the Golden Horn. Then they greased the planks and passed the entire Ottoman navy through their own territory and Genoese land and into the middle of Golden Horn in one night!

When the Romans woke up, the Ottoman fleet was in their backyard. Their surrender was immediate. The unconquerable city had at long last been conquered.

Progressives, that's exactly what we're going to do to the establishment. Remember, progressives are invisible to the establishment. Our fleet has been built where they cannot see it. And it's already in their backyard. Their surrender is much closer than you realize. They think we barely exist, when in reality, their time is almost up. Poor sons of bitches aren't going to know what hit them.

We're soon going to go from invisible to invincible.

The story of the conquest of what is now known as Istanbul is legendary. The details are fuzzy and some of the stories are surely apocryphal. It's a good tale passed on through the generations. But the essence of it is certainly true because the city is not called Constantinople anymore and the Roman Empire is in fact dead and buried. Let's note that Gramps, at a minimum, was one of the badasses who ended the Roman Empire.

Now wait, I never explained how Grandpa got his name (obviously this was dozens of generations ago, but you get it when I call him Gramps). Apparently, every day the sultan would come by and ask his admiral, "How is our plan to take over Constantinople going?" And every day, Grandpa would say . . . slowly. That's how he came to be known as Commander Slowly.

So, my dear readers, do not get discouraged. It appeared that Constantinople was taken in a day. But Rome was neither built nor conquered in a day. The plan to take the city was so gradual that its author was literally named "slowly." You know that old line from Ernest Hemingway about how change happens gradually, and then all of a sudden? We're at the gradual part, but we're rolling up on all of a sudden.

I told you in the beginning of this book that we would win. That our victory was inevitable. In fact, progressives always win. Because it's impossible to stop change. Even if you have a mighty chain and fierce cannons, someone will find a way around. The establishment has the mighty media and powerful political forces inside D.C., and it's still not going to work; they're not going to be able to stop us. We are change. We are inevitable.

Doesn't that feel great? To be on the winning side of history? Not only are we the good guys, but we are also the strong ones. The ones destined for success. On any given day, our progress appears to be slow and victory seems like an unreachable mirage in the distance. But that is exactly why the James Russell Lowell lines go, "Truth forever on the scaffold, Wrong forever on the throne,—/ But that scaffold sways the future. . . ."

The force of tradition, legacy, and the status quo are always in charge until—all of a sudden—they're not! And the city is ours.

Before my right-wing friends have a heart attack, let me remind them that this is an analogy! As I said earlier, when we win, we will bring you with us, not exclude you. The Ottomans aren't actually going to take over Washington. Louie Gohmert is not correct, Barack Obama was not re-constituting the Ottoman Empire. In fact, you know what happened to them? They died off, just like the Roman Empire. The Ottomans had a mighty empire, one of the largest in the history of the world, that lasted five hundred years. It peaked in the 1700s and took about two hundred years to dwindle away, until one day, all of a sudden, it was gone.

The only constant is change.

So we will win. Then we will calcify and become the new establishment. Money will creep in again, as it always does. Then new groups will arise and they will challenge our power. They will craft a way around our chains and cannons. And new progressives will be born. And then they will win. Because destiny is on their side.

But for now, my fellow progressives, destiny is our date. We are ascendant. We have built our fleet and all of a sudden is around the corner. Our path has been slow and steady, but our victory is certain. The good news is that no matter what they do, and whether they like it or not, justice is coming.

ACKNOWLEDGMENTS

I want to acknowledge some people for their help and patience during the writing of this book—and throughout my life. My mom and dad have been the best parents anyone could ask for. My mom, Nukhet, was a constant source of unconditional love. My wish for any of you is to have someone like that in your life. My dad, Dogan, was such an inspiration without having to say a word. Through my dad I saw the value of hard work, the strength of a provider, and the unceasing compassion of a man with a giant heart. My dad was strong enough to carry our family our whole lives and kind enough to help everyone in his path. I couldn't have asked for better role models. I'm the luckiest man alive.

My wife, Wendy, and my kids, Pro and Joy, were so patient throughout the four years it took to write this book. It cost us many weekends, but they were incredibly considerate throughout. I appreciate them so much it's hard to put into words, even for a guy who just wrote a three-hundred-page book. I also want to thank my wife for convincing me to have kids. That turned out to be an excellent decision.

Of course, there are too many other people to thank and I don't want to leave anyone out. But I do I have to thank the TYT crew for both their patience and their inspiration, especially my co-host Ana Kasparian. I want to thank my dear friends who believed in what we were doing enough to spend a big chunk of their lives helping me build TYT: Dave Koller, Ben Mankiewicz, Steve Oh, Praveen Singh, Jesus Godoy, Jayar Jackson, John Iadarola, Aaron Wysocki, Judith Benezra, Bora Saman, Kenan Turnacioglu, and Jack Gerard. Without them, there would be no TYT.

And finally, to all my friends who yelled at me to write a book. Well, here you go.

NOTES

Introduction

1. "NBC News Exit Poll: Most Mississippi Democrats Support 'Medicare for All'," Mar. 17, 2020, https://www.nbcnews.com/politics/2020-election/live-blog/march-10-primaries-live-updates-democratic-presidential-candidates-face-6-n1153296/ncrd1154931#liveBlogCards.
2. "Live Results: Mississippi Presidential Primary 2020," *The New York Times,* Mar. 17, 2020, www.nytimes.com/interactive/2020/03/10/us/elections/results-mississippi-president-democrat-primary-election.html.
3. "Climate Deniers in the 117th Congress," The Center for American Progress, Mar. 30, 2021, https://www.americanprogress.org/article/climate-deniers-117th-congress/.
4. Derek Seidman, "The Anti–Green New Deal Coalition," Public Accountability Initiative, Feb. 28, 2019, public-accountability.org/report/the-anti-green-new-deal-coalition/.
5. Frank Bass, "Green New Deal Opponents Get 24 Times More Campaign Cash from Big Oil Than Supporters," Fast Company, April 3, 2019, https://www.fastcompany.com/90329231/green-new-deal-opponents-get-24-times-more-campaign-cash-from-big-oil-than-supporters.
6. Mike Lee, "Remarks on the Green New Deal," Mar. 26, 2019, www.lee.senate.gov/2019/3/remarks-on-the-green-new-deal.
7. Lee, "Remarks on the Green New Deal."
8. Lee, "Remarks on the Green New Deal."
9. Lee, "Remarks on the Green New Deal."
10. Lee, "Remarks on the Green New Deal."
11. "Overpopulation and Climate Change, from the Center for Biological

Diversity," Blue Planet United, n.d., https://blueplanetunited.org/archives/population press/overpopulation-and-climate-change-from-the-center-for-biological-diversity/.

12. "Cooper Mocks GOP Lawmaker's Use of Props on Senate Floor," CNN, Mar. 27, 2019, www.cnn.com/videos/politics/2019/03/27/ridiculist-anderson -cooper-mike-lee-political-props-green-new-deal-sot-ac360-vpx.cnn.

13. Caroline Kenny, "Giuliani Says 'Truth Isn't Truth,'" CNN, Aug. 19, 2018, www.cnn.com/2018/08/19/politics/rudy-giuliani-truth-isnt-truth/index.html.

14. Cary Funk, "Republicans' Views on Evolution," Pew Research Center, Jan. 3, 2014, www.pewresearch.org/fact-tank/2014/01/03/republican-views-on -evolution-tracking-how-its-changed/.

15. "Top 10 Advertisers by Network," Center for Media Engagement, University of Texas at Austin, 2020, https://mediaengagement.org/wp-content /uploads/2020/12/Top-Advertisers-on-Cable-and-Nightly-Network-News -Programs-1.pdf.

16. Steve Inskeep, "Candidates and Political Action Committees Spent Nearly $17 Billion on Midterms," *Morning Edition*, NPR, Nov. 10, 2022, www.npr.org /2022/11/10/1135718986/candidates-and-political-action-committees-spent-nearly -17-billion-on-midterms.

17. Carlos Maza, "CNN Treats Politics Like a Sport—and That's Bad for All of Us," *Vox*, Apr. 17, 2017, www.vox.com/videos/2017/4/17/15325172/strikethrough -cnn-espn-trump-surrogates.

18. Ross Douthat, Twitter, Sep. 25, 2015, twitter.com/douthatnyt/status /647401086056271872.

19. Liz Spayd, "Why Readers See the *Times* as Liberal," *The New York Times*, July 23, 2016, www.nytimes.com/2016/07/24/public-editor/liz-spayd-the-new-york -times-public-editor.html.

20. James Fallows, *Breaking the News* (New York: Pantheon, 1996), p. 5.

21. Ben Terris, "Can the Bennet Brothers Save the Establishment?" *The Washington Post*, Oct. 29, 2019, www.washingtonpost.com/lifestyle/2019/10/29/can -bennet-brothers-save-establishment/.

22. Mugambi Jouet, *Exceptional America* (Oakland: University of California Press, 2017), p. ix.

23. Sahil Chinoy, "What Happened to America's Political Center of Gravity?" *The New York Times*, June 26, 2019, www.nytimes.com/interactive/2019/06/26 /opinion/sunday/republican-platform-far-right.html.

24. Dylan Scott, "House Republican: My Donors Told Me to Pass the Tax Bill 'or Don't Ever Call Me Again,'" *Vox*, Nov. 17, 2017, www.vox.com/policy-and -politics/2017/11/7/16618038/house-republicans-tax-bill-donors-chris-collins.

25. Rebecca Savransky, "Graham: 'Financial Contributions Will Stop' If GOP Doesn't Pass Tax Reform," *The Hill*, Nov. 9, 2017, thehill.com/policy /finance/359606-graham-financial-contributions-will-stop-if-gop-doesnt-pass -tax-reform/.

26. Marisa Schultz, "GOP's Big Donors Threaten to Close Wallets If Tax Reform Isn't Passed," *New York Post*, Nov. 6, 2017, nypost.com/2017/11/06/gops -big-donors-threaten-to-close-wallets-if-tax-reform-isnt-passed/.

27. Rick Perlstein, "Exclusive: Lee Atwater's Infamous 1981 Interview on the Southern Strategy," *The Nation,* Nov. 13, 2012, www.thenation.com/article /archive/exclusive-lee-atwaters-infamous-1981-interview-southern-strategy/.

28. Emily Stewart, "Donald Trump Rode $5 Billion in Free Media to the White House," TheStreet, Nov. 20, 2016, https://www.thestreet.com/politics/donald -trump-rode-5-billion-in-free-media-to-the-white-house-13896916.

CHAPTER 1: AMERICA IS PROGRESSIVE

1. Aaron Blake, "Trump Just Comes Out and Says It: The GOP Is Hurt When It's Easier to Vote," *The Washington Post,* Mar. 30, 2020, www.washingtonpost .com/politics/2020/03/30/trump-voting-republicans/.

2. Adam Payne, "Lindsey Graham Says the Republicans Will Never Win Another Presidential Election If They Don't 'Do Something' About Mail-in Voting," *Business Insider,* Nov. 10, 2020, www.businessinsider.com/us-republican -president-mail-in-voting-lindsey-graham-warns-2020-11.

3. Timothy Smith, "How Voter Suppression Threatens Our Democracy," *The Washington Post,* Sep. 20, 2018, www.washingtonpost.com/outlook/how -voter-suppression-threatens-our-democracy/2018/09/20/c1dd3b8a-aad3-11e8 -b1da-ff7faa680710_story.html.

4. Jeff Nesbit, "Who Are We Preparing to Fight?" *U.S. News & World Report,* Jan. 8, 2016, www.usnews.com/news/blogs/at-the-edge/articles/2016-01-08 /americans-love-their-guns-but-why.

5. "U.S. Voters Oppose Trump Emergency Powers on Wall 2–1 Quinnipiac University National Poll Finds; 86% Back Democrats' Bill on Gun Background Checks," Quinnipiac University Poll, Mar. 6, 2019, https://poll.qu.edu /Poll-Release-Legacy?releaseid=2604.

6. Victor Agbafe, "The Vast Majority of Americans Support Universal Background Checks. Why Doesn't Congress?" *Harvard Political Review,* Harvard Institute of Politics, n.d., https://iop.harvard.edu/get-involved/harvard-political -review/vast-majority-americans-support-universal-background-checks.

7. Timothy Cama, "Poll: Majorities of Both Parties Support Green New Deal," *The Hill,* Feb. 17, 2018, thehill.com/policy/energy-environment/421765 -poll-majorities-of-both-parties-support-green-new-deal/.

8. Eliza Relman and Walt Hickey, "More Than 80% of Americans Support Almost All of the Key Ideas in Alexandria Ocasio-Cortez's Green New Deal," *Business Insider,* Feb. 14, 2019, www.businessinsider.com/alexandria-ocasio-cortez -green-new-deal-support-among-americans-poll-2019-2.

9. Sean McElwee, "People Actually Like the Green New Deal," *The New York Times,* Mar. 27, 2019, www.nytimes.com/2019/03/27/opinion/sunday/green -new-deal-mcconnell.html.

10. Miranda Green, "Poll: Climate Change Is Top Issue for Registered Democrats," *The Hill,* Apr. 30, 2019, https://thehill.com/policy/energy-environment /441344-climate-change-is-the-top-issue-for-registered-democratic-voters/.

11. "Memo: U.S. Voters Strongly Support Bold Climate Solutions," YouGov

Blue, Mar. 19, 2019, https://www.dataforprogress.org/the-green-new-deal-is
-popular.

12. Isabelle Gerretsen, "Global Climate Strike: Record Number of Students
Walk Out," CNN, May 24, 2019, https://www.cnn.com/2019/05/24/world/global
-climate-strike-school-students-protest-climate-change-intl/index.html.

13. Somini Sengupta, "Protesting Climate Change, Young People Take to
Streets in a Global Strike," *The New York Times,* Sept. 20, 2019, www.nytimes
.com/2019/09/20/climate/global-climate-strike.html.

14. "Half of Youth Voted in 2020, Increase from 2016," Center for Information & Research on Civic Learning and Engagement, Tufts College, Apr. 29,
2021, https://circle.tufts.edu/latest-research/half-youth-voted-2020-11-point
-increase-2016.

15. Lisa Friedman, "Climate Could Be an Electoral Time Bomb, Republican
Strategists Fear," *The New York Times,* Aug. 2, 2019, www.nytimes.com/2019/08/02
/climate/climate-could-be-an-electoral-time-bomb-republican-strategists-fear.html.

16. Laura Barrón-Lòpez and Zack Colman, "Republicans Could Have a Green
New Deal Problem," *Politico,* May 3, 2019, www.politico.com/story/2019/05/03
/republicans-climate-change-2020-1299883.

17. Emily Atkin, "Corporate America Is Terrified of the Green New Deal,"
The New Republic, May 21, 2019, newrepublic.com/article/153953/corporate
-america-terrified-green-new-deal.

18. Ben Geman, "Poll Shows Strong Backing for Biden's $2 Trillion Climate
Plan," *Axios,* Oct. 21, 2020, https://www.axios.com/2020/10/21/biden-climate
-plan-energy-2020-trump.

19. Hiroko Tabuchi, "Manchin's Donors Include Pipeline Giants That Win in
His Climate Deal," *The New York Times,* Aug. 7, 2022, www.nytimes.com/2022
/08/07/climate/manchin-schumer-pipeline-political-funding.html.

20. Brian Schwartz, "Companies, Executives Donated Nearly $300,000 to
Manchin's Campaign After He Rejected Biden's Build Back Better Bill," *CNBC
Politics,* Jan. 31, 2022, www.cnbc.com/2022/01/31/joe-manchin-campaign-gets
-big-donations-from-corporations-executives.html.

21. "Howard Schultz: The Green New Deal Is Fantasy," Fox Business, Mar.
26, 2019, video.foxbusiness.com/v/6018101551001#sp=show-clips.

22. "The Trailer: Mike Bloomberg, Howard Schultz, and the Battle of the Billionaires," *The Washington Post,* www.washingtonpost.com/politics/paloma/the
-trailer/2019/01/29/the-trailer-mike-bloomberg-howard-schultz-and-the-battle
-of-the-billionaires/5c4f23211b326b29c3778ce9/.

23. Corbin Hiar and Niina Heikkinen, "Dem Leaders Fundraise, and Profit,
from Fossil Fuel Industry," *E&E News,* Dec. 15, 2019, www.eenews.net/articles
/dem-leaders-fundraise-and-profit-from-fossil-fuel-industry/.

24. Ben White, "Soak the Rich? Americans Say Go For It," *Politico*, Feb.
4, 2019, https://www.politico.com/story/2019/02/04/democrats-taxes-economy
-policy-2020-1144874.

25. Ruth Igielnik, "70% of Americans Say U.S. Economic System Unfairly Favors the Powerful," Pew Research Center, Jan. 9, 2020, https://www.pewresearch

.org/fact-tank/2020/01/09/70-of-americans-say-u-s-economic-system-unfairly-favors-the-powerful/.

26. Sharon Zhang, "Poll Finds 83 Percent of Americans Want to Expand Social Security," Truthout, July 11, 2022, https://truthout.org/articles/poll-finds-83-percent-of-americans-want-to-expand-social-security/.

27. "American Voters Share Cross-Partisan Consensus on Wide Range of Federal Policies, Polling Shows," The Appeal, Jan. 8, 2021, https://theappeal.org/the-lab/polling-memos/american-voters-share-cross-partisan-consensus-federal-policies-polling/.

28. Gregory Svirnovskiy, "Paid Leave Is Incredibly Popular—Even with Republicans," Vox, June 7, 2021, https://www.vox.com/2021/6/7/22380427/poll-paid-leave-popular-democrats-republicans-covid-19.

29. Justin McCarthy, "Same-Sex Marriage Support Inches Up to New High of 71%," Gallup News, June 1, 2022, https://news.gallup.com/poll/393197/same-sex-marriage-support-inches-new-high.aspx.

30. Justin McCarthy, "Record-High 70% in U.S. Support Same-Sex Marriage," Gallup News, June 8, 2021, https://news.gallup.com/poll/350486/record-high-support-same-sex-marriage.aspx.

31. Daniella Diaz, Clare Foran, and Kristin Wilson, "House Passes Bill to Protect Same-Sex marriage in Landmark Vote Sending It to Biden," CNN, Dec. 8, 2022, https://www.cnn.com/2022/12/08/politics/same-sex-marriage-vote-house/index.html.

32. Ted Van Green, "Americans Overwhelmingly Say Marijuana Should Be Legal for Medical or Recreational Use," Pew Research Center, Nov. 22, 2022, https://www.pewresearch.org/fact-tank/2022/11/22/americans-overwhelmingly-say-marijuana-should-be-legal-for-medical-or-recreational-use/.

33. Juliana Menasce Horowitz, Anna Brown, and Kiana Cox, "Race in America 2019," Pew Research Center, Apr. 9, 2019, https://www.pewresearch.org/social-trends/2019/04/09/race-in-america-2019/#majorities-of-black-and-white-adults-say-blacks-are-treated-less-fairly-than-whites-in-dealing-with-police-and-by-the-criminal-justice-system.

34. Claire Brockway and Carroll Doherty, "Growing Share of Republicans Say U.S. Risks Losing Its Identity if It Is Too Open to Foreigners," Pew Research Center, July 17, 2019, https://www.pewresearch.org/fact-tank/2019/07/17/growing-share-of-republicans-say-u-s-risks-losing-its-identity-if-it-is-too-open-to-foreigners/.

35. Bradley Jones, "Majority of Americans Continue to Say Immigrants Strengthen the U.S.," Pew Research Center, Jan. 31, 2019, https://www.pewresearch.org/fact-tank/2019/01/31/majority-of-americans-continue-to-say-immigrants-strengthen-the-u-s/.

36. "Immigration," Gallup, n.d., https://news.gallup.com/poll/1660/immigration.aspx.

37. "Immigration."

38. Yoni Blumberg, "70% of Americans Now Support Medicare-for-All—Here's How Single-Payer Could Affect You," CNBC, Aug. 28, 2018, https://www.cnbc.com/2018/08/28/most-americans-now-support-medicare-for-all-and-free-college-tuition.html.

39. "Poll: 69 Percent of Voters Support Medicare for All," The Hill, Apr. 24, 2020, https://thehill.com/hilltv/what-americas-thinking/494602-poll-69-percent-of-voters-support-medicare-for-all/.

40. Michael McCarthy, "U.S. Poll Finds Strong Support for Medicare and Medicaid," BMJ, July 22, 2015, https://www.bmj.com/content/351/bmj.h4010.full.

41. "New Public Opinion Poll Finds Strong Support for Home Health, Choose Home Care Act," Partnership for Quality Home Healthcare, Sept. 14, 2021, https://pqhh.org/article/new-public-opinion-poll-finds-strong-support-for-home-health-choose-home-care-act/.

42. Lindsey Copeland, "New Poll Shows Considerable Public Support for Proposed Medicare Changes in the Build Back Better Plan," Medicare Rights Center, Oct. 14, 2021, https://www.medicarerights.org/medicare-watch/2021/10/14/new-poll-shows-considerable-public-support-for-proposed-medicare-changes-in-the-build-back-better-plan.

43. "Kansas Abortion Amendment Election Results," The New York Times, Sept. 28, 2022, www.nytimes.com/interactive/2022/08/02/us/elections/results-kansas-abortion-amendment.html. See also Ben Flanagan, "Most Americans Strongly Oppose Abortion Ban, ABC Poll Says," AL.com, Sept. 25, 2022, www.al.com/news/2022/09/most-americans-strongly-oppose-abortion-ban-abc-poll-says.html, and "Brent Welder on Kansas' Historic Abortion Win," The Young Turks, Aug. 29, 2022, www.youtube.com/watch?v=JyTYyd5WKf4.

44. Abigail Tracy, "Republicans Lost Big on Abortion Ballot Measures. Now They're Trying to Change the Rules," Vanity Fair, Nov. 21, 2022, www.vanityfair.com/news/2022/11/republicans-abortion-ballot-measures-ohio.

45. "6. Economic Fairness, Corporate Profits and Tax Policy," Pew Research Center, Oct. 5, 2017, https://www.pewresearch.org/politics/2017/10/05/6-economic-fairness-corporate-profits-and-tax-policy/.

46. Juliana Menasce Horowitz, Kim Parker, Nikki Graf, and Gretchen Livingston, "Americans Widely Support Paid Family and Medical Leave, but Differ Over Specific Policies," Pew Research Center, Mar. 23, 2017, https://www.pewresearch.org/social-trends/2017/03/23/americans-widely-support-paid-family-and-medical-leave-but-differ-over-specific-policies/.

47. Kenny Stancil, "80 Percent of US Voters Want Government to Enact Paid Family and Medical Leave." Truthout, Sept. 25, 2022, truthout.org/articles/80-percent-of-us-voters-want-government-to-enact-paid-family-and-medical-leave/. See also Ellen Francis, Helier Cheung, and Miriam Berger, "How Does the U.S. Compare to Other Countries on Paid Parental Leave? Americans Get 0 Weeks. Estonians Get More Than 80," The Washington Post, Nov. 11, 2021, www.washingtonpost.com/world/2021/11/11/global-paid-parental-leave-us/.

48. Svirnovskiy, "Paid Leave Is Incredibly Popular."

49. Rick Perlstein, Reaganland: America's Right Turn 1976–1980 (New York: Simon & Schuster, 2020), 387.

50. "Presidential Candidates Debate," CNBC, Oct. 15, 2008, www.c-span.org/video/?281744-2/2008-presidential-candidates-debate.

51. "Transcript of First Presidential Debate," CNN, Sept. 26, 2008, www.cnn .com/2008/POLITICS/09/26/debate.mississippi.transcript/.

52. Sam Tanenhaus, "Conservatism Is Dead," *The New Republic,* Feb. 18, 2009, newrepublic.com/article/61721/conservatism-dead.

53. Joe Eaton, M. B. Pell, and Aaron Mehta, "Lobbying Giants Cash In on Health Overhaul," NPR, Mar. 26, 2010, www.npr.org/2010/03/26/125170643 /lobbying-giants-cash-in-on-health-overhaul.

54. Jonathan Cohn, "Drug Deal," *The New Republic,* Aug. 25, 2009, newrepublic.com/article/68671/drug-deal.

55. "'The Banks Own the Place'—Senator Dick Durbin," YouTube, Apr. 29, 2009, www.youtube.com/watch?v=CZbC_IqWEJY.

56. Cohn, "Drug Deal."

57. Cohn, "Drug Deal."

58. Paul Blumenthal, "The Max Baucus Health Care Lobbyist Complex," Sunlight Foundation, June 22, 2009, sunlightfoundation.com/2009/06/22/the -max-baucus-health-care-lobbyist-complex/.

59. Rick Perlstein, *Reaganland: America's Right Turn 1976–1980* (New York: Simon & Schuster, 2020), 387.

60. Igor Volsky and Jeff Spross, "FLASHBACK: Two Years Ago, GOP Predicted 'Armageddon' If Health Reform Became Law," ThinkProgress, Mar. 23, 2012, https://archive.thinkprogress.org/flashback-two-years-ago-gop-predicted -armageddon-if-health-reform-became-law-36df865958a1/.

61. Sonia Smith, "Another Day, Another Controversial Proclamation from Louie Gohmert," *Texas Monthly,* Jan. 21, 2013, www.texasmonthly.com/news -politics/another-day-another-controversial-proclamation-from-louie-gohmert/.

62. Bertha Coombs, "Obamacare as We Know It May Be Done For," NBC News, www.nbcnews.com/storyline/2016-election-day/obamacare-we-know-it -may-be-done-n681441.

63. Ira Stoll, "Affordable Care Act's Unpopularity Helped Trump Win 2016 Election," *Reason,* Nov. 14, 2016, reason.com/2016/11/14/affordable-care-acts -unpopularity-helped/.

64. Sarah Kliff, "Trump and the GOP Can Absolutely Repeal Obamacare— and 22 Million People Would Lose Health Insurance," *Vox,* Nov. 9, 2016, www .vox.com/2016/11/9/13487772/trump-obamacare-repeal.

65. Edward Morrissey, "How the Failure of Obamacare Helped Turn the 2016 Election," *The Fiscal Times,* Nov. 10, 2016, www.thefiscaltimes.com/Columns /2016/11/10/How-Failure-Obamacare-Helped-Turn-2016-Election.

66. Nelson Lichtenstein, "Who Killed Obamacare?" *Dissent,* Spring 2017, www.dissentmagazine.org/article/who-killed-obamacare-aca-failures-successes -lessons.

67. Steve Peoples, "Donors to GOP: No Cash Till Action on Health Care, Taxes," Associated Press, June 26, 2017, apnews.com/article/north-america-ap-top-news -tax-reform-health-care-reform-politics-1286e57772224f4080139c191412ee14.

68. MJ Lee and Eric Bradner, "Anger Erupts at Republican Town Halls,"

CNN, Feb. 10, 2017, www.cnn.com/2017/02/10/politics/republican-town-halls
-obamacare/index.html.

69. "Gohmert Responds to Group Calling for Town Hall Meeting," Feb. 21, 2017, gohmert.house.gov/news/documentsingle.aspx?DocumentID=398419.

70. Ben Kamisar, "Spicer: Town Hall Demonstrations Include 'Professional' Protesters," *The Hill,* Feb. 22, 2017, thehill.com/homenews/administration/320665 -spicer-town-hall-demonstrations-include-professional-protesters/.

71. Dena Battle, "Health Care Change, Not Chaos," *U.S. News & World Report,* Feb. 27, 2017, www.usnews.com/opinion/policy-dose/articles/2017-02-27 /town-hall-protesters-cant-shout-their-way-to-obamacare-reform.

Chapter 2: What Is a Progressive?

1. Matt Lavietes and Elliott Ramos, "Nearly 240 Anti-LGBTQ Bills Filed in 2022 So Far, Most of Them Targeting Trans People," NBC News, Mar. 20, 2022, www.nbcnews.com/nbc-out/out-politics-and-policy/nearly-240-anti-lgbtq -bills-filed-2022-far-targeting-trans-people-rcna20418.

2. Justin McCarthy, "Same-Sex Marriage Support Inches Up to New High of 71%," Gallup News, June 1, 2022, https://news.gallup.com/poll/393197/same -sex-marriage-support-inches-new-high.aspx.

3. Dan Avery, "Support for Gay Marriage Reaches All-Time High, Survey Finds," NBC News, Oct. 21, 2020, https://www.nbcnews.com/feature/nbc-out /support-gay-marriage-reaches-all-time-high-survey-finds-n1244143.

4. Emily Ekins and David Kemp, "Poll: 72% of Americans Say Immigrants Come to the United States for Jobs and to Improve Their Lives," Cato Institute, Apr. 27, 2021, https://www.cato.org/blog/poll-72-americans-say-immigrants-come -us-jobs-improve-their-lives-53-say-ability-immigrate.

5. Ben Steverman, "The Wealth Detective Who Finds the Hidden Money of the Super Rich," *Bloomberg Businessweek,* May 23, 2019, www.bloomberg.com /news/features/2019–05–23/the-wealth-detective-who-finds-the-hidden-money -of-the-super-rich?leadSource=uverify%20wall.

6. Kevin McCoy, "Billionaires Compared with the Rest of Us, by the Numbers," *USA Today,* Nov. 8, 2017, https://www.usatoday.com/story/money/2017 /11/08/billionaires-compared-rest-us-numbers/844720001/.

7. Ben Steverman, "The Wealth Detective Who Finds the Hidden Money of the Super Rich," Bloomberg, May 23, 2019, https://www.bloomberg.com/news /features/2019-05-23/the-wealth-detective-who-finds-the-hidden-money-of-the -super-rich?leadSource=uverify%20wall.

8. Emmie Martin and Yoni Blumberg, "Harvard's Freshman Class Is More Than One-Third Legacy—Here's Why That's a Problem," CNBC, Apr. 11, 2019, www.cnbc.com/2019/04/07/harvards-freshman-class-is-more-than-one-third -legacy.html.

9. Jeffrey J. Salingo, "Why Do Colleges Still Give Preference to Children of Alumni?" *The Washington Post,* Apr. 7, 2017, www.washingtonpost.com/news/grade -point/wp/2017/04/07/why-do-colleges-still-give-preference-to-children-of-alumni/.

10. Adam K. Raymond, "Jared Kushner Shows There's a Shady-Yet-Legal Way to Get Rich Kids into College," *New York,* Mar. 12, 2019, nymag.com/intelligencer /2019/03/jared-kusher-college-admissions-story-shady-but-legal.html.

11. Dylan Matthews, "How Many Americans Live on $2 a Day? The Biggest Debate in Poverty Research, Explained," *Vox,* Jun. 5, 2019, www.vox.com/future -perfect/2019/6/5/18650492/2019-poverty-2-dollar-a-day-edin-shaefer-meyer.

12. "State of Homelessness: 2022 Edition," National Alliance to End Homelessness, n.d., https://endhomelessness.org/homelessness-in-america/homelessness -statistics/state-of-homelessness/.

13. Sam Pizzigati, "The 'Self-Made' Hallucination of America's Rich," Institute for Policy Studies, Sept. 24, 2012, https://ips-dc.org/the_self_made_hallucination_of _americas_rich/#:~:text=On%20%E2%80%9Cthird%20base%2C%E2%80%9D%20 with,earn%E2%80%9D%20their%20Forbes%20400%20status.

14. Victor Davis Hanson, "Dueling Populisms," Hoover Institution, Apr. 12, 2018, www.hoover.org/research/dueling-populisms.

15. Victor Davis Hanson, "The Fifth American War," *National Review,* July 18, 2017, www.nationalreview.com/2017/07/fifth-american-war-blue-state-vs-red -elites-vs-populists-egalitarianism-vs-liberty/.

16. "Social Inequalities Explained in a $100 Race - Please Watch to the End. Thanks," YouTube, revised Oct. 3, 2018, https://www.youtube.com/watch?app =desktop&v=4K5fbQ1-zps.

17. Ashley Fantz, "Outrage over 6-Month Sentence for Brock Turner in Stanford Rape Case," CNN, June 7, 2016, https://www.cnn.com/2016/06/06/us/sexual -assault-brock-turner-stanford/index.html.

18. Amanda Holpuch, "Louisiana Court Upholds Black Man's Life Sentence for Trying to Steal Hedge Clippers," *The Guardian,* Aug. 7, 2020, https://www .theguardian.com/us-news/2020/aug/07/lousiana-court-denies-life-sentence-appeal -fair-wayne-bryant-black-man-hedge-clippers.

19. Chris Nichols, "Mostly True: America's Prison Population Has Skyrocketed 500 Percent in 40 Years," PolitiFact, Sept. 16, 2016, https://www.politifact.com /factchecks/2016/sep/16/kamala-harris/mostly-true-americas-prison-population -has-skyrock/.

20. "Drug Arrests Stayed High Even as Imprisonment Fell from 2009 to 2019," Pew, Feb. 15, 2022, https://www.pewtrusts.org/en/research-and-analysis /issue-briefs/2022/02/drug-arrests-stayed-high-even-as-imprisonment-fell-from -2009-to-2019.

21. "Report: The War on Marijuana in Black and White," ACLU, 2020, https: //www.aclu.org/report/report-war-marijuana-black-and-white.

22. Meena Venkataramanan, "'Medicare-for-All' Program Could Cost $32 Trillion but May Also Save $2 Trillion," ABC News, July 31, 2018, https://abcnews.go.com /Politics/32-trillion-price-tag-sanders-medicare-program-koch/story?id=56938226.

23. "U.S. Health Insurance Industry Analysis Report: 2021 Annual Results," National Association of Insurance Commissioners, 2022, https://content.naic.org /sites/default/files/2021-Annual-Health-Insurance-Industry-Analysis-Report.pdf.

24. Susan Heavey, "Study Links 45,000 U.S. Deaths to Lack of Insurance,"

Reuters, Sept. 17, 2009, https://www.reuters.com/article/us-usa-healthcare-deaths/study-links-45000-u-s-deaths-to-lack-of-insurance-idUSTRE58G6W520090917.

25. Willem Roper, "Productivity vs. Wages: How Wages in America Have Stagnated," World Economic Forum, Nov. 10, 2020, www.weforum.org/agenda/2020/11/productivity-workforce-america-united-states-wages-stagnate.

26. Lawrence Mishel and Josh Bivens, "Identifying the Policy Levers Generating Wage Suppression and Wage Inequality," Economic Policy Institute, May 12, 2021, https://www.epi.org/unequalpower/publications/wage-suppression-inequality/.

27. Colleen Doyle and Eric Dirnbach, "In a Single Year, $1.78 Trillion Was Stolen from the Working Class," *Common Dreams*, Feb. 2, 2022, www.commondreams.org/views/2022/02/03/single-year-178-trillion-was-stolen-working-class.

28. Franklin D. Roosevelt, "Acceptance Speech for the Renomination for the Presidency, Philadelphia, Pa.," June 27, 1936, www.presidency.ucsb.edu/documents/acceptance-speech-for-the-renomination-for-the-presidency-philadelphia-pa.

29. Roosevelt, "Acceptance Speech for the Renomination for the Presidency."

30. "President Franklin Roosevelt's Annual Message (Four Freedoms) to Congress (1941)," Jan. 6, 1941, www.archives.gov/milestone-documents/president-franklin-roosevelts-annual-message-to-congress.

31. Richard V. Reeves and Eleanor Krause, "Raj Chetty in 14 Charts: Big findings on Opportunity and Mobility We Should All Know," Brookings Institution, Jan. 11, 2018, www.brookings.edu/blog/social-mobility-memos/2018/01/11/raj-chetty-in-14-charts-big-findings-on-opportunity-and-mobility-we-should-know/.

32. Annie Nova, "Despite the Economic Recovery, Student Debtors' 'Monster in the Closet' Has Only Worsened," CNBC, Sept. 22, 2018, www.cnbc.com/2018/09/21/the-student-loan-bubble.html.

33. "Elizabeth Warren's Free College Plan Is Highly Irresponsible: Ben Stein," Fox Business, Apr. 23, 2019, video.foxbusiness.com/v/6028867469001#sp=show-clips.

34. Kristin Myers, "Amazon Will Pay $0 in Taxes on $11,200,000,000 in Profit for 2018," Yahoo! Finance, Feb. 16, 2019, finance.yahoo.com/news/amazon-taxes-zero-180337770.html.

35. Dogan Uyghur, *The Original Young Turk: Stories and Life Lessons from an American Dream Come True* (Bloomington, Ind.: Archway Publishing, 2020).

36. Adam Hughes, "5 Facts About U.S. Political Donations," Pew Research Center, May 17, 2017, www.pewresearch.org/fact-tank/2017/05/17/5-facts-about-u-s-political-donations/.

37. Natalie Jones, "Midterm Big Spenders: The Top 20 Political Donors This Election," *The Guardian*, Nov. 2, 2018, www.theguardian.com/us-news/2018/nov/02/midterm-spending-top-political-donors-sheldon-adelson.

38. "Candidates and Political Action Committees Spent Nearly $17 Billion on Midterms," NPR, Nov. 10, 2022, https://www.npr.org/2022/11/10/1135718986/candidates-and-political-action-committees-spent-nearly-17-billion-on-midterms.

39. Anu Narayanswamy, Chris Alcantara, and Michelle Ye Hee Lee, "Meet the Wealthy Donors Pouring Millions into the 2018 Elections," *The Washington Post*, Oct. 26, 2018, www.washingtonpost.com/graphics/2018/politics/superpac-donors-2018/?utm_term=.2dd7310c4c62.

40. Jones, "Midterm Big Spenders."

41. Paul Kiel and Jesse Eisinger, "Who's More Likely to Be Audited: A Person Making $20,000—or $400,000?" *ProPublica*, Dec. 12, 2018, www.propublica .org/article/earned-income-tax-credit-irs-audit-working-poor.

42. Jesse Eisinger and Paul Kiel, "Why the Rich Don't Get Audited," *The New York Times*, May 3, 2019, www.nytimes.com/2019/05/03/sunday-review /tax-rich-irs.html.

43. "Understanding the Inflation Reduction Act of 2022," *Thomson Reuters Tax and Accounting*, Oct. 7, 2022, https://tax.thomsonreuters.com/blog /understanding-the-inflation-reduction-act-of-2022-irs-funding/.

44. Paul Kiel, "IRS: Sorry, but It's Just Easier and Cheaper to Audit the Poor," *ProPublica*, Oct. 2, 2019, www.propublica.org/article/irs-sorry-but-its-just-easier -and-cheaper-to-audit-the-poor.

45. Andrew Johns and Joel Slemrod, "The Distribution of Income Tax Noncompliance," graphics8.nytimes.com/images/2010/04/13/business/Tax_Noncompliance.pdf.

46. Ben Steverman and Sophie Alexander, "Richest in U.S. Have a Few Tricks to Avoid Democrats' Tax Plans," Think Advisor, Jan. 30, 2019, https://www.thinkadvisor .com/2019/01/30/richest-in-us-have-a-few-tricks-to-avoid-democrats-tax-plans/.

47. David Barstow, Suzanne Craig, and Ross Buettner, "Trump Engaged in Suspect Tax Schemes as He Reaped Riches from His Father," *The New York Times*, Oct. 12, 2018, www.nytimes.com/interactive/2018/10/02/us/politics/donald -trump-tax-schemes-fred-trump.html.

48. Catherine Rampell, "Opinion: For Every Extra Dollar Invested in the IRS, the Government Could Be Getting $6 Back," *The Washington Post*, March 25, 2021, https://www.washingtonpost.com/opinions/want-to-shrink-deficits-or-fund -bidens-spending-plans-give-the-irs-more-money/2021/03/25/2959bcd8-8d90-11eb -9423-04079921c915_story.html.

49. "Trends in the Internal Revenue Service's Funding and Enforcement," Congressional Budget Office, July 2020, https://www.cbo.gov/publication/56467.

50. Bernie Becker, "Just Wait 'Til Next Year (Maybe)," *Politico*, Sept. 26, 2022, www.politico.com/newsletters/weekly-tax/2022/09/26/just-wait-til-next -year-maybe-00058780.

51. Peter Roff, "The Democrats Love to Promise Voters Free Stuff That Isn't Free at All," *Newsweek*, June 28, 2019, www.newsweek.com/democrats-love -promise-voters-free-stuff-that-isnt-free-all-opinion-1446580.

52. Steve Leisman, "Majority of Americans Support Progressive Policies Such as Higher Minimum Wage, Free College," CNBC, Mar. 27, 2019, www.cnbc .com/2019/03/27/majority-of-americans-support-progressive-policies-such-as -paid-maternity-leave-free-college.html.

53. "Romney's Speech from Mother Jones Video," *The New York Times*, Sept. 19, 2012, www.nytimes.com/2012/09/19/us/politics/mitt-romneys-speech -from-mother-jones-video.html.

54. Rush Limbaugh, "A Golden Opportunity for Mitt Romney," *The Rush Limbaugh Show*, Sept. 18, 2012, www.rushlimbaugh.com/daily/2012/09/18/a _golden_opportunity_for_mitt_romney/.

55. Rose Gordon Sala, "Conservative Response to Romney Fundraiser Remarks Mixed," NBC News, Sept. 18, 2012, www.nbcnews.com/news/world/conservative -response-romney-fundraiser-remarks-mixed-flna1b5957334.

56. Ben Craw and Zachary D. Carter, "Paul Ryan: 60 Percent of Americans Are 'Takers,' Not 'Makers,'" *HuffPost,* Oct. 5, 2012, www.huffpost.com/entry /paul-ryan-60-percent-of-a_n_1943073.

57. Maeve Reston, "Romney Attributes Loss to 'Gifts' Obama Gave Minorities," *Los Angeles Times,* Nov. 15, 2012, www.latimes.com/local/la-xpm-2012 -nov-15-la-na-romney-donors-20121115-story.html.

58. Mitt Romney, "Remarks at the NAACP Convention in Houston, Texas," July 11, 2012, www.presidency.ucsb.edu/documents/remarks-the-naacp-convention -houston-texas.

59. Alexander Burns, "Mitt: I Didn't Pander to NAACP," *Politico,* July 12, 2012, www.politico.com/blogs/burns-haberman/2012/07/mitt-i-didnt-pander-to -naacp-128721.

60. Barstow, Craig, and Buettner, "Trump Engaged in Suspect Tax Schemes as He Reaped Riches from His Father."

61. Scott Yenor, "Limousine Liberalism Goes Mainstream," *American Greatness,* Nov. 30, 2018, amgreatness.com/2018/11/30/limousine-liberalism-goes -mainstream/.

62. Sheelah Kolhatkar, "The Ultra-Wealthy Who Argue That They Should Be Paying Higher Taxes," *The New Yorker,* Jan. 6, 2020, www.newyorker.com /magazine/2020/01/06/the-ultra-wealthy-who-argue-that-they-should-be-paying -higher-taxes.

63. Jennifer Calfas, "President Trump Says He Doesn't Want a 'Poor Person' in Cabinet Role," *Time,* June 22, 2017, time.com/4828157/donald-trump-cabinet -iowa-rally-poor-person/.

64. Chris Sanchez, "Trump Defends Wealthy Cabinet Picks: I Want People Who 'Made a Fortune,'" *Business Insider,* Dec. 8, 2016, www.businessinsider .com/trump-i-want-people-who-made-a-fortune-wealthy-cabinet-2016-12.

65. Taylor Gee and Visual Capitalist, "The Gold-Plated Cabinet," *Politico,* Mar./Apr. 2018, www.politico.com/magazine/story/2018/03/09/trump-wealthiest -cabinet-members-217336/.

66. Gustavo Grullon, Yelena Larkin, and Roni Michaely, "Are U.S. Industries Becoming More Concentrated?" Aug. 2017, https://mendoza.nd.edu/wp-content /uploads/2019/01/2017_fall_seminar_series_gustavo_grullon_paper.pdf.

67. Matt Krantz, "Chasing Right Stocks to Buy Is Critical with Fewer Choices but Big Winners," *Investor's Business Daily,* Nov. 27, 2020, https://www.investors .com/news/publicly-traded-companies-fewer-winners-huge-despite-stock-market -trend/.

68. "U.S. Corporate Profits After Tax," YCharts, 2022, https://ycharts.com /indicators/corporate_profits_usgdp.

69. Hunter Blair, "Corporate Profits Are Way Up, Corporate Taxes Are Way Down," Economic Policy Institute, Sept. 22, 2016, https://www.epi.org/publication /corporate-profits-are-way-up-corporate-taxes-are-way-down/.

70. Alexandra Jaffe, "Sanders Calls for Breaking Up Big Agriculture Monopolies," Associated Press, May 5, 2019, apnews.com/article/fbf1ebc0dff34251b6 4f53bf5a7273c2.

71. Benjamin Fearnow, "MSNBC Host Chris Matthews Ties Bernie Sanders to Fears of Socialist 'Executions in Central Park,' Fidel Castro," *Newsweek*, Feb. 8, 2020, www.newsweek.com/msnbc-host-chris-matthews-ties-bernie-sanders -fears-socialist-executions-central-park-fidel-1486375.

CHAPTER 3: WHY REPUBLICANS SUCK

1. Mike Allen, "RNC Chief to Say It Was 'Wrong' to Exploit Racial Conflict for Votes," *The Washington Post,* July 14, 2005, https://www.washingtonpost .com/archive/politics/2005/07/14/rnc-chief-to-say-it-was-wrong-to-exploit-racial -conflict-for-votes/66889840-8d59-44e1-8784-5c9b9ae85499/; Elyse Siegel, "Michael Steele: For Decades GOP Pursued 'Southern Strategy' That Alienated Minorities," *HuffPost*, June 22, 2010, https://www.huffpost.com/entry/michael-steele -for-decade_n_547702.

2. Zeke J. Miller, "Hillary Clinton Says Half of Donald Trump's Supporters Are in 'Basket of Deplorables,'" *Time*, Sept. 10, 2016, time.com/4486437/hillary -clinton-donald-trump-basket-of-deplorables/.

3. Glenn Kessler, "State of the Union 2018 Fact Check: Biggest Tax Cut in U.S. History?" *The Washington Post,* Jan. 30, 2018, https://www.washingtonpost .com/politics/2018/live-updates/trump-white-house/fact-checking-and-analysis-of -trumps-state-of-the-union-2018-address/fact-check-biggest-tax-cut-in-u-s-history/.

4. Emily Horton, "The Legacy of the 2001 and 2003 'Bush' Tax Cuts," Center on Budget and Policy Priorities, Oct. 23, 2017, https://www.cbpp.org/research /federal-tax/the-legacy-of-the-2001-and-2003-bush-tax-cuts.

5. CNN Deputy Political Director Paul Steinhauser, "CNN Poll: Did Obama Act Stupidly in Gates Arrest Comments?" Aug. 4, 2009, https://politicalticker.blogs .cnn.com/2009/08/04/cnn-poll-did-obama-act-stupidly-in-gates-arrest-comments/.

6. Alexander Bolton, "McConnell Throws Shade on Graham's Proposed National Abortion Ban," *The Hill*, Sept. 13, 2022, thehill.com/homenews/senate /3641225-mcconnell-throws-shade-on-grahams-proposed-national-abortion-ban/.

7. Jessica Glenza, "'Historical Accident': How Abortion Came to Focus White, Evangelical Anger," *The Guardian*, Dec. 5, 2021, www.theguardian.com /world/2021/dec/05/abortion-opposition-focus-white-evangelical-anger

8. "The Persistence of QAnon in the Post-Trump Era: An Analysis of Who Believes the Conspiracies," PRRI, Feb. 24, 2022, https://www.prri.org/research /the-persistence-of-qanon-in-the-post-trump-era-an-analysis-of-who-believes-the -conspiracies/.

9. "Understanding QAnon's Connection to American Politics, Religion, and Media Consumption," PRRI, May 27, 2021, https://www.prri.org/research/qanon -conspiracy-american-politics-report/.

10. Joshua Green, *Devil's Bargain: Steve Bannon, Donald Trump, and the Storming of the Presidency* (New York: Penguin Press, 2017), 105.

11. Green, *Devil's Bargain,* 105.

12. Alma Cohen, Moshe Hazan, Roberto Tallarita, and David Weiss, "The Politics of CEOs," *Journal of Legal Analysis* 11 (2019): pp. 1–45, papers.ssrn.com /sol3/papers.cfm?abstract_id=3355690.

13. Corey Robin, *The Reactionary Mind: From Edmund Burke to Sarah Palin* (New York: Oxford University Press, 2011), 4, 8.

14. Alexander Hertel-Fernandez, Matto Mildenberger, and Leah C. Stokes, "Congress Has No Clue What Americans Want," *The New York Times,* Oct. 31, 2018, www.nytimes.com/2018/10/31/opinion/congress-midterms-public-opinion.html.

15. Hertel-Fernandez, Mildenberger, and Stokes, "Congress Has No Clue What Americans Want."

16. Hertel-Fernandez, Mildenberger, and Stokes, "Congress Has No Clue What Americans Want."

17. Hertel-Fernandez, Mildenberger, and Stokes, "Congress Has No Clue What Americans Want."

18. Hertel-Fernandez, Mildenberger, and Stokes, "Congress Has No Clue What Americans Want."

19. David E. Broockman and Christopher Skovron, "Bias in Perceptions of Public Opinion Among Political Elites," *American Political Science Review* 112, no. 3 (2018): 542–63, https://www.cambridge.org/core/journals/american-political -science-review/article/bias-in-perceptions-of-public-opinion-among-political-elites /2EF080E04D3AAE6AC1C894F52642E706/share/1bd83a8a05b6ac177c51e7a1 9aee1c55f3ef4b97.

20. David E. Broockman, Nicholas Carnes, Melody Crowder, and Christopher Skovron, "Why Local Party Leaders Don't Support Nominating Centrists," *British Journal of Political Science* 51, no. 2 (April 2021): 724–49, https://www .cambridge.org/core/journals/british-journal-of-political-science/article/abs/why -local-party-leaders-dont-support-nominating-centrists/1C6967FB44F7D3B5A7 546BE02E20D32A.

21. Derek Robertson, "Washington, D.C.: The Psychopath Capital of America," *Politico,* June 23, 2018, www.politico.com/magazine/story/2018/06/23/washington -dc-the-psychopath-capital-of-america-218892/.

22. Lauren Aratani, "Trump Calls for Fox News Journalist to Be Fired for Report on War Dead Scandal," *The Guardian,* Sept. 5, 2020, www.theguardian.com /us-news/2020/sep/05/trump-fox-news-journalist-jennifer-griffin-soldiers-losers.

23. Robertson, "Washington, D.C.: The Psychopath Capital of America."

24. Michael Kazin, "Bernie Sanders Has Already Won," *The New York Times,* Feb. 12, 2020, www.nytimes.com/2020/02/12/opinion/bernie-sanders-campaign .html.

25. "This Midterm Ad Is Straight Out of an Episode of 'Veep,'" *All In,* MSNBC, www.youtube.com/watch?v=Wf-p0FWDZ8U.

26. "This Midterm Ad Is Straight Out of an Episode of 'Veep.'"

27. "This Midterm Ad Is Straight Out of an Episode of 'Veep.'"

28. James Hohmann, "Pryor: 'I Believe in God,'" *Politico,* Dec. 4, 2013, www .politico.com/story/2013/12/mark-pryor-religious-beliefs-100653.

29. Aric Mitchell, "President Obama: Democrats Lost Over 1,000 Seats During His Presidency," INQUISITR, Sept. 7, 2017, https://www.inquisitr.com/3848721/president-obama-democrats-lost-over-1000-seats-during-his-presidency.

30. "Presidential Approval Ratings—Donald Trump," Gallup, n.d., https://news.gallup.com/poll/203198/presidential-approval-ratings-donald-trump.aspx.

31. Lydia Saad, "Trump and Clinton Finish with Historically Poor Images," Gallup, Nov. 8, 2016, https://news.gallup.com/poll/197231/trump-clinton-finish-historically-poor-images.aspx.

32. Caitlin Dickson, "Poll: Two-Thirds of Republicans Still Think the 2020 Election Was Rigged," Yahoo! News, Aug. 4, 2021, news.yahoo.com/poll-two-thirds-of-republicans-still-think-the-2020-election-was-rigged-165934695.html?guccounter=1.

33. Summer Lin, "Half of Republicans Say Biden to Blame for Trump Supporters Storming Capitol, Poll Says," McClatchy DC, Jan. 8, 2021, https://www.mcclatchydc.com/news/politics-government/article248376620.html.

34. Laura Santhanam, "Most Americans Blame Trump for Capitol Attack but Are Split on His Removal," PBS NewsHour, Jan. 8, 2021, https://www.pbs.org/newshour/politics/most-americans-blame-trump-for-capitol-attack-but-are-split-on-his-removal.

CHAPTER 4: HOW WE LOST OUR DEMOCRACY

1. Angela Carella, "Founding fathers worried about corporate clout," *Stamford Advocate,* June 12, 2012, www.stamfordadvocate.com/local/article/Angela-Carella-Founding-fathers-worried-about-3628729.php.

2. James Chace, "Excerpt: *1912*," *The New York Times,* May 9, 2004, www.nytimes.com/2004/05/09/books/chapters/1912.html.

3. Franklin D. Roosevelt, "Address at Oglethorpe University in Atlanta, Georgia," May 22, 1932, www.presidency.ucsb.edu/documents/address-oglethorpe-university-atlanta-georgia.

4. "President Franklin Roosevelt's Radio Address Unveiling the Second Half of the New Deal (1936)," www.archives.gov/milestone-documents/president-franklin-roosevelts-radio-address.

5. "Remarks by President Biden on the Continued Battle for the Soul of the Nation," Sept. 1, 2022, www.whitehouse.gov/briefing-room/speeches-remarks/2022/09/01/remarks-by-president-bidenon-the-continued-battle-for-the-soul-of-the-nation/.

6. Lionel Trilling, *The Liberal Imagination* (1950; repr., New York: New York Review Books, 2008), xv.

7. "Endorsement: Christy Smith Is the Best Choice to Replace Katie Hill in Congress," Editorial Board, *The Los Angeles Times,* Feb. 12, 2020, https://www.latimes.com/opinion/story/2020-02-12/endorsement-christy-smith-for-congress.

8. Dwight D. Eisenhower, "Letter to Edgar Newton Eisenhower," Nov. 8., 1954, teachingamericanhistory.org/document/letter-to-edgar-newton-eisenhower/.

9. Emma Roller and *National Journal,* "Can Democrats Ever Win Back State

Legislatures?," *The Atlantic,* Feb. 14, 2015, www.theatlantic.com/politics/archive/2015/02/can-democrats-ever-win-back-state-legislatures/455358/.

10.   Rick Perlstein, *Reaganland: America's Right Turn 1976–1980* (New York: Simon & Schuster, 2020), 201.

11.   Lewis F. Powell Jr., "The Memo," Aug. 23, 1971, www.reuters.com/investigates/special-report/assets/usa-courts-secrecy-lobbyist/powell-memo.pdf, 6.

12.   Powell, "The Memo," 11.

13.   Jane Mayer, *Dark Money: The Hidden History of the Billionaires Behind the Rise of the Radical Right* (New York: Doubleday, 2016), 76.

14.   Mayer, *Dark Money,* 73.

15.   Powell, "The Memo," 20–21.

16.   Jacob S. Hacker and Paul Pierson, "The Powell Memo: A Call to Arms for Corporations," excerpt from *Winner-Take-All Politics* (New York: Simon & Schuster, 2010), billmoyers.com, Sept. 14, 2012, billmoyers.com/content/the-powell-memo-a-call-to-arms-for-corporations/2/.

17.   John B. Judis, *The Paradox of American Democracy: Elites, Special Interests, and the Betrayal of Public Trust* (New York: Pantheon, 2000), 124.

18.   Powell, "The Memo," 30.

19.   Powell, "The Memo," 17, 18–19.

20.   Powell, "The Memo," 32.

21.   Powell, "The Memo," 24–25.

22.   Powell, "The Memo," 32–33.

23.   Powell, "The Memo," 24.

24.   Powell, "The Memo," 26.

25.   Richard Nixon, "Statement on Signing the Federal Election Campaign Act of 1971," Feb. 7, 1972, www.presidency.ucsb.edu/documents/statement-signing-the-federal-election-campaign-act-1971.

26.   *Buckley v. Valeo,* 424 U.S. 1 (1976), supreme.justia.com/cases/federal/us/424/1/#tab-opinion-1951588.

27.   Adam Lioz, "*Buckley v. Valeo* at 40," Demos, Dec. 15, 2015, www.demos.org/research/buckley-v-valeo-40.

28.   Ellen L. Weintraub, "Overturn *Buckley v. Valeo,*" *Politico,* 2019, www.politico.com/interactives/2019/how-to-fix-politics-in-america/corruption/overturn-buckley-valeo/.

29.   Powell, "The Memo," 26.

30.   *Buckley v. Valeo,* 424 U.S. 1 (1976).

31.   *First Nat'l Bank of Boston v. Bellotti,* 435 U.S. 765 (1978), supreme.justia.com/cases/federal/us/435/765/.

32.   Luke Wachob, "*First National Bank of Boston v. Bellotti:* Protecting the Right to Hear Others," Institute for Free Speech, Apr. 26, 2018, www.ifs.org/research/first-national-bank-of-boston-v-bellotti-protecting-the-right-to-hear-others/.

33.   Video available at Lauren Windsor tweet, April 15, 2022, https://twitter.com/lawindsor/status/1514986946908639236.

34.   *First Nat'l Bank of Boston v. Bellotti,* 435 U.S. 765 (1978).

35. "Opioids," National Institute on Drug Abuse, nida.nih.gov/research-topics /opioids.

36. Theodoric Meyer, "How Much Did Sheldon Adelson Really Spend on Campaign 2012?" ProPublica, Dec. 20, 2012, https://www.propublica.org/article/how -much-did-sheldon-adelson-really-spend-on-campaign-2012; Peter Stone, "Sheldon Adelson Spent Far More on Campaign than Previously Known," HuffPost, Dec. 3, 2012, https://www.huffpost.com/entry/sheldon-adelson-2012-election_n _2223589.

37. Brendan Cole, "Sheldon Adelson Gave Trump and Republicans Over $424 Million Since 2016," *Newsweek*, Jan. 12, 2021, https://www.newsweek .com/sheldon-adelson-donald-trump-republicans-donations-1560883; Fredreka Schouten, "Adelsons Provide $75 Million Cash Infusion to Trump's Reelection Effort," CNN, Oct. 15, 2020, https://www.cnn.com/2020/10/15/politics/sheldon -adelson-funds-trump-super-pac/index.html.

38. "GOP Donor Sheldon Adelson's Company to Pay $9 million in Bribery Case," Reuters, April 7, 2016, https://fortune.com/2016/04/07/sheldon-adelson -sec-bribery/.

39. Beth Jinks and Deirdre Bolton, "Las Vegas Sands' Adelson 'Morally Opposed' to Online Betting," Bloomberg, June 30, 2013, https://www.bloomberg.com /news/articles/2013-06-20/las-vegas-sands-adelson-morally-opposed-to-online -gambling?leadSource=uverify%20wall.

40. Rachel M. Cohen, "Sheldon Adelson Got a Surprise Gift in the Middle of the Government Shutdown," *The Intercept*, Feb. 8, 2019, https://theintercept .com/2019/02/08/sheldon-adelson-online-gambling/.

41. Kyle Roerink and Eli Segall, "In Talk at UNLV, Adelson Insists He's 'Very Socially Sensitive,'" *Las Vegas Sun*, May 6, 2014, lasvegassun.com/news/2014 /may/06/talk-unlv-billionaire-adelson-insists-hes-very-soc/.

42. Cohen, "Sheldon Adelson Got a Surprise Gift."

43. "Did Money Win?," Open Secrets, n.d., https://www.opensecrets.org /elections-overview/winning-vs-spending.

44. http://www.script-o-rama.com/movie_scripts/t/trainspotting-script -transcript-danny-boyle.html.

45. Martin Gilens and Benjamin I. Page, "Testing Theories of American Politics: Elites, Interest Groups, and Average Citizens," *Perspectives on Politics* 12, no. 3 (Sept. 2014): 564, scholar.princeton.edu/sites/default/files/mgilens/files/gilens _and_page_2014_-testing_theories_of_american_politics.doc.pdf.

46. "George Carlin on Corporate America," Films for Action, n.d., https:// www.filmsforaction.org/watch/george-carlin-on-corporate-america/.

47. Gilens and Page, "Testing Theories of American Politics," 576.

48. Gilens and Page, "Testing Theories of American Politics," 572.

49. "Fundraising and Spending in U.S. Presidential Elections from 1976 to 2016," Statista Research Department, www.statista.com/statistics/216793/fundraising -and-spending-in-us-presidential-elections/.

50. "Fundraising and Spending in U.S. Presidential Elections from 1976 to 2016."

51. "2020 Election to Cost $14 Billion, Blowing Away Spending Records," Open Secrets, Oct. 28, 2020, https://www.opensecrets.org/news/2020/10/cost-of-2020-election-14billion-update/; "Candidates and Political Action Committees Spent Nearly $17 Billion on Midterms," NPR, Nov. 10, 2022, https://www.npr.org/2022/11/10/1135718986/candidates-and-political-action-committees-spent-nearly-17-billion-on-midterms.

52. Jay Yarow, "New Jersey Car Dealer Slams Tesla: 'This Musk Guy, He Wants All the Profits for Himself,'" *Business Insider,* Mar. 20, 2014, www.businessinsider.com/new-jersey-car-dealer-on-tesla-2014-3.

53. Gary M. Fink and Hugh Davis Graham, eds., *The Carter Presidency: Policy Choices in the Post–New Deal Era* (Lawrence: University Press of Kansas, 1998), 4.

54. Rick Perlstein, *Reaganland: America's Right Turn 1976–1980* (New York: Simon & Schuster, 2020), 424.

55. Perlstein, *Reaganland,* 334.

56. Gregg Easterbrook, "The Business of Politics," *The Atlantic,* Oct. 1986, www.theatlantic.com/past/docs/politics/polibig/eastbusi.htm.

57. Easterbrook, "The Business of Politics."

58. Bob Secter, "Tony Coelho's Dramatic Rise Means a New Style in Democratic Leadership," *The Los Angeles Times,* Jan. 11, 1987, https://www.latimes.com/archives/la-xpm-1987-01-11-tm-3587-story.html.

59. Easterbrook, "The Business of Politics."

60. Robert Kuttner, "Ass Backward," *The New Republic*, April 22, 1985.

61. Marjorie Williams, "The Fall of the House of Coelho," *The Washington Post,* Jan. 8, 1995, www.washingtonpost.com/archive/lifestyle/magazine/1995/01/08/the-fall-of-the-house-of-coelho/35b3b035-2795-415a-b2a6-8e5b47ca0a44/.

62. Williams, "The Fall of the House of Coelho."

63. Williams, "The Fall of the House of Coelho."

64. Williams, "The Fall of the House of Coelho."

65. Williams, "The Fall of the House of Coelho."

66. Mark Jannot, "A Rahm for the Money," *Chicago,* Aug. 3, 1992, www.chicagomag.com/chicago-magazine/august-1992/rahm-emanuel-during-the-bill-clinton-years/.

67. "The Tony Coelho Factor," *The Washington Times,* Jan. 17, 2006, www.washingtontimes.com/news/2006/jan/17/20060117-092150-3845r/.

68. Daniel Schlozman, "Finance and the Democrats: Coalition Politics and the End of the Anti-Finance Coalition," prepared for presentation at the annual conference of the American Political Science Association in Philadelphia, Pennsylvania, Sept. 3, 2016, https://static1.squarespace.com/static/540f1546e4b0ca60699c8f73/t/57cc7ef52e69cf21021febed/1473019638194/Schlozman+APSA+2016.pdf.

69. Daniel Schlozman, "Democrats and Labor Unions Are Doomed Without Each Other—and So Are We," *The Hill,* September 1, 2015, https://thehill.com/blogs/congress-blog/labor/252333-democrats-and-labor-unions-are-doomed-without-each-other-and-so-are/.

70. Robert Kuttner, "Champions of the Middle Class," The American Prospect, Feb. 8, 2011, https://prospect.org/special-report/champions-middle-class/.

71. Schlozman, "Finance and the Democrats."

72. Thomas Frank, *Listen, Liberal: Or, What Ever Happened to the Party of the People?* (New York: Metropolitan Books, 2016), 29.

73. "Why Democrats Are Perpetual LOSERS?," *The Young Turks,* YouTube video, April 23, 2016, https://www.youtube.com/watch?app=desktop&v=iYwA4n8be0E.

74. Williams, "The Fall of the House of Coelho."

75. James B. Stewart, "Volcker Rule, Once Simple, Now Boggles," *The New York Times,* Oct. 21, 2011, www.nytimes.com/2011/10/22/business/volcker-rule-grows-from-simple-to-complex.html.

76. Stewart, "Volcker Rule, Once Simple, Now Boggles."

77. Isaac Arnsdorf, "Trump Won with Half as Much Money as Clinton Raised," *Politico,* Dec. 8, 2016, www.politico.com/story/2016/12/trump-clinton-campaign-fundraising-totals-232400.

78. Williams, "The Fall of the House of Coelho."

79. "Campaign Finance Reform and the 2016 Election: Remarks from Lawrence Lessig," American Enterprise Institute, Nov. 13, 2015, www.aei.org/wp-content/uploads/2015/10/Transcript3.pdf?x91208.

80. Sam Pizzigati, "American Billionaires Show US Is #1 in Creating Grotesque Inequality." *Common Dreams,* Oct. 9, 2022, www.commondreams.org/views/2022/10/09/american-billionaires-show-us-1-creating-grotesque-inequality.

Chapter 5: The Matrix

1. Nathan Pinger, "Home Field Advantage: The Facts and the Fiction," *Chicago Booth Review,* June 15, 2015, https://www.chicagobooth.edu/review/home-field-advantage-facts-and-fiction.

2. Eric Alterman, *What Liberal Media? The Truth About Bias and the News* (New York: Basic Books, 2003), 14.

3. "Topline Results for the October 2022 Times/Siena Poll of Registered Voters," *The New York Times,* Oct. 18, 2022, www.nytimes.com/interactive/2022/10/18/upshot/times-siena-poll-toplines.html.

4. Tara Golshan, "The 4 Fights That Make Up the Medicare-for-All Debate," *Vox,* Nov. 4, 2019, https://www.vox.com/policy-and-politics/2019/11/4/20948117/warren-sanders-medicare-for-all-cost-voxcare.

5. Brian Stelter, "Sharpton Appears to Win Anchor Spot on MSNBC," *The New York Times,* July 20, 2011, https://www.nytimes.com/2011/07/21/business/media/sharpton-close-to-being-msnbc-anchor.html.

6. "Some Critical Media Voices Face Censorship," Fairness and Accuracy in Media, Apr. 3, 2003, fair.org/press-release/some-critical-media-voices-face-censorship/.

7. "Some Critical Media Voices Face Censorship."

8. Timothy Dumas, "Truth and Consequences," *New Canaan–Darien Magazine,* Jan.–Feb. 2009, web.archive.org/web/20150217100254/http://www.newcanaandarienmag.com/n/January-2009/Truth-and-Consequences/index.php?cparticle=4&siarticle=3#artanc.

9. Jim Rutenberg, "From Cable Star to Face in the Crowd," *The New York Times*, May 5, 2003, https://www.nytimes.com/2003/05/05/business/from-cable-star-to-face-in-the-crowd.html.

10. Nick Wadhams, "U.S. Persuades Iraq to Quash Siemens Deal in Favor of GE," Bloomberg, Oct. 17, 2018, https://www.bloomberg.com/news/articles/2018-10-17/u-s-persuades-iraq-to-quash-siemens-power-deal-in-favor-of-ge; "GE Snaps up $3B Iraq Power Contract," TradeArabia, Dec. 16, 2008, https://www.tradearabia.com/news/OGN_153762.html.

11. Peter Wade, "Chris Matthews' Wild Rant Connects a Bernie Sanders Win with Public Executions," *Rolling Stone*, Feb. 8, 2020, https://www.rollingstone.com/politics/politics-news/chris-matthews-bernie-sanders-public-executions-949802/.

12. Eric Alterman, "The Many Man-Crushes of Chris Matthews," *The Nation*, Mar. 22, 2007, www.thenation.com/article/archive/many-man-crushes-chris-matthews/.

13. Alterman, "The Many Man-Crushes of Chris Matthews."

14. Alterman, "The Many Man-Crushes of Chris Matthews."

15. "'Hardball with Chris Matthews' for Dec. 13," NBC News, Dec. 19, 2005, www.nbcnews.com/id/wbna10533719.

16. Glenn Greenwald, "Chris Matthews on Fred Thompson's Sexiness and Smells," *Salon*, June 14, 2007, www.salon.com/2007/06/14/matthews_17/.

17. Danny Shea, "'I Felt This Thrill Going Up My Leg' as Obama Spoke," *HuffPost*, Mar. 28, 2008, www.huffpost.com/entry/chris-matthews-i-felt-thi_n_86449.

CHAPTER 6: HERE COMES THE REVOLUTION

1. Frank Luntz, "Young Voters Spell Doom for GOP," *USA Today*, Mar. 10, 2016, www.usatoday.com/story/opinion/2016/03/10/frank-luntz-young-voters-spell-doom-gop/81534530/.

2. Luntz, "Young Voters Spell Doom for GOP."

3. Luntz, "Young Voters Spell Doom for GOP."

4. Frank Luntz, "Memorandum," Feb. 18, 2016, static.politico.com/bc/7c/c808106e44eaa8855a3a12553bb7/snapchat-generation-release.pdf.

5. Luntz, "Young Voters Spell Doom for GOP."

6. Luntz, "Memorandum."

7. Luntz, "Young Voters Spell Doom for GOP."

8. "Poll: 69 Percent of Voters Support Medicare for All," *The Hill*, Apr. 24, 2020, https://thehill.com/hilltv/what-americas-thinking/494602-poll-69-percent-of-voters-support-medicare-for-all/.

9. "Sanders Banked on Young Voters: Here's How the Numbers Have Played Out," *PBS NewsHour*, Mar. 11, 2020, https://www.pbs.org/newshour/politics/sanders-banked-on-young-voters-heres-how-the-numbers-have-played-out.

10. "Memo: U.S. Voters Strongly Support Bold Climate Solutions," Data for Progress, Mar. 19, 2019, www.dataforprogress.org/the-green-new-deal-is-popular.

11. "Ahead of National School Walkout Day, Anniversary of Columbine Massacre, Harvard IOP Youth Poll Finds Stricter Gun Laws, Ban on Assault Weapons

Favored by Two-thirds of Likely Midterm Voters Under Age 30," Harvard Institute of Politics, n.d., https://iop.harvard.edu/about/newsletter-press-release/harvard -iop-youth-poll-finds-stricter-gun-laws-ban-assault-weapons.

12. Hannah Gilberstadt, "More Americans Oppose Than Favor the Government Providing a Universal Basic Income for All Adult Citizens," Pew Research Center, Aug. 19, 2020, https://www.pewresearch.org/fact-tank/2020/08/19/more -americans-oppose-than-favor-the-government-providing-a-universal-basic-income -for-all-adult-citizens/.

13. Ibram X. Kendi, "Stop Blaming Young Voters for Not Turning Out for Sanders," *The Atlantic,* Mar. 17, 2020, www.theatlantic.com/ideas/archive/2020 /03/stop-blaming-young-voters-not-turning-out-sanders/608137/.

14. "Politics," *Oxford Essential Quotations* (4th ed.), www.oxfordreference.com /display/10.1093/acref/9780191826719.001.0001/q-oro-ed4-00008442;jsessionid =750E64D6BE57ABA4F57DC115AC2DEAC2.

15. Duane F. Alwin, Ronald L. Cohen, and Theodore M. Newcomb, *Political Attitudes over the Life Span: The Bennington Women After Fifty Years* (Madison: University of Wisconsin Press, 1991), 64.

16. Yair Ghitza and Andrew Gelman, "The Great Society, Reagan's Revolution, and Generations of Presidential Voting," Working Paper, Columbia University, June 5, 2014, http://www.stat.columbia.edu/~gelman/research/unpublished /cohort_voting_20140605.pdf.

17. "The Generation Gap and the 2012 Election, Section 1: How Generations Have Changed," Pew Research Center, Nov. 3, 2011, www.pewresearch .org/politics/2011/11/03/section-1-how-generations-have-changed/.

18. "The Generation Gap and the 2012 Election, Section 1: How Generations Have Changed."

19. Caleb Ecarma, "Joe Biden, Revenant, Was an Irresistible Media Story—and It Helped Him Win Super Tuesday," *Vanity Fair,* Mar. 4, 2020, www.vanityfair .com/news/2020/03/joe-biden-media-story-helped-win-him-super-tuesday.

20. Juan Caicedo and Sarah Lazare, "CNN's Coverage of Sanders was 3X More Negative Than Biden Following Their Big Primary Wins," *In These Times,* Mar. 9, 2020, inthesetimes.com/article/cnn-bernie-sanders-joe-biden-media-spin -candidates-negative-mentions.

21. Caicedo and Lazare, "CNN's Coverage of Sanders was 3X More Negative Than Biden Following Their Big Primary Wins."

22. Caicedo and Lazare, "CNN's Coverage of Sanders was 3X More Negative Than Biden Following Their Big Primary Wins."

23. Caicedo and Lazare, "CNN's Coverage of Sanders was 3X More Negative Than Biden Following Their Big Primary Wins."

24. Jeremy Barr, "Can Cable News Win Over Young Viewers? At MSNBC a 40-Year-Old New President Is Going to Try," *The Washington Post,* May 24, 2021, https://www.washingtonpost.com/media/2021/05/24/msnbc-rashida-jones/.

25. Stef W. Kight, "70% of Millennials Say They'd Vote for a Socialist," *Axios,* Oct. 28, 2019, www.axios.com/2019/10/28/millennials-vote-socialism -capitalism-decline.

26. Kight, "70% of Millennials Say They'd Vote for a Socialist."

27. Alex Griffing, "Gallup Records Highest Ever Level of Americans with No Trust at All in Mass Media as GOP Numbers Crater," *Mediaite,* Oct. 19, 2022, www.mediaite.com/news/gallup-records-highest-ever-level-of-americans -with-no-trust-at-all-in-mass-media-as-gop-numbers-crater/.

28. "Whoopi Goldberg Attacks Justice Democrats," *The Young Turks,* Nov. 16, 2018, https://www.youtube.com/watch?app=desktop&v=USpVL3jzXsU.

29. Ryan Grim, *We've Got People: From Jesse Jackson to AOC, the End of Big Money and the Rise of a Movement* (Washington, D.C.: Strong Arm Press, 2019), 356.

30. Alexandra Glorioso and Marc Caputo, "Democrats: Medicare Fraud Is 'Fungus' Scott Will Never Get Rid Of," Aug. 30, 2018, *Politico,* https://www .politico.com/states/florida/story/2018/08/30/democrats-medicare-fraud-is-fungus -scott-will-never-get-rid-of-573155.

31. Susan Heavey, "Study Links 45,000 U.S. Deaths to Lack of Insurance," Reuters, Sept. 17, 2009, https://www.reuters.com/article/us-usa-healthcare-deaths /study-links-45000-u-s-deaths-to-lack-of-insurance-idUSTRE58G6W520090917.

32. Robert Barnes, "Rulings Offer Glimpse into What Kind of Justice Gor- such Would Be," *The Washington Post,* Mar. 17, 2017, www.washingtonpost .com/politics/courts_law/rulings-offer-glimpse-into-what-kind-of-justice-gorsuch -would-be/2017/03/16/47e461be-081d-11e7-b77c-0047d15a24e0_story.html?utm _term=.1612aade9d5d.

33. Joan Biskupic, "What the Case of a Killer Whale Tells Us About Brett Kavanaugh," CNN, Aug. 25, 2018, www.cnn.com/2018/08/25/politics/brett -kavanaugh-killer-whale-chevron-regulations/index.html.

CHAPTER 7: WHAT HAPPENS WHEN PROGRESSIVES WIN

1. Emily Moss, Kriston McIntosh, Wendy Edelberg, and Kristen Broady, "The Black-White Wealth Gap Left Black Households More Vulnerable," Brookings, Dec. 8, 2020, https://www.brookings.edu/blog/up-front/2020/12/08/the-black -white-wealth-gap-left-black-households-more-vulnerable/.

2. Phil Owen, "Tucker Carlson Says Biden Wants to 'Make You Drink Star- bucks Every Day' (Video)," *The Wrap,* Nov. 6, 2020, www.thewrap.com/tucker -carlson-says-biden-will-make-you-drink-starbucks-every-day-video/.

INDEX

abortion, 35–36, 71, 108–13
Abrams, Al, 185
A/B testing, 115–16, 136
accumulated power, 141–43
Adelson, Miriam, 171
Adelson, Sheldon, 114, 135, 167–72, 248
advertising, 10–11, 157, 161, 196, 243–44
affirmative action, 59
"affluenza," 64
Affordable Care Act (Obamacare), 24, 40–49, 90
Alterman, Eric, 196
"alternative facts," 9, 33
American Conservative Union., 182
American Enterprise Institute, 155
American Greatness (journal), 91
American Legislative Exchange Council (ALEC), 22
American National Election Studies (ANES), 121
American Petroleum Institute, 119, 120
Angelou, Maya, 18
antifa, 119, 149

anti-immigrant sentiments, 1, 32–33, 40, 53, 124, 125, 127, 134–35, 136
anti-Semitism, 110, 114, 135–37, 171
Appleton, Jim, 176
Apprentice, The (TV show), 17
Atlantic, The, 14, 123, 150, 184–85, 224
"Attack on American Free Enterprise System" (Powell), 153–58
Atwater, Lee, 16–17

Bacon, Don, 128
Banfield, Ashleigh, 205–8
Baucus, Max, 43
Beck, Glenn, 44
Bennet, James, 15
Bennet, Michael, 9, 34
Bezos, Jeff, 180
Biden, Joe
    Build Back Better Plan, 38
    Capitol riots and Republicans, 132, 138, 139
    climate plan, 6, 27, 28
    election of 2020, 2, 13, 26, 34, 50, 127–28, 139, 187, 224, 227–28, 263–64

Biden, Joe (*continued*)
  failure to fight back, 146–47
  health care and, 2
  Inflation Reduction Act of 2022, 6,
    27, 38, 83, 85, 192
  Nides as ambassador to Israel, 186
  polling as threat to democracy,
    198–99
  "socialist" label, 67
  tax policy, 106
  undocumented immigrants and,
    124
Big Business, 142–43, 153–54, 182,
  265–66. *See also* corporate
  interests
Big Lebowski, The (movie), 172–73,
  193
Big Pharma, 42–43. *See also* drug
  companies
bin Laden, Osama, 213
bipartisanship, 25, 188, 197–98,
  246–49
Black, Diane, 47
Black Lives Matter, 22, 66, 77
Blitzer, Wolf, 233–34
Bloomberg, Michael, 28
Boehner, John, 44
Boston Tea Party, 141
bothsidesism, 9–12, 14–15
Bowman, Jamaal, 9, 236
Breaking the News (Fallows), 14–15
Brennan Center for Justice, 82
bribery, 16, 27, 121, 142, 160,
  163–72, 247–48
British Empire, 141, 253
Broockman, David E., 120
Brooks, Mo, 163–65
Broun, Paul, 44
Bryan, William Jennings, 95, 124
Buckley, James, 159
Buckley v. Valeo, 159–60, 161, 163,
  165, 175, 189
Build Back Better, 38
Burke, Edmund, 116, 117
Bush, Cori, 9, 236

Bush, George H. W., 106, 150
Bush, George W., 211–14, 225
  Iraq War and, 107, 211–13
  mainstream media and, 196, 211–14
  marijuana use of, 64–65
  Richards quip on, 88
  tax cuts, 92, 106, 125, 127
Bush, John Ellis "Jeb," 114

California Assembly Bill 5, 73
campaign contributions.
  See corporate political
  contributions; PACs
Campbell, Jay, 86–87
Camp David Accords, 180
capitalism, 93–96
  democratic, 98–100, 142, 220
  polling on young voters on,
    220–21, 230–31
  Smith and, 95, 166, 200
Capitol riots of 2021, 132, 138, 139,
  140
Carlin, George, 174
Carlson, Tucker, 33, 104, 202,
  263–64, 265–66
Carter, Jimmy, 79, 124, 152, 180–83,
  184
Carter Presidency, The (Fink and
  Graham, ed.), 181–82
Carville, James, 21
Casar, Greg, 236
Center for American Progress, 4–5
Center for Biological Diversity, 8
center-right country, myth of, 2, 12,
  22, 24, 31–32, 33, 35–36, 48–49,
  115, 118–25, 256
Chamber of Commerce, 119–20,
  142, 153, 154–55, 158, 160, 180
Chavez, Linda, 227
Cheney, Dick, 196
Cheney, Liz, 196
Chomsky, Noam, 150, 198, 225–26
Christian Democratic Union, 16
Churchill, Winston, 224
circle of liberty, 51–54

Citizens United v. FEC, 82, 160,
    162, 165, 174
civil rights, 15, 17, 72–73, 92, 102,
    123, 149
Civil Rights Act of 1964, 101, 102, 149
Civil War, 103, 139
class warfare, 57, 59, 61–62, 77
Clean Energy Fuels Corp., 29
climate change, 3–9, 15, 25–29, 117
climate deniers, 3–5, 6–9, 26
Clinton, Bill, 79, 126, 189, 193, 225
    election of 1992, 21
    Friedman and, 6
    marijuana use of, 64–65
Clinton, Hillary, 183, 189, 208
    election of 2016, 84, 104, 109, 131,
        190, 191, 193, 194, 228, 233
Closet, the, 204–9
Clyburn, James, 96–97, 227
CNN, 2, 9–12, 13, 196, 201, 203,
    216, 227–28, 229, 232, 233–34
Coelho, Tony, 152, 184–90, 191,
    193–94
Cohen, Leonard, 212
Cohn, Jonathan, 42
colleges and universities
    free education, 79–82, 86, 97–98
    legacy admissions at, 59
    Powell on public speech at, 155
    progressives-are-lazy thesis and,
        90–91
Collins, Chris, 16
Columbia/HCA Medicare fraud case,
    241–43
Comcast, 11
Confederate flags, 138–39
Conservative Party (Britain), 16
conspiracy theories, 11, 108–9,
    113–14, 136, 171, 234
Constitution, U.S., 56, 160, 249,
    250, 252
Consumer Financial Protection
    Bureau, 191–92
"consumerism," 152, 153, 156
Conway, Kellyanne, 9, 33

Cooper, Anderson, 9–10
Cooperative Congressional Election
    Study, 120–21
corporate interests, 11–12, 13,
    141–94, 198, 218–19
    Adelson primary, 168–72
    capitulation of Democratic Party,
        179–84
    Coelho as Patient Zero, 184–90
    creating income inequality, 82–85
    first horsemen of apocalypse,
        144–45
    impact of, 173–77
    loss of hope, 158–63
    more money and more problems,
        163–65
    mortal danger from, 165–68
    Powell's memo, 153–58, 179, 201
    rewriting the code, 177–78
    rise of corporations, 141–44
corporate political contributions,
    12, 117, 241, 247–48. *See also*
    corporate interests *above*
    climate denialism and fossil fuel
        industry, 4–5, 27–28, 117, 120,
        239
    PACs, 82–83, 159, 168–69, 186,
        219
    role of Supreme Court, 142–43,
        144–45, 159–63, 165–66, 175,
        249–50
corporate media. *See* mainstream
    media
corporate pay, 194
corporate profits, 37, 77, 78–79,
    93–94, 129, 163, 171–72
corporate taxes, 30–31, 171, 231,
    252
corporatism, 93–96
corruption, 5, 16–17, 21–22, 28–29,
    46, 121, 168–72, 174–75, 176,
    186, 190, 198, 247–48
Couch, Ethan, 64
Covid-19 pandemic, 3, 14, 22, 24,
    68, 86, 116, 131, 235

Credibles, the, 203–4
criminal justice, 32, 63–66, 77–78,
    259–60
Cross Country Pipeline Supply Co.
    Inc., 29
Crowley, Joe, 233, 238
Cruz, Ted, 114, 178–79, 248
cuckoo for Cocoa Puffs, 137–40

Data for Progress, 25, 222
Davis, J. C. Bancroft, 144–45
Deason, Doug, 46
DeLay, Tom, 188
democracy, loss of. See loss of
    democracy
democratic capitalism, 98–100, 142,
    220
Democratic Congressional Campaign
    Committee (DCCC), 152, 184–88
Democratic Party (Democrats)
    capitulation of, 179–84
    center-right myth, 118–25
    Coelho as Patient Zero, 184–90
    fighting back, 91–92, 147–51
    focus on corporate money, 172–77,
        191–94
    history of, 145–51
    loss of Democrats, 151–53
    making the case, 125–30
    media and the Closet, 204–9
    young voters and, 25–26, 220–26
democratic socialism, 96–98
"deplorables," 104
DeSantis, Ron, 53
Disraeli, Benjamin, 224
Dodd-Frank Wall Street Reform
    and Consumer Protection Act,
    191–93
Dole, Bob, 132
Donahue, Phil, 206
Donnelly, Joe, 125–26, 127, 241
Douglass, Frederick, 122, 258–59
Douthat, Ross, 12
drug companies, 10, 33, 42, 70, 162,
    166–67

drug crimes and criminal justice,
    64–65
drug pricing, 42, 166, 172, 192
Dukakis, Michael, 149, 150
Duke, David, 136
Durbin, Dick, 42

Earned Income Tax Credit (EITC),
    83–84
Easterbrook, Gregg, 185
Eastman, Kara, 128
Ecarma, Caleb, 227
economic justice, 74–77, 238
    productivity and worker's
        compensation, 75–77, 76
education, 63–64. See also colleges
    and universities
    free college, 79–82, 86, 97–98
    legacy admissions, 59
Egyptian revolution of 2011, 204–5
Einstein, Albert, 1
Eisenhower, Dwight, 123, 149
elections
    public funding of, 10–11, 114, 219
    total spending on, 82, 175, 176–77
    1912, 145
    1936, 147
    1964, 149–50
    1968, 102
    1980, 17, 182–83, 184, 189
    1988, 189, 190, 225
    1992, 21
    1994, 193
    2000, 151
    2004, 173, 189
    2008, 17, 23, 40, 41, 126, 189
    2012, 40–41, 87–90
    2014, 126
    2016, 12, 17–18, 84, 85–86, 104,
        114–15, 131, 135–36, 168,
        178–79, 190, 208, 220–21, 226,
        228
    2018, 126, 194
    2020, 2, 21–22, 34, 50–51, 52, 67,
        86, 96–97, 105, 124, 127–28,

131–32, 147–48, 168–69, 175,
203, 216, 224, 226–28, 239,
250, 263–64, 268
2022, 10, 82, 128, 150, 175, 247
Emanuel, Rahm, 187
Embassy of the United States,
Jerusalem, 170–71
Environmental Protection Agency
(EPA), 123, 150, 152, 158
equality of opportunity, 58–59
Equal Rights Amendment, 251
Erickson, Erick, 88–89
Estonia, paid family leave, 39
evolution, 10
Exceptional America (Jouet), 15–16
Expanding Circle, The (Singer), 54
ExxonMobil, 239

Fallows, James, 14–15
Fauci, Anthony, 10
Federal Election Campaign Act
(FECA) of 1971, 158–60
Federal Election Commission (FEC),
28, 117, 159–60
Federal Reserve, 183, 191
Federal Trade Commission (FTC), 151
Fetterman, John, 128
Field, Stephen J., 144–45
financial crisis of 2007–2008, 95
First Amendment, 161, 252
first horsemen of apocalypse, 144–45
*First National Bank of Boston v.
Bellotti*, 161–63, 165, 175, 189
Fitzpatrick, Brian, 26
Floyd, George, 33, 92, 121
Ford, Gerald, 152, 159
Foreign Corrupt Services Act of
1977, 169
47 percent, 85–89
fossil fuel industry, 3–5, 27–29, 120,
239
founding fathers, 54–56
Fourteenth Amendment, 144–45
Fox News, 1–2, 4, 6, 32, 43, 56, 154,
196, 201, 218, 228, 229, 248

framing, 91, 99, 128
Frank, Barney, 191–94
Frank, Thomas, 189
free college, 79–82, 86, 97–98
"freedom from want," 80
freedom of speech, 24, 80, 161–63
free trade, 116
French, Lauren, 238
Friedman, Thomas L., 3, 6

Gabbard, Tulsi, 202
Gaetz, Matt, 247
"gaffes," 87
Gates, Henry Louis, Jr., 107
gay marriage, 32, 53
Gelman, Andrew, 224–25
Generation Z, 230–31
genetics, 1
Ghitza, Yair, 224–25
GI Bill, 97–98
gig economy, 73
Gilded Age, 194
Gilens, Martin, 173–74
Gingrich, Newt, 150, 168
Giuliani, Rudy, 9, 212, 213
global citizenship, 53–54
Gohmert, Louie, 44, 47, 272
Goldberg, Whoopi, 237–38
Goldwater, Barry, 131, 150
Gore, Al, 151, 189
Gorsuch, Neil, 249–50
Graham, Lindsey, 12, 16, 22,
197
Grassley, Chuck, 132
Great Depression, 146
Green, Joshua, 115–16
Green New Deal (GND), 3–4, 5,
6–9, 25–29, 237–38
Grey Poupon, 66, 91–92
Griffin, Phil, 204
Grijalva, Raúl, 42–43, 236
Grim, Ryan, 229
Guinea worm disease, 180–81
Guizot, François, 224
gun control, 22–23, 25, 119, 222

Hanks, Tom, 14
Hannity, Sean, 57, 238
Hanson, Victor Davis, 62
Hardball (TV show), 212–16
hardware and the brain, 1
Hargan, Eric, 46
Harris, Kamala, 14, 67
health care, 1–2, 24, 33–35, 67–72.
    See also Medicaid; Medicare
    cost considerations, 69–72
    mainstream media and, 2, 69–70,
        97, 200
    Medicare for All, 2, 33–35, 69–71,
        97, 167, 201, 222, 228
    Obamacare, 24, 40–49, 90
    public polling on, 25, 33, 35
Heritage Foundation, 22, 40,
    154–55
Hertel-Fernandez, Alexander, 118–19
Hezbollah, 124
Hilton, Paris, 61
Hollywood Reporter, 11
homelessness, 56, 57, 59
Hoover, Herbert, 96
Hugo, Victor, 224
Hurricane Harvey, 4
Hurricane Katrina, 24, 214

identity politics, 91, 102, 116,
    132–33, 263, 266–68
immigration and immigrants, 1,
    32–33, 57, 115–16, 124,
    134–35, 136, 261, 266–67
    Muslim ban, 53, 134
    public polling on, 33
    Romney and election of 2012, 40
inequality, 52, 58–59, 62, 79, 80,
    194, 262
    creating, 82–85
    the 47 percent, 85–89
Inflation Reduction Act of 2022, 6,
    27, 38, 83, 85, 192
Intercept, The, 170, 229, 240
interest groups, 42, 119–20
International Monetary Fund, 183

invisible hand of the market, 13,
    199–202, 208
Iran-Contra affair, 123–24
Iraq War, 6, 12–13, 98, 107, 205–6,
    211–13
IRS enforcement, 83–85
Israel, 170–71, 180, 186, 266–67
Istanbul, 270–71
"It's the corruption, stupid," 21–22

Jackson, Andrew, 142
James, LeBron, 107
Japan, 39, 40
Jayapal, Pramila, 236
Jefferson, Thomas, 55, 141, 142
Jesus Christ, 56–58, 107–8
jobs guarantee, 31
Johnson, Lyndon, 101–2, 149–50,
    225
Jordan, Michael, 195
Jouet, Mugambi, 15–16
Justice Democrats, 3, 115, 173, 187,
    194, 233–34, 236–41
justice for all, 72–78
justice system. *See* criminal justice

Kansas abortion referendum of 2022,
    36
Kasich, John, 114
Kasparian, Ana, 201, 203
Kavanaugh, Brett, 250
Kazin, Michael, 124
Kelly, John, 123
Kendi, Ibram X., 224
Kennedy, Edward Moore "Ted,"
    182–83
Kerry, John, 149
Khanna, Ro, 9, 236
King, Martin Luther, 268
Kinsley, Michael, 87
Kirk, Charlie, 155
Koch family, 46, 47, 69, 114, 171–72
K Street Project, 188
Kurdish uprising, 266
Kushner, Charles, 59

Kushner, Jared, 59
Kuttner, Robert, 186, 188

Laffer Curve, 104
Lamb, Conor, 96–97
Langone, Ken, 28
Las Vegas Sands Corporation, 168, 170–72
Law, Steven, 16
Lee, Mike, 3–5, 6–9, 13, 15, 26
Lee, Summer, 236
Leggitt, Lance, 46
Leisman, Steve, 86–87
Lemon, Don, 216–17
Lennon, John, 90
Lessig, Lawrence, 194
Lever, The, 229
Levin, Mark, 115
LGBTQ+ rights, 32, 52–53, 57, 117
"liberal"
   neoliberalism, 182–84, 188
   use of term, 183
liberal media bias, myth of, 2–16, 196
Lichtenstein, Nelson, 45
Lieberman, Joe, 44, 197
Limbaugh, Rush, 88
limited liability, 143–44
Lincoln, Abraham, 101, 102
Listen, Liberal (Frank), 189
lobbying, 5, 42–43, 46, 154, 156, 163–64, 247
Los Angeles Times, 148
"loss aversion," 48
loss of democracy, 141–94
   Adelson primary, 168–72
   capitulation of Democratic Party, 179–84
   Coelho as Patient Zero, 184–90
   first horsemen of our apocalypse, 144–45
   history of progressives, 145–51
   impact of corporate interests, 172–77

loss of Democrats, 151–53
loss of hope, 158–63
more money and more problems, 163–65
mortal danger of corporate interests, 165–68
Powell's memo, 153–58, 179, 201
rise of corporations, 141–44
love, 266–69
Lowell, James Russell, 272
Luntz, Frank, 26, 220–21, 222, 225, 233

McAuliffe, Terry, 228
McCain, John, 12–13, 17, 41, 48
McCarthy, Kevin, 85
McCaskill, Claire, 126, 241
McConnell, Mitch, 4, 16, 108, 197, 253
McElwee, Sean, 25
McGovern, George, 152, 228
McGregor, Ewan, 173
Maddow, Rachel, 199–200
Madison, James, 142, 143
mainstream media (MSM), 9–15, 18–19, 156–217, 218, 223–38.
   See also specific media
   abortion issue and, 36
   advertising and, 10–11, 70, 157, 161, 196, 243–44
   bothsidesism, 9–12, 14–15, 122
   center-right myth, 31, 33, 118–19, 122, 123, 196
   Chomsky and manufacturing consent, 198, 223–24, 225–26
   the Closet, 204–9
   the Credibles, 203–4
   invisible hand of the market, 199–202
   liberal bias, myth of, 2–16, 196
   Matthews and *Hardball*, 209–17
   new media vs., 226–35
   tax policy and, 256–57
   universal health care and, 2, 69–70, 97, 200

makers vs. takers, 89–92
malware, 1, 4
Manchin, Joe, 4, 6, 27–28
Manifest Project, 16
Mankiewicz, Ben, 60, 206–7
Manufacturing Consent (Chomsky), 198
marijuana, 32, 64–65, 77
Markey, Ed, 6
Marshall Plan, 24
Martinez, Chuey, 66
Masterson, Walter, 136
Matrix, the. *See* mainstream media
Matthews, Chris, 98, 210–17
Mayer, Jane, 153–54
media. *See* mainstream media
media neutrality, 13, 14–15, 18, 70
Medicaid, 41, 45, 68–69, 150
Medicare, 24, 35, 41, 48, 150, 166
    Scott and Columbia/HCA fraud case, 241–43
Medicare for All, 2, 33–35, 69–71, 97, 167, 201, 222, 228
Meet the Press, 9
Mehlman, Ken, 102
Mehmet II, 270–71
Mercer family, 114, 171–72, 178–79
meritocracy, myth of, 59, 60–65
Mildenberger, Matto, 118–19
"military-industrial complex," 123
millennials, 25–26, 87, 220–26, 230–31
minimum wage, 24, 74–75, 126, 129
Mississippi, 2, 17
Moonves, Les, 11, 13
Moral Majority, 22
Morse, Alex, 240
Moyers, Bill, 167
Mr. Potato Head, 104, 255–56
MSNBC, 12–13, 196, 199–200, 201, 204–8, 228, 229, 232
    Matthews and *Hardball,* 210–17
Mubarak, Hosni, 204–5
Munch, Edvard, 166
Murphy, Ryan, 122–23

Musk, Elon, 176, 181
Muslim ban, 53, 134

Nader, Ralph, 151–53, 158, 265
National Association for the Advancement of Colored People (NAACP), 89–90
national deficit, 30, 45, 84, 106
National Federation of Independent Business, 155
National Journal, 41
National Republican Campaign Committee, 184–85
National Republican Senatorial Committee, 242
Native Americans, 139, 260
Neal, Richard, 240
neoliberalism, 182–84, 188
Netanyahu, Bibi, 266
Newburgh and New York Railway, 144
New Deal, 24, 124, 146, 147, 188, 225. *See also* Green New Deal
New Democrats, 150–51
new media, 229–35
New Republic, The, 26, 41, 43, 186
Newsweek, 85
New Yorker, 92
New York Times, 2, 3, 6, 12, 13–14, 15, 25, 26, 27, 41, 84, 90, 198, 204, 208, 231, 243
Nichols, Tyre, 33
Nides, Thomas, 186
Nixon, Richard, 17, 24, 32, 102, 123–24, 150, 151–52, 158–59
Norway, 81, 99
NRA (National Rifle Association), 23, 119
Nunberg, Sam, 115

Obama, Barack, 79, 143
    birther conspiracy, 11, 14
    Egyptian revolution of 2011 and, 204–5

election of 2008, 17, 23, 40, 41, 189, 215, 221
election of 2012, 40–41
failure to fight back, 146, 151
Gates incident, 107
marijuana use of, 64–65
"socialist" label, 67
tax policy, 92, 106, 191
undocumented immigrants and, 124
Obamacare, 24, 40–49, 90
Ocasio-Cortez, Alexandria (AOC), 9, 57, 233
climate change and Green New Deal, 3, 6, 9, 25
election of 2016 and Trump, 115
election of 2018 and Crowley, 233, 236, 238
election of 2020 and, 128
Pelosi sit-in, 237–38
Occupational Safety and Health Administration (OSHA), 123, 152, 158
Occupy Wall Street, 56
Odyssey Investment Partners LLC, 29
Olbermann, Keith, 205–6
O'Malley, Martin, 233
Omar, Ilhan, 115, 236
O'Neill, Thomas "Tip," 121, 188, 215
online gambling, 170–71
opioid epidemic, 166–67
Original Young Turk, The (Uygur), 82
Osefo, Wendy, 66
"others," 52–53, 54, 117–18, 133–34
Ottoman Empire, 44, 270–71, 272
"owning the libs," 134
OxyContin, 166
Oz, Mehmet, 128

PACs (political action committees), 82–83, 159, 168–69, 186, 219
progressive, 235–54

Page, Benjamin I., 173–74
paid family leave, 37–40, 67
paid maternity leave, 86
party loyalty, 25, 245–46
Paul, Ron, 179
Pelosi, Nancy, 143, 253
climate change and Green New Deal, 29
corporate donations and, 197, 249
election of 2020, 132, 147
failure to fight back, 147, 151
mainstream media and, 196, 237–38
Pelosi, Paul, 29
Pence, Mike, 132
Perlstein, Rick, 152–53
pharmaceutical companies. See drug companies
Piker, Hasan, 232–33
police brutality, 32–33, 65–66, 77, 260, 261
political campaign contributions. See corporate political contributions
political correctness, 12, 14–15
Powell, Lewis, 142–43, 153–58, 160, 161, 162, 164, 172, 175, 250
power and justice, 257–63
Preserve America, 168–69
presidential elections. See elections
press. See mainstream media
Pressley, Ayanna, 115, 236
Price, Thomas, 46
privatization, 67–68
productivity and worker's compensation, 75–77, 76
Progressive Era, 149–50, 194, 257
progressive PACs, 235–54
Rebellion PAC, 239–45
Wolf-PAC, 239–40, 245–54
progressives, 18–19, 21–49
the Credibles, 203–4
criminal justice system, 63–66
defining principles of, 50–100
democratic capitalism, 98–100
democratic socialism, 96–98

progressives (*continued*)
  equality of opportunity, 58–59
  expansion of the circle of liberty,
    51–54
  facts as stubborn things, 30–37
  founding fathers, 54–56
  free college, 79–82, 97–98
  Green New Deal and, 25–29
  health care, 69–72
  history of, 145–51
  how they win, 255–72
  income inequality and, 82–85
  justice for all, 72–78
  makers vs. takers and, 89–92
  myth of meritocracy, 60–63
  Obamacare, 40–49
  paid family leave, 37–40
  religion and Jesus, 56–58
  Republican voters, 32
  "socialist" label, 50–51, 67–69
  universal health care, 33–35
  use of term, 50–51, 183–84
  47 percent and, 85–89
progressives-are-lazy thesis, 89–92
projection, 113–14
Pryor, Mark, 126
psychopathy, 122–23
Public Accountability Initiative, 5

QAnon, 108–9, 110, 136, 234

race and racism, 18, 92, 137–38,
    257–63
  criminal justice system, 63–66,
    77–78, 259–60
  power and justice, 257–63
  public polling on, 32–33
  Romney and election of 2012,
    89–90
  Southern Strategy, 16–17, 101–8,
    124–25, 138
  Trump and, 132–34, 259
Rather, Dan, 229
Reactionary Mind, The (Robin),
    117

Reagan, Ronald, 7, 123–24, 125,
    150, 209–10, 225
  election of 1980, 17, 184
  tax cuts, 105–6, 210
  War on Drugs, 32
Reaganland (Perlstein), 152
Rebellion PAC, 239–45
redistribution of wealth, 12, 57, 59,
    76, 104, 252, 261
referees, 195–96
regulations, 94–95, 116, 129, 188,
    189, 191–92, 264, 265
Reich, Robert, 43
Reid, Harry, 149
religion and Jesus Christ, 56–58,
    107–8
Republican Party (Republicans),
    101–40
  abortion lie, 108–13
  Adelson primary, 168–72
  center-right myth, 118–25
  crookedness of, 113–14
  cuckoo for Cocoa Puffs, 137–40
  the 47 percent, 85–89
  makers vs. takers, 89–92
  political extremism of, 15–18
  public polling on, 9–10
  Southern Strategy of, 101–8,
    124–25
  Trump and popularity myth,
    130–37
  voters vs. politicians, 114–18
Respect for Marriage Act, 32
Richards, Ann, 88
right wing, myths of the, 2–16,
    31–32
Robin, Corey, 117
Roe v. Wade, 35–36, 108–9
Roff, Peter, 85–86
Rolls-Royce Republican., 91–92
Roman Empire, 56, 270, 271, 272
Romney, George, 150
Romney, Mitt, 40–41, 87–90, 150,
    168
Romneycare, 40

Roosevelt, Franklin Delano (FDR), 80, 92, 124, 145–47, 149, 225
Roosevelt, Thedore "Teddy," 142, 145, 159
Rose, Max, 128
Rubio, Marco, 12, 115, 137, 208
Ryan, Jonah, 125
Ryan, Paul, 89

same-sex marriage, 32, 53
Sanders, Bernie, 80, 95–99, 182
    democratic socialism of, 96–98
    election of 2016, 194, 208, 221, 233, 236
    election of 2020, 194, 203, 226–28, 236–37, 239, 244, 268
    grassroots funding, 187, 236–37, 239, 244
    mainstream media and, 98, 198, 208, 211
    "socialist" label, 50–51, 67
    universal health care, 2, 97
Santa Clara County v. Southern Pacific Railroad, 144–45, 160
Santorum, Rick, 44, 45
Scarborough, Joe, 139
Schlozman, Daniel, 188
Schultz, Howard, 28
Schumer, Chuck, 149
Scott, Rick, 241–43
Scream, The (Munch), 166
seat belts, 127, 151, 265
Second Amendment, 139–40
Securities and Exchange Commission (SEC), 95
Senate Leadership Fund, 16
September 11 attacks (2001), 9, 139, 212–13
shadow banning, 232
Shapiro, Ben, 155
Shapiro, Neal, 208
Sierra Club, 119–20
silent majority, 24, 234
Sinclair, Upton, 184
Singer, Peter, 54

Sirota, David, 229
Skovron, Christopher, 120
slavery, 55, 101, 103, 144, 259–60
Smith, Adam, 95, 166, 200
socialism, 67–69, 220, 230, 233–34
    democratic, 96–98
"socialist," 50–51, 67–69
social justice, 72–78
Social Security, 24, 31, 35, 48, 50, 147, 150
software and the brain, 1–2
Soros, George, 114, 135, 171
Southern Railroad Company, 144
Southern Strategy, 16–17, 101–8, 124–25, 215, 245
Soviet Union, 124
Spanberger, Abigail, 96–97
Spayd, Liz, 13–14
Spicer, Sean, 47
Stannard, Paula, 46
Starbucks doctrine, 263–66
Steele, Michael, 102
Stein, Ben, 81
Stevens, John Paul, 160
Stokes, Leah C., 118–19
Sunlight Foundation, 43
Supreme Court and corporate interests, 142–43, 144–45, 159–63, 165–66, 249–50
Sweden, 39, 81, 99
Syria, 82, 211–12

Taiwan, 99
takers vs. makers, 89–92
Tanenhaus, Sam, 41
Tapper, Jake, 238
tax audits, 83–85
tax policy, 30–31, 74, 86, 92, 104, 105–6, 256–57
    Bush tax cuts, 92, 106, 125, 127
    corporate taxes, 30–31, 171, 231, 252
    Trump tax cuts, 16, 30, 104, 105–6, 171
    wealth tax, 256–57

Tea Party, 47
Thompson, Fred, 210, 214–15
Till, Emmett, 139
Tlaib, Rashida, 115, 236
Too Strong Coffee, 264
top 1 percent, 58–59
Trainspotting (movie), 173
transgender rights, 52–53, 74, 91
Trilling, Lionel, 147
Trump, Donald, 92, 259
  Adelson and, 168–72, 248
  border wall, 125, 127, 134
  climate denialism of, 4
  corruption of, 16–17, 43, 90, 92, 115
  election of 2016, 1, 11, 12, 13,
    17–18, 84, 85–86, 89, 114–16,
    131, 135–36, 168, 178–79, 190,
    191, 208, 226
  election of 2020, 21–22, 50, 52,
    67, 86, 89, 105, 115, 131–32,
    168–69, 228, 250
  FBI search of Mar-a-Lago, 77
  health care and, 46–47
  mainstream media and, 202, 203,
    208, 211–12, 213
  the "others," 52–53, 54, 115–16,
    133–34
  popularity and populism myth, 88,
    130–37, 202
  porn star mistresses of, 56
  psychopathy of, 123
  Southern Strategy, 102, 103, 105
  supporters and voters, 103, 104,
    115–16, 132–37, 198
  tax cuts, 16, 30, 92, 104, 105–6, 171
  as threat to democracy, 198
Trump, Donald, Jr., 90
Turner, Brock, 63–64

unconscious, 1
United Nations, 24
universal background checks, 22–23
universal health care, 1–2, 15,
    33–35, 57, 67, 228. *See also*
    Medicare for All

universities. *See* colleges and
    universities
Unsafe at Any Speed (Nader), 151
Uygur, Dogan, 60, 81–82
Uygur, Dukhet, 270

Vandewalker, Ian, 82
Ventura, Jesse, 206–7
Vietnam War, 24
View, The (TV show), 237–38
Volcker rule, 191–92
voter suppression, 21–22
Voting Rights Act, 101

Wallace, Nicolle, 196
Wall Street Journal, 41
Walmart, 265
War on Drugs, 32
Warren, Elizabeth, 80, 96, 191, 256
Washington, George, 55
Washington Post, 34, 186–87
Watergate, 159
wealth tax, 256–57
Weber, Vin, 188
"wedge issues," 74, 115–16
Weigel, Dave, 34
Weintraub, Ellen, 160
West, Kanye, 135
Weyrich, Paul, 22, 108
What Liberal Media? (Alterman), 196
White, Byron, 160, 165, 166, 167
Williams, Marjorie, 186–87, 191
Wilson, Woodrow, 145
Windsor, Lauren, 164–65
Wolf-PAC, 239–40, 245–54
Women's March, 22
Wu, Brianna, 243–44
Wyden, Ron, 83

Young Turks, The (TYT), 60, 81–82,
    136, 152, 156, 201, 214,
    229–35, 237, 238

Zeleny, Jeff, 228
Zucker, Jeff, 11